CASEBOOK ON
READING DISABILITY

Also by the author:

How to Increase Reading Ability

CASEBOOK ON
READING DISABILITY

EDITED BY

Albert J. Harris

DAVID McKAY COMPANY, INC.
NEW YORK

LIBRARY OF CONGRESS CATALOG CARD NUMBER: 70-114763
MANUFACTURED IN THE UNITED STATES OF AMERICA

Preface

THIS COLLECTION of sixteen case reports is intended to fill a long-felt need for descriptions of reading diagnosis and remedial help in lengthy case reports. It is anticipated that the book will be useful in a variety of ways: as a text or collateral text in advanced courses in diagnosis and treatment of reading disabilities; as required or supplementary reading in basic courses in reading diagnosis and remediation; as supplementary reading in a variety of professional education and special education courses; and as personal reading for reading specialists, psychologists, members of other professions interested in reading disabilities, school administrators, supervisors, teachers, and parents.

A certain amount of technical terminology has been unavoidable, especially in presenting the results of medical and psychological examinations. The editor has inserted parenthetical explanations of many of the technical terms, but probably has missed some that will be new to many readers. This should not, however, prevent the reader from understanding the main features of the case.

Many psychological and educational tests are mentioned in these reports. Basic information about these tests and their publishers is given in Appendixes A and B, which have been reproduced by permission of the publisher from: Albert J. Harris, *How to Increase Reading Ability*, Fifth Edition. New York: David McKay Co., 1970.

The editor is happy to acknowledge his deep gratitude to all of the authors. Their job of reading through the hundreds of pages of material in the records of many of these cases and selecting the information and integrating it into its present form has taken scores of hours for each report. The authors have accomplished this task despite the fact that all of them are very busy people with many other responsibilities.

Albert J. Harris

June, 1969

Contributing Authors

FRANCES BERRES, PH.D. (University of California at Los Angeles), is Associate Head of the Fernald School on the campus of U.C.L.A. She was successively psychologist, supervisor of remedial instruction, and assistant head of the Fernald School, and, before that, was in charge of remedial instruction in a high school. She is qualified as a psychologist, a family and marriage counselor, and a high school teacher. In addition to several articles on the evaluation of the treatment of learning disabilities, she is co-author of the *Deep Sea Adventure Series,* widely used in remedial programs.

DOROTHY KENDALL BRACKEN, M.A. (Southern Methodist University), is Director of the Reading Clinic, Southern Methodist University, which she started in 1948. Other experience has included classroom teaching, demonstration teaching, and lecturing at such universities as Chicago and Columbia. She is in demand as a speaker and workshop leader on reading. She is a past president of the International Reading Association and is coordinator of international tours for that organization. She has also been very active in the Texas Association for the Improvement of Reading. Co-author (with Ruth Strang) of *Making Better Readers,* she has also authored twenty-two other books including textbooks in English and social studies, adult non-fiction, and children's books.

WILMA BUCKMAN, M.S.W. (University of California, Berkeley), is Associate Clinical Professor of Psychiatric Social Work, University of California Medical Center in San Francisco. Her background includes positions as an elementary school teacher, principal of a child care center, psychiatric social worker, and case work supervisor. She is Secretary of the Association of Family Therapists and a member of the American Association of Social Workers. She is co-author of several articles in the *American Journal of Diseases of Children.*

STELLA S. COHN, M.A. (City College of New York), organized the first multi-disciplinary reading clinic in the New York City public schools in 1955 and has been Director of the Bureau of Special Reading Services ever since, with thirteen clinics now under her direction. She started as a classroom teacher and has been a supervisor of classes for the mentally retarded, a guidance coordinator, and a coordinator of special projects. She has taught courses in several universities, has directed reading conferences, institutes, and workshops, and has spoken at several conventions of the International Reading Association. She is co-author (with David Cohn) of *Teaching the Retarded Reader,* and has written several papers for *The Reading Teacher.*

EDWIN M. COLE, M.D. (Harvard), worked with Dr. Samuel T. Orton following a neurological residency. He organized the Language Clinic at Massachusetts General Hospital in 1934 and was its director until his very recent retirement to private practice. He is a Diplomate in Neurology, and has been Associate in Neurology at Harvard Medical School for many years. He has also been a consultant to several universities and private schools. He is the author of articles on reading disability which have appeared in medical journals and the *Bulletin of the Orton Society.*

JOYCE TAYLOR EYER, B.A. (San Diego State College), is Supervisor in the Fernald School at U.C.L.A. She previously was a demonstration teacher in that school. A member of the International Reading Association and the Council for Exceptional Children, she is president of the South Pasadena Education Association.

MARIANNE FROSTIG, PH.D. (University of Southern California), is Executive Director of the Marianne Frostig Center of Educational Therapy and Clinical Professor in the School of Education, University of Southern California. A former school psychologist, she has also taught at Los Angeles State College and San Fernando Valley State College. She is a Fellow of the American Psychological Association, the American Orthopsychiatric Association, and the Society for Projective Techniques, and is on the Advisory Board of the International Association for Children with Learning Disabilities. She is on the editorial boards of the *Journal of Learning Disabilities* and *Child Development.* She is author or co-author of the *Marianne Frostig Developmental Test of Visual Perception,* the *Frostig Program for the Development of Visual Perception,* and about fifty papers on learning difficulties in professional journals.

LAWRENCE GOLD, PH.D. (New York University), is Director of the Reading Clinic and Associate Professor of Education at Kent State University, Kent, Ohio. He was most recently Director of the Learning Center at Binghampton, New York; before that, Assistant Professor of Education, Division of Teacher Education and Hunter College of the City University of New York, supervisor in the Reading and Study Center at Adelphi University, a school reading consultant, and a secondary school teacher of English, social studies, and special education. He is co-author (with Albert J. Harris and others) of the final report on the CRAFT Project, and has presented several recent papers on developmental dyslexia at professional conventions, including that of the International Reading Association.

ROSE GREENE, M.S.S.A. (University of Louisville), is a School Social Worker in the Bureau of Special Reading Services, Board of Education of the City of New York. She has had previous positions as a psychiatric social worker.

ROSA A. HAGIN, PH.D. (New York University), is Assistant Professor in Clinical Psychology, Department of Psychiatry, New York University School of Medicine. She has been director of special services in two school systems, a school psychologist, and a psychologist in a mental hospital. She is Secretary of the Division of School Psychologists of the American Psychological Association, and a Fellow of the American Orthopsychiatric Association. She is chairman of a task force of the Interdisciplinary Committee on Reading Problems. She has been closely associated with Dr. Archie A. Silver in research and writing on reading disabilities and has been co-author with him of several important research papers.

ALBERT J. HARRIS, PH.D. (Harvard), is Professor Emeritus in the Division of Teacher Education, The City University of New York. He was successively Assistant Professor and Supervisor of the Remedial Reading Service at The City College, Director of the Educational Clinic and Professor of Education at Queens College, and Director of the Office of Research and Evaluation, Division of Teacher Education, all within The City University of New York. He is a past president of the International Reading Association, the National Conference on Research in English, and the Division of School Psychologists of the American Psychological Association. He is a Fellow of the American Psychological Association and the American Orthopsychiatric Association, a Diplomate in Clinical Psychology, and a certified school psychologist. He is a member of the executive committee of the Interdisciplinary Committee on Reading Problems. He is author of *How to Increase Reading Ability, Effective Teaching of Reading*, and the *Harris Tests of Lateral Dominance;* senior author of the Macmillan Reading Program; editor of *Readings on Reading Instruction;* author of numerous articles in periodicals, yearbooks, and encyclopedias; and speaker at many reading conferences.

JIMMYE DOBBS HAYS, M. ED. (University of Houston), is a reading consultant in the Region XII Educational Service Center in Waco, Texas. She was a clinician in the Reading Clinic at Southern Methodist University for several years. She also has taught in primary, intermediate, and junior high school grades and has been a reading consultant in public schools. She has been president of the Cen-Texas Council of the International Reading Association, and is co-author (with Dorothy Bracken) of the *S.R.A. Listening Skill Builders*.

LAURA M. HINES, M.A. (New York University), is a School Psychologist in the Bureau of Special Reading Services, Board of Education of the City of New York. She was previously a psychologist in mental hospitals, and a consultant to the Free School Association of Prince Edward County, Virginia. She is a member of the American Psychological Association.

MARJORIE SEDDON JOHNSON, ED.D. (Temple University), is Associate Director of the Reading Clinic and Professor of Psychology and Educational Psychology, Temple University. She has been associated with the Laboratory School of the Reading Clinic since 1948; before that she was a high school teacher. She has been a visiting professor and a speaker, demonstrator, and workshop leader at many reading conferences. She is author or co-author of over fifty papers and publications on reading and reading disability, including the *Reading Education and Development* Series. She and Dr. Roy A. Kress have collaborated on a large number of projects, including the editing of *The Reading Teacher*.

Roy A. Kress, Ph.D. (Temple University), is Chairman of the Reading
Department, Director of the Reading Clinic, and Professor of Psychology and Educational Psychology at Temple University. His service at Temple University, which began in 1949, was interrupted by
three years as director of a private school for exceptional children,
and five years at Syracuse University as associate professor, director
of the diagnostic and remedial services of the Reading Center, and
coordinator of the annual reading conference. He has been a member
of the Board of Directors of the International Reading Association
and the National Conference on Research in English and belongs to
many other professional organizations. He is co-editor of *The Reading Teacher* and author or co-author of over fifty papers and publications, including the *Reading Education and Development* series. He
and Dr. Marjorie S. Johnson work closely together on many projects
and publications.

Beatrice Levison, M.S. (Yeshiva University), is a Remedial Therapist at
the Northside Center for Child Development. A member of the
American Orthopsychiatric Association and the Council on Exceptional Children, she wrote an article on school phobia which was
published in *Exceptional Children*.

Donald Neville, Ph.D. (University of Florida), is Professor of Psychology and Education, George Peabody College for Teachers. He was
until recently Director of the Child Study Center at that institution.
Former positions include reading clinician and reading resource
teacher. He is a member of the International Reading Association
(former state organizational chairman), the American Psychological
Association, and the American Educational Research Association. He
is the author of papers in the Conference Proceedings of the International Reading Association. Currently he is directing a pilot project
for training child development consultants, for the National Institute
of Mental Health.

Ralph C. Preston, Ph.D. (Columbia), is Professor of Education and Director of the Reading Clinic at the University of Pennsylvania, a
position he has held for many years. He was an elementary school
teacher before moving to a university setting. An educational psychologist, he is a member of the International Reading Association,

the American Psychological Association, and the American Educational Research Association. He has written numerous articles on reading in the social studies, and the comparative reading skills of German and American children.

GILBERT B. SCHIFFMAN, ED.D. (University of Maryland), is Director of Instruction, Board of Education of Prince George's County, Maryland. Previous positions include Supervisor of Reading in the Maryland State Education Department and diagnostic work in the Children's Evaluation Clinic, University of Maryland Hospital. Trained in optometry and psychology as well as education, he has written numerous periodical articles and has been a contributor to eight books and monographs.

ARCHIE A. SILVER, M.D. (New York University), is Associate Clinical Professor of Psychiatry in the New York University-Bellevue Medical Center, psychiatrist in charge of the Children's Section, Bellevue Hospital Mental Health Clinic, and in private practice. A Diplomate in Psychiatry and Child Psychiatry, he is a Fellow of the American Psychiatric Association, the American Orthopsychiatric Association, and the New York Academy of Medicine. He is general chairman of the Interdisciplinary Committee on Reading Problems. He and Dr. Rosa A. Hagin have co-authored many research reports on the causation and treatment of reading disability.

SISTER M. JULITTA, O.S.F., M.A. (De Paul University, Chicago), is Professor of Education and Director of the Reading Clinic at Cardinal Stritch College in Milwaukee, where she has been since 1944. Before that, she was a first grade teacher. She has served on several committees of the International Reading Association and is a past president of the Wisconsin State Council and the Milwaukee Area Council. She is the author of papers in the Proceedings of the International Reading Association and the University of Chicago Annual Reading Conference, and in the *Catholic School Journal.*

HELEN K. SMITH, PH.D. (University of Chicago), is Associate Professor at the University of Miami in Coral Gables, Florida. She has been Associate Professor at the University of Illinois at Chicago Circle, and Director of the Reading Clinic and Assistant Professor at the

University of Chicago. She is a member of the International Reading Association and the American Educational Research Association and is a member of the Executive Committee of the National Conference on Research in English. She is co-author of annual summaries of research on reading which have appeared in the *Reading Research Quarterly;* co-author (with Helen M. Robinson) of *Clinical Studies in Reading,* Vol. III; and editor of *Perception and Reading,* published by the International Reading Association. Her dissertation was awarded a prize by the International Reading Association and was published in the *Reading Research Quarterly.*

GRACE S. WALBY, PH.D. (University of Chicago), is Head of the Reading Department of the Child Guidance Clinic of Greater Winnipeg, Manitoba, Canada. Starting as a teacher in rural schools, she became an adjustment teacher and psychometrist before starting doctoral studies in reading. She is past president of the Greater Winnipeg Council of the International Reading Association and a member of the Manitoba Association of Psychologists. She is author of papers in several volumes of the Proceedings of the University of Chicago Annual Reading Conferences, and is Canadian Editor of the Collier-Macmillan Reading Program.

ALICE J. WHITSELL, A.B. (San Francisco State College), is Director of the Pediatric Reading and Language Development Clinic, University of California Medical Center in San Francisco. Starting as a teacher of the deaf, she has been educational director and director of the remedial reading program in a private school. She is a member of the Orton Society. She is author of papers that have appeared in *The Reading Teacher* and the Proceedings of International Reading Association Conventions. She works closely with her husband, Dr. Leon J. Whitsell.

LEON J. WHITSELL, M.D. (Stanford), is Assistant Clinical Professor of Pediatrics and Neurological Consultant to the Child Study Unit and the Pediatric Reading and Language Development Clinic of the University of California Medical Center in San Francisco. He was previously Assistant Professor of Medicine at Stanford University, and has been a neurological consultant to the Veterans Administration for many years. A Fellow in the American Psychiatric Association and the Association for Research in Nervous and Mental Disease, he was recently vice president of the Orton Society. He is chairman of one of the task forces of the Interdisciplinary Committee on Reading Problems, and has written several recent papers on reading disability that have appeared in *The Reading Teacher* and other journals.

MARGARET F. WILLSON, M.S. in Ed. (University of Pennsylvania), is Assistant Director of the Reading Clinic and Lecturer in Education at the University of Pennsylvania. A member of the International Reading Association and the American Speech and Hearing Association, she is the author of a recent article on remedial reading in *The Reading Teacher*.

BEVERLY BARTH ZENGA, M.S. in Ed. (Bank Street College of Education), M.A. in Sociology (American University), has been a Reading Counselor in the Special Reading Services of the New York City Board of Education for several years. Previously she was an instructor and research assistant in sociology and a teacher in a day treatment center for exceptional children.

Contents

Cases from Medical Settings

List of Tables

List of Figures

Introduction

THIS BOOK is the result of the Editor's recognition, in teaching courses on the diagnosis and treatment of reading disabilities for many years, of a need for a collection of varied case reports, presented in detail and at length. Printed materials can provide vivid examples of how diagnosis, planning, remediation, and evaluation are carried out in leading centers. Published case reports, however, have not been numerous, and most of them have been presented nontechnically or in a brief and compressed way, due to the limitations imposed by the professional journals in which they have appeared.

The plan that has been followed involved the assembling of long case study reports, with each author (or authors) encouraged to present the case in detail. The suggested maximum of 8,000 words corresponds to about twenty-five printed pages. The authors were selected, first of all, as highly regarded specialists whose writings and research have attracted wide and respectful attention, or as staff members of organizations that have developed superior reputations. The ones to whom invitations were sent were selected not only for the known quality of their work, but also to represent variety in location, auspices, and points of view regarding diagnosis and treatment.

The authors were asked to provide, in each report: (1) a section on diagnosis; (2) a section on remedial treatment; (3) an evaluation of progress made; (4) follow-up information if available; and (5) discussion of any aspects of the case that seemed to deserve it. Beyond that, they were encouraged not to follow a fixed pattern, but to write up the case in the way that seemed to them to provide the most effective presentation. There is quite a variety in the organization of the reports. Some authors have given diagnostic findings in great detail while others have reserved most of their space for treatment details. In different case reports one can find detailed descriptions of the findings of psychological testing, neurological and other medical examinations, psychiatric examinations and interviews, oral and silent reading tests, etc. The sections on remediation sometimes present single lessons with *verbatim* quotations, sometimes summarize a year's work in a paragraph or two. These variations reflect the emphases chosen by the authors.

Each author was asked to supply two or more cases in brief outline form, one of which was quite representative of the reading disability cases treated in that setting, and one or more which were somewhat exceptional but seemed to have desirable teaching possibilities. The editor chose the final cases from among those submitted, and tried to see that there was sufficient variety in age, sex, degree of severity of the reading problem, kinds of related or causal handicaps, and type of treatment program used. Most of the cases chosen had severe reading disabilities, as one would expect in clinical centers; the children with ostensibly mild reading problems were either struggling hard in school or were already failing.

Although the cases were chosen with variety as one of the criteria, there should not be any assumption that they represent a statistical cross-section of children with reading disabilities. They have been grouped according to the type of setting: full-time remedial school, multi-disciplinary clinic, remedial reading clinic or center, or medical setting. The sequence in which they are arranged is an arbitrary one that seemed reasonable to the editor.

More than half of these children were considered to have some neurological difficulty. In one case this was attributed to brain damage in early childhood, resulting from an accident (Case 11). In other cases, the presence of other persons with reading problems in the family raised the question of an inherited tendency (Cases 3, 10, 15, 16). In still others, neurological and psychological examinations suggested or indicated the presence of neurological immaturity and/or brain damage (Cases 2, 4, 13, 14, 15).

It is also significant that the majority of the children showed emotional difficulties, ranging from discouragement and inferiority feelings through depression, anxiety, and tension, to childhood schizophrenia. In several cases treatment involved psychotherapy as well as remedial teaching. Sometimes psychotherapy was started first, sometimes they were begun together, and sometimes the need for therapy became clearly evident after a considerable period of remedial teaching. The degree of parental involvement varied not only in the plans and facilities available, but also in the ability and willingness of the parents to participate. In one case the parents were the only ones in psychotherapy (Case 15), and in one case a very interesting type of "conjoint therapy" was used, with parents and child seen together (Case 14). Sometimes efforts to involve parents in therapy did not succeed (Case 5).

Even when psychotherapy as such was not used, the remedial program was often planned with as much attention to the child's emotional and social problems as to his cognitive handicaps. In several cases printed materials were avoided for considerable periods of time because the child had developed an aversion to them (Cases 2, 4, 10). The selection of individual or small-group instruction, the avoidance of a school-like atmosphere, tolerance and acceptance of disruptive behavior (Case 2), insurance of success, and the development of a comfortable relationship between teacher and pupil have been given at least as much attention as the instructional details.

While nearly all of these children needed help in learning how to identify printed and written words, there was little similarity in their psychological patterns. The I.Q.s of the children ranged from superior to borderline at the time of the diagnostic study. Some had higher verbal than performance I.Q.s, some had higher perfomance than verbal I.Q.s, and some showed no disparity between the two. In some children, specific weaknesses were evident in visual perception or memory, in auditory perception or memory, in ability to make associations across modalities, or in directional orientation and sequencing, but there was no consistent pattern of low abilities. Incomplete or mixed hand dominance seemed to be related to directional confusion and reversals in some cases. Difficulty with other phases of language such as listening and speaking were also present in some (Case 10), justifying the use of a term such as language disability, but these were few; in most, oral and aural skills were normal.

Visual difficulties were present in several cases. One child had gone without needed glasses until very shortly before the diagnostic study, and the glasses obtained were found to be incorrect (Case 12). An older boy with a residual problem from corrected strabismus was given glasses to equalize the vision of his two eyes, and this corrected the fusion difficulties that had been interfering with his reading (Case 9). One child had previously been given orthoptic training to correct an eye muscle difficulty and was found to have normal vision at the time of the diagnostic study (Case 16). Another child seemed to have an uncorrected eye difficulty at the time of the diagnostic study, but since the child was under the continuing care of an eye specialist, the only vision recommendation made was to reexamine at regular intervals (Case 11).

A combination of teaching methods was used with most of these children, for example, teaching the visual recognition of common words while also teaching phonics, and devoting part of the lesson to oral and silent reading. The Gillingham method of phonics instruction was followed in Cases 4, 14, and 16, and was sometimes combined with kinesthetic procedures (Case 10). The Fernald kinesthetic or VAKT method was employed in several of the cases, usually with some modification. For example, in Case 2 the child's lack of fine motor control made writing difficult, so typing was substituted. A language experience approach utilizing the child's own dictation was employed at the beginning in several cases, at times combined with reading of very easy printed material (Case 1). In printed materials, books written with mature interest appeal and low vocabulary were generally preferred to basal readers.

Direct teaching of perceptual skills, sequencing, etc., was involved in Cases 2, 4, 14, and 15. Motor training emphasizing large-muscle skills and balance was an integral part of the remedial program for one child (Case 4). In none of the cases was an attempt made to change a dominant hand or dominant eye and thereby influence central cerebral dominance. Also, none of the cases involved attempts to promote neurological organization through such activities as creeping and crawling, or sleeping in a particular position.

Medication was a significant part of the treatment plan in three cases. In one of these (Case 2), it was discontinued after several months because it did not seem to be doing any good. In another it played a helpful but minor part (Case 11). In the third (Case 14), in which hyperactivity and distractibility interfered greatly with learning, both medication and dosage were changed until a marked improvement in behavior and ability to learn were evident.

Some of the children progressed in reading to a point at which it was necessary to place the major emphasis of the remedial help on comprehension and study skills. The description of these upper-level remedial procedures should be of particular interest to those working with older children and adolescents (Cases 11, 15).

The Editor has greatly enjoyed the privilege of being the first to read all of these case reports. His editing has been restricted mainly to minor stylistic changes, and cutting some non-essential material out of a few of the reports that had gone over the maximum length allowed. No changes have been made in the factual accounts or the opinions expressed by the authors.

Authors were requested to make sure that all names of the children and their families were changed, and that any other information that might help to identify a particular child was modified. Thus dates, place and school names, and similar items have been altered without influencing the essential facts of the case. As a final step, the Editor has represented all family names (even when already altered) by an initial letter only, as a continuing reminder that identification of a particular child and family is not intended. Authors have also held back on some facts, divulged to them in strict confidence, which had no direct relation to the child's reading problem.

Each case report begins with a brief description of the setting from which the report comes. Most of these sections were written by the Editor from information supplied by the authors, and in a few instances are quoted word for word from that information.

Each case report ends with some brief comments by the Editor, whose task in writing these comments was made difficult by two self-imposed restrictions. The first restriction was to keep the final comments very brief, so as to save as much space as possible for the case reports themselves. There were so many points in each case which interested the Editor that he would have had little difficulty in commenting at great length. With a self-imposed maximum length of one typed page, each section of comments is necessarily highly selective. The second restriction was to avoid the strong temptation to second-guess the authors—to wonder what might have happened if a different diagnostic procedure or a different treatment plan had been followed. Comments of that kind would hardly be fair to the authors. The Editor's comments are intended, then, to point up some of the special features of each case.

Now, let the case reports speak for themselves.

CASEBOOK ON
READING DISABILITY

Martin

BY ROY A. KRESS, Ph.D., AND
MARJORIE SEDDON JOHNSON, Ed.D.

Setting

The Reading Clinic of Temple University in Philadelphia is the service and laboratory facility of the graduate program in the Psychology of Reading, one of the largest programs for the training of reading specialists in the world. The Reading Clinic provides diagnostic and instructional services to large numbers of children and adults. Its two main units are the Diagnostic Division and the Laboratory School.

In the Diagnostic Division, several hundred diagnostic studies are conducted each year, more than half of them by graduate students under supervision, the rest by staff members. The diagnostic program includes psychological testing, detailed analysis of reading and related skills, screening tests of vision and hearing, and referral for special examinations when indicated.

The Laboratory School provides full-time schooling on a highly individualized basis in classes of nine to twelve children, and operates a six-week summer session in addition to the regular school year. A thorough diagnostic examination must precede admission to the Laboratory School.

The Reading Clinic also provides corrective reading courses for secondary school students, college students, and adults.

Diagnostic Study

LIKE MANY OTHER YOUNGSTERS with severe learning problems focused in the area of reading, Martin had been examined a number of times by various psychologists and physicians before he arrived in the Diagnostic Division of the Temple University Reading Clinic for a reading evaluation. The referral had been made by the director of another clinic who had evaluated Martin some two years earlier. He had recommended, on the basis of his findings, placement in a small private school where he felt the boy's individual needs would be met. At the time of referral to Temple, when the parents had again consulted him for advice, he felt that the "normal school situation" supplemented by special remedial instruction in reading would not meet the boy's needs and that he should be transferred to a full-time remedial school. Martin was 8 years 2 months old when he came to the Diagnostic Division.

Case History

When the case history was taken, with Mrs. E. giving the information, it was apparent that there had been no obvious deviations in the developmental pattern before Martin entered nursery school. He had suffered no significant illnesses or injuries. He had one older brother and two younger sisters. Although Mrs. E. had not been conscious of any great differences between Martin and her other children as infants or in the very early years, she did report that Martin's learning difficulties had been apparent from the time he entered nursery school. His behavior in the school situation, and sometimes at home, was reported as very variable. At times his actions seemed to reflect "extreme shyness"; at other times he showed a decided tendency to act out all his feelings in rather extreme silliness and loudness. In addition to his acting "like a frightened rabbit" in his shy moments and his being objectionable to others with his silly loud behavior, his mother reported that there were times when he seemed "to go blank and to lose track of everything." The same reported behavior was linked, in his teacher's comments, by the statement that he often came out of his "blank" periods with "shock" and covered up with acting out.

Referral Report

In the referring psychologist's report, based on both the findings of the psychological examination and the report of a neurologist to whom Martin had been referred, his case was diagnosed as "a specific dyslexia or at least relatively isolated cognitive defect, based upon an impaired cerebral physiology." Actually the results of the electroencephalogram (electrical recording of brain activity) were described as "entirely within normal limits" although the examining neurologist felt that there might well be some organic base for his problem which available techniques were inadequate to detect. The report also suggested that psychotherapy might well be necessary at some future time and there was a real emotional involvement.

The analysis of projective tests pointed to "fairly adequate ego organization" and a conscience adequate to the task of helping Martin control and direct his impulses but not overly strong or constrictive. Motivational patterns were considered typical for a boy his age. There was evidence reported of "unfulfilled needs for affection and much indecision and ambivalence with respect to how to deal with his strong, outgoing masculine aggressive energies." The conclusion at the time was that there was evidence of continuing overidentification with the mother, whom he seemed to view as the dominant parent, rather diffuse anxiety and tensions, problems with relations and communication with the father generally, but that the time was not ripe for intervention from the emotional standpoint.

The results of an individually administered test of intelligence indicated that Martin was currently functioning in the high average to superior range of the general population, with a Full Scale I.Q. on the WISC of 118. Previous evaluation, using the WISC, had resulted in a Full Scale I.Q. of 107, a Verbal I.Q. of 90, and a Performance I.Q. of 124. It was felt that his potential was probably considerably greater since there was clear evidence of the interference of problems in attention and concentration.

Testing in the Diagnostic Division

The reading evaluation, which was done at the Diagnostic Division of the Reading Clinic, also included tests of specific capacities such as associative learning and memory span as well as an updating of information on vision, hearing, and academic achievement.

In spite of the earlier diagnosis of dyslexia, Martin did not show the typical associative learning problem which one might expect in such a case. However, he did show the beginnings of an emotional resistance to wordlike symbols. His ability to make associations was tested in a number of different situations (*Gates Associative Learning Tests*). He very easily and accurately made associations to non-wordlike symbols, regardless of the amount and nature of the sensory stimulation provided. However, on the wordlike symbols he had greater difficulty, with marked improvement when auditory stimuli were added to the basic visual stimuli.

Although no basic associative learning problem appeared to exist, the fact that Martin was beginning to resist tasks involving wordlike materials was certainly significant in terms of his reading problem. The anxiety which was evident in dealing with the wordlike materials was symptomized in his hesitance to respond to some of these items on subsequent trials even after he had successfully made the correct association. In all, on the section of the test in which he had to associate a picture with a wordlike form with no auditory stimulus, he had twenty-six refusals in contrast to five errors. Even when he had the additional help of auditory clues, he had seventeen refusals in contrast to eight errors. When his task had been one of making associations with geometric rather than wordlike materials, the same tendency had been somewhat apparent. On neither of these sections did he give an incorrect response, although he made a total of twelve ommission "errors" before he reached his top score of eight out of ten on the visual-visual association and six omissions before he mastered the ten items involving visual-auditory clues.

On the tests of memory span which were administered, all his scores were below both his chronological age (8 years 2 months) and his mental age (9–6) with the exception of his span for visual objects. This test yielded a mental age score of 9–11. The next highest span score was for letters presented visually (8–0), tending to indicate that he had no basic problem in dealing with visual stimuli in spite of his lower scores on completely visual association tasks. In descending order were his memory span scores for oral directions (7–9), digits forward (7–0), auditory related materials (5–0), auditory unrelated materials (3–5), and digits to be repeated in reverse (3–0). The summary statement in the diagnostic report said of his memory span performance: "Results of the memory span battery taken from the *Detroit Tests of Learning Aptitude* indicate that Martin has severe difficulty attending and concentrating in a number of different situations. Martin can concentrate better than attend to a task. This is not necessarily a good state of affairs since Martin must work hard to get the sort of learning most youngsters get effortlessly. Martin can also function better on a concrete rather than an abstract level. One of his lowest scores was on a test most vulnerable to anxiety."

The results of a verbal opposites test tended to confirm the picture of generally restricted achievement. His score on the specific tests from the *Detroit Tests of Learning Aptitude* placed him at the 8–0 mental age level.

In contrast to the memory tests, measures of visual and auditory discrimination revealed no problem. His scores were perfect on each of the tests (*Gates Reading Diagnosis Tests* and *Betts Ready to Read Tests*) and he appeared to have no difficulty with the tasks. Screening evaluations in the areas of vision and hearing also revealed no problems.

Reading. The evaluation of levels of achievement and the specific strengths and weaknesses in reading painted a rather typical picture of the contrasts shown by standardized and informal tests. On the *Gates Primary Reading Tests* Martin was able to score within the second-grade level on all three sections. His grade scores ranged from 2.3 on Paragraph Reading to 2.7 on Sentence Reading. On each of these subtests his performance was somewhat erratic, with errors on some of the easier items and correct responses on harder ones. It was obvious from analysis of the responses that he was highly dependent on the picture clues that were a part of the tests, and on his oral language background. On the word recognition section he showed some definite knowledge of sound-symbol relationships although he was overdependent on the initial part of the word. Some responses showed that he also attended to word endings, but that he apparently ignored the medial parts of the words.

On the informal reading tests, his difficulties in reading were much more apparent. On the recognition of words presented in isolation, he was able to perform perfectly only with the list of preprimer words. Beyond this point he began to run into considerable difficulty with the flash presentation and was not able to correct all of his responses even when he was given unlimited time. In the word recognition test, as during the psychological evaluation, Martin was reluctant to respond unless he was quite sure he was right. When a word was exposed to him for only a momentary glance, he responded, rightly or wrongly, if he felt that he actually knew the word. Once he realized that he had been wrong, he rarely responded with another try. Therefore, although there were small improvements, there were never marked differences between his flash and untimed scores on the lists of words. At primer level he had a flash score of 72 percent, gave the word *into* without another exposure of it, and corrected two errors when he saw the words for an untimed period, *went* for *what* and *run* for *ran*. This gave him an untimed score of 84 percent. At first-reader level he missed eight words out of twenty-five for a 68 percent score. He made second attempts, when these words were reexposed, on only three of them, correcting just one, *now* for *new*. His other responses on the untimed presentation were to change his response *say* to *set* for *stay*, and *then* for *them* after no response. His untimed score was 72 percent. By the time he reached second-reader level, he was able to recognize immediately only 40 percent of the words, with one error, *his* for *hide*, and an exceedingly slow response to *everything*. On the untimed presentation he responded to three words to which he gave no response on the flash presentation, but corrected no errors, for a total score of 56 percent. At third-reader level, he made no attempts on the flash presentation, and was able to recognize only one word, *love,* on the untimed.

An informal reading inventory was administered, beginning at the preprimer level. On oral reading at sight Martin made only one error, a substitution of *here* for *her,* which he corrected with no help from the examiner. He was able to answer all the comprehension questions. During the silent reading at this same level he evidenced lip movement throughout the reading and was able to achieve only a 50 percent comprehension score. His oral rereading, however, showed good ability to locate the appropriate part of the material to support an idea, and he read with good rate and rhythm.

At primer level, his oral reading at sight was quite poor and was accompanied by finger pointing. He substitued *to* for *the* and repeated the whole sentence, read *fat* for *funny, are* and then *ran* for *run,* and had to ask the examiner for the word *pretty.* On two of the five comprehension questions he made no attempt at an answer. Overall on the 26-word selection, he had only 85 percent accuracy in word recognition and 60 percent comprehension. At this same level on the silent reading, he attempted answers to only two questions, one of them wrong, for a comprehension score of 16 percent.

A check of his hearing comprehension revealed that he was able to understand adequately materials at second-reader level when they were read to him by the examiner, but at third-reader level his performance was very poor. He again resorted to answering, "I don't know," to most questions and was able to give correct responses to only about a third of the questions.

Thus, in spite of the second-grade level standardized test scores that he had attained, Martin was not able to function independently in reading with any materials, even those at preprimer level. In fact he had some real instructional needs at that level and showed no readiness to profit from instruction at a higher level at the moment. In view of his performance at primer, he would have to be considered frustrated there.

A sampling of words from a first-grade spelling list was administered. Of the twenty words, Martin attempted only nine. On two of these he tried only the initial letter of the word. The six words which he wrote correctly for his score of 30 percent were *he, A, can, see, I,* and *at.*

Certain characteristics were rather consistently shown in both the psychological tests and those of specific reading functioning. As soon as he began to run into any kind of difficulty, his performance dropped off precipitously. Rather than the gradual decline in performance which many children show as they go on to harder tasks, Martin appeared to "fall apart" virtually all at once. The fact that he frequently gave no response, or said that he did not know rather than take a chance, always left the examiner with the feeling that he probably had more learnings than he was able to use on a consistent basis. His anxiety about failure appeared to lead to unwillingness to take a chance and virtual paralysis of those abilities he did have.

An almost overwhelming lack of self-confidence seemed to pervade all of his reactions. The clinician who did all the testing characterized him as "an extremely shy youngster who was reticent but cooperative. . . . Even with encouragement Martin would not venture an answer he was not completely sure was correct." In the recommendations, emphasis was placed on his need to experience success in reading activities and to judge himself in terms of the progress he was making rather than in terms of how far he still had to go. The prognosis in his case was considered fair to good provided he was in the proper educational setting. The opinion of the psychologist who had referred him was reaffirmed in that a full-time program in the Laboratory School of the Reading Clinic was recommended so that he could have a program based on his needs in a therapeutic environment. No recommendation for concurrent psychotherapy was made at that time.

Remedial Program

First Summer

The parents followed the recommendations, and Martin began his full-time remedial program just two weeks after the evaluation. This action was not taken without some "sacrifice" because the family ordinarily spent summers at the shore.

During the six weeks of this first session Martin displayed many of the characteristic behaviors that had been reported in both the case history and the results of various examinations. When he was first taken to his classroom to meet his teachers and the other children, he immediately showed his shy, reserved side. He showed no interest in meeting or becoming involved with the children. For the first week or so he shuffled into the room each morning, displaying total indifference to those who were already there. He made it clear that he did not care to enter into discussion, either before or during school. Generally, when someone attempted to start a conversation with him, he would set his lips, look away, and say nothing. He worked in a rather perfunctory manner, yawned frequently, and gave the impression of being very tired. The only evidence on his daily record sheets of an active show of feelings came in reports of impatience with himself and with certain demands placed on him, of strong resistance to the procedures he had to follow in word learnings, and of expression on repeated occasions of "I don't know" or "I can't learn that" even before he had tried.

Martin's program during the summer session was based primarily on the language experience approach, although he also did some directed reading, in a small group situation, using basal materials. In the first group in which he worked on a reading activity, he felt that the other members did better than he did and this brought strong negative reactions. He was far more overwhelmed and frustrated emotionally than he actually was academically, although some of the group were more advanced in word recognition. Because his self-confidence was already at such a low ebb, it seemed important for him not to feel inferior. Therefore, he was changed to a group in which he was actually the most capable. Here he could see that he "knew more words" than did the other children. Before long he was feeling definitely superior, a feeling he had probably never experienced in an academic situation. It was obvious that this was a more comfortable situation for him than being what he perceived as "low man," and he seemed really to begin to enjoy working. However, he obviously did not know how to cope with his new view of himself and he often fell into silliness as his mode of operation. In this group, a preprimer from a basal series was used, with the children reading both the actual book material and experience records based on the characters, illustrations, etc., but reflecting the children's own reactions to them and their language. There was a marked difference in Martin's attitude toward the actual book material and the stories the group composed cooperatively. He read the book material in an unnatural manner, but handled the material that utilized the children's own language, interests, and concepts much more effectively. He seemed almost to be embarrassed by the immaturity of the book material although he reveled in being successful with it, and he dealt with his embarrassment by making fun of the material.

The language experience reading activities were of two types. In the first, Martin worked individually with a teacher, explored topics of his own choosing, and reported his ideas about them in written form. In order to allow him to express his ideas more freely, he was allowed to do the creative part of his composition orally and only when this was done did he begin the physical job of writing. In order to learn the words he needed for writing these reports, he used a visual-auditory-kinesthetic-tactile technique (VAKT). It was felt that this technique would help him in two specific ways. First, it would give him an opportunity to experience success in word learning and therefore to reverse the negative trend of his reactions to wordlike forms. Second, the completely structured procedures of the technique would make the tasks of attending and concentrating easier for him in the word-learning situation. In his other language experience reading activity, he worked in a group situation. Here the children selected topics of interest to them and worked cooperatively on solving problems, answering questions, and extending their conceptual backgrounds relevant to these topics. No special word-learning techniques were employed. However, in both situations, follow-up materials were prepared to provide reinforcement of sight vocabulary, development of elementary word-analysis skills, and extension of comprehension abilities.

In the first type of language experience setting, in which his work was done individually with a teacher, Martin chose to learn and write about various sea animals. No attempt was made to push him to explore the topics any more deeply than he felt prepared to do. At first, probably because of his lack of confidence, he was unwilling to delve into any subject with any depth. In fact, his first series of "reports"—written about the shark, the porpoise, and the swordfish—contained not more than two sentences each.

Martin's word-learning activities through VAKT drew their content from two sources, these "reports," and the words that were needed for his daily recording of his activities. It was immediately evident as he began to use the VAKT technique that much of his performance would be the result of his attitude at the moment, once he had learned the basic procedures. If he went into the learning of a particular word with the attitude indicated in his statements "I can't learn that one," or "I knew this would take forever," he performed very erratically—resisting the training, asking for many demonstrations, and making numerous errors of a procedural nature in both the tracing and the writing trials. On the other hand, if he approached the learning task eager to show himself and

others what he could do, he required little demonstration and few tracings, and made a minimum number of errors. Particularly in the early
stages of his work, he hated the idea of having to relearn a word that he
had not retained—as if this were concrete evidence of his inadequacies.

The Kinesthetic Method (VAKT). When he was first introduced to the
VAKT technique, he chose *globe* as the first word he would like to learn.
After the clinician wrote the word for him on a large slip of paper, she
demonstrated how he was to trace it. Immediately he showed his reluctance to try unless he was sure he would be right. He allowed her to trace
the word six times for him before he felt he could do the same thing. To
learn the word, he traced it six times, twice incompletely because he was
stopped when he made procedural errors. His first two attempts at writing the word after these six tracings were incorrect, once because of procedural error and once because he began to make a *d* for *b*. After this he
made two successive correct copies. The next four words he learned were
ones he needed for his daily record sheet—*opening, writing, recess,* and
July. The number of tracings and trials on these words varied considerably and two of the words had to be relearned on subsequent days
when he was again unable to write them correctly on his clipboard sheet.
July was learned with no tracings necessary. He learned the word by
simply looking at the teacher-written copy and saying it.[1]

During his third day of using the VAKT technique, he planned a one-
sentence "story" he wanted to write. Even though it was only one sentence he insisted on its having a title.

The Shark

The Shark has a fin sticking out of the water.

The only words he did not have to learn by VAKT were *the, a,* and *of.*
In addition to the six words for the story itself, he had to learn *room* for
the identifying heading on his paper. The first day after he had planned
his story, he wrote the heading and the title. He was already showing less
need for demonstrations before he would try tracing words, perhaps because he was anxious to get on with the writing of his story. He had
begun to object to learning the words for his clipboard records and, in
fact, had on occasions tried looking back to copy them from previous
sheets.

On the second day with the story, he was able to write *shark* again,

[1] For another description of the kinesthetic method, see Case 2.

changing to the lower case letter, with no need for relearning. He learned *has,* wrote *a* independently and learned *fin.* The following day, after relearning *opening* and *writing* very easily, he had considerably greater difficulty with *sticking* and added only that one word to his story. The next day he finished the sentence, learning *out* and *water* relatively easily, and planned a two-sentence "story" on the porpoise. After revision which he made as he wrote, this story read: "The porpoise has a sort of curved fin and his back shows out of the water. I would like to ride on the back of a porpoise." He had to learn *porpoise, sort, curved, back, shows, out, of, would, ride,* and *on.* Although he had to relearn *back* for the last sentence, he was able to rewrite *porpoise* spontaneously. He worked on this eight different days before he completed it. Then in four days he wrote two more sentences. This time about the swordfish: "The swordfish is big. It has a sword sticking out of its head." For this he learned *swordfish, big, has, sword, sticking, out, its,* and *head.* As he was finishing, he said, "This time it will be about whales," and began planning a series of reports on different kinds of whales.

While he had been working on these stories a marked change had occurred in his approach to himself and the word-learning process. A real sense of achievement was evident and he talked about his pride in his work. "See? I can write *July* now. Remember how hard it was before? It's easy to write now." Another day he reported that he had now learned twelve words. He counted only those which he had learned for his stories, not those learned for keeping his daily records. At the same time he began to talk more freely, showed less reluctance to trace as he realized he was gaining success through doing it, and started evaluating and revising what he had planned to write. He continued to be annoyed at any necessity for relearning. As he began his report on whales he was able to show his enthusiasm quite openly, even clapping his hands when he felt he learned the word *whales* quite easily. That same day he expressed some concern about another boy's learning words that Martin considered harder than his, but he immediately listed his own credits— "I've learned two words today, haven't I?" "This is a good story, isn't it?" Although he was obviously asking for reassurance, he was also becoming self-propelling. The next day when time for writing came around, he said to his teacher, "Let's get to our story—quick—so we don't waste any time. We want to learn new words, don't we?"

At the end of the six weeks, Martin still needed to trace most words he was learning, but made many fewer errors in the tracing and writing process. The only words he did not trace were ones he had learned previously and could relearn by looking at and saying the word. He still was very reluctant to try to write a word on his own, and instead of making an attempt immediately, said he did not know how to write it and went on to learn it through VAKT.

In his other language-experience activity during the summer session, the one in which he was part of a group, the focus of attention was also on the natural science area. The group settled on insects as a topic for study. At first he participated in the evolution of the topic and the preparation of the materials only as a listener. Gradually he became much more vocal, contributing information from an obviously wide background and drawing comparisons between his previously formed ideas and those which were presented by other members of the group. He evaluated ideas, accuracy of information, etc., and stated his ideas with confidence. From the first, however, it was apparent that he was more interested in insects than in reading about insects. When he did try to read and met any momentary frustration, he reacted with, "Do we have to read this? Why don't we just get on with it?" This attitude was certainly not completely overcome during the six weeks, but he did do the reading more willingly and actually began to make use of the finished word to clarify his ideas on a topic of importance to him. His contributions came from what he was reading as well as from his background of information.

The reading materials were basically of three types. The first was drawn directly from the children in the group, either from their previous backgrounds or from listening experiences. The following article illustrates this type of material:

> Some insects look like sticks.
> One that looks like a stick is the walking stick.
> The walking stick can be more than a foot long.
> The walking stick is wider than your finger.
> The walking stick is brown.
> The walking stick looks like a tree branch.
> The walking stick has six legs.
> The walking stick has two "feelers" that look like twigs.

A second type of material was teacher-written, based on what had come from the children but often extending beyond it or giving a somewhat different slant. The third type of reading material was also teacher-developed and was designed for the individual child's use as a follow-up of the group reading activity. These materials, in addition to providing an opportunity for further contact with the particular words that were being used, were formulated so that they demanded application of particular skills and abilities which were being taught.

Other areas of his summer's work were arithmetic and art. Here he showed much the same kind of reaction as in the specific language instruction. He evaded reading tasks when possible, showed himself capable of solid, original thinking, and increased in self-confidence during the period.

By the end of the summer Martin was taking real pride in his learnings in all areas. He had kept a tally of the number of words he learned through VAKT and showed open pleasure in his ability to read the materials in the group language-experience activity. He continued to show real annoyance when he had difficulty with retention of words in either situation. He also had not gone beyond the use of initial sounds in attempting to analyze words and rarely tried any word analysis unless he was directed closely in his efforts. His participation was more active in every area of school life. He finally brought in an insect as so many others in his group had been doing. The first show of interest in doing so was to come in making a joke of the idea, pointing to an embroidered insertion on his shirt pocket and saying, "See? I brought an insect." The next day, however, he came bearing a large bee in a box. All he said was, "I brought a bee," not without some show of embarrassment, but he was obviously pleased with the excitement the large specimen created in his group.

Results. The reevaluation completed at the end of the six weeks period did not reveal dramatic gains in scores obtained on the various tests. In the word recognition area he showed improvement through second-reader level in his untimed recognition. He was obviously disturbed by the idea of being tested, but was able to settle down to making a real effort to do his best. His only real efforts at word analysis were with initial parts. During the informal reading inventory he was still dependent on examiner help and showed many of the symptoms of difficulty he had evidenced during the diagnostic study. On standardized reading tests his scores ranged from high first- to low third-grade level, although the reading inventory showed that he still had needs at preprimer level.

One of the biggest changes seen was in Martin's ability to try. For example, although he had just 52 percent of the words on the first-grade spelling test correct in comparison with 30 percent at the time of diagnosis, there were no omissions here or at the next two levels. Through third level, he successfully represented many of the initial parts of the words dictated and produced some easily recognizable though incorrect "phonetic spellings."

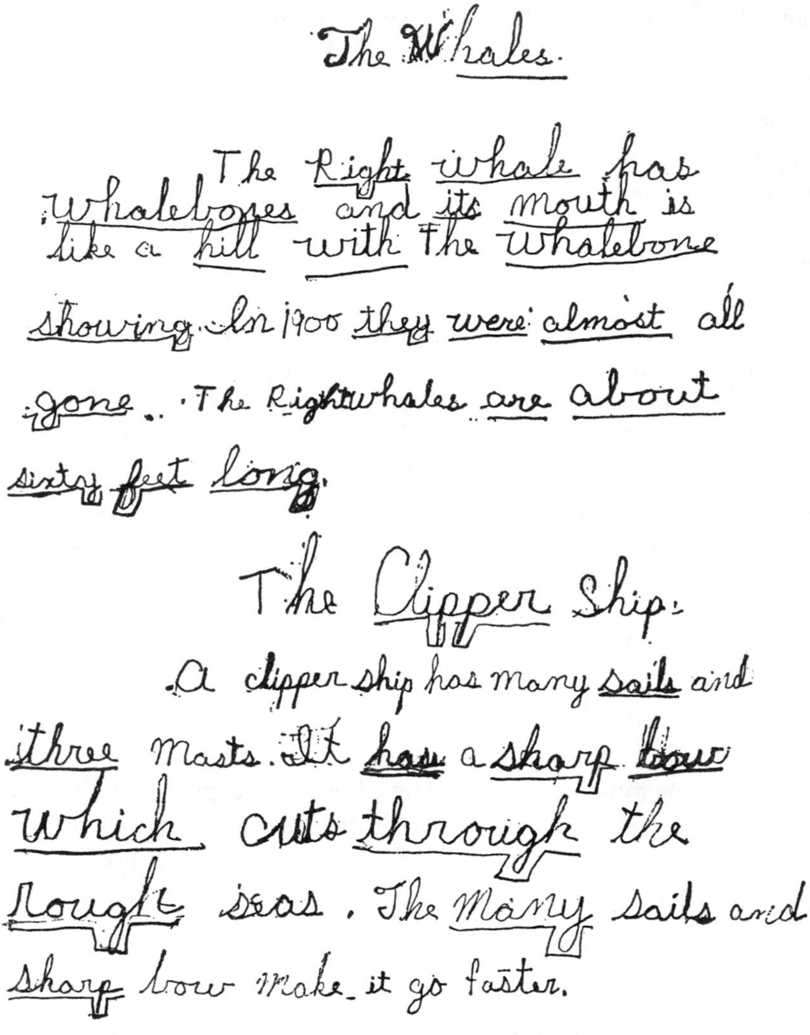

The Whales.

The Right whale has Whalebones and its mouth is like a hill with the whalebone showing. In 1900 they were almost all gone . . . The Rightwhales are about sixty feet long.

The Clipper Ship.
A clipper ship has many sails and three masts. It has a sharp bow which cuts through the rough seas . The many sails and sharp bow make it go faster.

Fig. 1. Two samples of Martin's stories.

Perhaps Martin's crowning achievement at the end of the six weeks was his climbing a tree in the play yard. Throughout the summer he had been torn between wanting to climb it and his fears that he might be unsuccessful or even suffer some physical harm. On the last day it seemed he just had to do it, and he did.

First Full Year

When Martin returned in the fall to begin his first regular year program, he continued with basically the same kinds of instructional activities. At first he continued to depend on tracing for almost every word he learned in the writing situation and rarely was willing to try a word unless he was quite sure he knew it. Gradually, he began to show evidence of increased confidence in his ability to work out words and to learn certain of them by looking at them and saying them in parts rather than depending on the tracing, especially if the word was one he had previously traced.

Martin's interest in sailing ships sparked the story about the clipper ship (see Fig. 1). He had models at home and brought in a large clipper to show to his classmates. His explanation of it was a very satisfying experience for him. This story is one written during the period of time when Martin was actively undergoing a transition from the dependence on tracing to complete independence of it. All underlined words were learned.

South was the first word that was written for Martin on a 4 by 6 card in small script rather than on a 4 by 12 slip in large script suitable for tracing. It had been evident that he was doing the tracing purely for confidence rather than for actual learning of the words. Because it seemed important for him to have proof that he really did not need this added support, it seemed necessary to move away from the larger learning copies. It is interesting that there was not only no increase in his errors at attempting to write the words after studying them when he could no longer trace, but an actual marked decrease. He continued throughout the rest of the year using basically the second stage of the VAKT technique, with words learned from a teacher-written copy but with no tracing. Occasionally, he learned a word directly from print when he and his teacher checked it in the dictionary. A decreasing percentage of the words had to be learned or relearned as his repertoire of word analysis skills and his willingness to apply them increased.

During the fall term, Martin's other reading instruction, as well as that in the VAKT-VAK setting, was on an individual basis. It seemed necessary for him to work in this one-to-one relationship with a teacher in order to give him a real chance to develop confidence in his ability to learn and perform. Even at the end of the term it was still evident that, although he had much greater confidence and consequently was able to give his full attention to the learning task rather than to his anxieties, the presence of visitors, or any sign that he was being observed or his progress evaluated, was enough to bring on tension, irritation, and inability to concentrate. Basal reader and other materials at preprimer and primer levels had been used in the individual instructional situation and Martin had been able to handle them very well. He had begun to work successfully with word analysis skills involving initial consonant symbol-sound relationships, rhyming elements, and a number of variant endings. In the area of comprehension, instruction and practice emphasized purposeful reading, precise factual recall, following directions, anticipating outcomes, getting main ideas and supporting details, appreciating sequence, and making and supporting inferences. Although there were still self-doubts which kept cropping up, he was able to surmount them in the day-to-day activities. He came to the point where he could do follow-up work which had been prepared for him on his own with no difficulty. He also began to do some easy independent reading, choosing materials relevant to his science interests, and willingly applied his word analysis skills.

Results. The end of the term testing, however, certainly showed that Martin had far from overcome his fears about his own competence. He was again very tense during the testing, and to compound the problem, he had been absent for three days just before informal reading inventory was scheduled. Even his daily work was usually affected by any time away from school, but he seemed to settle on this as the whole reason for his poor test performance, at least as it compared to what he did day-by-day. He was inconsistent in both word recognition and comprehension and really met the criteria for an instructional level only at preprimer. He explained his difficulty by saying, "When I am out of school a day or two and come back, I forget everything. I wonder why it does happen, really." In spite of all this he showed a much improved attitude over what he had displayed in the August testing. His scores on word recognition in isolation were greatly improved, and he showed real progress in application of word analysis skills as well as in extension of his immediate recognition vocabulary. The fact that he was able to go to second-reader level before he was completely frustrated was also encouraging even though the instructional level remained the same.

The first real breakthrough in test performance came when Martin was tested in June of that first year. He had continued through the second semester to get all his reading instruction individually, using materials at primer and then at first-reader level. On the informal reading inventory in June, he achieved an independent level at first-reader, an instructional range from second to third reader, and a frustration level at fourth grade. His word recognition continued to improve markedly; he was able to work out 68 percent of the words at fourth-reader level. In January, the testing had been stopped at third because of the drop-off at that level. In the spelling inventory, he tried all the words through the sixth-grade range and, although he showed independence only at first-grade level, he had three words right even at sixth.

Throughout this testing period, Martin made periodic remarks such as "Hey! this sounding out does work!" or a loud "I know it!" when he finally worked out a word using his own resources. He was very much interested in reading orally with good expression and in truly understanding what he read. He even was able to relax enough to react to ideas as he was reading (as he read that frog's eggs looked like black dots in jelly, he said, "Hey! Yes they do!"). A daily problem, that of reading more than necessary when he was asked to prove a point, did not escape him as his spontaneous comments show: "Only two sentences needed" and "Too much! I should have read only one part." Even his standardized test scores showed marked improvement and, in fact, higher-level tests had to be administered to get a real measure of his achievement. On the *Gates Advanced Primary Tests,* he scored at middle third- to middle fourth-grade level.

The Second Summer

Martin attended summer session again because it still seemed unwise to risk losses from three months away from school. Even with only a three-week break between the spring semester and the summer, some of the old fears did actually reappear. He was sure he had forgotten everything, deprecated his performance constantly, and began to resort much more regularly to acting silly and showing off as cover-up for his feelings of inadequacy. Whereas he had become quite active in his peer group during the spring term, he could not seem to adjust to new children who entered the school during the summer. He took some consolation from the fact that his "friends" would be back in the fall. However, the fact that his attitude toward himself could regress so greatly seemed to point to a real need for a more concerted attack on the problem of his self-concept. Particularly evident as a necessary instrument in the attack was the opportunity to make a strong identification with a male adult. His daily performance seemed to have slipped below the levels it had reached by June. Only toward the end of the six-week session did he seem to regain momentum, and then only when certain of his activities were halted in favor of meeting other needs that seemed more pressing—those in the self-concept and male identification areas. He worked on the repair and setting up of a previously leaky classroom aquarium. Getting his hands dirty with the sticky, black aquarium cement seemed quite enjoyable to him despite great initial reluctance. While this project was taking place, opportunity was also provided for ballplaying and a certain amount of roughhouse with the male instructor.

Results. The "proof of the pudding" seemed to come not only in better cooperation and academic productivity in the waning days of the summer, but also in his attitude toward the end-of-session testing. After his work with second- and third-reader level materials, basal and science-oriented experience, he showed gains on the August informal reading inventory. For the first time he performed perfectly with preprimer materials, showed independence at second, and had an instructional level at high third. Further work was obviously necessary as far as attitudes and emotional adjustment were concerned, as well as in the academic area. In the final report on the session, a strong plea was made for reappraisal of Martin's readiness to profit from direct help in the emotional area and for home cooperation, with the attempt to provide the needed identification with a male figure.

The Second Year

The portions of Martin's full-time remedial program described thus far constitute the periods of slowest movement toward overcoming his problem, on the one hand, and the periods of most dramatic movement, on the other. Fairly typical of children with severe reading problems was his going through a complete summer session plus a complete fall term before his informal test results actually reflected marked gains in his instructional level. All the while, however, he was showing small but steady increments of progress in his actual skills and abilities. In terms of his emotional status and its impact on his achievement, he is also not atypical. After a full year, he could still show great regressions in adjustment but, most important, he was actively inquiring into the reasons for his reactions and seeking help openly. Finally, through it all he could continue to learn and to apply his learnings. Because he seemed, after this period, really to have found the door open to his overcoming his problems, the succeeding two years which were necessary before he was ready to return to a regular school situation can be described in somewhat less detail.

During the fall term of the second year, Martin continued with his writing activities about topics of interest to him, using VAK for word learning. By the end of the term he was learning most words directly from print rather than from teacher-written copies. His topics were ones that were connected with class activities, including the building of a heart model and a subsequent study of other parts of the human body. Many times when he made an error in an attempt to write a word, he was able to correct it himself. Even on the words he ultimately had to learn, his first attempt was usually a sensible "phonetic" representation.

This same evidence of his increasing appreciation of sound-symbol relationship was evident in his recognition of words in a variety of settings. In his directed reading activities, which during the fall term were at third-reader level in social studies and science areas, he often made "close" substitutions of words in his oral rereading, and the errors were almost always self-corrected. From practice exercises for which he had to write responses, a good illustration came on one in which he had to make pictures of "ten animals or objects shaped for greater speed" and to label each. He labeled a Jaguar correctly, wrote *rockit* for *rocket,* and *motersikol* for *motorcycle.* His strengths in word analysis were also shown as he read reference materials, directions, etc., in connection with his projects. He would read a word like *ventricles,* for instance, at sight with no help. In both comprehension and word analysis he was showing sufficient gains to lead his instructor to write on his daily record sheet such comments as "with prodding and encouragement, he can do anything, but he must be pushed" and "excellent skills apparent when effort is unobstructed."

Emotional Difficulties. All was not perfect, however, during these months. Martin was still having severe problems from the emotional standpoint. His father had begun to build a closer association with him, particularly through joint participation in a variety of activities, and there were positive results evident. However, no move was made on his getting professional help until late in the semester. Meantime, his self-protective silliness continued, an increasing amount of violence was being expressed in a multitude of drawings, digressions from his work were apparent from time to time, and the old "I can't do it" pervaded all activities on certain days. All of those symptoms occurred on an irregular basis, with the exception of the drawing, and many of them seemed to take the place of frustration-induced hostility, saying, "We must never be hostile." The drawings, on the other hand, were usually filled with open expression of violent hostility but were almost invariably based on some facet of his schoolwork. Thus a study of volcanoes or a study of colonial life in America could, one as easily as the other, afford him the opportunity to dress up his basic illustration with shooting, violent eruptions, etc.

Another development was what seemed almost to be deliberate "baiting" of instructors. Some of his silliness was very deliberately acted out in a feminine way when he was working with the male instructor most actively involved in handling Martin's male identity problems. He was successful with the baiting to a point that his instructor had moments of doubt about whether Martin's identification with him, which had seemed such a promising development, might not actually be standing in the way of his establishing a real sexual identity for himself. Even saying to his instructor, "Oh, you men!" in a very feminine way, for instance, served his purposes well. With another instructor, with whom he worked in math, he made himself deliberately annoying in other ways which he knew would "get to" her. If she sent him back to his desk, he looked as pleased as he could be. He had done it! He blamed his difficulties in writing on some imaginary man who had invented our language, and brought to school a "lucky elephant" to help him with his reading. The fact that he stated, "He helped me in nursery school. I want to depend on him," seemed to make such actions a thinly veiled attempt to go in the opposite direction from that for which his instructors were striving. He almost seemed to be saying, "I should grow up and be a man so instead I'll be a dependent little girl." On one occasion he was somewhat more open and direct, making a picture of his male instructor in which his head was being bombed by a plane. He kept it hidden away for a time, but ultimately had to show it to its subject.

Finally, toward the end of the term, he started psychotherapy. When the idea of getting some help in the emotional area was first discussed directly with Martin, he brought out many things on which he obviously needed assistance. For example, he expressed his desire to return to a regular school, in fact quite specifically to the public school in his home area. At the same time he said he was sure he was stupid and would not really be able to succeed there. His fears and aggressions were also very troublesome to him and he seemed entirely ready to accept aid. On the day after the first visit he volunteered that he had liked it and said that he had drawn pictures and answered questions about anger. Very soon his "I can't do it" was being replaced with "My trouble is that I don't have self-confidence." He also tended to become much more open in his attempts to challenge teacher authority and even was able to make himself so openly obnoxious in a reading activity being directed by his favorite male instructor that he had to be put out of the group. The first time that this happened was shortly after another boy was added to both Martin's directed reading activity and his writing period at the beginning of the spring term.

There were many difficult periods for Martin through that winter and spring. The battle that he was fighting within himself seemed sometimes to be almost tearing him apart. He was fearful about the aggressive feelings that had come to the fore because he still clung to the idea that he should not be aggressive. He did not like himself as he now was—"a bully" in his own eyes—instead preferring the embarrassed, shy boy he had once been. It was difficult for him to communicate these feelings to others and, therefore, for him to get reassurance that many of his feelings were quite normal concomitants of growing up. Many times he was on the verge of tears. He continued to use his drawing, both at school and in therapy, as an expression for his feelings. In both music and art classes he seemed to be able, however, to use a variety of media for other expressive purposes than letting out his troublesome feelings. Here he seemed to take genuine pleasure in letting his creative abilities come forth in fluent, original expression and was able to recognize his own competence far sooner than he could in other areas.

As the year went on, he began to work himself slowly but surely to the surface of his pool of despair and fearfulness. He began to enjoy his aggressive feelings and expressed them in acceptable boyish ways such as wrestling with his peers. He became more communicative with adults, especially about his true feelings. He started, for instance, to talk about things he and his father were doing and even to share the results of them with his classmates. After a number of fishing sessions, for instance, Martin came in one day fully prepared to demonstrate for the group his ability to make flies. As they gathered around him, he made samples for them and dispensed them proudly. At the same time, he began to respond to pressure to try in academic areas without the extensive teacher help he had required and to take errors in his stride and in positive fashion. When another child was complaining one day about how hard his work was, the "new" Martin told him to stop feeling sorry for himself.

His academic performance was generally inconsistent, ranging from a high degree of competence to almost complete inability to function. He had difficulty handling his competitive feelings toward the other boy who worked with him. Some days they led him to analyze words quickly and effectively, as if to show up his competition, and even to give unwanted help to the other child. On such days his oral rereading was rushed, though accurate and expressive, as if he wanted to be sure his work partner would not take the opportunity away from him. Sometimes his problems seemed to block his thinking; other times he displayed excellent initial thinking skills and could get right to the heart of a concept. He continued to work primarily with social studies materials at high third-reader level in the small group reading activity and showed excellent grasp of both historical and geographic concepts.

Results of Second Year. Testing done at the end of the second year placed Martin at third-reader level for independent work and at fourth for instruction. He was able to go to sixth-reader level before the material was completely frustrating to him. His standardized test scores in reading averaged middle fourth-grade level; in social studies and science, middle fifth; in arithmetic, beginning fifth; in language, beginning fourth; in spelling, low third. He was 10 years old at that time.

The Third Year

Generally, Martin seemed to be on the right path to face his adolescent years and the challenge of a regular school situation. There appeared to be no reason to feel that he would suffer appreciable academic losses over the summer if he were not in school. Instead, it seemed that a camp experience would actually be more profitable for him, and this was recommended. This appears to have been a good decision. Although early in the third year there were some evidences of inability to handle work independently and to do effective inferential thinking, Martin seemed to get back on the track rather quickly in these respects.

In his writing activities during this year, Martin learned all words he could not work out by looking them up in the dictionary and studying them from the print there. By far the main effort in the supervision of his writing activities was on getting him to function independently, applying the skills which he had developed. The number of words he actually had to learn through the VAK third stage was minimal. In addition to the supervised writing activities, he was given independent writing assignments which grew out of his social studies work. He gathered information for reports and wrote them up, giving additional information on people, places, and events that were studied. It was clear from these reports that he was still far from over his spelling problems and, in fact, had not reached the point at which he could recognize and correct his own errors when he reread his material. However, he was able to organize his materials effectively and, in oral presentation, his reports were certainly satisfactory.

Reading instruction during this third year began at fourth-reader level and went on to fifth. Social studies materials were used, again emphasizing both historical and geographical concepts. After a somewhat slow start while he was getting used to a new male instructor and learning to live with his concerns about his ability to take his place in a regular school the following year, he made a good adjustment. For quite a time he appeared to be expending an excessive amount of energy and time on each academic task for the results he was achieving, particularly on those which were to be done independently. Many of the assignments which he should have accomplished effortlessly he turned into major projects. While this was going on, he was also quite constrained in his behavior and responses.

The first breakthrough seemed to come in the area of sports and other non-academic associations with his peers. Especially in organized games, he began to join the normal "give and take" and to develop more directness in his associations generally. Finally the same sort of increased relaxation began to emerge in academic situations. The greater his overall self-confidence and comfort with himself as a person became, the better able he was to function on his own resources in learning activities.

Results of Third Year. By June the plans for the coming year had been solidified. He was going to enter sixth grade in the local public school. He was to carry on with reading through the summer according to a plan worked out with the school supervisor, but was not considered to need summer school. The final testing showed that he had very few needs in word recognition through fifth-reader level (the highest tested). There were still needs in the area of inferential thinking, but Martin easily met the criteria for an instructional level at fifth reader. In spelling he now had an instructional range from third- to fourth-grade level and was close to readiness for instruction at fifth. His lowest standardized test score was still in spelling, but he now rated at high fourth-grade level even in that area. Aside from this, his lowest score was at middle fifth-grade level on one general vocabulary test and his highest was middle ninth-grade level on a social studies subtest. The average of all his standardized sub-test scores was above middle sixth-grade level. He was 11 years old.

Follow-Up

BECAUSE OF THE CONFIDENCE that Martin had gained and the freedom to learn and apply his learning which came with the resolution of his emotional difficulties, there was no reason to be fearful about his chances of success after he left the Laboratory School. Again, experience proved the point. Martin did make a real success of his sixth-grade year, having come from the status of a virtual non-reader as an eight-year-old and having spent his third-, fourth-, and fifth-grade years in a full time remedial program.

Editor's Comments

This vividly portrayed case offers an interesting problem in differential diagnosis, with continuing experience during the remedial program tending to reinforce the importance of emotional disturbance, and, by implication, raising doubts concerning the reality of the "impaired cerebral physiology" considered probable in a previous diagnosis. Psychotherapy begun late in the second year may have been more timely then than it would have been earlier, since Martin had already been strengthened by ample evidence of his progress in learning to read, and by relief from public school standards.

The authors' comments on the disparities between Martin's performance on informal reading inventories and on standardized tests deserve careful reading, since misleading conclusions about instructional levels are often drawn from standardized reading test scores. The point that, in the early stages of remedial teaching, considerable progress can be made that is not shown in tests is also convincingly made.

Although stress was placed on the language experience, kinesthetic approach, it may be noted that some use of basal reader material was made from the beginning, that phonics was introduced early, and that a variety of comprehension skills were taught throughout.

John

BY FRANCES BERRES, Ph.D., AND
JOYCE TAYLOR EYER

Setting

The Fernald School of the University of California at Los Angeles, formerly called the Clinic School, is named after its founder, Dr. Grace M. Fernald. A thorough diagnostic examination is required before an application is reviewed. The remedial school offers a regular session and a summer session.

During the regular session, students of average or better intelligence but seriously deficient in basic school skills attend for a full school day, five days a week. Classes are limited to fifteen to twenty students, and an individual remedial program, including physical education, is formulated for each student. The amount of individual help that can be provided is amplified by the presence of interns and graduate and undergraduate student helpers. Individual, group, and family counseling are available as additional remedial procedures when required. Each student is expected to continue until he has attained grade level and can return to and function satisfactorily in his regular school.

The six-week summer session has an intensive remedial program for students with mild to serious difficulties in school achievement. Students attend three hours a day, five days a week.

Other arrangements that are possible include a half-day program in small groups, which allows students to attend their regular schools part-time, and individual and small-group tutoring on an hourly basis.

Diagnostic Study

WHEN JOHN, DEFEATED, TROUBLED, AND ANGRY, was 14 years 2 months old, application was made for him to attend the Fernald School at UCLA. A Negro boy, reared in an integrated, middle-class neighborhood, he had a long history of school problems, both academic and emotional. John's father expressed great concern regarding John's future if adequate academic and behavioral skills were not acquired. John's mother, although divorced from Mr. D. and living apart from him and John, also showed concern. Both parents were cooperative and talked freely during intake interviews.

Intake Data

Intake data revealed that John's family, whose identification with middle-class society appeared strong, included his mother, his father, and a 16-year-old sister. The maternal grandfather, an alcoholic, lived with the family until his death, which occurred when John was 10. According to the father, the presence of the grandfather was a negative influence in the home, not only because of his drinking, but also because of the preoccupation of the mother with his well-being. As reported, Mrs. D.'s affection was mainly directed toward her father and she was never warm with the children.

The conclusion that John's relationship with his mother was an unhappy one was borne out by statements from both parents that there were frequent clashes between mother and son, that John was hostile toward his mother, that he would "blow up" when she made a request of him, and that he tried to withdraw from her whenever possible to avoid her constant lecturing. The parents agreed that the mother favored John's sister, a good student who was domineering and aggressive toward John, and of whom John was both jealous and resentful. By contrast, the father and son were highly compatible and companionable, seeming to find in each other solace from perceived neglect and rejection. Mother and father both reported that Mr. D. favored John and tended to overprotect, "baby," and make excuses for him.

John's parents were divorced when he was 11 years old. John went to live with his father and the sister with his mother. The father made many attempts to find appropriate means of improving John's learning skills and behavior. These included consultation with school personnel, enrollment in special private schools and special classes in public schools, psychological and physical diagnostic examinations, eye examinations with prescribed exercises, and private tutoring.

There was no history of familial congenital diseases or neurological defects. Medical history indicated that birth was normal and early development was reported by the parents as "average" in spite of chronic asthma and some allergy to foods and pollens. John had the usual childhood diseases. Measles, which occurred when he was 4 years old, was accompanied by a high fever. Although his parents considered him somewhat hyperactive, this was not regarded as a problem or in any way abnormal until he entered school.

School records showed that in kindergarten John was unable to conform to the classroom setting, couldn't follow directions, and exhibited immature muscle control. In the first grade it was noted that peer relations were poor, that behavior was unacceptable, that there was no appreciable improvement in learning or carrying out a task. Limited progress was reported during the second grade and the school administration recommended that John repeat the grade. A *Stanford-Binet,* given by the school when he was 7, showed an I.Q. of 99. For about a year John was given help in addition to his regular classroom work, with no discernible improvement either in reading or adjustment to school. Throughout the third and fourth grades his behavior became increasingly disruptive and provocative. For example, when placed in isolation at the rear of the classroom, he would hide under the desk and howl like a wolf, or roll on the floor and yell. A *California Reading Test* given by the school when John was 9 showed a reading grade of 1.7.

A year later the principal stated to the parents that it was impossible to contain him in a regular classroom and suggested additional efforts to diagnose his problem. A *Wechsler Intelligence Scale for Children* (*WISC*) was administered with a resultant Verbal I.Q. of 103, a Performance I.Q. of 96, and a Full Scale I.Q. of 99. *Wide Range Achievement Test* scores at that time showed Reading at 1.5, Spelling at 1.0, and Arithmetic at 2.2. The *Bender Visual Motor Gestalt Test* revealed faulty visual-motor performance and distorted spatial relations. Although John had poor recall of visual stimuli, his responses to auditory stimuli were superior. The examiner noted that John was ambidextrous and unsure of which was his right or left hand. A summary of teacher observations disclosed poor work habits, lack of friends, poor social adjustment, and minimal progress in all basic skills. Although he had a good speaking vocabulary, a high level of oral comprehension, and had received much extra help, he made no improvement in reading. The guidance department recommended that John be excluded from school specifically because of his uncontrollable behavior.

At that time, Mr. D. took John to a child guidance clinic for further diagnosis and assistance. A neurological examination disclosed a somewhat abnormal and poorly organized EEG (electroencephalograph) pattern. Medication was recommended, used for a few months, and discarded because it apparently had no effect. Wrist (carpal) examination and X-ray revealed immature bone development. Eye tests showed a visual functional disorder or "drift" of the left eye with difficulty in sustaining focus in tracking.

Psychologists found John to be neurologically handicapped with severe perceptual distortion. A *Revised Stanford-Binet* administered at that time placed his I.Q. at 113. It was felt that his problem behavior in school was undoubtedly exacerbated by his awareness of his inadequacies and disabilities. In addition, it was stated that his desire for acceptance and recognition appeared to be at the root of his provocative and disruptive behavior as much as his deficit in academic skills. Psychotherapy was initiated at the clinic. John was sent to an optometrist for eye exercises and at the same time, was enrolled in a private school for educational therapy.

During John's attendance at that school, the staff observed that in addition to his perceptual problem, he was suffering from an inability to recall symbols of any kind. They reported that it was exceedingly difficult for him to distinguish between letters of the alphabet, the various numerals, and most geometrical forms and designs. A *WISC* administered at the school showed a Verbal I.Q. of 127, a Performance I.Q. of 101, and a Full Scale I.Q. of 113. Initially John was placed on a one-to-one student teacher basis and attended school twice weekly, but soon thereafter he was permitted to attend full-time in a group of three. The staff reported he needed much support, affection, and understanding, and he responded to this approach, beginning to make real effort. His teachers reported that John's behavior had improved greatly, he was now able to recognize nearly all the letters of the alphabet, but he was still unable to read. Tuition at the school had largely been met by scholarship funds and loans made for this purpose. However, after a year, financial pressures became too great and Mr. D. had to remove John, now 11 years old, from that school.

The school district to which they moved administered a *WISC* with resultant scores of Verbal I.Q. 106, Performance I.Q. 104, Full Scale I.Q. 106. John was enrolled in an ungraded class, where he remained for about a year. Staff comments indicated that he was "well spoken" and "much more intelligent than his scores suggest." They further remarked that "severe perceptual distortion affected his reading, school work, and consequently, his behavior."

Again circumstances necessitated a school change. Authorities (teacher and principal) in the new school district interpreted John's problem as mental retardation and wanted to place him accordingly. Mr. D. felt that this would be wrong for John and, consequently, placed him in a fifth/ sixth grade combination class in a private church school. He also employed a tutor twice weekly, and although some progress was noted, John continued to perform inadequately and received poor grades in school.

Clumsy, thin, and tall for his age, John was particularly embarrassed at that time, according to his father, because he was almost four years older than most of the students in his class, bigger, and yet unable to perform academically as well as even the least able in the group. Temper outbursts and inability to accept classroom standards flared anew. John made no friends and continued to be unhappy and unsuccessful in school. At the end of his third semester John was once again requested to leave because the school could no longer cope with his inappropriate behavior. Mr. D., on the advice of the principal, applied for entrance for John at the Fernald School.

Fernald School Evaluation Data

At the initial screening interview required of applicants to the school, John showed a good command of English, was cooperative, and made quite a point of appearing nonchalant, assuring the examiner that he had "done this many times" and was "very good at it."

Tests administered included the following: WISC (Verbal I.Q. 95, Performance I.Q. 80, Full Scale I.Q. 87); *Stanford Achievement Test* (Elementary Form J, Paragraph Meaning 1.4, Word Meaning 2.0, Spelling 1.6, Arithmetic Computation 2.2); *Gray Oral Reading Paragraphs* (Grade Score 1.9); *Thematic Apperception Test; Sentence Completion Test; Draw-A-Person; Rorschach; Bender Visual Motor Gestalt; Benton Visual Memory;* various motor skills tests.

Test findings were reported as follows:

1. John's intellectual functioning, as measured by the WISC, is in the Dull Normal range (Full Scale I.Q. 87). This is appreciably below previous results in which I.Q.'s were reported from 99 to 113. The current

WISC pattern is highly erratic, with lows on Coding and Block Design and highs on Similarities, Vocabulary, and Object Assembly, but is fairly consistent with reported patterns of previous *WISC* tests, suggesting that there may be a stable kind of intellectual impairment or deficit. Eye-hand coordination seemed poorly developed, although the evidence of organicity was not pronounced. Although the present test may reflect John's current functioning level correctly, it grossly underestimates his intellectual potential, possibly because of interfering emotional and neurological factors.

2. Achievement: Reading and spelling tested at about first- to second-grade level and arithmetic fundamentals were at second grade. John had to count on his fingers. Lack of word attack skills, little association between letter form and sound, reversals, and a painfully laborious working through of basic arithmetic processes, as well as high anxiety and lack of confidence, were noted.

3. Personality Factors: The projective tests seemed to suggest a lack of ego-involvement and lack of motivation for achievement. There were indications of pronounced immaturity and poorly developed emotional controls. Self-esteem appeared very low with a deep underlying depression. He seemed angry with himself and with the world for his predicament, and there was evidence of self-destructive fantasies as a way of escaping his unhappiness. He seemed pessimistic about his future, feeling that no amount of effort on his part would bring results. In general, he appeared to be a fairly disturbed adolescent.

4. Perceptual-Motor Skills: Eye-hand coordination was poor, and mild visual perceptual difficulties were exhibited; visual memory was very poor. Auditory perception was found to be good, auditory memory adequate. Motor skills, including balance and laterality, were weak but adequate.

During the testing, John cooperated well but exhibited great anxiety, was hyperactive, and tended to give up easily. He made many self-deprecatory remarks and constantly watched the examiner for cues to see if he had given a correct answer. During the achievement tests, after the first few minutes he stopped trying and marked answers at random. These test findings were a good measure of John's functioning level but certainly not of his potential.

A report of a recent medical examination, including eye and ear checks, showed John to be in good physical health with normal sight and hearing. The "drift" of the left eye reported earlier was no longer apparent. The report also indicated that medication to alleviate hyperactivity had been prescribed from time to time but discontinued because no effective results were obtained.

In summary, John was seen as a physically healthy boy of at least average intellectual potential whose intellectual functioning level was impaired, possibly by emotional and neurological factors. Seriously educationally handicapped and rather disturbed emotionally, John appeared to be a victim of minimal cerebral dysfunction, and the emotional overlay of early failure experience. In addition he was coping with the residue of what had probably originally been severe visual-perceptual retardation and difficulty with fine and gross motor skills. John's rejection by mother and sister, continued school failure, expulsion from two schools, and being Negro in predominantly white classrooms, undoubtedly contributed to his low self-image and feelings of inadequacy. These feelings were possibly underscored by his father's constant over-protection and "babying."

A full-time remedial school placement and psychotherapy (if no improvement in the first six months) were recommended. A new school term began approximately three months after testing and at that time John was enrolled at the Fernald School.

Remedial Program

The First Year

A program was planned for John, based on the Fernald School's philosophy of a holistic, multidisciplinary approach. Psychosocial, biological, and educational factors were considered in attempting to create an atmosphere conducive to optimum learning. These factors were also considered when setting long- and short-range goals with both academic and behavioral objectives. As the school is committed to the idea that each person has his own style of learning and that no one approach is effective for all learning styles, an individualized program was designed.

Each student was called in for interviews and presemester educational testing the week before school started. John then had the opportunity of meeting the school staff, his teacher, the physical education director, and many of his classmates on an informal basis. The *California Achievement Test* was given, and additional informal surveys of John's academic performance were made by the school staff. John's teacher, a young woman with unusual ability to relate to and understand adolescents, listened to him read orally so that notes could be made regarding his needs in the area of reading. She checked John's math skills and also had him write a brief sample paragraph so that handwriting and language usage could be evaluated. This type of conferencing not only served to acquaint the staff with John's learning style and academic skills, but also gave John the chance to become acquainted with his teacher. In addition, the teacher had an opportunity to learn about John's personal interests and activities, his feelings and attitudes about school.

John's low self-esteem and depression, as observed by the examiner during psychological testing, were also notably evident to the school staff. His voice was strident and tense, his movements were jerky and his eye contact shifty. He seemed to anticipate both teacher hostility and personal failure. He was slow speaking, self-conscious about his work, and had a very short attention span. His math skills were at second-grade level and, for all practical purposes, he was a non-reader and non-speller.

Results of the tests, informal surveys, and anecdotal remarks were entered in a folder that became a part of John's continuous record to be used by those who would become involved in working with him, i.e., teacher, psychologists, social workers, and university students in training.

John was assigned to a classroom with fifteen other boys, ranging in age from 14 to 16. Included in the class were two other Negroes and two Mexican-Americans. They would attend from nine to three daily and receive help from a classroom team consisting of a supervising staff working with a demonstration teacher, a teacher's aide, university graduate students from the disciplines of psychology, education, and social welfare, as well as from ten to fifteen undergraduates training in the field of learning disorders.

The first day of school gave the staff an opportunity to observe John's behavior in a group. His initial attitude indicated that he was immune to teacher persuasion and his acute auditory perception skills were turned off as far as responding to an academic environment was concerned. He clumped noisily in the room, poked people, made strange noises, and during the rare times that he was seated, tapped incessantly on the desk top with his pencil, head darting from one side to the other, mouth slightly open most of the time and body tense as if to spring up in defense at any sign of danger.

Obviously the first challenge that had to be met with John was helping him to see himself differently so that he could learn to function in the classroom. Since it had been already established that medication was not indicated, various techniques were employed that dealt with his problems realistically but at the same time permitted him to be accepted as a worthwhile person and establish for himself a good reputation. For example, school records showed John's hyperactivity had always caused him problems in the classroom; therefore his program was built to utilize it constructively. His classroom schedule was arranged so that a good deal of freedom of movement was acceptable. Tasks scheduled were of short duration and various areas in the room were designated as work areas. John was given a choice of tasks to do and a choice of areas in which to work. He was permitted to sit at a desk, on the floor, or to stand up if he felt that this enabled him to concentrate on his work better. In this way, he had a structural freedom that met his need to move about, but was also acceptable activity as far as classroom standards were concerned.

Also, in addition to the regularly scheduled physical education period, John went to the athletic field at least twice each day, or more often if he or the teacher thought it necessary. During this time John circled the field at full speed or punched a punching bag for five or ten minutes until he felt relaxed enough to work again within the classroom structure.

Because of the unique classroom setting, where many adults were available for working with the students, it was quickly established with John that if he did not understand his work, or had any feeling of insecurity or inadequacy, he could request and receive help immediately. He, as a consequence, had the opportunity to see that it was not necessary to resort to his usual pattern of disruptive behavior. John was told that since the classroom was a place to work, any time he felt angry or wanted to complain or "sound off," he was most welcome to present himself to the Supervisor's office where he could howl, yell, make strange noises, jump, or swear to his heart's content without disturbing the class. John availed himself of this privilege at first, no doubt less out of a spirit of cooperation than out of curiosity to see if he really would be allowed to do it. When he found that he could indeed avail himself of these outlets and that they were helpful to him, he learned to make use of them. As he gained in maturity, self-confidence, and skill, he found they were no longer necessary.

John's academic program was aimed at developing the basic skills.

Various techniques were used and specialized materials introduced as a means of helping him to achieve successfully. Evaluation of work included immediate feedback to John with the opportunity for him to take part in making the plans for subsequent work. In this way he could, within limits, suggest techniques to be used, make choices in terms of which work should be done next; he could feel that he had some responsibility for and control over what he was doing and thus, hopefully, become an active participant in the teaching-learning process.

Assignments were designed to be limited in scope and relatively short in length so as to provide little anxiety and immediate success. Even so, any academic task at first was met by John with violent negative reactions. He made it quite clear that he couldn't care less about such things. Therefore, the goal for the first few weeks was to establish relationships, diminish John's anxiety, and help him to feel secure and trust the staff. Monitor-type jobs were devised and a good deal of informal talk and exchange of ideas were encouraged. John could begin to see himself as a helpful person who could fit into a school setting and be respected there.

John's experience with reading and books had been totally negative and his tension had been so great that he broke out in a cold sweat on being presented with a book during the first evaluation session. Therefore, adhering to a practice long found successful at the Fernald School, John was not given any books or asked to work with them at all initially. In spite of his ability to put up a good front at the intake interview and talk about wanting to reach grade level and consider college, once confronted with classroom tasks John assured everyone within hearing distance that he wouldn't do "that junk," it was "stupid and too easy," it was "for sissies, not for me."

Utilizing a Specific Interest. As relationships with the staff became easier, and he realized no one was expecting "impossible" performance from him, he relaxed and began to enjoy informal conversations with various staff members. He revealed his interests and this gave the staff an opening for presenting tasks he might accept. He confided that not only did he hate "that junk" but he really didn't need it because he planned to be a plumber like his father and "plumbers don't need all that stuff." This provided the important clue for John's program planners. Without directly debating the point that plumbers, as all others in our society, do indeed need academic skills, they inaugurated a program of involving his interest by helping John to "become a plumber." Materials in all skill areas were prepared utilizing the plumbing theme. Pictures, measuring devices, pipe lengths, and cutting materials were brought in, as well as sales slips, invoice records, account books, and catalogues of samples.

Arithmetic instruction took the form of figuring out how much to charge when taking into account hourly rates and basic expenses, or figuring feet of pipe needed in various building or repair jobs. John at first did the problems in his head even though they were far more complicated than the 2.2 grade level he achieved on standardized arithmetic tests. Soon he discovered it was easier in many instances to write down figures and to check them; he even discovered a practical use for memorization of addition and multiplication facts.

Reading skill development started with staff members and trainees devising stories about plumbers and discussing with John their activities and usefulness to others. Soon John was initiating the discussions and making up stories too, as well as relating true incidents he experienced when he accompanied his father to work on numerous occasions. This gave John the courage to start dictating stories to a teacher so that other students could read them. Of course the plumber was always the hero of the tale. He rescued a small dog from drowning when a water heater burst in the basement; he helped pipe water to a desolate spot where wild horses were perishing during a drought; he aided an irate homeowner to overcome insomnia by fixing the drip-drip-drip of the bathtub faucet; and incidentally he made Jack the Plumber a very popular fellow among students and staff—gaining acceptance and recognition for John at the same time.

Incorporation of a student's interest into this type of a project framework within which academic skills can be taught had a number of advantages. In John's case:

1. Because of his sincere interest in the subject matter and because it was a completely different approach than he had ever known, it intrigued him and thus permitted him to lower his defenses.

2. It incorporated both his experiential background and his goals for the future and, therefore, was extremely meaningful to him. John responded when he could see that what he was doing related directly to his life and could be of some use to him.

3. This approach gave John the opportunity to instruct others regarding various facts related to his interest and in so doing he gained in self-confidence, self-respect, and feelings of adequacy.

4. John found that in order to continue with the project he really needed arithmetic and reading and writing and, thus motivated, gained the courage to attempt tasks that were more academic (while the staff in the process of preparing lessons and listening to John learned a great deal about plumbing!).

The Kinesthetic Method. The process of helping John to progress from his highly negative attitudes toward learning and assisting him to become a successful student is easier to describe than it was to accomplish. His first reaction to any suggestion was a highly emphatic "No! I'm not gonna." However, once he reached the stage of wanting to read, he accepted warily but more or less willingly the kinesthetic approach to reading and writing.

Based on and incorporating the methods developed by Grace M. Fernald, the techniques use writing to teach reading. Stories are written on topics of interest to the student. Words needed for the stories are learned initially through auditory, visual, kinesthetic, and tactile channels, a multisensory approach that ensures a successful learning experience and furnishes an excellent focusing device. In addition, it provides an interesting, meaningful way to learn because the writing is related to something about which the student wants to communicate.

John's first writing activities involved making out itemized bills and invoices for "plumbing services." The first word he wanted to learn was "tools" because he was going to fill in an order blank.

While John watched and listened, the teacher wrote the word in large script on a 3- by 11-inch newsprint slip with black crayon, saying it simultaneously. After the word was written the teacher repeated it so John could see and hear it as a unit and John looked at the word and said it.

Next John took the tracing slip and, using the first two fingers of the hand with which he wrote, simultaneously traced and said the word. He used finger contact as though he were writing with a pencil, carefully outlining the word and crossing the "t." He traced and said "tools" until he could successfuly reproduce it on the back of his tracing slip without copying and then wrote it from memory on his order blank. When he finished filling out his order blank, John filed his tracing slip in a file box with alphabetical dividers. The box remained on his desk so that he could pull out and relearn the word any time it was necessary.

The tracing technique was novel to John and he enjoyed carefully saying and tracing the words. He didn't even seem to mind writing them, although his poor fine motor coordination prevented him from making them very legible. He could see that going through the process helped him to recognize words he wanted to know.

Story writing was now introduced. Each day John was asked to write a story about anything that interested him. Any words he needed were supplied on tracing slips and John learned these words using the technique described above. When a story was completed, John and the teacher went over it to catch any possible errors, and then it was typed. The next day it was returned for him to read.

Each day, after he had read the typed copy of his story aloud to a teacher, he read the new words he had learned the day before. These were listed for him out of context at the bottom of the page and were reviewed each day until John recognized them successfully for three consecutive days. Any words not recognized were pulled from his file box and relearned.

For most students this technique not only helped with the reading process but was also an effective technique for learning to spell and to improve handwriting. In John's case, poor fine motor coordination made it very difficult for him to write legibly and the writing process was slow and painful. Furthermore the experience was extremely anxiety-provoking because, after John had finished writing, the product was so illegible that there was very little he had put down on paper that he could read. After John had used the technique for two months it became apparent that its use would have to be adapted to accommodate his problem.

The tracing and immediate writing of words was obviously effective in helping John to recognize them and to build up a sight vocabulary. Therefore the painful story-writing process was eliminated and in its place was substituted the previous dictated story technique which had been successful and enjoyable. Now after the story was dictated, it was typed and the next day John was asked to read it. Those words he could not recognize he learned using the kinesthetic technique, and he was given practice in recognition of these words until he could recognize them successfully on three consecutive days.

After approximately seven months, John no longer needed to trace all new words in order to recognize them. He was able to look at a word carefully, say it, and write it from memory on a card. The card was filed in an alphabetical card file to be used again if needed. Occasionally, when John found a word particularly difficult to recognize, he went back to the tracing technique and used it to good advantage.

John "wrote" many stories and described numbers of true incidents, and these, his own literary products, became his first reading materials which he eventually put all together in book form, and for which he made illustrations and drew and labeled diagrams. Eventually, as he gained skill and confidence, John began to read from books—initially animal stories and eventually any assigned topic.

It should be noted that many types of materials were tried and discontinued. For example, the Sullivan programmed materials were presented. As long as John had a teacher working with him, he responded to the lesson. However, any time he was left alone, using this or other aids such as *Reader's Digest Skill Builders* or *Reading for Meaning*, a behavioral crisis would occur or the time would be wasted. Because of his coordination problem John had difficulty forming letters and filling in spaces or writing words, so that without continued support he would become extremely anxious and would revert to some of his old habits.

Teacher-prepared materials, typed copies of his own stories and eventually high interest, low-vocabulary books such as the *Wild Life Adventure Series,* the *American Adventure Series,* and the *Deep Sea Adventure Series* were acceptable to John because he found them interesting and didn't consider them "babyish"—a term he used for any materials he didn't care for or considered beneath his dignity.

Various kinds of activities were used to facilitate John's reading. New words to be read in a lesson or any words John didn't recognize while reading were learned kinesthetically. Each day he spent ten to fifteen minutes going through a portion of his tracing slip file or his card file, reviewing the words for recognition; those he had forgotten he relearned. Phonics lessons and drill were used as John needed them to further his understanding of word structure. By the end of the first year at Fernald School, John could successfully analyze and pronounce most words at beginning fifth-grade level and comprehend reading material at middle fifth-grade level.

Second Year

During the second year John began to read with the *Controlled Reader,* which he liked from the very beginning and considered one of his favorite activities (partly due to the fact that he worked in a special room with one teacher during this time). Exercises were given using the tachistoscope; short phrases were flashed on the screen in order to help him to focus and to accustom him to reading with minimum regression. As he participated in these lessons, it was evident that he was pushing himself both in speed and comprehension because he would request that the teacher speed up the machine, or go back so that he could understand something that he had missed.

John's attitude toward reading during this second year was excellent. He said he knew he was doing "pretty well," but he confided to his teacher he still couldn't read well enough to read the Edgar Allan Poe stories, something he had always wanted to do! The teacher decided that reading such material might be a positive rather than a negative experience for him, since he was at the point where missing a number of words was not necessarily defeating to him and he was willing to try hard if it was something he really wanted to do. Therefore, they went to the library and picked out a collection of Poe stories. John's teacher prefaced the reading of the new material by assuring him that it was all right if he didn't know all of the words and that she would tell him any words he needed. Both of them were surprised and pleased at how well John did and both felt that John's positive attitude made for his success.

John became an avid reader and, by the time he was ready to leave the Fernald School, he was reading some classics, and literature concerning politics and social reform, in which he was particularly interested.

Mathematics. The second year was not completely clear sailing for John, however. There were many factors that plagued him. For example, his first enthusiasm for mathematics lagged considerably as the processes became more difficult. Math concepts were learned only by extremely slow and laborious means. Consistent use of concrete materials, "putting the problem on the table" so that John could manipulate, count, and practice again and again helped him to show some gains. Cuisenaire rods, flannel boards, and, of course, the plumbing materials added interest and motivation. John had much difficulty, however, when he was presented with even the most simple written directions. He refused to read them, glanced at them hastily, then started to work, usually using the wrong process. Two ideas, used consistently, helped him to progress; first, making certain that all math processes were originally introduced orally and that all directions were clearly understood; second, presenting simple written directions and problems and insisting that John explain them to the teacher before he started working.

John's motor coordination was a prime source of difficulty and prevented him from clearly and legibly putting problems on paper. Graph paper was used so that there would be identifiable spaces in which to place the correct number. However, the multitude of small lines were confusing and this paper was abandoned in favor of plain paper with grids drawn under the problem to guide proper placement of the answer. This served to reduce the field stimuli and was found to be effective. Eventually John was asked to imagine the lines in order to keep the numbers in the right spaces. All numbers were written in a large size and only a few problems were presented at one time, as John felt very pressured when he saw a whole page of problems ahead of him, and would then refuse to work. A great deal of repetition and encouragement was needed and it was also always necessary to find new and challenging ways to introduce new processes and to sustain John's interest.

Writing. Gradual improvement took place in mathematics as it had in reading, which was most encouraging to John and his teachers. His most severe difficulty, however, still centered around his writing and spelling skills. As early as kindergarten, he had been identified as a child with a fine motor skills deficit. At 15 he still could not write legibly in either manuscript or cursive. Even he had no idea, ten minutes later, what he had written. Standard handwriting procedures were introduced and discarded as ineffective.

While tracing and writing, even though illegibly, obviously helped John with his reading vocabulary, these techniques had very little effect on John in handwriting and spelling. One teacher tried using different colored pencils to help him to identify and distinguish between the letters. This had no effect. Raised letters, tracing in sand, marking in clay, and templets were presented for practice with only a glimmer of improvement. Although cursive writing is generally preferred in the use of kinesthetic techniques because it presents the word as a unit, John was encouraged to print. Even this was a slow and laborious task for him because of his motor deficit, but he was able to produce a more legible product than with cursive writing.

The staff conferred frequently, evaluated, and sought new ways to help John. He had become well able to express his ideas orally and was adept at following orally presented lessons. The facts that writing was such a tedious process for him and that he couldn't spell were extremely discouraging to him.

The real breakthrough came when the teacher gave John a list of basic spelling words and suggested that he type them. John did this, starting slowly and painfully. He discovered for the first time that he could read what he had written. This was a revelation for him and he now saw some connection between reading, spelling, and writing. He was so greatly encouraged that he made a real effort to develop better spelling skills. In addition, he started to learn to type properly and began to use the typewriter for other written assignments, such as math.

This breakthrough, although encouraging, was no cure-all for John's problems. There were many instances when typing was not appropriate nor a typewriter available. If this was the case, John used printing, even though it was laborious. However, this was a real turning point as far as John's attitude toward his spelling and handwriting deficiencies were concerned. He worked to improve his spelling and could now accept what he had thought was an insurmountable disability in handwriting as merely an unfortunate detail. He was able to accept the deficiency because he had found a way to compensate.

John continued to progress and learned outlining and note taking skills, became familiar with the dictionary and encyclopedia, and was now able to type his own stories and research papers. Because he had been one of a few Negro children in predominantly white classrooms all of his school life, it was felt that the opportunity to learn about Black history and culture would help to give John a sense of pride and enhance his feelings of adequacy. He enjoyed this and did an excellent project on Black history.

Specific problems still remained with punctuation and syllabication. The teachers presented these skills as the need occurred in his story writing and as the points in question were appropriate to his level of understanding. As he progressed, this type of instruction continued but was implemented with more formal instruction in punctuation, grammar, and usage. When John was almost ready to leave the Fernald School, formal instruction was used entirely and self-correction of indicated errors was expected, as it would be in a regular school setting.

As John began to have school success, he felt more confident; his general attitude regarding peers changed from hostility to acceptance and tolerance. He began to establish good relations with other boys and showed an unusual degree of sensitivity and perception for their problems. Whereas earlier he had resisted and fought group participation, he eventually became a leader and took an active part in seminar sessions and class activities. Teachers in the classroom and physical education field supervisors saw the changes almost simultaneously.

Other Curriculum Areas

The physical education training, as part of the holistic approach, was an integral part of John's program. The physical education supervisor worked closely with John's teacher at all times. The program consisted partially of exercises to develop good muscular response, laterality, and spatial orientation, practice on a balance board, and opportunity to gain experience in following directions and obeying rules. Initially John had refused to participate in group sports. Rather he preferred to remain on the periphery, often making snide comments which led him into conflict with the other boys.

The assistant coach worked with John individually for a while, practicing throwing baskets, catching balls, running, playing ping-pong, and in general helping him to develop skills and to be at ease on the athletic field. When John seemed ready he was encouraged to join with a group of two other boys who were functioning at approximately the same level in terms of skills and confidence. Then, as continued success was evident to John and the coach, large group activities were introduced. These usually were a Fernald School version of the sport of the season. John's size was advantageous to him, particularly in basketball and other sports, and it was a great day for the entire school when John, acting as a fielder at a faculty-student baseball game, caught the first fly!

John refused at first to get involved in the Fernald School art program. His first art experience in kindergarten, because of his perceptual motor and fine motor coordination difficulties, had been extremely unsuccessful, reinforcing his feelings of inadequacy. As a consequence, during his school career he refused to do any sort of art work. At the Fernald School the goals of the teacher were not only to provide a pleasant art experience for the students but also to help them to learn to complete a task and to encourage feelings of adequacy. Each student was provided with paper, water colors, pastels, or charcoal. The teacher might sketch a scene while at the same time discussing some art technique such as perspective, color contrasts, or symmetry. The students were encouraged to begin their art work at any time, and choose the media that they preferred. Each student had only one piece of paper and was encouraged to finish the "picture" during the art period. The subject matter of the art production could be that of the scene being discussed, or any other of the student's choice, including abstract or free form.

Some weeks passed before John became engaged in any art activity. He was interested when he saw that students who had trouble getting started were given personal instruction by the teacher and those who made mistakes on their papers were shown how to change or add to make the picture satisfying. John chose a fountain as his first subject. He was exceptionally pleased when, with the teacher's help, he completed the picture and it really looked like a fountain. He became a willing participant in the art program. Possibly because of his long-standing difficulty with fine motor control, he seemed to be particularly proud when he was able to reproduce on paper an object that others could recognize.

Parent Guidance

When John had been at the Fernald School for six months, a social welfare graduate trainee was assigned to work under the supervision of a social worker with John and his father in an attempt to accelerate John's behavioral and academic progress. The trainee made several home visits and reported that John and his father had an excellent relationship, but that the father's anxiety concerning John's success was an inhibiting factor to his progress. Mr. D. was so concerned for John that he unknowingly took on too many of John's responsibilities. While constantly urging John to help at home, do school work such as read and practice spelling words, John's father usually gave in to John's reluctance and procrastination. Mr. D., exhausted from trying to convince his son to do the work, would either do the task himself or accept John's excuses. It was made clear to Mr. D. that he could be of more assistance by giving John clearly structured, reasonable household tasks with a time limit set and have appropriate consequences consistently meted out. Both John and his father needed to see that John had to take responsibility for himself and his actions. In keeping with Fernald School's policy, it was recommended that Mr. D. forget about having John do academic tasks at home until he was mature enough and ready to do them on his own. Mr. D., continuing in his concern for John, cooperated fully and shortly thereafter remarked to the teacher that this was the first time since John had been of school age that he felt free from constant anxiety about him.

Helping a Younger Boy. At the beginning of the second year additional responsibility was also placed upon John at school. He was selected as one of the older students who might function as a successful tutor for one of the younger students. The needs and strengths of both students were carefully assessed and personality traits were considered before John was given his assignment. He had the responsibility (under supervision) of working with an 8-year-old boy during the reading period. His duties consisted of reading to a pupil and then having the pupil read aloud to him and answer questions concerning the material covered. John was given a specific time and was totally responsible for getting to the pupil's classroom, arranging the seating area, conducting the lesson, leaving the classroom neat, and returning to his own class on time. He was expected to keep simple records and report progress to his pupil's teacher. Eventually he was able to take part in selecting interesting and appropriate material for his pupil. This responsibility was met, and both boys profited greatly from the experience.

Transition to Public School

At the end of three years of attendance at the Fernald School, John's reading was at eighth grade, math at sixth, although spelling (as previously indicated, one of John's weakest areas) was only at fourth-grade level. It was decided that John had progressed both academically and behaviorally to the point where he could try to function in a regular school setting and should have an opportunity to "try his wings."

A program was arranged with the local public high school so that John could remain at the Fernald School in the morning to continue work on his basic skills, and attend physical education and shop classes at the high school in the afternoon. The morning program was structured so that the class activity simulated the regular high school curriculum. John was encouraged to do homework, keep a notebook, was given dictated assignments with greater academic responsibility, as well as being exposed to competitive situations with other students in his group. He continued with this program for a semester which he completed successfully. The following semester John remained part time at the Fernald School, but, with the cooperation of counselors and the high school principal, was permitted to take one academic course at the high school as well as physical education and shop. At the end of the year, John tested at grade level on the *California Achievement Test* in reading and mechanics of English, at seventh grade in math, but only at fifth grade in spelling.

Follow-Up

THE FOLLOWING YEAR a concentrated program at the high school was arranged for John so that he could meet graduation requirements. Special arrangements permitted John to use a typewriter or take oral examinations when essay questions were required. He returned to Fernald School each afternoon for one hour of supportive tutoring. This not only gave him the opportunity to develop better study and organizational skills, but also served as a source of encouragement and reinforcement whenever John needed it. His grades for the last year were B's and C's and he had excellent reports in citizenship.

John had the benefit of the high school vocational counseling service and had many opportunities to discuss his future with Fernald School staff members. Various careers were discussed and investigated, but he decided to continue toward his original goal. After he graduated he took a job as a plumber's helper for the summer months. In the fall he enrolled in the city trade school program to pursue his ambition to become a plumber like his father. When John left Fernald School he was invited (as are all students) to feel free to come back to visit or to discuss any problems that might arise. John visited several times and apparently from his reports was making good progress and a satisfactory adjustment in his world.

Summary and Conclusions

JOHN FITS CLASSICALLY into the much discussed category of minimal brain dysfunction. He exhibited many of the symptoms: 1) hyperactivity, 2) confusion in laterality, 3) clumsiness, 4) violent outbursts, 5) coordination difficulties, 6) visual perceptual retardation, and 7) a consistent pattern of deficiencies on several WISCs administered over a period of years. In addition, results of EEG readings indicated abnormalities.

Although maturation lag is sometimes used synonymously with minimal brain dysfunction, it was hypothesized that John actually suffered from both conditions. He was socially immature, exhibited perceptual problems sometimes found in younger children but usually outgrown by 9 or 10, and early wrist X-rays showed delayed development.

Added to these factors were John's home difficulties. His unfortunate interaction with his mother and rejection by her, along with the overprotection supplied by the father, could only have caused conflict and confusion for the child.

Immature, hyperactive, and unprepared to accept direction or responsibility, John's problems when he started school were exacerbated by perceptual distortion and poor coordination. Having to function in a classroom before he was ready, and being unable to meet the demands of kindergarten, he both gave and received an image of himself as a "bad boy." This image was reinforced as he grew older and continued to have severe difficulties and few satisfactions or successes. Nonproductive habits and hostile emotional reactions to school and learning, as well as a negative self-image and deep feelings of inadequacy, were well established by the time John was enrolled at the Fernald School.

Treatment procedures described in the present report reflected an holistic approach to the remediation of learning problems and maximized remedial instruction techniques by individualizing them to fit the needs of the particular student. This required an eclectic approach in which contemporary learning theory as applied to behavior modification was used. However, the present approach went beyond conventional behavior modification procedures in that it attempted to utilize insofar as possible the inner resources and growth potential of the individual student and continually evaluated and reevaluated methods of achieving target behaviors.

Remediation for John had to begin with his feelings and attitudes. He needed to be respected and given a good reputation to live up to so that he could see himself as an adequate, worthwhile human being. Certain behaviors had to be extinguished and others reinforced or initiated. However, concomitantly, John needed to know that he had the capability of succeeding academically. Techniques by which he could learn and subject matter which was interesting and meaningful to him, as well as encouragement and a supportive school staff, were imperative.

Important also in the remedial process was the integrated functioning of school and home. It was necessary for John's father to become aware that John was not a different person in school than he was out of school, and that as a parent he had to assist in helping John to take responsibility for himself and his actions.

Functioning in a therapeutic school setting where he no longer felt isolated or a failure, the temporary minimizing of competition, the success experiences, and the opportunity to be of help to others, all contributed to John's progress.

John entered the Fernald School severely impaired behaviorally and emotionally. Academically he was almost completely disabled. Dramatic changes occurred in personality and self-concept as well as in the ability to function independently and to assume responsibility. In addition, John became an adequate, interested student.

Although John has never overcome his fine motor coordination handicap, he has learned to live with it quite comfortably. He is pursuing occupational plans of a realistic nature in which he is genuinely interested and for which he has the potential.

John's history indicates that the prognosis for many children with minimal brain dysfunction can be viewed optimistically and that efforts to help adolescents with learning problems—sometimes considered to be relatively hopeless—can produce positive results.

Editor's Comments

This case is a most impressive example of what can be done for a child whom several schools had expelled for intolerable behavior, and who had made practically no academic progress up to the age of 14. Particularly noteworthy is the careful planning to meet John's personal and social needs, as well as to provide instruction adapted to his special handicaps.

A consideration of causation indicates that John's learning disability resulted from much more causation than is needed to produce a learning disability. There is strong evidence of minimal cerebral dysfunction which could be based on brain damage, of delayed and irregular neurological development, or in this case probably a combination of both. His ambidexterity and directional confusion, his visual problem, his very poor fine motor coordination, and his severe visual-perceptual retardation, all could be aspects of a basic neurological difficulty. On the other hand, the stresses of his family situation in early childhood were sufficient to provide a causal explanation based on emotional disturbance. The combination of constitutional and environmental handicaps was overwhelming, and the resulting disability was very severe.

The difficult problem of successful transition back to a regular school program allowing high school graduation was sensibly met by making the change a very gradual one. The high school deserves much credit for being so flexible in adapting to an exceptional boy's requirements. The final outcome is a success story in which the father's persistent determination to find the solution to his son's problems should be recognized as an essential ingredient, without which John would have remained a total educational failure.

· 3 ·

Jim

BY MARIANNE FROSTIG, Ph.D.

Setting

The Marianne Frostig Center of Educational Therapy is a nonprofit institution which has three main functions: service, professional training, and research. Psychiatrists, psychologists, social workers, and educational therapists combine their efforts to diagnose children with learning difficulties and plan a comprehensive program to help them achieve their full learning potential. Full-day and part-day educational programs provide highly individualized learning in very small classes. Individual training and tutoring, psychotherapy, and counseling are provided for children and parents as needed.

Children of elementary school age are taught in very small groups. The standard California curriculum is followed whenever possible, but the needs and disabilities of each child determine the classroom experience. Special training in lagging abilities, such as perception, language, or coordination and muscular skills, is given to all children enrolled. Playground activities, arts and crafts, and a summer day camp are also available.

Fellowship and internship programs are provided for experienced teachers and psychologists. The center's research program is concerned with developing new ways to evaluate learning difficulties and methods of treatment.

Introduction

THIS CASE HISTORY is the longitudinal study of a child with a familial language difficulty characterized by, but not restricted to, a reading difficulty.

The treatment and results that are reported covered a span of eight years. A follow-up report is also given on Jim's current status after one and a half semesters in a junior college.

There is much controversy about the success that can be expected in cases of familial dyslexia. The decision as to whether the treatment was successful may depend on the point of view of the person who judges the results. If adjustment to school and functioning in society and *improved* reading ability are the criteria, then Jim's treatment was successful. If the achievement of *average* reading ability is considered the only acceptable goal, the results must be regarded as a proof of failure.

The present adjustment of this youngster has resulted from close co-operation between a large public school system and a private clinical school. This aspect of the management of the case might serve as a pattern for similar arrangements in the treatment of children with severe learning disabilities who cannot improve in the available public school setting.

The case history also illustrates the role of direct training of the abilities that are involved in learning to read.

Diagnostic Study

Background Information

Jim came to us in November, 1960, when he was just 11 years old, and in fifth grade. He was a handsome, chubby boy with a round face that showed three dimples when he smiled (a permanent one in his chin and two in his cheeks), but he smiled rarely. He had completely "given up," and sat in school without responding. His movements were very slow; his face had an anxious expression; he was depressed, withdrawn, and defeated. At the request of the public school psychologist, Jim was seen by a psychiatrist who diagnosed a severe learning problem and referred him to us.

Interview with Mrs. C., November, 1960. Mrs. C. reported that she, herself, had learning difficulties as a child, especially in reading. She was not very good in math but was able to get by. Although she spoke very fluently during the interview, she still felt that verbal expression was hard for her and that she did not know how to use certain words. She said that her vocabulary was "lacking," although this was not apparent. She said that she had an inferiority complex because of her former reading and language difficulties. Her father had expected her to be perfect in school but, she said, she "just wasn't the perfect type." At the time of referral she was so worried about the children that she had arranged to have a few counseling sessions with a psychologist.

Mrs. C.'s father had himself been excused from further school attendance when he was 14 years old. He had said that he had been expelled for using foul language, but Mrs. C. did not know if this was the true explanation. He certainly had no reading difficulties later on, because he educated himself by reading. He was very proficient technically. He invented machines and learned electronics by looking at diagrams and reading. He could do arithmetic but not advanced math. He was color blind, and she wondered if this caused difficulty in school.

Mrs. C. reported that her mother was good at languages. The rest of the family were farmers and working people, and she did not know anything significant about their school performance.

All of her own children had trouble in school, not only Jim. Robert, 13, the oldest, had had remedial reading in grammar school for two or three semesters, but continued to be a poor reader. Arithmetic was also difficult for him. John, 12, the second son, had less difficulty than Robert, but still found reading very difficult. Donald, two years younger than Jim, also had some difficulties in reading and in math. The youngest child, Catherine, 4 years old, was not yet in school.

Mrs. C. believed that her husband had problems in English and in reading. She described him as a very slow reader, who often mispronounced words unknowingly. His vocabulary was quite limited.

Jim's Difficulties at the Time of Referral

At the time of referral, November, 1960, Jim was unable to name any letter, nor did he know any letter sounds. He was color blind and tone deaf. On the *Frostig* visual perceptual tests, he showed disturbances in eye-motor coordination and perception of spatial relationships, although his performance in other areas of visual perception assessed by the test (figure-ground perception, constancy of perception, and perception of position in space) appeared to be adequate. He had no difficulties in directionality. Auditory perception was very poor. Jim was unable to hear differences or similarities between sounds whether they were isolated or in words. He could visually match letters but not words. His scores on the *WISC* showed a 22-point discrepancy between his Verbal I.Q. of 85 and his Performance I.Q. of 107; the Full Scale I.Q. was 95. Another *WISC* administered elsewhere had given a Full Scale I.Q. of 93. Subtest scores are shown in Table 1 (see p. 69).

At about this time the family doctor had put Jim on Dexedrine. Although Jim seemed more alert, the mother noticed that he lost weight and slept poorly at night; she therefore discontinued the medication. After a few weeks there was no noticeable change in behavior, although he seemed a bit more listless. Up to the present time, Jim has taken no other psychotropic drugs.

The task of the teacher was complex. Jim had difficulties in visual perception, in auditory visual integration, and in auditory perception. He showed a low energy level, hypoactivity, and emotional disturbances characterized by despair and listlessness secondary to his learning difficulty.

He showed all of the symptoms that one would expect in a child with such severe reading difficulties, with the exception of systematic reversals and difficulties in left-right discrimination. His language abilities were severely impaired; he had noticeable defects in expressing a thought, in remembering words, and in using correct grammar. As language disabilities also occurred in many other members of the family, one could hypothesize a hereditary defect.

Remedial Program

Elementary School

We began teaching Jim (in November, 1960) by using what is called the organic reading method. For learning to read and to spell, Jim was allowed to choose those words which were of the greatest significance to him. He at first chose only arithmetic words such as "add," "plus," "subtract," and "multiply," because he was proud of the rapid progress he made in his arithmetic skills after coming to our center.

His progress in arithmetic was indeed astonishing. His mother asserted that he could not count to more than thirteen when he came to us—and we found that he even made errors in this task. He must have had a severe block in this area, because after four months he was not only able to add and to subtract, but he had also begun to learn his multiplication tables through the fives. He quickly learned arithmetic signs (%, ", ', #) and to match them with the correct words (percentage, inch, foot, pounds) and to use measurement in arithmetic problems. After a few months (February, 1961) he was able to say, for example, which was larger, 42 feet or 54 inches, and by how much.

It was most interesting that at that time anything connected with arithmetic seemed to help him overcome his learning block, despite the extreme difficulty in learning letters. In the initial stage the teacher used a combined oral and manual kinesthetic method. Jim watched the teacher's mouth as she said a sound or a word, then he repeated it very carefully and slowly. He would then say it a second time while watching the teacher write it, and then he himself wrote the word. Finally, he overlearned words with the aid of flash cards, thus transferring from the kinesthetic to the visual channel. This method was at first indispensable for him in learning any word. He also tried to learn by tracing words, a combined visual-tactile-kinesthetic method which in this instance proved unsuccessful.

In March, 1961, the teacher began to work with Jim on a variety of language skills, such as punctuation and capitalization, explaining, for example, that the first word in a sentence was written with a capital letter, and when to make a period or a question mark or an exclamation mark. He also became acquainted with the dictionary and learned to refer to the index of a book. He learned simple opposites (e.g., black-white, big-little), and was told to watch for plurals while speaking, adding an "s" at the end of a regular noun used in the plural. He learned new words for his spoken as well as written vocabulary. He learned to use "was" and "were" correctly.

From the very beginning, even at the preprimer level, he was taught to read for comprehension, rephrasing the factual information, and making inferences whenever possible. We attempted to help him learn different symbols through the use of maps. He was asked to dictate stories for practice in the creative use of language. Various approaches to mastering oral, written, and printed language were thus used simultaneously. Also, from March, 1961 on, a phonic approach was started, at least to the extent of his listening for the first letter in a word.

At that time Jim showed extreme concreteness in all thought processes. For example, the teacher tried to teach Jim to write a statement which was not really true, but imaginary, and Jim refused to write down "a lie."

All the stories which Jim dictated were egocentric; that is, Jim was the hero and his ideas referred to something he himself had seen or done or was doing at the time or wanted to do immediately.

Arithmetic progress continued to be astonishing in comparison with his other progress. He was sometimes able to do quite lengthy computations, although he was exceedingly slow and often used his fingers. He could not solve any word problem that was written; it had to be given orally and pronounced slowly. Although he could add and subtract, he could not reverse the process, or understand that addition and subtraction have an inverse relationship. It seemed indeed that Jim had not yet reached Piaget's level of concrete operations. The teacher worked on number stories to help him comprehend reversibility.

After four months with us, Jim still did not know the names and the sounds of most of the letters, in spite of work with phonics. As the reading material in books within his range was too childish, he worked a great deal with his "own" book, a book written by the teacher with Jim's help. Imagery gradually developed and, through imagery, he became able to assume a less egocentric and less concrete attitude toward the world. For example, after writing on one occasion that he had taken his dog for a walk, he added a description of what the dog experienced and how it felt during the walk.

Penmanship was very poor at that time, but Jim slowly learned to form letters and, in fact, to write rather legibly. By the end of March he wrote sentences from memory, such as: "I can ride the pony," "I can see the sun," "I can see the tree." He still had to be prodded not to write about himself only.

Jim's attention was good, and he made progress. He mastered the pre-primer vocabulary by April, 1961, and began to read a primer. At the end of June he began with a high first-grade book, *On Cherry Street* (Ginn & Co.). Through the methods described above Jim seemed to be able to learn and retain new vocabulary, but the teacher still found the progress in reading to be slow in comparison with arithmetic.

The teacher's note from April 20, 1961, was as follows:

> In arithmetic he adds and carries very well, borrows from zero with no difficulty. Multiplication tables covered until 6, knows through 5 fairly well. Handles simple division easily, e.g., $10 \div 2$. Knows signs and symbols. Starting long division; shows good progress. In spelling and reading, visual as well as kinesthetic methods prove helpful but here the progress is still very slow.

The teacher's report seems to indicate more knowledge in arithmetic than Jim really had. He worked very slowly, still sometimes using his fingers for counting.

The semester report from June, 1961 (at that time Jim was 11 years and 8 months old), showed real improvement, which was verified by test results. The *California Achievement Test,* Lower Primary, Form W, was given as a power test, and his reading score was at the 2.6 grade level. In reality, however, he was not able to read above a high first-grade level.

He continued to make progress in arithmetic, and fractions were introduced in June, but computation remained a slow process. He tested at a 3.9 grade level, but this also was higher than he was able to function in the classroom. We have found frequently that group achievement tests tend to overestimate the achievement level of children with learning disabilities, especially at the lower levels.

Learning through listening, in spite of the poor auditory discrimination of speech sounds, was good when concrete and factual material was presented. Jim learned facts about the solar system. Plant and insect life were studied. Lectures were illustrated by pictures and graphs. Jim continued to work with maps. He made progress in all these areas. The learning of letter symbols was not facilitated by auditory methods, however, and connecting and retrieving sounds and meaning which corresponded to the printed letters and words was a painful process. Reading continued on a first-grade level all through the summer of 1961.

The teacher had introduced the use of "blind writing" and color cues early in the spring of 1961.[1] Blind writing and color cues were successful in that Jim learned to spell the words that he learned to read. Both methods are helpful in teaching a child to become aware of sequences of letters and of detail, and they help the child to visualize. We emphasized visualization and told Jim to write down words after visualizing them.

In July, 1961, Jim began to use color cues systematically and to attack words phonetically. The teacher was worried, however, because his performance was erratic; what he seemed to know one day, he was unable to do the next. Jim, himself, asked to learn every word by writing it with closed eyes. He said that he remembered it best in this way and could even "see" it. While he learned as well by "blind" writing as he had learned by the oral-manual-kinesthetic method, he did not learn by tracing. Tracing seemed to bore him and was of little help.

Everything was done to make the work of learning sounds and words more pleasurable. We introduced a study of the history of the letters of our alphabet, of how they came into being, and of how their form and

[1] Marianne Frostig, "Corrective Reading in the Classroom," *The Reading Teacher,* XVIII (1965), 573–580.

use changed throughout the years. For a child who has to overcome so many difficulties in learning, motivation is a key factor. Learning about ideas makes the learning of skills more interesting.

From the time Jim began work with us, there were no behavior problems. However, in public school he had been reprimanded and told that he was lazy, and in consequence had completely withdrawn and refused "to enter the field." We therefore found that Jim needed great encouragement to participate in group activities. He was first observed to do this voluntarily in October, 1961. In November, 1961, the teacher noted that Jim had become more self-confident and assertive. At times he even became aggressive toward other children.

Second Year. Jim began reading a second-grade book in the fall of 1961, after having been with us for about one year. His progress in this reader was very slow, but he wished to finish it, so the teacher decided to give him many very easy books to read at the same time. The massive reading of these easy books with much overlearning of missed words was helpful; Jim finished his second-grade reader, and a third-grade book a few months later (in January, 1962). Reading haltingly, with many mistakes, he insisted on reading in a fourth-grade book in January. Jim now knew the sounds and names of all letters and could sound out many words, but the reading of each paragraph took a very long time. The teacher had agreed to give Jim a fourth-grade book only because he desired it so much. He continued to read many very easy books simultaneously, and these were used for quickening his pace. A pencil was trailed across the page while he was reading to attempt to pace him.

Jim continued reading in a fourth-grade level book, still with great difficulty, throughout the spring of 1962. He seemed to be at a standstill. Easy books on a low second-grade level were also read, but even these books were read slowly word-by-word.

The teacher tried to quicken Jim's pace through the use of several techniques: flash cards of words and phrases; choral reading; the use of the trailing pencil; the use of a "Flash X" device; and self-competition. When reading aloud Jim used paper markers.

Jim was told to write his spelling words large and with a flowing movement, but he continued to write in a small, cramped style. He still seemed anxious. He expressed a great deal of concern over control, making such comments as, "Oh, we mustn't say that," or "We mustn't do that, that's dangerous."

The following is a teacher's progress note dated August 8, 1962:

> Several remarks of Jim indicated that while Jimmy's mother was very kind, Jimmy's father is very strict with the children. For instance, when I once raised my arm to put my hand on the back of Jim's chair, he flinched and said, "Don't you hit me." I questioned him about this and he mentioned that his dad had made a cat-of-nine tails. At first I didn't believe him, but he went on to describe it in some detail. He also said he knew how it felt.
>
> At times Jim has mentioned something about a boy running away. Currently his thoughts seem to center around deaths. In spite of this, he seems rather cheerful compared to previous occasions.

Third Year. Any interest Jim showed was used to make reading more interesting. In the fall of 1962, Jim expressed interest in learning about rocks and minerals. He was given a third-grade book on these topics.

Various skills continued to be taught simultaneously. Jim wrote summaries of the material that he read, and used the dictionary to find the spelling of some of the words. He read in the SRA series on the third-grade level and worked with phonic blends. Flash cards were used for intensive review of words he had learned and writing was emphasized. He also read a reader on the high fourth-grade level.

His *California Achievement Test* in November, 1962, Primary Form AA, showed a reading grade of 3.8 (Vocabulary, 4.1; Comprehension, 3.5).

Secondary School

In the spring of 1963, Jim had been with us for more than two years. He was now 13 years old. He had achieved a high third-grade level in reading as indicated by both his classroom performance and the reading test. In view of the severity of Jim's language difficulty, this progress can probably be regarded as substantial.

But Jim's future would have been bleak if it had not been for the cooperation of the Los Angeles city schools. Jim, as well as his colleagues who attended junior high school classes at the center, was permitted to take most of the academic courses at the center while taking non-academic courses in the public junior high school. Grades were given for the courses taken at the center, and transferred to the report card issued by the public school.

At the beginning of the spring semester of 1963, Jim was enrolled in the public junior high school, where he took art and Boys' Glee Club. In

Boys' Glee Club he received a D; the teacher wrote that "Jim's pitch problems make it hard for him to sing well." In art, he received a C.

At our center he took math, social studies, and remedial reading. Because of his slowness in reading, our teacher still used books on the third- and fourth-grade level, as well as a great variety of other simple reading material.

In the fall of 1963, Jim took basic math in public school. He did his math homework at our center, and struggled hard and valiantly with it. But he felt he was not succeeding, became more absorbed in his daydreams, and avoided contact with his peers. Accompanying his greater anxiety was a decrease in his reading skills. A review of fourth- and fifth-grade words was begun, five to ten words being given each day. (It was not necessary to use the former cumbersome methods for this review.) Jim wrote the words and then they were incorporated in stories written by the teacher. Jim read the words from flash cards, spelled them, and then wrote them in sentences. He agreed to review these words, but he had become so discouraged that for a whole month he would not touch any stories or reading books.

In November we gave Jim an achievement test. He worked so slowly that he did only one-third of it and refused to finish. We were therefore unable to enter any scores for him. Reports from public school showed a D in basic math, his only academic subject.

In reading, Jim seemed again to make some progress after the intensive overlearning of previously learned words. He was able to read very slowly without correction from his teacher, figuring out every word in an easy fifth-grade book. A power test in January, 1964, showed him reading on a fourth-grade level.

Systematic Ability Training. During the spring semester of 1964, ability training was systematically introduced in all classrooms of the center for the first time. Although our teachers had been previously familiar with the concept of training psychological functions, and had shared in the construction of the *Frostig Program for the Development of Visual Perception,* a systematic, careful step-by-step approach in developing perceptual and language abilities was not "operational" at the center until after suitable programs were available. The experimental work we had done in these areas was with younger children only.

Although Jim showed no low areas on the test for visual perception at this time, the teacher and the supervising psychologist knew from the initial test that visual perceptual difficulties had existed when Jim was younger. To help him in this area, his teacher introduced an astronomy unit which stressed spatial relationship and visualization. The ability to work with symbols was also developed further by diagramming science concepts, by outlining experiments, and by coding exercises. Phonic words were dictated daily to improve Jim's auditory perception. Games such as phonic lotto were used and Jim seemed to enjoy them.

Thus over two years after Jim came to us, a more comprehensive training was instituted that focused on his particular deficits in basic developmental abilities and was related to his reading and other basic skills. *The Metropolitan Achievement Test* (Form A, Intermediate Battery) administered as a power test in June, 1964, showed the effectiveness of this approach. During the six-month period from January to June, Jim gained 1.5 grade levels in word knowledge, about 2 grade levels in reading comprehension, 1.6 grade levels in spelling, 1.7 grade levels in arithmetic computation, and .5 grade levels in arithmetic concepts. His speed of perception remained slow, however.

In the spring of 1964, Jim read a variety of remedial materials in addition to working on exercises focused on the development of specific abilities. He now learned best by color coding the word and memorization as described before. He had daily drill in word analysis and grammar. The teacher also tried to increase Jim's store of information and his ability to comprehend. For this purpose selected materials from *Practice Readers, Standard Test Lessons in Reading,* and *Reading for Understanding* were used; the materials were at about a low fifth-grade level. Together with his teacher he also read more difficult books that he particularly liked, such as *Huckleberry Finn* and *The Old Man and the Sea.* He read voluntarily for the first time.

It seemed that Jim always had difficulty with one of the three or four subjects that he took in public school. In the spring semester of 1964 it was science, in which he received a grade of D; while in health education, graphic arts, and homeroom he had no difficulties.

The center began testing all children with the experimental edition of the *Illinois Test of Psycholinguistic Abilities* in 1964, and Jim was first given the test in June of that year. As expected, Jim's scores were very low in grammar ("auditory vocal automatic") and in short-term memory for auditory sequences ("auditory vocal sequences"). In the fall of 1964 his teacher began intensive use of exercises in grammar, in finding synonyms and opposites, and in memorizing auditory sequences of numbers, words, and sentences. One of the exercises used to help Jim with his difficulty in sentence structure was unscrambling "scrambled" sentences. Jim also practiced analyzing visually presented patterns by changing them to a different scale. The exercises in auditory discrimination and daily coding exercises were continued.

Multiple materials continued to be used for remedial reading. Skill building materials were used as well as those to help develop comprehension (for example, McCall and Crabbs' *Standard Test Lessons*, SRA's *Reading for Understanding*, Junior Level, January, 1965). *The Metropolitan Achievement Test*, Form B, Advanced Battery, administered as a power test indicated the following results: Word Knowledge, 5.8; Reading Comprehension, 5.3; (Grade 9, May 6, 1965).

Attempts to help Jim develop the ability to master thought processes were intensified. Science was taught to Jim by the discovery method. He participated in class demonstrations with actual weights and scales. Information was translated into a diagram on the blackboard and on paper, which helped him to develop abstract principles. He learned to draw diagrams and to write descriptions of what he had seen. He repeated the principles involved after the teacher, and later repeated them from memory. He was set a variety of thought problems, including many concerning pulleys and levers. Thus the teacher tried to develop Jim's ability to abstract, classify, and draw inferences through reading and science instruction. Observing his own progress, Jim was usually in a happy mood, and he became rather more active and alert.

The teacher decided that exercises that demanded careful listening and active verbalization were at this time the most important tasks for Jim, as his difficulties were in the language area in general and not just in reading. Language was still halting and he often groped for the correct term. The teacher reported: "I still attempt to improve Jim's automatic and sequential verbal skills."

Throughout the semester the teacher tried to help Jim to acquire more information by introducing him to a variety of topics, which also served to stimulate Jim to greater verbal expression in both oral and written form. Jim began to write with somewhat greater ease. He completed a number of compositions and made outlines, which helped him with the organization of ideas, sentence structure, and spelling. The teacher sparked an interest in recording and listening to parliamentary discussions. He was encouraged in every way to express himself informally, and to take part in class discussions.

For the first time, Jim's public school midsemester report showed no D's. He had C in physical education, B in woodshop, and C in art. He had been placed in a posture class for physical education because his slow tempo of movement made it impossible for him to keep up in the regular gym class. Jim's general slowness was a genuine handicap. His final semester report in January, 1965, showed a D in art, because he was unable to complete all of the assignments.

At this time, the teacher at the center wrote that he was continuing to stress auditory perception and verbal communication and to have Jim react to visual stimuli also. He combined visual and auditory stimuli and Jim was to communicate what he had seen and heard. Observing science experiments, spelling, and following a text while someone read aloud were used to promote visual-auditory integration.

In February, 1965, the teacher reported that Jim was working on the seventh-grade level in spelling, that his comprehension seemed to be much better, but that his responses were still very slow. He therefore decided to work with him on speed exercises in math. Jim was often given the same examples twice, but was told to solve them in reverse order; for instance, to add 345 to 697 and the next time to reverse the process.

In the spring semester of 1965, Jim again tried to take an academic subject in public school. This time it was life science, and he came with a failure note in March. Daily preparation for his science class was therefore begun at our center. Jim continued to work with diagrams, as well as writing short paragraphs about the concepts of life science, which were entirely new to him. He managed to pass this class at midsemester with a D, and his final grade was a C. The public school teacher stated that Jim had made great progress.

In June, 1965, the teacher at the center wrote that Jim's difficulties were still very evident, although slowly diminishing. Jim's slowness of response was a global problem. His language was still grammatically incorrect; Jim's difficulty in memory for auditory sequences of an abstract nature continued. His auditory perception was still very poor, and the teacher felt it would take continued effort to improve reaction time and speed. Reading was on a seventh-grade level but very slow.

Ability training was continued in the fall semester of 1965. In this semester verbal expression was greatly stressed. He was told to say something to himself, and then to write it down, as writing seemed to be as difficult as ever. For continued practice in work with symbols, Jim learned the Morse code. He still showed great difficulties in memorizing abstract sequential materials.

During the fall semester Jim took science, physical education, and arts and crafts in public school, and he received C's in all subjects. However, at midsemester in the spring of 1966, Jim failed in drafting, had D in physical education (because of his slowness in movement), and C in ceramics, a defeat that reactivated his withdrawal and listlessness. Another factor contributing to the resumption of his former attitude of hopelessness may have been a change of teachers which took place at the center late in 1965. The new teacher was less experienced in administering ability training, and at that time had not developed the training programs and prepared materials that are now available. The idea of systematically training underlying psychological functions to alleviate learning difficulties was then new.

Nevertheless the teacher learned, while working with Jim, how to help him. Jim wrote daily compositions. He worked on categorizing and sequencing exercises in which he classified things, seriated them on a logical basis, and practiced automatic sequencing as in repeating a series of numbers. But the symptoms of withdrawal and listnessness continued and the teacher decided that he had asked too much of Jim. Working with coding, auditory sequencing, and grammar was continued, but the written assignments were curtailed. Jim responded well to the diminishing of pressure. He began to make much better progress, and his final public school report in the spring of 1966 showed C's in all of his three subjects. We were delighted.

During the fall semester of 1966, oral language was again emphasized. Simultaneously with a variety of exercises integrating training in grammar and punctuation, sequencing, sentence completion, and learning antonyms and synonyms, he was asked to give an oral report daily, discussing his activities at home or what had happened at school, and so on. Spelling was practiced daily. Words and phrases were analyzed phonetically and structurally. Reference and outlining skills were stressed. Jim needed occasional help in math, which was again one of his subjects in public school. On one occasion he was immensely proud because he had received a grade of B for math. He said that he had almost an A, but the teacher had at one point given an explanation that was too quick for Jim to assimilate and he performed the task incorrectly. We all were very much impressed with him during this semester. He was much more talkative; he answered questions readily and the public school counselors reported better grammar and better speed and accuracy in his work. He again had no grade lower than C in public school.

Ability training was continued in the spring of 1967. Jim did group and individual exercises covering psycholinguistic skills, and continued to work on much skill material in reading. Jim was permitted to continue most of his academic high school courses at the Frostig Center.

Jim was not happy during this last year (1967–1968) at school. It became more and more a struggle for him to keep going to public school in the morning and to come to the center in the afternoon. He said that he was getting bored in public school and that he felt almost out of place at the center where he was the oldest of all the members of his class. But he had decided to go through high school and so he would finish it. Jim graduated from high school in June, 1968, receiving a public school diploma, although he had taken the majority of academic subjects at the Frostig Center. In the fall of 1968 Jim entered junior college. He was now on his own and was not to get any more remedial or supportive school work at the center.

Follow-Up

Interview with Mrs. C., February 15, 1969

In February, 1969, we asked Mrs. C. to come for a follow-up interview. Mrs. C. seemed relaxed and happy and quite satisfied that she could report on the progress of her children. When asked how all were getting along she began to talk first about the oldest child, Robert.

Robert had continued to work very hard while in high school so as to get a C in English. In other subjects he did well. The teachers explained to the mother that his comprehension of oral material was far above his reading ability. Robert is interested in electronics; he was trained in electronics in the Air Force, which he joined after completing high school.

John is preparing for college. He could not pass his college entrance exam because he failed the English test. He had to take a remedial course in English. Mrs. C. states that John still has difficulty in explaining what he wants, either orally or in writing. In written expression, his difficulty is particularly severe; if he is drawn out, he can finally get to the point and explain what he wants orally. Every time he has to write an essay he "falls apart."

Jim has begun his second semester in junior college. He does not know as yet what he wants to be. Mrs. C. feels that he is a little better than average in art. He managed to pass all courses during the first semester.

Donald, the fourth son, is still in high school. He passed algebra with a D, but Mrs. C. thinks the D was "the result of a combination of hard work and a nice teacher." His math is not as good as Robert's or John's. He quit some math courses—got "fouled up" in geometry. He also has reading trouble. He is majoring in photography and art in high school. He is now able to get Cs in English, but only in a slow moving class. He is the happy, not the "worrying type," and is very pleased when he gets through a school year.

The youngest child, Catherine, worries her most. She has severe reading difficulties. Mrs. C. knows Catherine will need tutoring soon.

Then Mrs. C. returned to her report on Jim. She said she likes to talk about the children because she likes to get "in the open," when she has a problem or is angered, but Jim won't argue; he is placid and becomes very quiet when worried. At certain times in the past, school had been a chore for him, and at times he just did not want to go at all. Mrs. C. is very happy that he is doing as well as he is.

Interview with Jim, February, 1969

It was a pleasure to see Jimmy enter the room. He is a tall, well-built boy, very handsome, with a broad grin and three dimples which by now are as permanent as his grin. His movements are still slow and somewhat halting and cautious. After greeting me, Jim, who was immaculately dressed, said, "Aren't these good clothes? But this sweater is my brother's, he already earns money. I can't afford such good clothes yet, but I wanted to look my best. My brother was kind enough to lend me his clothes."

After a few polite words on my part, Jim was asked to tell how he now felt about his many years in school. He answered that he still remembers that he had a "heck of a bad time" with reading in public school during the first school years. He said that he had felt terrible; that he had almost had a "nervous breakdown." He said that he began to hate the teacher because she had tried to make him read and he couldn't.

When he first came to us, he felt very nervous. After a week or so he "got used to the place," and to the people around him, and it seemed that life was somewhat easier. "It sure was a lot better than being forced to read." This remark is interesting because Jim read at the center from the first day on, but he only remembers that he learned the sounds of letters. He thought "this sure was fun," it "was only a game." He remembered that a few pupils worked together, and that it was sort of a contest of who could say the sound of the letters first.

Jim reports further that when he returned to public school on a part-time basis in eighth grade he had trouble settling down. He said all the old uneasiness returned because he was reminded of his former difficulties.

I told Jim that I remember an occasion when the school called because Jim was absent, and wasn't at home either. We were very anxious indeed, but when we spoke with his mother she wasn't perturbed at all and remarked, "Oh, he will come home." We thought that maybe he was exceedingly unhappy or discouraged, and we regretted sending him back to junior high school. Jimmy remembered the incident. He said that he had "just needed a day of rest." In public school he liked woodshop. He thinks the teacher in the metal workship didn't like him.

Jim has had no tutoring since entering junior college, but last semester he took a speed reading course. His speed was initially 100 words a minute, but by the end of the course he averaged from 175 to 200 words a minute. The teacher of the course "was good," and reassured him about his capabilities. "He was interested in how much I improved," said Jim, "not how well I did." Jim will continue with speed reading during the summer. Besides speed reading Jim also took a preparatory course in English, and courses in algebra, design, and drawing, all of which he passed. This semester he is taking another elementary English course (which involves him, he says, in reading essays, then writing essays about essays); and courses in police science, drawing, typing, and office machinery. In the course in office machines, he enjoys learning how to work with calculators, adding machines, and so on. His typing is slow, but he has mastered the layout of the keyboard. He feels that his typing is overcautious because he still feels so strongly about making mistakes that he will not risk a slip. Jim states that he enjoys college. He is glad that he no longer has to attend two schools at the same time, as he did in the past.

I asked what he would like to do after he finishes college. He told me he is not certain, but that he may become a policeman or an artist. He intends to concentrate upon police science and art during his four years as an undergraduate.

Comment

There are two points that I want to discuss: first, our methods in pursuing our goals with Jim, and, second, the evaluation of our results.

With regard to the question of procedures, it should first be emphasized that it is sometimes not possible to describe methods used with a child. Often, what a teacher does and what he thinks he does are different things. It is particularly difficult to decide which of the methods used were successful with Jim. But we can at least delineate the guidelines used in Jim's treatment.

1. The teachers initially worked from the premise that a child as defeated, listless, and hypoactive as Jim needed to be motivated. Motivation was not achieved by external means (by reward and punishment), but by satisfying Jim's interests and by using the advance of reading skills to change his self-image. We tried to help Jim by showing willingness to accept his feelings that reading was a very arduous task, but at the same time always making clear our confidence in his ability to learn and always encouraging him to have faith in himself. The caring, supporting role of the teacher helped Jim whenever his spirits sank.

2. The "organic" method was used, together with the provision of ideas instead of concentration only on the learning of skills. Also, the teaching of subject matter and of reading skills was combined so that Jim could pursue his particular interests.

3. Overlearning was stressed continuously. Overlearning is one of the most important methods in teaching reading to children with dyslexia.

4. Reading was regarded as but one aspect of the global language difficulty, and the teaching of all language skills was combined and integrated.

5. The methods used for the teaching of reading were multivaried, and new methods were added as Jim progressed.

6. Sound discrimination and phonics were taught consistently. Although learning was very slow, the methods used were successful. "Sounding out" is still Jim's main approach in reading. His reading skills are not fully

automatized. Phonics improved most strikingly when color cues were used consistently.

In my opinion, it is essential to teach sound recognition. But adequate auditory perception no more insures fluent reading than improvement in the visual channel alone. Jim's reading difficulties were the result of his global disabilities as well as of specific underlying disabilities in visual and auditory perception and abstract thinking. Above all, he was handicapped by a general slowness of reaction and a difficulty in retrieval from memory of abstract and sequential material, which made all learning a slow and laborious process.

7. Speeding-up exercises of various kinds were used, but were least successful in making reading an automatic performance. The tempo of Jim's reading is still exceedingly slow, despite improvement stemming from his enrollment in a speed reading course. We wonder if the present relative success reported in junior college is due to a new phase in his development; we wonder if some modification of our methods would have affected his reading speed more profoundly.

8. It was observed in Jim's case (as well as in other children with reading difficulties) that a multimodal approach did not work out initially. Jim was unable to learn by a combined kinesthetic, tactile, visual, auditory method, such as the Fernald method. We found that at first a combined oral and manual kinesthetic method and later writing with closed eyes (blind writing) worked best. Unimodal kinesthetic presentation was followed by exercises permitting transfer to the visual channel. Similarly, oral expression was used before transferring the verbal expression to written motor encoding. Integration of modalities and a multimodal approach in language teaching is of great importance, but in some cases unimodal presentation might have to precede methods of improving the child's intermodal integrative abilities.

9. In surveying Jim's progress at the center it becomes evident that he made his greatest academic advance when the teacher focused on his specific underlying difficulties. Ability training has to be an organized, multifaceted procedure. Systematic training was given to develop imagery, auditory and visual perceptual skills, thought processes, working with various symbols in a variety of situations, and in all lagging linguistic abilities. Such basic training seems indispensable for generalization of learned skills to occur.

10. In evaluating the factors that made Jim's progress possible, we

must take into account those circumstances that were extraneous to the center. Therapists often tend to ascribe the successful outcome of a situation to themselves, and failure to other circumstances. Parents are readily blamed for a child's failure, while their constructive role in the child's rehabilitation goes unacknowledged.

Jim's mother became confused and bogged down by the multiple problems stemming from her children's learning disabilities, and by her husband's punitive attitude. But when she was referred for counseling, at the time that Jim entered the center, she improved speedily. The therapist successfully rekindled her dampened spirits, and soon terminated treatment. She became a tower of strength to her family, and never relinquished her belief that all of her children could grow up to be adequate, successful, and happy adults.

Of crucial importance for Jim was the cooperation between the clinical and the public schools, which enabled him to continue through high school in spite of his difficulties in reading and verbal expression, and his general slowness.

It has been the experience of the teaching staff at the center that youngsters must be reintegrated into public school not later than the first two years of junior high school (seventh or eighth grade) to assure their continued high school attendance and the possibility of subsequent schooling. The center cannot provide a complete and well-rounded high school education by itself; too few children attend the secondary school program to permit either a sufficiently diversified program or sufficient interaction with groups of other youngsters. The center contributes a careful, individualized clinical approach essential for the remediation of learning difficulties, but it cannot provide workshops, sports, glee clubs, team debates, dances, or other social activities, which not only provide fun and educational advantages but also prepare the youngster for the social climate and social situation to which he must later adjust.

The cooperative attitude of the department of secondary education in the Los Angeles schools has been crucial for the successful rehabilitation of numerous children who, like Jim, attended a public school and the clinical school simultaneously. This collaborative procedure has proved a most successful innovation. The courage, patience, and flexibility of the counseling departments of the public schools with whom we have been involved has earned our deepest admiration.

So far we have discussed those circumstances that we feel were instrumental in Jim's rehabilitation. It is of equal importance to discuss where we failed and the alternative procedures that might have proved more successful.

Jim showed not only disabilities in language and thought processes, memory and perception, but also a general lack of alertness and a slowness of response, which was evident in all aspects of behavior. It seems to me in retrospect and on the basis of later experiences that this global underlying deficit could have been treated more intensively. Enhanced alertness, speed of reaction, and tempo of movement not only speeded up Jim's tempo, but also promoted better generalization of learned skills. Since Jim left the center, a comprehensive physical education program has been initiated that might have been of benefit to him. With regard to the reading process itself, it might have been possible to speed up his reading rate by emphasizing exercises to lengthen his eye span, and by teaching him how to scan and perceive materials presented tachistoscopically. In our experience, hypoactive children do develop more slowly than those with hyperactivity. It takes a great deal of time to speed up their tempo, and improvement occurs late, though it may continue after adolescence.

Evaluation of Results

There is much discussion in the literature as to whether familial reading deficiency can really be "cured." It seems to me that the answer depends on what one calls a cure. Jim's reading difficulty has been ameliorated, but only in part. He still is a slow reader, although at the present time he is able to pass his courses in junior college without outside help. He is happy in school and holds his own in spite of the many hours of effort his daily reading requires. He foresees a future for himself as either a policeman or an artist. Jim's intelligence test scores have shown a noticeable I.Q. gain from 93 and 95 in the first tests at the age of 11, to 115 at the age of 19.

Nevertheless, the pattern of subtest scores has not changed. The total scores have improved but the deficits are still evident. In spite of improvement in arithmetic, his last subtest in Arithmetic on the WAIS again showed a scaled score of only 6. Digit Symbol has remained steady at 7, despite the use of many coding exercises throughout the years. On the other hand, Jim's Information scores have improved from 5 to 9; and Block Design, Picture Arrangement, and Object Assembly are now 16

Table 1. Jim's Intelligence Test Results
at Ages 11 and 19

	WISC Date 10/60 C.A. 11–0 Scaled Score	WAIS * Date 3/28/69 C.A. 19–4 Scaled Score
Verbal Tests		
Information	5	9
Comprehension	10	14
Arithmetic	4	6
Similarities	10	12
Vocabulary	11	11
Digit Span	5	10
Performance Tests		
Picture Completion	18	13
Picture Arrangement	8	18
Block Design	12	16
Object Assembly	10	16
Coding or Digit Symbol	7	7
Verbal Scale I.Q.	85	105
Performance Scale I.Q.	107	127
Full Scale I.Q.	95	115

* 10/4/67 WAIS scores almost identical to above WAIS scores.

or above. It may be that Jim's work with maps and science experiments has paid off better than the coding exercises.

Familial reading difficulties are neurologically based. This substructure has not changed in Jim, but through his hard and consistent work he has been able to develop many of his abilities. From the withdrawn youngster who could neither recognize a word nor count to above 13 at 11 years of age, he has progressed to a boy who is doing passing work in junior college, who trusts in the future, and who has an iron will to succeed.

If a child's ability to learn skills is regarded as the main goal of educational therapy, then we have been only moderately successful. If, on the other hand, human happiness, the ability to help others, and a stable personality are the goals of education, we were successful. Jim's despair has vanished, and he has become a self-directing individual, satisfied with his progress and intending to continue to strive toward a worthwhile future.

Editor's Comments

In addition to the author's perceptive comments, it may be noted that at least one of Jim's areas of deficient functioning, auditory discrimination, remained a source of trouble after several years of training intended to strengthen it. Why auditory discrimination is less amenable to training than visual discrimination is a mystery that future research may resolve.

Another interesting point is that the conventional VAKT kinesthetic procedure did not seem helpful to Jim, while "blind writing" (guided tracing with the eyes closed, followed by tracing with eyes open) did help. It may be that some nervous systems become easily overloaded and benefit from adding modalities one at a time.

A final point is that remediation aimed at strengthening basic areas of psychological functioning (visualizing, abstract reasoning, grammar, etc.) is a very new development which has exciting possibilities, but is still too recent to be properly evaluated.

· 4 ·

Robert

BY GILBERT B. SCHIFFMAN, ED.D.

Setting

Prince George's County is a school system of approximately 150,000 pupils in suburban Washington. For a number of years, this county has provided two special programs for retarded readers. One program, called *corrective,* is typical of the corrective reading programs throughout the country. Experienced reading and study skill teachers offer additional reading instruction to small groups of pupils and utilize basically the same techniques employed in the regular classroom. The other program, labeled *remedial,* is a full-time, clinically oriented program employing special techniques in small group settings. This latter program, with its small class size, use of highly trained reading specialists, and supplementary services of psychologists and visiting teachers, is very expensive.

The following case study is about a child with a severe reading disability. Robert was referred to a children's evaluation clinic for an interdisciplinary diagnosis. Unfortunately, the school could not place the child into a *remedial* program at the start of the remediation process. The child did not make appreciable progress in the conventional *corrective* program but made substantial gains for the following three years in the clinic or center program.

The part of this report dealing with the remedial program describes the clinic center program in detail, rather than providing detailed information on the specific adaptations to Robert's needs, and his responses to the program.

Diagnostic Study

_____ Hospital,
Evaluation Clinic for Children

Preliminary Data

Name: Robert F., Grade 2 Race: White Sex: Male CA: 9–1
Parents: Jim and Sue F.

Referred By: Prince George's County Board of Education
Visit Date: July, 1964
Birth Date: June, 1955

Reason for Referral

Robert was referred through the Prince George's County Board of Education as a result of the school and the home's concern about the child's learning disability.

Robert has a reading disability. He knows all the letters, but is unable to put them together in any form. He does a lot of guessing, and the majority of what he reads the mother feels is done by memorizing. He seems to have special trouble in knowing the letter at the beginning of the word and starting it off right. He can spell some words, but if he is asked to write them down, he is unable to do so. Because of his reading difficulty, he was retained in the second grade last year. He has not passed, but is being moved on to third grade. He passed his other subjects.

Robert still sucks his thumb, and when someone hurts him he will come to his mother and cry rather than slap anyone back. He is a little nervous and cannot sit still very long.

He did not play well in a group until about six months ago. He usually came home crying when he did not get his turn, and still does that once in a while. However, there is marked improvement now.

According to his principal, Robert has to be called to attention constantly. He lives in a dream world of his own. The mother, however, has never observed a true staring spell. He also has not had any convulsions.

The father feels that Robert is like himself. He does not learn easily, and doesn't do anything about it. On the other hand, he will make anything in his father's machinist's shop that he wants to, clearly thinking it through and properly putting the parts together.

Family History

The mother is 41 years of age and in good health. She graduated from high school and is now a housewife.

The father is 37 years of age and in good health. He quit school in the eighth grade and failed several times. The father left home at the age of 16, because his father wanted him to go to school and he did not want to.

The father is a successful chief machinist. He makes about $180.00 a week. The family owns a home with six rooms and a bath in a residential area. Robert shares a room with three of his brothers. Robert's uncle (father's brother) never went to school. He learned to write his name but had no formal education.

Robert has five brothers. Three of his siblings are attending school, and two of the three are already demonstrating some difficulty with verbal materials.

Past Medical History

A. Prenatal and Natal

Mother is Rh negative, father is Rh positive. There was never any Rh incompatibility. Records indicate a normal, full-time pregnancy with no complications at any time. There also was no difficulty with the delivery.

B. Development

Mother reported that Robert smiled at three months and walked by himself at one year of age.

C. Illnesses

During the first two years of age, Robert had many ear and throat infections, with high fevers up to 103° and 104°. He did not experience any unexplained fevers, hospitalization, or operations. When he first started walking he was very "aggressive" and he fell very badly a number of times. He would get stiff and perspire, as if holding his breath. These falls happened between the ages of 1 and 2 years.

Physical Examination

Robert is a very blond, pleasant, cooperative, 9-year-old boy. He is well built with good muscular development. He gets on the scale to measure his own weight, although it takes a little while until he catches on how to do it. He readily explains that he is about four feet and some inches tall. He knows that twelve inches are a foot; with some difficulty, however, he figures out how many inches three feet are. One has the feeling that he does not think things through.

His head is normal in shape and with normal hair distribution. The extraocular movements are normal. The pupils react normally to light and accommodation. The fundi are negative and the discs were well seen and outlined.

Consultations

A. Report of Psychological Examination

Date of Birth: 6-19-55
Date of Examination: 10-1-64

Tests Administered:

Revised Stanford-Binet, Form L, C.A. 9–2, M.A. 10–0, I.Q. 109
Wide Range Achievement Test, Reading Grade 1.7
Bender Gestalt
Man Drawing
Rorschach
Thematic Apperception Test

Summary:

Test results indicate that Robert is of at least average intelligence. There are no indications of organic involvement or of the kind of visual-motor difficulty that is often associated with reading disability. *Binet* test scatter was considerable (from 7 to 14 years) and raises the possibility of better potential. Highest test successes were in practical reasoning, memory, and spatial conceptualization. Robert is unable to function effectively at even an average level, however, because of marked personality constriction and anxiety. The *Rorschach* record is that of a child with strong unfilled dependent needs who feels unable to meet the responsibilities of growing up. He apparently perceives other individuals in the environment, particularly parent figures, not as warm and accepting but as cold and anxiety producing. Control has certainly been emphasized at the expense of spontaneity and development. Robert reacts to pressure —which he apparently experiences as rejection—and frustration with marked hostile feelings which are almost completely unacceptable to him and must consequently be repressed. In order to further insure that he will do the conforming, acceptable thing, he tends to withdraw from others. Angry feelings are not likely to be expressed more overtly than in passive, stubborn resistance. There are indications of some satisfactions from fantasies.

In Robert's *TAT* stories, all the adult characters are depicted as rather grim, exacting, punitive figures. The first several stories, which are quite restrained, center about children who are compelled to go to school against their wishes. (School seems to be equated with a lack of material things and having to work hard without reward.) More than half of Robert's stories center about father figures who are pictured either as killing or being killed in retaliation for disapproval and punishment. The hero never meets with any direct, easy satisfaction of his needs and wishes; the best he can hope to attain is a compromise involving sacrificing his own needs and goals.

B. Audiology and Speech Evaluation

Impression

1. Hearing: Normal bilateral end organ hearing minus 10 db pure tone. Auditory discrimination investigated by *Wepman Test*—normal.
2. Speech: Normal.
3. Language: Apparent normal functioning for verbal reception and expression of ideas.
4. Voice: Hoarse—probably due to utilization of a lower than suitable pitch for his physical growth. Will probably change with maturity.

Discussion

Reading disability superficially investigated. The boy has an apparent dysfunction in reading ability. This does not appear to be due to an auditory discrimination but more to a visual learning function, such as seeing reversals and not being able to correct them—"p" becomes "d," "d" becomes "g." There is no apparent scheme to this dysfunction as far as investigated. It is noted that a "m" looks like a "n," a "c" like an "h," yet an "h" can look like a "k" to him. Quite frequently two letters, the one seen and the one thought to exist, are confused even though there is no relationship in appearance between one and the other, such as in the case of a "c" for an "h." He is apparently taking general cues as in the case where there is a "n" with a letter following it at the end, he will invariably think of the combination "ng" in working out the word. Yet, there is not enough experience for him to actually decide on what word and quite frequently comes up with a ridiculous combination of letters for words. He has no basic concept of reading as shown by the fact that he has little insight into the phonics approach which may be due to some form of auditory memory process or visual memory process.

Recommendations

1. Remedial reading program on a diagnostic basis.
2. Investigation of ocular motor dysfunctions.
3. Investigation as to why the child needs to say "let me see" before giving an answer to a visual stimulus picture.

C. Ophthalmological Examination

The results of the ocular examination were within normal limits.

D. Report on Ear, Nose, and Throat

Chronic inflamed tonsils suggesting recurrent tonsilitis.

Remainder of the exam was essentially negative. The occurrence of an occasional earache suggests that the lymphoid tissue in the nasopharynx may well encroach upon his eustachian tube.

Recommendation

It is our recommendation that this child be scheduled for a tonsillectomy and adenoidectomy.

E. Electroencephalography Report

There is a fairly well-developed 8–9/sec. alpha appearing posteriorly mixed with small amounts of 5–7/sec. activity. Alpha appears less prominently anteriorly and is mixed with low voltage fast 5–8/sec. activity. The tracings from the two hemispheres are essentially symmetrical. There are no focal disturbances and no paroxysmal discharges. With hyperventilation, there is a moderate buildup of slow frequencies diffusely with prompt return to baseline.

EEG Interpretation

This record is within normal limits. There is no evidence to suggest brain damage.

F. Social Summary

Interviews with Parents

Interviews with Mr. and Mrs. F. revealed that Robert had a very frightening infancy and early childhood in which both parents were rigid and severe in their handling of Robert, to such a degree, in fact, that although their handling of the children is extremely rigid even now, both parents find it hard to forgive themselves for the unrealistic demands they made of Robert when he was 2 and 3 years of age.

Further exploration with the parents revealed that their own childhoods were unhappy because of their own parent-child relationships and each brought childhood conflicts to the marriage which are now acted out on each other and on their children. Mr. F. comes from a very rigid Baptist home in which smoking and drinking, "and even having fun," is wrong, and he finds it difficult to accept his wife's Catholic approach to these things. He resents deeply the children's being educated in the parochial schools.

Mrs. F.'s relationship with her own mother she describes as one in which the mother's answer was always "No." "If you did anything wrong you were punished. She would punish you a week later rather than think that you might have gone unpunished." Mrs. F. left home at sixteen "hating my mother." Mrs. F. is glad she has all boys—she does not like little girls (it was my feeling that Mrs. F. does not like herself and denies much in herself that is feminine and maternal).

In talking with me both Mr. and Mrs. F. were able to take responsibility for Robert's difficulty, although they had little insight into the effect their present rigidity and strict discipline are having on all of the children.

Referral to Child Guidance Clinic

Both Mr. and Mrs. F. would benefit from some help with their own feelings about their relationship to all of the children. Mrs. F. has expressed some concern that Richard, too, needs remedial reading, as well as some concern about Johnnie who, she says, is like Robert and like his father. Hopefully, if the parents could be less strict and less demanding, all of the children would move into learning situations with more spontaneity and more readiness.

G. Educational Report

Test Results

1. Individual Word Recognition Test

	Flash	Untimed
PP	94%	100%
P	70	75
1	75	75
2	60	65
3	24	30
4	10	15

2. Informal Reading Inventory

	Reading Readiness
Independent Level	
Instruction Level	PP
Frustration Level	1
Probable Hearing Capacity Level	3

3. Informal Spelling Inventory—Instructional Level 0

4. Standardized Capacity and Achievement Test
   Scholastic Mental Ability Test   I.Q. of 77
   California Reading Test   Comprehension   2.8
                                        Vocabulary   2.7

5. Verbal Opposites   M.A. 9–3

6. Word Learning—OK

7. Digit Memory Span—   Digit Forward   M.A. 9–0
                        Digit Reversed   M.A. 8–9

8. Oral Directions   M.A. 4–6 (*Detroit General Aptitudes Examination*)

9. *Ayres Handwriting* below second grade

Conclusions

Case Typing: Severe Corrective
Degree of Retardation: About three years

Recommendations

Full-time clinic placement with the employment of a multisensory language development pedagogical procedure.

Summary and Recommendations

Robert F. is a 9-year-old white boy who was referred to us by the Prince George's County Health Department because of a reading disability.

Robert is of at least average intelligence. His reading disability has no specific patterns of substituting letters and he does not use a phonics approach or visual memory process. However, in the *Rorschach* test he revealed strong unfilled dependent needs, with parent figures producing feelings of anxiety. Robert reacts to pressure and frustration with hostile feelings which are repressed and he tends to withdraw.

In an interview with the social workers, the parents separately have given many clues as to why Robert is the withdrawn child he is and what might be the source of his reading difficulty. We feel that the parents could gain much from counseling in a child guidance clinic. When they have learned to handle him better, and have gained more insight into their and his difficulties, he might benefit by psychotherapy himself.

The electroencephalogram was within normal limits for his age. There was no evidence that his difficulties are organic in origin.

Robert was found to have chronically enlarged tonsils. The lymphoid tissues were thought to encroach on his eustachian tube. Therefore tonsillectomy and adenoidectomy were considered advisable.

Further Diagnostic Study. Unfortunately, it was not possible for the local school system to provide a full-time clinic program for the 1964–1965 school year. Instead, Robert was provided small group supplementary tutoring for thirty minutes a day for five days a week in a typical corrective program. The school did not notice any apparent improvement at the end of the school year and Robert was referred back to the clinic's psychologist for further study.

More intensive exploration of Robert's visual motor functioning and visual memory reveals more marked difficulty than was apparent in 1964. Reproductions of *Bender* designs show a significant number of rotations, difficulty in angulation, and in left-right orientation. Reproductions of *Benton* designs from memory similarly contain reversals, rotations, and perseverative trends; they score in the borderline to defective range for Robert's chronological age. These findings, in a boy with overall average intelligence, are strongly suggestive of central nervous system dysfunction. It appears most likely that the reading disability has an organic basis. This is not to negate the contribution of apparently rigid environmental pressures previously cited to the basic problem. In this respect, it should be noted that Robert seems to be more spontaneous and less constricted than he was when seen previously.

When the staff received these findings it was felt that Robert's reading disability was not previously the result of an emotional disturbance but was on an organic or constitutional basis. Robert was then placed the following September (1965) into a full-time clinic program, in which he remained for three years.

Remedial Program

Description of Clinic Center

The children in this Clinic Center are functioning on an educationally retarded level. All of them have specific learning disabilities such as visual-motor problems, auditory perception problems, difficulty in dealing with symbols, impaired body image, spatial disorientation, figure-ground disturbance, impaired gross or fine motor skills, and other problems of language and communication. Some of the children have obvious physical problems, such as cerebral palsy, epilepsy, hearing and speech defects, lack of visual acuity, and congenital handicaps. Many also have obvious behavioral problems. They are excitable, easily confused or distracted, and require a great deal of personal attention from their teachers. They all give indication of either being neurologically impaired or behaving as neurologically impaired. The children usually have difficulty in more than one of these areas: physical, learning, and behavior. It therefore becomes necessary to determine which is the area of primary involvement that needs to be worked with before further learning can take place.

When a specific learning problem can be defined, individualized teaching methods, materials, and techniques are utilized to help these children to circumvent or to overcome their particular learning disabilities. How early the child with the learning problem is referred for help and whether or not there is an organic basis for the problem are two of the important factors affecting the amount of progress the child can be expected to make.

The pupil-teacher ratio is seven to ten children per teacher. One aide assists the teachers. Experience at this center seems to indicate that the program functions best with a maximum of fifty children.

After evaluating the records and reports, and talking with the parents and the child, the supervisors and the principal make the decision to place the child at this center. The children stay at this center for one to three years. During this time, close contact is maintained with other people who are working with each child. Evaluation conferences involving the faculty, supervisors, pupil personnel worker, public health nurse, and others, are held at least once a year to consider the growth, development, future plans, and placement for each child. Conferences are also held during the school year whenever a child is not benefiting from the program because he has needs that the center is not equipped to provide. The final decision about placement is necessarily that of the supervisors.

The role of this center is to develop and to improve the communication skills of each child. Because of neurological impairment, some of the children come here with no usable language; some come with severely disorganized language; and some come with confused language patterns. Therefore, it is necessary that the staff stabilize, as far as possible, the language and concepts used with each child. For example, before the concept of likenesses and differences is introduced in the Visual Perception Program, the teachers discuss and agree upon the exact vocabulary and the question forms that will be used. At the same time the concept is being developed in Visual Perception, it is also introduced in the Auditory Perception Program. The music and physical education teachers use the same concepts in their programs.

A basic premise of the teaching is that each child needs to work on his own developmental level. This level may be different for each area of learning. A sequentially progressive program determines the level of development, helps to define the problem, and indicates the next steps in the child's program. In grouping the children their levels of education and social development have been taken into account. From these basic class groupings, many children go to other rooms for work in a specific area. Teachers keep and compare anecdotal records on each child so that it is possible to see his growth and development. A continuing evaluation is made of each child to determine by what teaching methods he learns best. When this is determined, a future placement is recommended. Some of the children may go to trainable-retarded centers or into classes for the educable retarded. Many go into special learning classes where the problems previously described are best handled because of the limited number of children allowed in these types of classes. In some instances, residential placement is recommended.

Schedules

Lower Classes

Morning

Juice and Crackers
Pledge of Allegiance
Time Line and Calendar
Visual Perception
Arithmetic
Body Image and/or Physical
    Education
Recess
Auditory Perception
Lunch

Afternoon

Rest and/or Manipulative
    Experience
Language Development

Upper Classes

Morning

Juice and Crackers
Pledge of Allegiance
Calendar and Time Line
Visual Perception
Body Image and/or Physical
    Education
Arithmetic
Auditory Perception
Recess

Afternoon

Lunch
Social Studies, Language Develop-
    ment and/or Storytime
Afternoon Activities
Manipulative Experience

Reading—individually scheduled
Directed art experiences—one period a week
Library—one period a week
Assembly—one period a week

Each year begins with the schedule as listed. Since the Visual, Auditory and Body Image programs are the basis for this center's diagnostic evaluation, it is imperative that each child be scheduled for each of these programs.

The child's progress in these three basic programs will indicate his needs and whether a change in schedule is necessary.

Arrangement of Classrooms

Areas Provided—Lower
   1. Play
       a. doll corner
       b. block row
       c. open space for large muscle

Areas Provided—Upper
   1. Play—blocks, wheel toys
   2. Desk
   3. Table—for group activities, games, lunch

Arrangement of Classrooms

Areas Provided—Lower

    activities

    d. sand table

2. Work area—quiet activities
desks or tables
3. Place for upset child
4. Table area—group activities,
lunch can be same as work
area

Areas Provided—Upper

4. Table or special area—for individual instruction

The rooms are divided into definite areas using shelves, cabinets, wooden screens or movable bulletin boards for dividers. These are high enough so a child cannot see over them when sitting, but low enough so the teacher can see all areas of the room. The younger children need more confining areas with smaller passageways. Each child has his own labeled shelf, chair, desk, place at the table, and coat hook. It may not be necessary to have all of these things labeled for the older group.

The room is free of distractible objects, particularly in the rooms of the younger children. This includes few, if any, decorations or objects on the bulletin or chalkboards. In the room of the younger children, the blinds are drawn and the door closed.

A supervised area is maintained outside of the room where an upset child can be taken to engage in activities that are suited to his immediate needs.

Educational Program—Perceptual Training

Visual Perception

    Size

    Prepositions

    Placement (First, Second, Middle, Last)

    Left and Right

    Color

    Tactile

    Likenesses and Differences

    Block Designs

    Pegboard Designs

    Phono-Kinetic Printing

    Reproduction of Shapes

Auditory Perception
  Awareness of Sound
  Development of Auditory Memory
  Discrimination Among Gross Sounds
  Discrimination Among Words and Sounds

Body Image
  Fundamental Body Movement Routines
  Location, Identification, and Labeling of the Parts of the Body
  Drawing the Body

Language Development and Communication Skills

Speech and Language Therapy
Creative Language
Storytime
Play Experiences
Social Studies and Science
Reading
Arithmetic
Music
Directed Art Experiences
Guide to Art Activities

Physical Development

Bilateral Coordination Exercises
Skill Building
Stunts
Manipulative Experiences

Grouping of Children

The children are grouped into classes on the basis of their social-emotional development and educational level. Each teacher is responsible for helping each child in her room adjust to his classroom routine and daily schedule.

Before diversified grouping and team teaching can be programmed, there is a period of time provided when each teacher maintains a self-contained classroom. This period may extend from two to four weeks, during which the teacher has the opportunity to observe and to assess the needs and abilities of each child in the room.

After the varied levels of development have been determined, the children are regrouped within the program according to their needs.

Each one of the programs is scheduled for a certain time period. Regrouping is done in several ways. For example, children who are at the beginning level of visual perception are grouped together for a visual perception class regardless of their social-emotional grouping (their "home" room). The intermediate and advanced classes are similarly grouped. Each child's progress, relative to the rest of that class, is observed. If he is progressing too rapidly or too slowly in comparison with the others, he is changed to a more appropriate group. Regrouping is often necessary.

There are certain learning situations, such as in directed art experiences, in which all of the children work on the same subject at the same time with two teachers.

Children are also grouped on the basis of their level into small groups or individually for reading, speech therapy and any other area in which special attention is necessary.

Occasionally classes combine for a learning experience that provides larger group experiences and allows one teacher to be free to observe the interaction of the children and teacher. In this situation two classes combine and, as one teacher does the actual instruction, the other teacher is free to observe while assisting.

At least once a week all the children are involved in a total group social experience. All the teachers work together to provide such activities as movies, plays, singing, games, and dancing.

For lunch and recess, the children are grouped according to their age and social development.

Structure in Daily Situations. It is basic that an everyday routine be established to provide a consistent and stable environment for this type of child. It has been found that when the routine is stable the transition from one learning situation to the next is best handled without upsetting the child when he knows what to expect and what is expected of him. At the center, each child has a routine to follow that will not change until his needs change.

An important concept in planning is not only to plan for experiences and activities, but also to plan controls and limits before, during, and following, each experience. Movement in the classroom during the lesson must be highly structured. For example, during a reading lesson in moving from the desk area to the table area, it is necessary for the children to change places one at a time. This also applies to all movements within the routine. The limits and controls that are used must be consistent to help the child feel secure and to function effectively.

Occasionally a child needs time away from the group. For this child a special supervised place is provided which is equipped with books, puzzles, games, crayons, and paper. Occasionally a child becomes upset and needs to exert physical energy to overcome the frustration. For this child another supervised area is provided that is equipped with a punching bag, pounding boards, and bean bags. *The child is free to return to the group when he feels he is ready.*

Sometimes when a child needs time away from the group, he does not need to leave the room. If the group is distracting to him, he is given a place to continue working with the group, but physically apart from it. Some children are distracted from their individual work by others working around them. For this type of child an area is screened off from the rest of the room and designated as a "private office."

Choices are difficult for children who are neurologically involved. Some children must have choices made for them, and as they progress they may be able to make a choice between two things. For example, during manipulative time, in the beginning the teacher chooses the puzzle for the child. Later, he may choose between two puzzles. Eventually, he may choose between two activities such as puzzles and peg boards. In many cases the children need help in choosing words to express needs, feelings, or ideas. It is then necessary for the teacher to make the choice by supplying the needed vocabulary. This is very important for the child who needs help in learning how to play or interact in other ways with his peers.

Robert's Remedial Program

THE PROGRAM OF READING REMEDIATION for Robert centered around a multisensory language development approach. Robert was not exposed to basal readers for obvious reasons. He emotionally rejected these books because of years of repeated failure. The books whose readability level he could handle were of no interest. Therefore, a rich language experience approach was instituted. Robert was able to read material developed from his own vocabulary, his own backround, his own concepts, and his own interest. A "word bank" was developed from Robert's dictation and creative stories.

The words in Robert's "bank" were reinforced and made a permanent part of his sight vocabulary employing a modified Fernald kinesthetic, or VAKT, technique. In addition, Robert had a structured phonics program designed as a modified Gillingham approach, with a close association of visual, auditory, and kinesthetic elements.

As soon as Robert had developed a sufficient vocabulary he was given an opportunity to read many basal readers and trade books independently.

Results

Robert was reevaluated on 7–1–68 after three years in the Clinic Center. At this time his C.A. was 13–0. Data from his standardized and informal tests revealed the following growth:

	8–2–64	7–1–68
Informal Reading Inventory	*Grade*	*Grade*
Independent Level	PP	2
Instructional Level	P	5
Frustration Level	1	7
Capacity Level	4	8
Informal Spelling Inventory		
Instructional Level	0	3
Stanford Reading Achievement	3.1	7.2

The interdisciplinary team decided to place Robert in a slow moving seventh-grade class for the 1968–1969 school year. It was also recommended that Robert's parents, teachers, and Robert himself receive constant supportive help by the appropriate specialists. Only time will tell if the gains are sufficient and lasting to insure Robert's academic success.

Discussion

THE "AVERAGE" CHILD acquires adequate reading ability through visual and auditory clues with no kinesthetic stimulation except that involved in speech. Regardless of how much improved the program of instruction in reading is for him, some few very capable children will still not succeed.

These are the people who, for a variety of reasons, have unusual difficulty in forming associations between experience and printed symbols. The many factors that may be related to their disabilities have not always been recognized. Even when these people are exposed to a program of instruction through which people of similar mental age learn to read well, they may remain completely unable to look at a printed word or group of words and connect meaning with them. Unfortunately, these individuals have been given repeatedly, with no positive results, more of the same dose which had previously effected no cure. Consequently, they have sometimes been "given up" as impossible.

Children who have failed to progress under ordinary classroom methods must be taught, not by a repetition of techniques that have failed, but by new ones, carefully planned to capitalize on innate strength and to overcome individual weakness.

As the non-reader ascends through the primary grades, his problems multiply as all other subject matter is conditional on reading. Thus, he cannot solve the problems in arithmetic or social studies, even though he may have the skill to do so, because he cannot read the examination questions. The impression is one of general academic failure. He is likely to be considered mentally retarded or a lazy child with the view that "he could if he would." It is difficult to imagine a more chilling indictment of a confused child bewildered by his inability to learn despite earnest efforts to do so.

Failure by teacher, parent, and physician to recognize the key problem will have devastating results. The child is now attending a class conducted in what is for him almost a foreign language. Little wonder that a large group of non-readers are referred to the physician with the chief complaint of behavior disorder. Such a child may be disturbing the class with attention-seeking behavior or with hostile acts; he may be "lost in a cloud" or may become a truant. At home he may be surly and unwilling to do his homework. Or he may be of concern to his parents because of low self-esteem, withdrawal, and general apathy. Frustrated by his inability to learn, bored by class exercises he cannot follow, coerced by parents and teachers to do what he cannot, the non-reader has both the inner turmoil and the lack of constructive outlet to become a major problem at home and at school.

One of the major problems is the educator's limited resources to measure achievement and capacity in a school setting. This is particularly true with the group intelligence testing program.

Editor's Comments

The diagnostic study in this case has two parts. The first consists of a comprehensive set of examinations in a hospital out-patient setting, which found a severe reading disability accompanied by emotional problems, but did not find evidence of a neurological deviation. Parent counseling and a full-time remedial program were recommended, but neither could be carried out, and the corrective reading program in school that was tried for a year was ineffective. Psychological reexamination disclosed problems in visual-motor and visual memory functioning that led to a changed diagnosis emphasizing the probability of an organic (neurological) basis.

The author has chosen to describe the clinic center program rather than present details about the particular way in which Robert was taught, and his reactions. The results of the three years of full-time clinic center attendance include a gain of about four years in reading ability and two to three years in spelling. Progress in other curricular areas is not reported.

The clinic center program as described differs from most remedial reading programs in the emphasis placed on visual perception, auditory perception, and body image development, and in the stress on controls and limits for behavior. These emphases may be very helpful to brain-damaged children. From the facts given, it does not seem possible to determine whether all aspects of this program were relevant to Robert's needs, or whether elements other than remedial reading instruction were instrumental in his progress.

Marion and Melissa, Twins

BY STELLA M. COHN, ROSE GREENE,
LAURA HINES, AND BEVERLY ZENGA *

Setting

The Bureau of Special Reading Services of the New York City Board of Education operates thirteen clinics, each serving an area containing many elementary schools. These clinics are intended to serve children whose reading problems are so severe, or are so complicated by social and emotional difficulties, that they are not good prospects for help by the more than 400 corrective teachers who work in the schools.

Every child referred is given a comprehensive reading diagnosis, a clinical diagnosis (involving psychologist, psychiatrist, and social worker), a physical examination, an eye examination, and a speech examination. Recommendations are worked out in conferences involving the clinicians, the reading counselor, and the classroom teacher.

Children are usually seen in groups of six to eight for reading instruction, for one hour twice a week. Individual help is given to children too disturbed to work in a group. Teaching procedures are eclectic and emphasize the development of motivation for learning. Remedial teaching is supplemented by parent workshops and seminars, and in some cases by psychotherapy for the child.

Diagnostic Study

Referral Data

Marion and Melissa R., tall, slim, attractive Negro 10-year-old fraternal twins, were referred to the Bureau of Special Reading Services clinic by

* This case material was written by Rose Greene, Psychiatric Social Worker, Laura Hines, Psychologist, and Beverly Zenga, Reading Counselor. Stella M. Cohn, Director, planned, reviewed, edited, and coordinated the case study. Appreciation is extended to Joseph Patalano, Supervising Social Worker, and Marion Meyrich, Coordinator of the reading clinic which the twins attended, for their assistance in reviewing this material.

their respective classroom teachers. Both children evidenced reading retardation, generalized learning difficulties, and poor social adjustment.

Melissa was reported to be an extremely depressed child who was
easily upset and given to frequent mood swings. These moods were
characterized by refusal to participate in classroom activities, or by a
complete disruption of the classroom situation which would require her
removal.

Marion, on the other hand, appeared less depressed. She gave the
impression of being a much more outgoing and defiant child. Her classroom behavior was not as disruptive as Melissa's.

At the time of referral, Melissa was in the fourth grade. She had repeated third grade. Her reading level was 2.6 with a 70 percent accuracy
rating. This represented a retardation of 2 years and 2 months.

When Marion was referred to the Bureau of Special Reading Services a
year later, she was already a fifth-grade student who was reading on 3.9
grade level with 50 percent accuracy, representing a 2.1 retardation level.
She had been held over in the second grade.

Interview with Parent by the Social Worker

It was hoped through this first interview to determine, if possible, from
the mother, some of the underlying factors contributing to Melissa's social
and emotional problems and also to her learning difficulties.

The impressions the mother gave in the first, as well as subsequent
interviews, was of a forceful, aggressive, bright woman who was fighting
desperately for all the symbols that would give her middle-class status.
She seemed to have difficulty with her own identity and sense of security
and was seeking all the outer symbols for reassurance and a sense of
belonging.

When the family first became known to us, they had lived in this area
for about a year, having moved from an overcrowded apartment in a low
socioeconomic, poverty- and problem-ridden neighborhood. She had
wanted to move for a long time and felt they could afford it. The father,
however, objected. He was comfortable, had his cronies there and really
resented the move. They fought about this a great deal and finally the
father gave in. As she went on, it became more and more apparent that
the relationship between the parents was a most difficult one. The father
ran around a great deal, was home very little, and, other than providing
for the material needs, was not really available to her or the children.
The mother demanded the material needs, was most angry with him even

when she got them, but seemed only superficially aware of what she really needed from the relationship. Thus, there was constant stress in the home.

This was Mrs. R.'s second marriage. She had been married at an early age to a man she described as infantile and irresponsible. She had two sons by that marriage. These boys were living on their own but they managed to involve the total family in their severe emotional problems. She stated that she did not want to repeat the experience of a divorce and having to care for children on her own. This she implied was what kept her from separating permanently from her present husband. She has four girls (the twins, a daughter a year older, and a daughter a year younger) from this marriage. The twins and the younger sister were in the same grade when we got to know them, although not in the same class. During the initial interviews, she denied any difficulty with either of the other girls.

We reviewed the twins' school experience. They started in kindergarten together, in the same class. This worked out very poorly. They both conspired to do what they wanted in class and seemed to feed and get support from each other. There were many complaints and they were finally separated. In first grade they were in different classes. They had no trouble, or at least Mrs. R. heard no complaints. In the second grade Marion was very upset. She cried a great deal and the mother blamed the teacher for handling her poorly. The teacher babied her and let her sit on her lap according to Mrs. R. The child refused to do her work, and once she disappeared on a class outing.

Marion also, at that time, complained to the teacher and the school nurse that she heard noises in her head and had pains in her stomach. The mother was referred to the local hospital for a complete work-up. According to the mother, after thorough medical examinations, they determined that there was nothing physically wrong. They did recommend a psychiatric diagnostic interview but the mother said she did not pursue it. When asked why, she said that she had many pressures at the time and just forgot. Marion was held over in the second grade and there was no further difficulty. They moved when Marion was in the latter half of the third grade.

Melissa, too, had her difficulties at school, but they were not as dramatic. She did her work poorly, was withdrawn, and was held over in the third grade. The mother tended to blame the previous school for the twins' learning difficulties and felt they were making progress in their new school.

The mother stated that the girls were fraternal twins. The pregnancy was normal and uneventful. Melissa's was a normal delivery but Marion's was a breech birth. They each weighed well over eight pounds at birth. Melissa was born with a slightly twisted foot and had to wear a cast from 9 to 13 months of age. Marion was walking at 1 year but Melissa did not walk until 15 months. Melissa began to talk at about the same time; Marion, a little earlier. They both still sucked their fingers at times, and Melissa, at 10 years of age, still occasionally wet the bed.

When talking of one twin, the mother always compared her with the other. Initially, she had a tendency to compare all the girls and almost lumped them together, so that the interviewer had to spend some time in separating them out to make certain that we knew which one she was talking about. She described the relationship between the girls in such a way that she saw Marion as the dominant one and Melissa as almost fearful of exposing the fact that she was being dominated. The first impression was that Melissa seemed to be more favored by the mother. The referral and history was discussed with the psychologist who saw Melissa in order to determine eligibility for our program.

Psychological Report: Melissa

Techniques Used: *Rosenzweig P-F Study, Bender Visual Motor Gestalt, Rorschach, Thematic Apperception Test, Wechsler Intelligence Scale for Children.*

Melissa was seen for an initial psychological evaluation following the interview with her mother by the social worker. Her previous school records showed that she had been given a *Pintner-Cunningham* test that revealed an I.Q. of 87. Later, she had been given a *Lorge-Thorndike* on which she obtained an I.Q. of 67, and a subsequent *Otis Alpha* revealed an I.Q. of 81. In view of the discrepancies on these tests and the fact that the referral data had indicated that the child appeared to be quite depressed and that she "needed much encouragement," she was now given a *WISC* to determine her current level of functioning.

Melissa came to the examining room willingly. Throughout the first session, she was cooperative and apparently enjoyed the exclusive attention of the examiner. On this occasion, she was neatly dressed and gave the appearance of being somewhat shy and timid. Her general approach to the test material was slow and hesitant. For example, if she felt she did not know an answer, she would not hazard a guess. If she were later urged to "try," it often turned out that she had some knowledge of what was required. There was quite a tendency to ramble. This tendency persisted throughout ensuing sessions.

As previously stated, her initial appearance was neat. However, on subsequent occasions her appearance often reflected her mood. She could be extremely unkempt, and at times her clothes were very dirty. On these occasions she appeared to be aware of her shoddy appearance, but unable to do anything to correct it.

Her response to test materials also generally reflected her mood. Once she became involved, however, she was often able to function adequately. On the WISC, Melissa obtained a Full Scale I.Q. of 85, with a Verbal I.Q. of 89 and a Performance I.Q. of 83. These scores place her in the Dull Normal range of intelligence. The summary scores have little or no meaning in understanding Melissa because they really mask her erratic performance. There was one score which was significantly low and that was a scaled score of 5 on Object Assembly. This represents an inability to anticipate part-whole relationships and a lack of flexibility in working toward a goal that may at first be unknown. This inability to organize parts into global wholes and to project in this manner frequently shows up in her hesitancy to approach new materials. Although she also did poorly on Block Design, which is generally regarded as a test of perceptual analysis, synthesis and reproduction of abstract designs, she did not otherwise show any signs of visual-perceptual dysfunctioning. Low scores on these two subtests suggest some difficulties in spatial relations but these did not prove to be significant.

With one exception, Melissa performed below her age level on all subtests. She achieved a scaled score of 11 on Coding, indicating an ability to learn new materials fairly quickly. This assumption held up throughout her stay in Special Reading Services. She appears to learn quickly but does not easily retain what has been learned.

Projective materials revealed an extremely depressed child who was totally unable to cope with her difficulties. One of her chief problems centered around her inability to relate to people and her conflict about her parents. She experienced deep feelings of inadequacy and suffered from overwhelming, disorganizing anxiety that she did not understand and was unable to do anything about. All of her efforts to relate to the environment on an emotional basis were forced. She perceived the world as hostile and unfriendly, yet she would lean on it to satisfy her dependency needs. She had very little in the way of adjustment resources, little drive, and only a slight indication of adjustment potential. She seemed unable to find a source of satisfying her needs within herself. At the same time, she was afraid to act out the satisfaction of her needs in her social milieu. She tried hard to adhere to an impersonal and objective interpretation of her world in order to guard against psychological trauma. She constantly attempted to avoid emotional involvement with people around her, inhibiting her basic drives. This dependent, sensuous child was in a serious conflict situation. She could not channelize her energy inwardly, on the other hand she could not seek help from the significant figures in her external environment because of the threatening impact these persons held for her. There was a tremendous amount of hostility directed toward both her mother and father. She saw them both as cold, indifferent people who were incapable of meeting her needs and, as has been mentioned, she was not able to make the necessary demands upon them.

Melissa was fearful and suspicious of all people in authority. She automatically assumed an aggressive attitude towards them. She could not give such people a chance to demonstrate their real character since she automatically assumed they were all alike.

This child showed some paranoid ideation, expressed in terms of people watching her; at one point, she felt sure that her conversation with the psychologist was being taped. She stated that she could not see a tape recorder but she knew that one was there.

Since this child appeared to be aware of the need for help and to be reaching out for it, a team consultation was held. It was agreed that Melissa would be taken into the program for reading instruction.

Clinical Follow-Up. From the test results and the conferences with the reading counselor it was obvious that Melissa needed some therapeutic intervention which would help relieve some of the anxiety she was manifesting. Consequently, she was seen regularly by the psychologist who helped her ventilate some of her confused feelings.

Mrs. R., too, was seen several times during this period and the child's progress in the reading program and the classroom was discussed.

Approximately one year later, Marion (her twin) was referred to the Bureau of Special Reading Services and subsequently accepted into the service after completion of the intake procedures.

Psychological Report: Marion

Techniques used: *House-Tree-Person, Thematic Apperception Test, Rorschach.*

Marion R. is a tall, slim, attractive child whose appearance also fluctuates from very neat to unkempt and disheveled. Her appearance, too, reflects her mood. When she is happy she looks very good. At these times, her hair is neatly groomed and she wears makeup. At other times, she looks as if she could barely make it to school.

When she initially came to the examining room, she appeared to be quite apprehensive. She sat quietly and responded only when spoken to. She appeared to be pleased that she was being seen because she knew that Melissa was also getting attention. She made reference to the fact that they were twins, but that she was an individual and wanted to be treated as such. She stated that she was not doing well in school and that she needed a lot of help, especially in arithmetic. She felt that she was doing well in reading. She did not, however, want to go on to junior high school when she finishes here. She could think of no alternative, she just "won't go."

At her initial interview, she was given a *House-Tree-Person Test.*[1] She drew quickly and easily but made no comments about her drawings. When she was next seen, an attempt was made to administer the *Thematic Apperception Test.* On the first card, she said, "This is a violin, right? I can't think of a story." She subsequently rejected the next three cards. No further attempt to give this test was made. She became quite sad and began to cry. She stated that she was sensitive but was unable to explain further.

Later, when presented with *Rorschach* cards, Marion became quite animated and extremely verbal. She appeared really to enjoy this test. She was not given a formal intelligence test; it had been previously determined that she was a bright child who was functioning below her capacity. There were no evidences of gross perceptual motor difficulties.

The projective materials revealed a very depressed child who felt extremely inadequate to deal with day-to-day situations. Although, as has been previously stated, she was potentially very bright, she spoke of herself as being stupid and unable to grasp things quickly. She had a very rich fantasy life and good imagination which could be used for creative

[1] *House-Tree-Person.* Beverley Hills, Calif.: Western Psychological Services.

or constructive purposes. However, her fantasy life served mainly as a depository for her many feelings of frustration and hostility towards her parents which could not be openly expressed. She was extremely sensitive and easily upset and frustrated by things happening around her. Potentially, she was a warm, emotionally alive person. She was currently, however, very withdrawn and depressed. Her self-concept was extremely ambivalent. She alternated between being rebellious and being very passive. She had strong feelings of both warmth and hostility.

This child also had mixed feelings about her parents. She saw them as rather cold people who were not sufficiently involved with her problems. Her father, a cold, detached person, unable to satisfy her needs, was nevertheless seen as strong and powerful. Although her mother appeared to be a domineering force in the home, she was a completely ineffectual force who was seen as a competing teen-ager, not fulfilling her role as a mother.

Marion had difficulties relating to her siblings. Her greatest problem was Melissa. She resented being a twin, yet there were times when she was extremely protective and eager to identify as such. She resented the "success" of an older sister who is a performing artist of a sort.

There were also problems in the sexual area. There was a lot of guilt associated with her feelings and at some time she may have either fantasied or observed some sexual behavior. Projective materials suggested some masturbatory guilt.

This child was venting feelings of frustration associated with the home and her school failure. She would like to "do well" in school but she was stymied by her inability to divorce herself from her immediate problems. She had good potential capacities for adjusting to the world and for relating to other people. However, there were times when her reality testing was very poor.

Clinical Follow-Up

Subsequent to testing, Marion was seen on several occasions by the psychologist, but this was felt to be unsound therapeutically in the light of both children's needs to be "individual." Separate therapists were deemed advisable, with a more meaningful therapeutic plan for both girls. A psychiatric diagnosis was discussed but held in abeyance temporarily.

When Marion was approached with the idea of being seen by someone else, she initially rejected the idea. Since she felt so rejected at home and by her classroom teacher, the psychologist would continue with Marion until a smooth transition could be effected.

In the meantime, on-going conferences with the reading counselor revealed behavioral problems in the classroom. It was felt that seeing Mrs. R. on a weekly basis for counseling could possibly have an ameliorative affect. The mother agreed to the sessions but soon began to miss appointments. When faced with her resistance to coming, she gave all kinds of reasons why she could not come. One time she said that she had to go to work because of a bad deal that the father had entered into. At other times, she became involved in her older son's domestic crisis and had no time to come in.

When seen, she talked at length about her background in her parents' home. She was raised in a small suburban town where her family, although not rich, was considered a notch higher on the social scale than other families around her. However, she grew up very aware of what it meant to be of another color and how this was used economically and socially. She talked a great deal around feelings rather than about them and used discussion of the outer social scene rather than how she felt about it. She seemed to get away from her own feelings.

When talking of the girls, she was intellectually aware of their needs and even some of their problems, but the impression conveyed was of an impersonal view rather than a real emotional involvement. She experienced much turmoil and inner confusion; this is what came through to the children. She had developed a very fragile balance in her relationship with her husband and she was afraid of upsetting it. She constantly used this to express her resistance to change.

In further evaluating how much of a contribution Mrs. R. could make to helping her twins, in view of her own deprivation, it was felt that direct work with the twins would be attempted. The psychiatric consultation which had previously been discussed was now felt to be necessary.

Psychiatric Report

Interview with Mother. Mrs. R. arrived promptly for her appointment. Mother is an attractive Negro woman. She was meticulously dressed in what appeared to be expensive clothes and the first impression is that of a narcissistic, exhibitionistic woman who is extremely concerned with herself and her effect on other people. She spoke well, intelligently, and, although initially guarded, she soon lost this and spoke quite freely. She expressed concern about her children's behavior. She was involved in an egocentric way only because they were not meeting certain of her standards. She gave the following history:

She was the only child of middle-class parents, whom she described as follows: Her father was a laborer. He always earned good money and provided for his family well financially but was totally uninvolved emotionally. He was an alcoholic and she remembers being constantly embarassed by his stumbling down the street. The relationship between her parents was poor with frequent arguments and bickering. This situation persisted until his death. Her mother was described as a cold woman who tried to engage the daughter in a symbiotic relationship which Mrs. R. resisted and eventually solved by leaving home and marrying early. Apparently the atmosphere in the home was one of a family that was aspiring towards middle-class ideas and values but at the same time there was the fact that they did not quite make it because of the father's alcoholism. His lack of education and his inability to meet his wife's standards contributed towards their dissension.

Interview with Father. Mr. R. was a very verbal man, impulsive and outgoing. He stated that he is one of a large family. His father left the home, and in spite of the fact that his parents were separated, apparently there still was a great deal of strife between them. The father was a "high liver" and had money which he spent on other women and good times. His mother was a hard working woman who was unable to meet the needs of her children because of her own depression and her concern about realistic things like providing food and shelter for them. Mr. R. identified with his grandfather with whom he apparently had a warm relationship. He felt that he remained detached from the two parents and their disputes but he was friendly with both. He seemed totally unaware of his own personality problems. He was a truck driver who is extremely aggressive on his job. He was interested in getting ahead and fighting for "Negro rights."

He could not see this as a projection of his own aggressive drives and his own needs to be cared for and protected. He was dressed in an extremely meticulous manner and his clothes also appeared to be quite expensive. This he admitted is very important to him. He is trying to give to himself and to his children, again in a monetary way, the things that his father did not provide for him. He sees himself as a responsible family man.

Interview with Marion. Marion is a verbal child of 13. The striking contrast in her dress as compared to her parents was immediately apparent. She had made some effort to make herself attractive, but she said that she fixes her own hair and picks out her own clothes. They were obviously inferior to those of the parents. She was an extremely anxious child who seemed extroverted, admitted to her problems readily, and was eager for help. She was quite frightened by her sexual feelings and hinted at some acting out. She had poor relationship with her parents, was threatened by what she perceives as her father's firmness (violence), and was extremely depressed by the realistic knowledge that her mother is not involved with her in a healthy, maternal-child relationship.

Interview with Melissa. Melissa was a shy, infantile, withdrawn, depressed girl of 13 who was trying to deny that she was unhappy. But she was extremely emotionally labile and went from ready tears to relating and talking in a fairly free way. She attempted to deny any problems at home. It is obvious that her needs were not being met.

Summary of Psychiatric Findings. This mother was brought up in a home where her own dependency needs were not met. She was given material things instead of the emotional nurturing that she needed. She experienced her mother as cold, rejecting, and unwilling to allow her to grow. She identified with her mother and has become a driving, aggressive person. Her father was not a strong male figure and she was denied the support of a real fathering person. Her Oedipus Complex is still unresolved because she was involved in pairing off one parent against the other while at the same time being unable to cope with these feelings in this milieu. Because of her need to compete, to attract handsome men, to bolster her own self-concept, and to act out essentially what was the problem at home, she has chosen men who are attractive to other women and who play around. It is important that she always is able to win them back after these interludes. The father, on the other hand, is a dependent man who is extremely depressed and angry. He tends to act out his feelings in a very impulsive way and does not have the inner controls necessary to handle his problems. He is reacting to a mother who was either unable or unwilling to meet his dependency needs and a father who essentially abandoned him. His sorrow and rage at this are apparent in his behavior. The two parents are involved in an insoluble situation. Each one looks towards the other to satisfy his needs while at the same time having chosen a person who is unable to do this. The father provides the mother with money as her father did. He thus feels that he has discharged his responsibilities. At the same time, he is trying to get from her the mothering that he needs. He is acting out his ambivalence towards his mother on his wife. Mrs. R., in her way, is doing the same—looking to a man who is emotionally unable to meet her needs and then being very angry with him when he cannot do so.

The children are being squeezed in this situation. Their own needs have been ignored and lost in the hostile dependency needs of both of their parents. The father sees his role as one providing money, but otherwise he does not have any idea of how to be a father; at the same time, he resents their needing him. When they demand that he satisfy their emotional needs, he becomes punitive and frightened and tends to clamp down on them in a very severe way. Apparently, Marion's aggressive acting out behavior is threatening to him because of his own poorly controlled impulses. He is extremely punitive with her. There is a great deal of competition between these children. There are two older boys by the mother's previous marriage. They are out of the home. The younger of these boys is apparently mentally ill but little of the details are known to this examiner.

Marion and Melissa, although twins, have reacted to their problems in overtly different ways, although basically, the problems are the same. Both of them are infantile 13-year-olds who have been severely deprived emotionally. They have extremely ambivalent feelings towards a cold, rejecting mother who needs them to satisfy her own needs. Father is out of the home most of the time and is unable to relate to them in any real way. Melissa has withdrawn and has stayed out of the home as much as possible. Academically underachieving, she acts out her own dependency needs by babysitting a lot. On weekends she goes out of the house and stays with her brother and sister-in-law where, again, she babysits. She uses them as substitute parents, attempting to satisfy some of her infantile desires. She is extremely depressed and uses denial and projection with a resulting rich fantasy life. Her defense to her strong sexual feelings is to completely deny them and to appear not interested in boys at all, at least overtly. She has few friends, an extremely poor self-concept, and is unable to function at this time except on a very marginal level.

Marion, on the other hand, with the same needs and reactions, tends to act out, to run around with a lot of boys although she says she "does not go all the way." She is much more aggressive. They both hate being twins, feeling that their own individuality has been lost and that there is too much confusion. There is a tendency to be much more competitive with each other than with the other siblings, against whom they both feel they have little chance of winning.

Recommendations of the Psychiatrist. The need for treatment was explored with mother and father. Mrs. R. stated that she was interested and ready to go. Mr. R. was quite resistant and he said that he will not be involved except on a marginal level. It is important that the two girls and the mother be treated. In spite of the amount of pathology present, there are many positives. There is the fact that the mother is interested in helping and is extremely guilty about her own role as a mother and a woman, and it is felt that her motivation is good. The two girls also should be good candidates for psychotherapy because both are aware that something is wrong with them and with the family situation. Although they have fairly weak egos, they are both above average in intelligence. It is my feeling that with intensive treatment the prognosis will be good, although it will be a difficult case because of the multiplicity of problems. Mr. R. will be seen again to arrange details of the treatment.

Psychotherapeutic Treatment

Clinical Follow-Up

As a result of the diagnostic conference, after the psychiatric evaluation, both girls and mother were recommended for therapy in an outside agency. The mother refused to accept this for the time being, saying that at this point she could not afford it. We got the impression there was a good deal of financial manipulation. She said she would probably be able to work it out in a few months. She did not deny that the girls needed help. Since the girls were in desperate need of help, and the mother, at the time, refused to accept referral elsewhere, it was decided that Marion and Melissa would be seen by us for therapy. Mother was also seen once monthly. The mother, as previously stated, missed several appointments. She seemed to be involved with many activities outside of the home. The oldest daughter was mentioned frequently. We got the feeling that this was her most satisfying child, although she was having some problems with her, too.

Marion was to be seen by the social worker and Melissa would remain with the psychologist. Highlights of their therapy sessions are reported here.

Psychologist's Treatment Notes on Melissa

Melissa was having much more difficulty in her classroom in terms of her disruptive behavior. She had, at the time of psychiatric consultation, decided that she no longer wanted to come to the Special Reading Services. She felt that she was being singled out and did not want to be "different." Her first real therapy session came on a day when she had refused to remove her coat in the classroom. She came to the therapy room in a very sullen mood and also refused to take off her coat. She began talking and said that her mother had said she had to go to a "physical and mental doctor." She also said that she would refuse to go. We discussed her anger and she began to cry. She asked if she could come again the same day. Permission was granted and she returned, still refusing to remove her coat.

At another time, Melissa had been sent to the principal's office because of her behavior. Her mother had been called but was not available. Melissa was then sent to the psychologist's office. She sat, rocked back and forth continually, and viewed the whole incident as "stupid and silly." She had allegedly called one of her classmates "cock-eyed." This she said was completely untrue. She had merely been "talking to herself." Later the same day, she was again sent out for "disruptive behavior." She came in and began to cry. She cried continuously for about an hour. During this time, she expressed anger with everyone. She would like to go someplace and sleep and do nothing else (not even eat). She often eats very little, and at times refuses to eat. On this day, she said she felt that she was crazy. She has two relatives in a mental hospital and her father is a "maniac." She described the behavior of an older relative, saying that he "sucks his thumb and rocks." Incidentally, Melissa does the same thing. When she returned to her classroom, she continued to cry.

Generally, Melissa spoke freely. She was able to discuss her true feelings, often acting them out in our sessions. As her sessions progressed she began to show signs of feeling much less angry and more interested in her appearance. She had several outbursts but was able to come and discuss her problems. Although she refused to continue in the reading room, she frequently read to the therapist.

It is interesting to note that although both girls had been quite insistent upon being recognized as individuals, rather than twins, and the fact that they made every effort to dress differently, there was one instance when they decided to wear identical dresses and coats. This was for their graduation. This, they decided, was something quite special. We, too, treated this as a very special event. Both girls reacted quite emotionally.

Melissa was generally conscientious and consistent in coming to therapy sessions. She gained some insight and was able to maintain herself in the classroom until the end of the term. Although her general attitude about herself had improved and she appeared much more relaxed, a little less angry, and somewhat more able to sustain interpersonal relationships on all levels, she still needed a great deal of help. At the end of the sessions, the team felt that if there were no continuation and involvement, the child would experience a great deal of difficulty in junior high school.

Social Worker's Treatment Notes on Marion

At the start Marion was seen once weekly. It soon became apparent that this left too much time in between for her to sustain herself. We then began to see her for forty-five minutes twice weekly. This seemed to work out much better, although at first she still tended to come in between times and try to involve the worker in some of her difficulties with teachers and others. As we continued, this became less and less frequent until we really saw her only at the alloted time with occasional popping in just to say "hello."

Marion is a tall, slender, very attractive girl. Her manner was always soft and low-keyed. Although she was usually conscious of her appearance, this did not always help her to look well. She knew this and was able to express it. She cried a great deal, many times smiling and saying she didn't know why she was crying. She talked about being all mixed up. She often said she hated the fact that they had moved—things had been easier in the old neighborhood. In this house, you had to keep cleaning all the time; the furniture was new and if you scratched it, either parent would be down on her, the father because it cost so much money and the mother because she wanted the house to look nice and to keep everything intact. This conflict of what her mother thought was proper and what she saw around her in the immediate family seemed to be most burdensome to her. Her world was not clear but full of conflicting standards. She talked at great length about herself, her family and friends. She was acutely aware of the world around her and most sensitive to how others saw her. For a while, she considered learning and good marks as closely related to the mother with whom she was in conflict. She saw getting along in school as what her mother wanted as part of the status seeking.

We got the impression that she felt that if she learned, it would be a disloyalty to the old neighborhood and group.

She got the opportunity to discuss all this and somehow gained the recognition that she could separate fighting her mother from the school situation. She began, as she became more proficient in reading, to enjoy it and separated the learning process from her feelings towards her mother. She also began to enjoy writing stories and poetry, so that learning and the use of language became a satisfaction in itself.

Although towards the end of her therapy with us she seemed to get along better with her peers and twin, she still needed a great deal of help with her feelings towards her parents and towards the outside world. Her view of men was hostile, since the three men around her, father and two older half-brothers, were described as severely disturbed. She saw women as pushy, aggressive, and as manipulating the male.

Social Worker's Treatment Notes on Mrs. R.

Work with the mother centered on helping her to see the girls and their needs. We felt that intellectually she was able to accept this, but because of her own needs, she was unable to do anything about it. The impression was that she was hoping the problems would just go away and that the strong recommendation for her to obtain therapy for both herself and the girls had little chance of being carried out after their promotion to junior high school.

Diagnostic Evaluation by the Reading Counselor

AFTER IT HAD BEEN AGREED by the clinical and instructional staff members to accept Melissa, a fourth-grade pupil, into the reading program, a diagnostic evaluation was given; a *Metropolitan Elementary Reading* had been administered during the screening procedures. Melissa worked slowly on her test, making few errors. She did not complete it and obtained a grade score of 2.6 with 70 percent accuracy.

As appears earlier in this study, Marion (Melissa's twin) was referred to the Bureau of Special Reading Services about a year later, when she was in the fifth grade. Marion, too, was given the *Metropolitan*. She showed an erratic test pattern, missing easier items and succeeding with the more difficult ones. Her accuracy was 50 percent, which indicated that her functioning reading level was considerably lower than the grade score of 3.9 that she achieved.

In describing the instructional program, it is important to point up that it was the considered opinion of the full team that each girl be assigned to a different reading counselor. Despite the time disparity of their acceptance into the reading clinic program, the description of the remedial program will involve both girls.

Several diagnostic tests were used to determine whether the twins showed perceptual deficits. In tests of visual memory and word matching (from the Slingerland *Screening Tests*) the twins performed within average limits.

Marion evidenced a slight immaturity on the *Wepman Auditory Discrimination Test*. Melissa performed within the normal range.

Both girls showed mastery of consonant sounds and two-letter blends on the Roswell-Chall *Diagnostic Test of Word Analysis Skills*. Marion had difficulty with short and long vowels. Neither girl could isolate short vowel sounds.

Their scores on listening comprehension were considerably higher than their scores on silent reading, based on the *Diagnostic Reading Scales* by Spache. Marion demonstrated considerable skill in grasping the main idea of a reading passage but often was careless about details.

In oral reading both girls omitted word endings, and substituted medial vowels and at times consonants, especially *b* for *d* and *n* for *m*. At the third-grade level of this Spache test, Melissa made five errors; at the fourth-grade level, Marion made seven errors.

Results of the pattern of errors on the various tests were summarized for each child on the Check List of Reading Difficulties of the Bureau of Special Reading Services. Continuing diagnostic evaluations were made on this form every three months, to provide an on-going picture of growth in reading skills and an analysis of the skill sequences to be taught.

On the *Harris Tests of Lateral Dominance*, Marion was rated moderately right and Melissa as strongly right-sided. Without hesitation, each child could follow directions involving the concepts of right and left in relationship to her own body and to another person. They were able to cross-pattern accurately—e.g., each could touch her left ear with her right hand.

The diagnostic examination of Melissa by the speech improvement teacher showed that word endings were often omitted. There were a few consonant substitutions such as *d* for *t*. The examiner noted that Melissa spoke in a barely audible voice. Marion also omitted several word endings.

There was a slight distortion of the *s* and a substitution of *f* for the *th* sound.

On the audiometer test, neither girl evidenced any impairment of hearing.

Marion was given an eye examination. Glasses were recommended and obtained. However, Marion was quite reluctant to wear them. Frequently she left her glasses in the classroom or at home and resisted putting them on in the reading room. "I look horrible," she commented. In subsequent sessions, the reading counselor, who wore glasses herself, used several opportunities to discuss, humorously, with the reading group her own resistance as a child to wearing glasses. She remarked that when she was a young girl, she would put on her glasses in the movies only when the theater was darkened. Another time, she told about her experiences at football games, not being able to follow the action because she couldn't see without her glasses. "But now," the reading counselor emphasized, "people who don't even need glasses are wearing them to look more fashionable and more interesting. Glasses, today, are so much more attractive and colorful." After a time, evidently, Marion became convinced that glasses could be attractive and she began to wear them.

Findings from the medical examinations given by the school doctor were reported as, "No symptoms noted." Both girls were somewhat under-weight; Marion's classroom teacher reported that Marion sometimes re-fused to eat for a day or so. At parties in the reading rooms, each of the girls refused to taste anything.

Remedial Program

Recommendations for the Instructional Program

Many conferences were held between reading counselors and clinic team members regarding the most effective procedures for upgrading the reading level of each of these girls. An underlying factor was that each girl needed a highly motivated, highly stimulated learning situation, ac-companied by an enormous sensitivity to their constant demands. The learning program had to be eclectic and had to stress visual, auditory, and kinesthetic pathways—all being strengthened in the learning experience.

In order to minimize competition and to emphasize differentiation of the girls, each twin was assigned to a different reading counselor. Remedi-ation was scheduled twice a week in a small group situation.

The Instructional Program: First Year

Melissa began remedial reading sessions in a group of all girls. Cooking was at that time the group's main interest. Recipes were used to build word attack skills involving short and long vowel principles, to develop vocabulary, and to give practice in following step-by-step directions. Melissa came willingly, but would not taste the food that the girls prepared. Some days she would join the group's project of looking through recipes to find words with short or long vowels, write the word on a card, and place the card in the correct pocket on a vowel chart. Other days, she would watch the girls' activities without participating.

Frequently, she left her classroom early to stand by the door of the reading room until it was time for her group to assemble. After school, she might stop by to show the reading counselor a new dress, a new pair of shoes, and sometimes even a poem she had written.

In October, when Marion was accepted into the reading program, she did not relate immediately to her reading counselor. During the first month of the reading sessions she was quiet, unresponsive to questions, and aloof. Her answers, when given, were usually limited to a minimal *yes* or *no*. A teacher-prepared chart on feelings stimulated her first real participation. The heading on the chart was "Our Feelings" and adjectives such as happy, angry, disappointed, proud, and jealous appeared below. Marion spoke about how angry she became at various times; once when a boy annoyed her, or another time when someone had thrown a rock at her, or when her sister bothered her; also when her sister wore her clothes without even asking her for permission. She willingly joined in as each child chose a card presenting a highly charged emotional situation and took her turn reading to the group. This was followed by the group reading *Our Emotions and How They Work* by J. Beim. Reading skills related to this learning situation included how to use the dictionary, selecting the appropriate meaning, the place of synonyms, and language skills in using newly acquired vocabulary.

The reading counselor's supportive attitude towards the children's right to express their feelings opened up further communication. Typical complaints from Marion centered around the family situation.

"It's no fun at my house," Marion blurted out. "My mother gives my sisters everything they want. I get only old, ugly, second-hand things, only broken down stuff. It's great at my aunt's. I wish I could stay there all the time." The impression Marion gave was that she enjoyed her visits there because her aunt was more permissive, and so there were few restrictions.

Frequently Marion showed open hostility. A conference with the classroom teacher disclosed that Marion often teased a girl in the school who took pride in looking very neat and well-dressed, although Marion herself was usually nicely dressed. Marion was suspected of being part of a group who had defaced a new building in the neighborhood. When the reading counselor questioned the group about the vandalism and asked why people might want to break windows or scribble on walls, Marion volunteered: "I'd rather live in an old slum building because in my house everybody is too fussy."

The girls' general adjustment in the classrooms and reading rooms was discussed at a team conference. It was decided that the twins should receive psychotherapy on a regular basis from the Special Reading Services clinic team.

During this period when Marion was acting out much of her hostility, Melissa became increasingly withdrawn and sullen. Communication was limited to complaints. She was annoyed that Marion would not let her eat dinner "peacefully" and that another sister had slammed a door on her hand. "Now it hurts when I write," and "My teacher blames me for things I don't do. Yesterday, she said that I took my friend's pen." In the reading room, her typical posture was to sit with her chair pushed back from the table and her head down. When the reading counselor asked her to push her chair in, she might comply for a few minutes, and then gradually would sink back into her former, typical position of "head down." If she did not understand the directions for a task, she would cry. Some days she accepted help from the reading counselor and worked on teacher-prepared rexographed material; other days, she would refuse. A characteristic response to work was: "I'm a nit-wit, anyway. I can't learn these words. They are too hard."

During this time, she also would leave her classroom if the teacher corrected her for anything. A conference with the classroom teacher disclosed that Melissa often teased a handicapped child and even made inappropriate sarcastic comments about the teacher.

For several sessions, Melissa came to reading but refused to read aloud or answer questions. The reading counselor devised a lesson, *Our Five Senses,* partly to make the point with Melissa that she could learn by listening. Her participation improved when she realized that silence was not a weapon and was acceptable.

She became involved in a book about a boy, Pascal, and his red balloon.

The reading counselor brought in a bag of balloons and gave these directions to the group: "Pretend this balloon is you. Where could the balloon travel? What will the balloon see?" Melissa responded, "The balloon could fly around all the tall buildings and look into people's houses." Reading Counselor, "What do you think you could see?" Melissa, "Oh, probably kids fighting."

The reading counselor proceeded with the reading lesson which stressed drawing inferences and formulating conclusions, how to use imagination, and the use of synonyms to vary dialogue. Creative writing was stressed to further stimulate the use of imaginative experience.

Getting Melissa to practice specific word analysis skills was often difficult. She did not want to use workbooks or even teacher-prepared materials. Finally, after many and varied attempts with different materials, an audio-visual machine stimulated her interest and broke down some of her resistance (Bell and Howell *Language Master*).

Melissa practiced words with short vowel sounds; then a word would be read from the programmed cards and she could check her pronunciation with the audio-component of the machine. Blank cards were available for her to record her own responses under the supervision of the reading counselor. Phrases and sentences were programmed around her interests. Melissa seemed able to accept the machine's authority and "correction" more easily than direct suggestions from a teacher, perhaps because of the machine's objective and impersonal aspects.

Melissa's reaction to games was apt to be explosive. Taking turns and sharing word cards might demand more maturity than she was capable of, especially if she were in an angry mood. A game called "Find Your Partner," which had as its goal the principle of the final "e," was disrupted by her when she grabbed another child's card. When the reading counselor stopped the game, Melissa sulked and attempted to leave the room.

More positive responses were elicited by use of the tape recorder. Melissa enjoyed reading orally into the recorder and playing back her tapes. In this way she could evaluate her progress in mastering fifth- and sixth-grade words, in reading accurately, and in using appropriate phrasing and expression. Some days, she taped her own stories or poems—a valuable way to promote her self-expression and allow some ventilation of her turbulent feelings.

The question of biographies arose in Marion's group after the group watched the story of Helen Keller on TV the night before. The pupils were fascinated by Helen Keller. It amazed them that a woman who could not see, was unable to speak, and could not hear did succeed in learning to read. Beyond that, they were also intrigued by the fact that she turned her sad experiences into avenues in which she could help others face their tragedies through her lectures and her writings. The reading counselor used Helen Keller's biography as a means of stimulating interest by reading parts of it to the group at each session; a book in Braille was brought in. Codes and books on codes were investigated. Teacher-prepared charts on prefixes and suffixes were studied. Comprehension exercises were rexographed. The unit was culminated with each member writing and illustrating her own short autobiography. The reading of biographies became a highlight in this group, especially with Marion. From then on she borrowed every biography she could secure. This became another turning point in her reading progress.

Results. In May the twins were tested again. Melissa's score on the *Metropolitan Achievement Test,* Elementary Reading, was: Word Knowledge 5.8; Reading Comprehension 5.2, accuracy 60 percent. She worked slowly on this test and resisted completing the reading paragraphs. "These stories are too long. I don't like to bother reading such big stories on tests. I don't care what score I get because I'm stupid, anyway." Despite this attitude of self-denigration, Melissa's reading performance had grown 2 years and 9 months from September until May, a period of eight months.

Marion also showed reluctance about taking standardized tests. She would put her pencil down, stare at the ceiling, or gaze out of the window. When encouraged by the reading counselor to continue, she would make a face, pick up her pencil, and go on for a short time. After reading two or three paragraphs, she would put her pencil down again. Marion's test results on the *Metropolitan Achievement Test,* Elementary Reading, were: Word Knowledge 5.5; Comprehension 5.5, accuracy 66 percent. Her gain after eight months of remedial instruction and therapy was 1 year and 6 months.

In summarizing Marion's progress for the year, her classroom teacher commented that her reading showed much improvement, especially in word recognition skills, comprehension, and fluency. There seemed to be an overall improvement in her study skills and personal-social patterns. She showed self-direction, and when given a task that she could do on her own without much supervision, was able to give it sustained attention.

Melissa's teacher stated in June, "She is now reading a great deal in class and asking questions about fables and myths, which interest her. At times she relates what she reads to her own life situation—finding similarities between members of her family and characters in books. Although her grammar and spelling could be improved, she writes in a colorful, imaginative style." The teacher elaborated more about Melissa's poems and compositions and was impressed with the child's talent.

As to peer relationships, the teacher described some trouble between Melissa and two boys in class. "These boys, in particular, are apt to make her angry, and she sometimes screams at them if they say anything to her. She occasionally has crying spells, but not as often as at the beginning of the term."

Remediation: Second Year

Melissa. When school reopened in September, Melissa had a new reading counselor because of staff reorganization. Melissa, for whom any important change could be theatening, found it difficult to establish a new relationship. This is best illustrated by the following incident:

Entering the reading room on the first day of the new term Melissa commented: "Anyway, this room still looks pretty." However, she resisted reading orally. After some encouragement from the reading counselor, she read in a whisper. When asked some questions about the lesson from a children's newspaper which the group was reading, Melissa refused to answer. Some days she was the only girl in the group, which made her uncomfortable. She did respond positively to the reading counselor's suggestion that she sit next to her, "so we two girls can be together."

For several weeks after this incident, she came willingly and especially enjoyed using the tape recorder. She often brought the reading counselor a poem or a story she had written, as she had done with her former reading teacher. At this time, the reading counselor felt that there had been considerable improvement in Melissa's reading. Perhaps there should be a tapering off of this instructional service followed by her joining the alumni.[2]

A team conference was held and it was recommended that Melissa be given a standardized test to determine her reading level and to terminate service in the reading group if she were on grade level. She would continue to receive clinical services. On *Metropolitan* Intermediate Reading, she received a grade score in Word Knowledge of 6.7 and a Reading

[2]All pupils who graduate out of the Service become members of the alumni group and are seen twice a month by the reading counselor.

grade score of 8.7, with an accuracy rating of 70 percent. She became an alumna of Special Reading Services.

Marion. Marion continued to come to the reading room on a regular basis. In her classroom, however, she was full of complaints. She described the work as "baby work." "It's too easy for me," she moaned. At this point, the reading clinic team suggested to the principal a possible change in class placement. A short time later, Marion was transferred to a more advanced class with a teacher who was especially skillful in handling her occasional resistance to assignments and her temperamental outbursts.

The group had been learning the techniques of how to read a newspaper. The necessary skills, vocabulary, and actual handling of a newspaper were taught. Books on the subject were read, e.g., *Let's Visit a Newspaper*, and *The Horse Who Wanted His Picture in The Paper*, and various parts of a newspaper were investigated. Opinion versus fact was a much discussed topic. Various types of newspapers were studied and discussed as to the type of reporting. Marion became especially involved with current events and important people in the news.

On the anniversary of the birth of Israel, the Minister of Education from Israel came to visit the Bureau of Special Reading Services. He visited Marion's reading room and talked with the children. Marion was fascinated. She and the group began to read books about other parts of the world including, *The First Book of Israel, The First Book about Negroes,* books about Japan, Mexico, and Africa. This was an important milestone for Marion, because until then she had been unable to accept hearing anyone use the word Negro. After reading these books about other ethnic groups, she began to be able to verbalize differences in people.

During the spring term, Marion's classroom teacher reported that Marion's reading skills had grown considerably and that she had become very much interested in learning new and difficult words that she had previously refused to try. This was most heartening because much work had been done on syllables and syllabication. However, the teacher also pointed out that there were days when Marion resisted doing her class assignments and was "seething with anger." "On these days it is difficult to keep her from distracting the other children. She made faces, giggled and said silly things."

Results. At the final conference in June, the classroom teacher reported that Marion now shows considerable self-direction and a more constructive attitude towards work. "However," she continued, "Marion still shows erratic behavior. When she is unhappy or angry, she will not concentrate on a school task. Lately she complains that she is not sleeping well, and there are days when she cries." Her work pattern was still very much dictated by her own feelings. She would work when *she* decided that she wanted to accomplish something.

Resistance to taking tests continued up to the last month in school. Although her final test, which was given in a small group, showed excellent reading progress, the reading counselor had to prod her to keep her working. She sucked her fingers, stared at the ceiling, and looked unhappy during much of the test. On the *Metropolitan Achievement Test,* Intermediate Reading, her grade score on Word Knowledge was 11.1; Reading Comprehension, 8.7; accuracy 81 percent.

She was then graduated from the sixth grade to junior high school. Marion was able to take a foreign language upon admission to the junior high school. She chose French after much deliberation and discussion. This attainment represented a new level of success and seemed to reflect itself in her demeanor and new feelings of self-worth.

Follow-Up and Evaluation

A FOLLOW-UP VISIT was made to the junior high school when both girls were in the eighth grade. The girls were seen, as well as their guidance counselor and some of their teachers. Although erratic in their achievement, neither girl had failed any of her subjects. Their reading scores on standardized tests fluctuated from fifth- to eleventh-grade reading, with their teachers' subjective estimation that the level veered more to the higher grade than the lower.

Both Melissa's and Marion's teachers felt that the girls needed extra prodding to achieve. They responded to the learning processes more in terms of how they felt than what went on around them. At one grading period, Melissa did so well that she was put on the Honor Roll. Promptly after that she began to act up and had to be suspended for five days. It was our feeling, in reviewing the episode with the clinic staff, that this child reacted with panic and fear to a very real manifestation of her strengths and potency. It seemed almost terrifying to her that she could succeed and had succeeded. The realization that this may enable her to release repressed anger may have triggered off the acting up.

The girls were pleased to see us and the impression was that the warm relationship that had been set up in the therapeutic situation persisted. Marion has been able to transfer it. She had, when in difficulty, turned to a male teacher who was now helping her with mathematics. She also talked with him when she was troubled and confided many of her problems to him. We felt strongly that both girls were ready to move into therapy. As feared, no therapy had been obtained for them by the parents.

These girls illustrated so graphically the interrelationship between the emotional and the learning process. Everyone concurred that the twins reacted to their moods. It was extremely difficult to interpret this fact to some of their teachers. They were often unable to accept the fact that the girls' performances were not within their conscious control. When they were well-motivated, felt good about themselves, and had support, they could and did achieve. The support they received often counteracted their feelings of low self-esteem, enabling them to perform well at times.

The fact that they lacked the inner strengths necessary for self-maintenance and productivity was evidenced constantly in their school achievement and behavior. This fact illustrated the need for therapeutic intervention where such strengths could be built up and sustained. Our recommendations were thoroughly discussed with the current guidance counselor, who stated that the parents would be seen and that every effort would be made to follow through with our recommendations for continued therapy.

In conclusion, it is important to note that both Marion and Melissa maintained their reading gains and carried these achievements into the other curriculum areas. What is the matrix of progress that brought about this growth in learning? One could suggest such variables as: a constructive relationship with their reading counselors and therapists; a highly motivated, carefully planned program of remediation; small group instruction; and a high level of involvement and stimulation in school projects. Certainly all of these were operative and it is difficult to determine how one affected the other. Yet as we ponder the why of the children's achievement we ask what role was played by the intense and involved interest of all the staff and how this intensity contributed to the children's growth in motivation.

Editor's Comments

This report of work with twin sisters is noteworthy for the vivid detail provided about the family background and the interplay of emotional life with school behavior and learning. The contributions of the social worker, psychologist, and psychiatrist are well portrayed. The title "remedial counselor" reflects the emphasis placed in this setting on a close relationship between guidance and teaching.

The need to sell Marion the idea that eyeglasses are attractive will seem familiar to many remedial teachers and clinicians. Often the effort to get eyes examined, and then to see that the family gets the glasses, is only the beginning.

Psychotherapy sessions once a week with a psychologist or social worker seemed to have helped both sisters, but as the report closes they were entering adolescence with no essential change in the family situation, and both were considered still to need intensive psychotherapy, which neither had received. Thus the outlook for future adjustment remains uncertain, despite quite satisfactory growth in reading skills.

· 6 ·

Raphael

BY BEATRICE LEVISON *

Setting

The Northside Center for Child Development is an independent, non-profit, mental health out-patient clinic located in the Harlem area of New York City. Founded in 1946, the Northside program puts main emphasis on diagnosis, psychotherapy, and educational remediation for the emotionally troubled child.

Northside's program includes psychological testing, a pediatric examination, individual or group or family psychotherapy, casework, and remedial education. Familiarity with the social, economic, and physical landscape of the ghetto marks the orientation of the interracial team of psychologists, psychiatrists, social workers, and teachers. Fees paid by parents amount to less than 1 percent of total operating costs.

Diagnostic Study

RAPHAEL WAS REFERRED TO NORTHSIDE by his school because of what was rather ambiguously described as "language difficulty." He was 8½ years old and repeating second grade. His teacher felt that he was "impossible and dull." According to her, he never spoke, couldn't do anything, didn't seem to understand anything that was said to him, and made no response to anything or anyone. He spent his time walking around the room, making noises, rotating his hands, and grinding his teeth. At times he was loudly disruptive. Earlier school reports gave a similar picture. After attending kindergarten for a few weeks when he was 5, he was withdrawn

* Mamie Phipps Clark, Ph.D., has been executive director of Northside since its founding and helped to select this case. Mrs. Jeanne Karp has been head of the reading department since 1952; she supervised the remedial instruction and helped in the case selection. Mrs. Levison, the remedial therapist who taught Raphael, wrote the report with the assistance of Miss Harriet Moskowitz, a coworker.

at the school's request. The teacher reported that he spoke to no one, ran around the room making loud screaming sounds, and was aggressive, hyperactive, and destructive. Reports at ages 6 and 7 were that he seemed to live in a different world, was unhappy, and couldn't be taught.

Early Development

An intake interview with his parents disclosed that Raphael was an unwanted child. His mother, a hairdresser, returned to work shortly after his birth, and he was cared for by an elderly neighborhood woman who came to the home daily. Raphael was slow in sitting up. At 1 year he stood up, much to the surprise of his family, and walked all around the room; then he did not walk again for several months. He also started talking at 1 year, but stopped abruptly when he was 2. His pediatrician felt that he was a retarded child and suggested that the parents arrange for a diagnostic evaluation, but this recommendation was not followed.

The mother related that from the time he was very small Raphael had had a passion for windows and beds, always talking about them and saving such pictures of them as he could find. Also from the time he was small he had what she called the habit of making rotating motions with his hands, hitting one against the other and simultaneously making a hissing sound. This might go on for hours.

Despite this history, the mother's attitude was one of denial of the possibility of any pathology. The father, too, gave the impression of lack of concern about the possibility of any serious disturbance. The mother attributed what she described as Raphael's misbehavior to the fact that the woman who took care of him did not bring him up properly.

Clinical Findings

Raphael was seen for psychiatric evaluation soon after the initial parent interview was held, and the diagnostic impression was one of childhood schizophrenia. Psychological tests were administered during the same period. Raphael attained an I.Q. of 76 on the *Revised Stanford-Binet*. A *WISC* could not be given because he did not seem to understand the questions. The *Wide Range Achievement Test* placed him at 1.3 level in Reading and 2.2 in Arithmetic. The examiner observed a great deal of scatter in Raphael's intellectual functioning, as well as inappropriate affect. Figure drawing and performance on the *Bender* were poor.

Raphael's responses on the *Rorschach* resembled those frequently observed in mentally retarded children, but some were of sufficiently high quality and level to make a diagnosis of mental retardation questionable. Some responses indicated that his reality testing was poor, and there were some signs of schizoid trends.

On the *Thematic Apperception Test* Raphael did not offer stories spontaneously. When pressed, he related rather long, unhappy tales in which adults were seen as violent and aggressive and he was the helpless victim who could not protect himself.

Remedial Treatment

First Year

Psychotherapy for Raphael and casework for his parents were recommended, and were begun a few months later. Remedial reading was also recommended, but because of the difficulty in finding someone to escort Raphael to and from the center it was not started for another few months, at which time he was scheduled for two 45-minute sessions per week.

When introduced to me by his psychotherapist, Raphael would not look up or take my hand although he rather willingly followed me to the room for our first session. He replied to none of my comments, and before sitting down he opened all the closet doors, investigated the closets, closed the doors, and then came to the desk.

I had planned to spend our first hour in trying to make him feel comfortable in what was for him a strange, new setting and to introduce some of the materials with which we were going to work. Appropriate books and games had been selected before his arrival and were displayed on my desk. The first thing he picked up was a spelling toy—a rotating wheel with pictures and words—which he immediately began to spin. He kept coming back to this device and the only conversation he made throughout the first session was, "I like this game." In the course of the session he examined everything else that was on the desk, punctuating his activity with frequent bursts of inappropriate laughter. From the Picture-Word card game he extracted all cards with pictures of beds and windows and, holding them in his hands, made rotating motions, accompanied by hissing sounds and other noises. He was also interested in what was under the desk and on several occasions hid there for a few minutes.

Despite his distractibility, hyperactivity, and shyness there were intermittent moments when he was able to become involved and focus on some of the material. I took advantage of these brief opportunities to see whether he could learn new words by sight from the Picture-Word card game. I let him select five words he wanted to learn. "Window" was his first choice. About five minutes were spent on this activity, at the end of which Raphael could recognize the five words without the related pictures. This was the only clue I had as to what might be useful in helping him learn.

The second session was pretty much a repetition of the first. I was curious to see whether he had retained the sight words previously learned and was pleased to discover that he remembered two of them, "window" and "floor." Raphael spent most of the session manipulating the Go Fish and Picture-Word game cards. Again he extracted all those with pictures of beds and windows, holding these in one hand while with the remaining cards he built card houses. An attempt to teach him to play Go Fish was unsuccessful; he could not understand either the purpose or the rules of the game. However he was able to understand simple instructions well enough to complete two pages in a beginning workbook.

It was impossible at that early date to make a formal diagnosis of either his reading level or relevant skills, since he could not sit still long enough to answer questions, nor did he understand at first what I was asking of him. During subsequent sessions he became a little more relaxed, and when he agreed to read for me it was quickly evident that he was most comfortable with a preprimer. He had a small sight vocabulary and knew the sounds of the consonants, but he would never attempt to attack an unfamiliar word. Since he seemed to be able to learn by sight and enjoyed the Picture-Word cards, I decided to concentrate on building a sight vocabulary that would enable him to read the primers.

Actually all decisions had to be tentative and flexible. There was no way at this point of knowing how much Raphael really knew, how much he would be able to learn, and what would be the most effective teaching approach. Goals were necessarily vague. Here, after all, was a child who was not profiting from schooling and whose life offered no satisfactions whatever. Any growth he could achieve, whether in intellectual or social areas, was in itself a valid objective.

Raphael's illness was discernible to even the most casual observer. He was physically ungainly and uncoordinated. His eyes were constantly shifting from one object to another, never focussing directly on a human being. The bizarre aspects of his appearance were compounded by signs of neglect: he looked unkempt and uncared for. His shoelaces were untied and his shirttails were hanging out. He seemed encapsulated and totally withdrawn. His verbalizations usually took the form of unintelligible muttering to himself. His response to as simple a question as "How are you today, Raphael?" might be, "Do you have a husband?" or "I flew over the buildings to get to the clinic." I never pursued his fantasies with him, but always let him know that I distinguished between fact and fancy.

A major problem during the early months was getting Raphael to sit still long enough to benefit from instruction. I began to realize that in my effort to make the program attractive to him, I was offering him precisely those inducements that were scattering his attention and heightening his distractibility—the wide variety of games, books, etc., spread out on my desk prevented him from focussing on any particular task. I therefore began to limit the exposed materials to two or three things I chose to work with on a given day. But more important, there was the problem of setting limits and structuring the sessions. I was at first timid and unsure of what to do—afraid that I might snap the rather tenuous thread that seemed to be holding Raphael to the remedial program. I knew that he liked to come. He was always early and began to come to look for me before I called him. He started to make comments, sometimes appropriate and relevant, sometimes not. He occasionally would tease me by purposely giving an incorrect answer in his workbook and would laugh loudly when I'd say, "You're fooling me again!" He clearly did not want to read but began to do so in order to please me.

In a conference with his psychotherapist, I raised a question about my handling of Raphael's hyperactivity and lack of attention. Should I put some pressure on Raphael in an effort to get him to adhere to some kind of structured program? The therapist's feeling was, "By all means, try it. You can't do any terrible damage. If it doesn't work now, maybe it will some other day."

The next time I saw Raphael I had an opportunity to test the new approach. When, in the middle of reading, he turned to the box of cards to look for the window picture, I took the cards from him and (not without some trepidation) said: "Now look, Raphael, if you want to keep coming here, you must finish the things you start. Otherwise I won't be able to work with you. You must finish reading this page." He looked up at me, smiled, and to my great amazement turned to the book and completed the page.

This was not, of course, a magical solution to the problem. Raphael continued to be easily distractible, noisy, and essentially noncommunicative. But, little by little, changes were noted. Toward the end of the year rotating motions of arms and body, as well as the accompanying noises and grinding of teeth, had markedly decreased. With his therapist Raphael had grown communicative and even a little affectionate. His relationship with me developed at a slower pace. During the early months of his treatment he had not seemed to be aware of me as a person. I was, rather, an object whose purpose was to supply him with pictures of windows and beds in the form of cards and illustrations in books. It was, therefore, gratifying indeed when, at the end of the year, I returned to the clinic after a short illness and was greeted by Raphael who ran in asking where I had been and what had been wrong. Since much of my effort during our sessions that first year had to be directed towards establishing a relationship with him, his progress in reading was not noteworthy.

Results. Test scores at the end of the year placed him at a high first-grade level. He had learned a few more sight words, read two primers, and started a first-grade book. He continued to be reluctant to read, yet gave me the distinct impression that he knew more than he was revealing —that he just wasn't going to let me know how much he could do. I might add that at this time he concealed from his parents his ability to read even the simplest material. In fact, they believed he was still a total non-reader.

However, from a highly disorganized child Raphael had become one who, in response to the structured character of the reading sessions, was able to devote some time each session to oral reading, workbook exercises, and simple games. Varying the tasks and keeping each one short enabled him to maintain interest in the work, and his disruptive habits and mannerisms were less conspicuous.

Second Year

In the fall Raphael started his second year of the psychotherapy and remedial work. The gains made the previous year had been retained over the summer and greater relatedness both to the teacher and his work were immediately apparent upon his return. It became possible to undertake systematic phonic instruction, and as his skills increased an effort was made to arouse his *interest* in reading. Raphael clung to books he could handle comfortably, like "Cat in the Hat," yet it was felt that he had the ability to read more difficult material which would also be more appropriate to his age and interest level. He had expressed some interest in skin diving, and a second-grade book, *The Sea Hunt,* part of a series called *Deep Sea Adventures,* was left on the desk one day when he was expected. After studiously avoiding it for a few minutes, he casually picked it up and began to study the illustrations. He was soon reading the first chapter and finally asked for it as his "reader."

Raphael's increased attention span and greater ability to organize his thinking now made it possible to introduce more complex games. During the first year, the rules for the game "Go Fish," which teaches single consonant sounds and consonant blends (the bl's, sl's, tr's, etc.), were difficult for him to follow. Attempts to play it had only increased his disorganization and generally left me holding the cards except the "b" for bed and "w" for window, which he appropriated. He now understood and enjoyed the game, playing it according to the rules. In fact, he became very annoyed one day when I accidentally tried to go out of turn. I suddenly realized that Raphael was demanding structure of me. This is not to say that game-playing was always a successful or productive activity. His reactions were still unpredictable, and there were times he would express excitement or irritation by flinging the cards wildly in the air.

Signs of his growing ease in the reading sessions began to multiply. He started to teach me Spanish phrases and showed amusement at my accent. Further, after consistently refusing the offer of a lollipop he unexpectedly announced, "I think I'll have a lollipop today," and from that point on helped himself freely. Although he still shied away from physical contact he began to take my hand when I called for him in the waiting room. Raphael also revealed greater capacity for involvement in an activity. This was startlingly expressed on one occasion when I prepared to shift him to a new task. He looked up at me with indignation and said, "But I'm not finished with this experience yet."

By the end of the second year he had read five first-grade books and one second-grade book. He enjoyed discussing them and made appropriate and intelligent comments.

Test scores at that time placed him at middle third-grade level. Improvement in oral reading was noted and he was able to employ his new phonic skills when confronted by unfamiliar words. His comprehension of the material read was excellent. A report received from Raphael's school confirmed these gains. It indicated that in science and social studies his oral response to questions was generally appropriate and his answers correct. However, his social adjustment was still poor. He was not involved with other children in school activities, refused to eat lunch with them, did not follow directions, and was noisy at times.

Third Year

At the start of his third year in remedial work he was in a slow fourth-grade class in public school. It now seemed realistic to set limited goals, both with respect to academic achievement and self-discipline. Raphael still functioned best in situations that did not require independent activity. For example, it was difficult for him to take a timed test because he could not stay with the task and work within a time limit; he also would forget that no assistance could be given during a test and kept asking for help. Similarly, most of his reading had to be done orally because he was too distractible to work without close supervision. A major goal, then, was to increase his capacity for independent work.

Analysis of his reading skills indicated that he now knew initial consonant sounds, long and short vowel sounds, and many of the consonant blends and vowel combinations. He had good sight vocabulary and made excellent use of context. He was ready to proceed to a more advanced level of phonic instruction. He was at this time reading a second-grade book with ease and was reluctant to try something new. While it was gratifying to see Raphael read *any* book with enjoyment, it seemed both necessary and possible to move him on to more challenging material.

He still maintained his previous year's interest in skin diving and after some coaxing he agreed to try the next book in the series he had started. This book was on a third-grade level, and once he accepted it, he was able to read it with fluency and comprehension.

As the year progressed Raphael's concentration span lengthened. He began to enjoy the process of learning. An incidental, but highly important, result of this was his awareness of me as a person. I was now someone with whom he could raise questions and discuss his opinions about the material read.

Toward the end of the year, SRA materials on a 3.5 level were introduced. He liked reading the selections and began to do some independent work on answering the questions dealing with comprehension and word meanings. He was able to discipline himself to stay with an assignment until it was completed.

Test results at the end of the year showed that he had made over one year's progress in both the *Wide Range* and the *Gates Advanced Primary* Silent Reading test. He was able, for the first time, to work on a timed test with no help from me. This was also the first time he attempted the Paragraph Meaning section of the test. He had previously refused to try this, saying that it was "too hard." He scored 5.0 on Paragraph Meaning. On the *Wide Range* he tried to read words through the sixth-grade level, coming very close on many of them (*element* for *eliminate*, *īmage* for *image* and *theorý* for *theory*).

As Raphael became more involved in the remedial process, distractibility and hyperactivity were the exception rather than the rule. A vacation or a period of tension at home or in school could result in a temporary recurrence of his old patterns. But he had by this time become very attached to his psychotherapist and her understanding and support enabled him to surmount these crises. Firmness and structure remained critical elements in the reading sessions. Raphael needed to learn that there were limits he could not exceed. And he *could* learn! Having once been dismissed early for refusal to pay attention during a session, he was careful to avoid having this happen again.

During this third year Raphael made an effort to establish some contact with his peers. He became involved with other children in the waiting room, knew their names, and referred to some of them as "my friends." He became more aware of himself as an individual, an awareness which resulted in his playing hookey from school for two or three days because he resented the fact that children were teasing him. He looked neat and well-groomed. Walking and running were done with greater coordination and bizarre mannerisms were rarely evidenced. Incidentally, whereas earlier he would not admit to his parents that he could read at all, he began to enjoy reading to them and demonstrating his skill.

Fourth Year

When he returned to remedial work in the fall, Raphael was in a fifth-grade class. He was reading comfortably on a high fourth-grade level with good comprehension. His excellent phonic and word analysis skills also enabled him to read fifth-grade material, but at this level comprehension began to decrease.

It was now time to place major emphasis on improving comprehension skills. SRA materials on a fourth- and fifth-grade level, which he accepted willingly, were used throughout the year. Raphael was encouraged to ask questions about words whose meanings he did not know and to use the dictionary as often as possible. He also enjoyed using the Syllaboscope because he felt that this was a "grown-up" device with an advanced vocabulary. Here, too, word meanings were discussed, and the new words were employed in constructing sentences. To encourage independent reading Raphael was given the use of our library, and he began to borrow books freely, reading them at home and reporting on them at the sessions.

His behavior was generally more mature and responsible. There were still periods when he reverted to some of his former behavior, becoming silly, making noises and being uncooperative. These episodes, as formerly, seemed to be related to an unsettled home situation. His parents separated during the year and this was a period of turmoil for Raphael. Despite these problems he began to demonstrate that he did have the ability to function in a completely independent manner. At various times he was given an assignment and left alone in the room to complete it. From an initial stage of being able to answer only one question during the entire work period, he reached the point of completing an SRA card without my assistance or presence.

Group Experience. In view of his progress both academically and in terms of inner controls, it was decided that Raphael should have the experience of working with other children. After several discussions with him, he overcame his initial reluctance and agreed to participate. He and two other boys were to be seen by me twice a week. I was also to continue seeing Raphael individually once a week. He still needed personal relationships with accepting adults, and at this time the only satisfying relationships he had were with his psychotherapist and with me.

The other two boys in the group, Martin and Alfred, were also children with whom I had been working individually. It was felt that each of the three boys had certain strengths from which the others could learn and certain weaknesses which a group might help them overcome. Martin and Alfred were serious, cooperative youngsters who might exert a stabilizing influence on Raphael and help him learn to work with peers. While they were slow and hesitant readers whose decoding skills were at high third-grade level, they were able to comprehend more difficult material. Raphael's problem was just the reverse: he read rapidly and fluently, but comprehension at a fifth-grade level was poor.

During the first session all were a little shy and subdued but seemed to like being together. Raphael was the fastest reader, Alfred the slowest, and Martin somewhere in between. Raphael behaved very well during the first session and derived great pleasure and pride from being the one to supply unknown words to the others. He was aware, however, that

Martin and Alfred could answer the questions more quickly and accurately than he could. All enjoyed playing Go Fish and it was interesting to see that Raphael, who prior to this would never hold all his cards in his hands at one time because "it was too hard to keep track of them," tried to do so as the other boys did, although somewhat clumsily.

Martin and Alfred had been prepared for the fact that Raphael was "different" from other boys, and while they were puzzled by some of his behavior, they showed amazing tolerance and willingness to accept him. Although Raphael was making an obvious effort to conform to the group, he had a tendency to make noises or talk nonsense when he felt embarrassed or uncomfortable. He also tended to be intolerant of the slow reading of the others and would mutter to himself about their slowness or call out the words without giving them sufficient time to try for themselves. He was spoken to about this privately. It was pointed out to him that when he held the others up while trying to answer a question they waited patiently for him to get through. This highlighted the necessity for patience and consideration for the needs of others, as well as the fact that Raphael, himself, had areas of weakness in relation to the other boys.

The understanding that the boys displayed towards Raphael was illustrated by remarks each made privately early in the year. Martin, commenting on Raphael's noises and silliness said "but maybe he's just nervous." Alfred, in that same week, said "He acts too silly sometimes. But I used to act that way till you gave me a talking to and told me I'd never learn that way. So he may change."

As the sessions progressed the boys became better able to work together. Martin and Alfred got along very well and tried to include Raphael as a member of their "gang." Raphael's slowness and disorganization when playing a game was rather trying, but they did their best to help him organize himself. Raphael, in turn, began to improve his functioning in games and also developed greater patience in permitting others to work at their own rates. He tended to become overexcited during games, but a warning from me that the game would have to be discontinued was usually sufficient to calm him down. During the games there was much shouting and horse-play, which Raphael particularly enjoyed. It was at these times that he gave the impression of feeling accepted. He would refer to Martin or Alfred as "my friend" when asking for a card. One one occasion some derogatory comments about Raphael's playing were made by the others but at the end of the game Martin voluntarily apologized to Raphael. After one particularly fruitful session Alfred turned to Raphael and complimented him on "not fooling around today."

The boys all looked forward to the group sessions. Raphael, particularly, seemed disappointed if someone were absent. He enjoyed leaving the clinic with the boys and, to use his expression, "horsing around outside" until they separated to go to their various schools. Since each of the boys was seen once a week individually for work on special needs, emphasis in the group was on improving comprehension and listening skills for all and some work in phonics, primarily for the benefit of Martin and Alfred who had particular difficulty with consonant combinations and short vowel sounds. *Phonics in Action* (Workbook 4 in The Happy Times with Sounds series) and *Go Fish* 2 were used for these skills. Brueckner and Lewis *Diagnostic Tests and Remedial Exercises in Reading* (Holt, Rinehart and Winston) *My Own Book for Listening* (SRA) and *Basic Reading Skills* (Scott, Foresman) were used for word meaning and comprehension. Work covered dealt with understanding the main points of a story, words that spoil the meaning, drawing conclusions, putting sentences in proper sequence, phrase and sentence meaning, categories, and words with more than one meaning. *My Own Book for Listening* was effective in getting the boys to concentrate on material read to them since the pressure of the group made them all eager to be able to answer the questions which were going to be asked.

The material involving listening to a story led to a revealing discussion. Martin and Raphael (Alfred was absent) named types of work in which it was important to listen. When asked what kind of work they wanted to do and whether listening would be important in that work, Martin reported that he wanted to be a biologist and listed a number of valid reasons for a biologists' need to listen. Raphael, who was always reluctant to participate in any personal discussion, replied that he would like to be a clown. He clearly expected this response to be taken as a joke and the subject closed, so he was very surprised when I took it seriously and asked, "Well, then is it important that a clown listen?" He was not only startled but quite angry to be taken at his word, particularly when Martin proceeded to tell why a clown would need to listen. Raphael suddenly interrupted Martin with a shouted "I don't want to be a clown . . . I want to be a businessman," and the discussion continued with Raphael thoughtfully describing why a businessman needs the ability to listen.

The school report at the end of the year was the most positive ever received. His teacher noted that Raphael was trying to improve in all areas. His vocabulary had grown tremendously and he was generally eager to learn. He was beginning to talk to the children sitting near him. She also noted that although Raphael read well and would read to her, he was still reluctant to participate in the reading group. She felt that he could now function in a regular classroom although he needed improvement in oral expression. An added note by the principal stated: "We have seen a great improvement in Raphael lately. His current teacher did not know him then, but I remember his days of crawling under the desk to withdraw from human contact! Raphael has actually initiated a few conversations with me this year; they have been short, but quite coherent, and he has been able to express his desires."

Fifth Year

When Raphael returned to reading in the fall it was the start of his fifth year in the remedial program. Martin had moved during the summer and it was decided to offer Alfred and Raphael a joint session once a week, plus two individual sessions. Raphael at this time was not happy in his new class at school. He was having problems with the children, who looked upon him as "a nut," and missed his former teacher to whom he had become attached. Raphael began to use his attendance at the clinic as an opportunity to stay out of school for the whole day, and towards the middle of the year a serious truancy problem developed. He was therefore scheduled for just two morning sessions a week—one individual and one with Alfred—and was told that the school would be notifying us if he did not return. His attendance improved but his unhappiness remained. He urgently needed a special all-day school where he would not be so markedly different from the other children, particularly since this was his last year in elementary school. Transfer to a junior high school was impending and it was felt that he would be unable to cope with the confusion of shifting classes and different subject area teachers. Exploration of the possibilities for placement in a special school was begun.

During the course of the year Raphael was exposed to a variety of materials aimed at improving comprehension. *McCall-Crabbs* (Book A) and SRA materials on fifth- and sixth-grade levels were used to check comprehension. Word meanings, synonyms, antonyms, words that spoil the meaning, prefixes, suffixes, descriptive phrases, and analogies were covered during the year. For this work, selected exercises from Brueckner and Lewis, and *Basic Reading Skills* were used. Test scores at mid-year indicated that he was able to read sixth-grade material accurately, with comprehension still lagging behind that level.

Raphael particularly enjoyed the joint sessions with Alfred and learned to conform to standards set for cooperative efforts. He related to Alfred with friendliness and derived a great deal of satisfaction from the fact that Alfred responded as a friend.

Toward the end of the year we learned that Raphael had been accepted by a small private day school for disturbed children which offered him a partial scholarship. He was told about this and although fearful about making a change, he by this time hated the public school so fiercely that he offered no resistance. The transfer was made, and once at his new school he established new relationships rather rapidly. This was due in part to the homogeneity of the group in which he was placed: all of its members were roughly similar to him in temperament, ability, and problem areas. Equally important, the school had prepared the group members for his entry, giving them some picture of his background and problems.

An early report from the school stated that while Raphael was deficient in math, writing, and oral expression, it was apparent that he had excellent phonic and word analysis skills. Remedial reading at Northside was at this time discontinued. He was, however, to continue seeing his psychotherapist once a week.

Summary and Discussion

TABLE 2 GIVES A SUMMARY of Raphael's test scores during the four years and seven months he was in the remedial programs.

An analysis of test scores reveals that Raphael learned most easily those skills involving word analysis and word recognition techniques. As soon as comprehension was introduced, he ran into difficulty—a difficulty that was probably a function of his emotional illness. His disorganization, his inability to make firm contact with reality, and the generally fragmented quality of his thinking made it impossible for him to focus on abstract concepts and derive something meaningful from them. This was particularly true in the early days of his psychotherapy. The learning of concrete skills, on the other hand, was relatively easy for him. Almost from the start he could understand and remember that certain letters or com-

Table 2. Raphael's Reading Test Scores During Five Years

Test	Diagnostic Study	First Year	Second Year	Third Year	Fourth Year	Fifth Year
Wide Range	1.3	1.7	3.5	5.0	5.5	6.6
Gates Primary						
Word	1.8	2.1	3.4			
Sentence	(Could not do . . . . . .)					
Gates Adv. Primary						
Word				4.5	4.7	
Paragraph				3.6		
Metropolitan Elem.						
Word Meaning					3.4	4.3
Reading					3.4	3.7

binations of letters make certain sounds. He could learn and apply rules. Exceptions to a rule were frequently taught as sight words or, since Raphael was intelligent, figured out from the context.

It should be pointed out that we never felt that the I.Q. of 76 was a valid measure of his potential. Although the gap between his potential and his comprehension never closed, it continued to narrow, reflecting the progress Raphael was making in therapy. As he became more related to, and part of, the world around him, he became less of an automaton and more of a thinking human being.

His fourth year scores showed a drop in silent reading when he was given the *Metropolitan Elementary* achievement test for the first time, but his taking the test, albeit reluctantly, was in itself a major achievement. Qualitatively this is a much more difficult test than the *Gates Advanced Primary* and involves reading longer and more complicated paragraphs. Yet Raphael stayed with it and completed the test within the given time limit. The following year, when the test was administered prior to his closing, Raphael took it willingly and cooperated fully.

When told that he no longer required remedial reading, Raphael had mixed feelings. He was pleased to learn that he could now "hold his own" in a sixth-grade class, but unhappy about ending our relationship. He was worried about his ability to function independently and greatly reassured when told that if he ever really needed it he could return for help.

Raphael has at this writing been at the special school for several years. He has continued in treatment with his psychotherapist at the clinic and has made visible progress. He is now being directed towards vocational training with the realistic expectation that he can become a self-sufficient and self-supporting individual. We occasionally run into each other at the clinic. The first time we met, about one year had elapsed. He looked at me and said, "You haven't changed a bit. Are you *still* a reading teacher?"

For the reading teacher, work with a child like Raphael is both challenging and rewarding. The objective in this case was not solely to teach reading. We also wanted to see whether in the process of helping Raphael learn to read we could help him emerge from his private world of fantasy and establish contact in a realistic manner with the world around him.

When he first came to the clinic, he was bewildered and terrified of the world and the people in it; he needed first of all the security of a relationship with a non-threatening adult who was able to remain part of the background until such time as he was ready to reach out for contact. Any early attempts to make physical contact with him—a hug, or even a pat—would have further increased his terror. Once having demonstrated that I would not hurt him—either physically or psychologically—the next step was to make him feel that I liked and accepted him. But this had to be done without falling into the trap of entering his unreal, fantasy world. All efforts had to be directed towards bringing him into contact with the real world. Thus, our reading materials never included fairy tales, fables, or stories in which animals spoke. There were already enough monsters peopling his imagination. In conversation, too, I would ignore or reject the imaginary events he related and focus on what was real and tangible in his life experience.

In Raphael's case, structure and firmness were preconditions for learning. At first he functioned in a scattered, disorganized manner. The external noises and motions were merely a reflection of the chaos operating internally. Despite my fears that he was too fragile and insecure to be able to accept limits, the truth was that he desperately needed them—in fact, welcomed them. Providing structure meant the orderly presentation of a minimum of materials at one time in a distraction-free environment. Simple tasks were set forth as units to be completed individually. This approach helped orient Raphael and provided concrete boundaries within which he was expected to, and could, function.

Once the importance of structure was recognized, it had to be adhered to with firmness. There would be no point in setting up a structure if

Raphael were permitted to depart from it capriciously. Initially this required that I impose discipline on him; ultimately he was able to impose it on himself.

For the teacher an important lesson to be learned from work with Raphael was to overcome the fear of trying something new. Many times during the year it was not without misgivings that new approaches were made. When they worked, many benefits accrued; when they didn't work, they were discarded, with no great harm done. A striking example of this was Raphael's inclusion in the group. There was no guarantee at the time that he would be able to function there—he was not functioning on any level with his peers in school. We were not certain whether he would be strengthened or further threatened by this experience. We were, however, never committed to it as a *must*. If it did not seem to be a positive one, we were prepared to admit it to ourselves—and to Raphael —that it had not been a good idea. If it had not been tried, Raphael would have been deprived of one of the few happy experiences he had up to that point in establishing contact with other children.

Finally, Raphael's story demonstrates the value of approaching even a seriously disturbed child with the expectation that he can be taught. Had we looked only at the low I.Q., the bizarre behavior, and the irrational responses, we would have prejudged the outcome and done Raphael a great disservice.

Editor's Comments

Raphael is a prime example of the value of patient, understanding, optimistic effort to help even severely disturbed children in a remedial reading program. Childhood schizophrenia used to convey an implication of hopelessness and a need for lifetime institutionalization. Now it is recognized that many of these children, even of those who are openly and obviously psychotic, can be helped to get a firmer grasp on reality and eventually to become self-sustaining adults. In this process, remedial reading has been found to be one of the most useful therapeutic tools.

Many a remedial teacher has assumed that an upset child needed freedom and self-expression, when the child really needed order, structure, and limits to help him to achieve some stability and to focus on specific learning tasks. Raphael was fortunate that his remedial therapist was not afraid to try alternatives, and discovered that he both needed and wanted limits.

The pattern of reading problems that Raphael displayed, with word recognition improving much more rapidly than comprehension, is quite common among emotionally disturbed children. It contrasts markedly with the difficulties that neurologically handicapped children tend to show in learning to recognize words.

The benefit to a child like Raphael of learning how to get along, and to become friends with, one or two other children in a small remedial group are amply shown in this report. The care needed in setting up such a group, and the maintenance of individual along with the group sessions, also are worthy of emulation.

7

Tony

BY GRACE S. WALBY, Ph.D.

Setting

The Child Guidance Clinic of Greater Winnipeg is a joint education and mental health project administered by the Winnipeg School Division No. 1. Any child attending public, private, or parochial school in Winnipeg City and specified adjacent suburban areas is eligible for referral. No direct charge of any kind is made for service rendered. The child may receive service from any of the five clinic departments (School Social Work, School Psychology, Reading, Speech and Hearing, Psychiatry) either singly or working together in whatever combination is indicated by the child's particular problems. Referrals are made by parents, school staff, other agency workers, physicians, nurses, and other professional persons. Self-referrals are accepted from older children.

The clinical work is conducted by the five departments: School Social Work, School Psychology, Reading, Speech and Hearing, and Psychiatry. In each area there is a department head who is responsible for the organization and operation of that particular department within the framework of the general policy of the clinic.

A reading diagnosis involves the integration of two types of information:
1. Information from other sources—a measure of the child's capacity and general aptitudes for learning provided by the Psychology Department; a picture of background experiences obtained from such sources as a school history, parent interview, medical report and information from other clinic departments which have had contact with the case; a screening of language development, speech, and hearing provided by the Speech and Hearing Department.
2. Analysis of performance in reading and related skills.

From this information an analysis is made of the extent to which the child is retarded academically, the probable causes of his difficulty, and recommendations for treatment. Recommendations may take the form of specific steps in remedial instruction or referral to another clinic department or agency for further investigation. This report is discussed with the parent, the classroom teacher, and other workers involved in planning for the child.

Remediation may take several forms: tutoring at the clinic, tutoring by field workers, tutoring by adjustment teachers, remedial reading teachers, private tutors, or modification of the classroom program. Contact is maintained with the parents and the school staff during the period of tutoring. Progress is reassessed at regular intervals.

Assistance involves developing a relationship with the child in which he knows that his feelings will be understood and accepted. In such a relationship he can be helped to clarify and modify his feelings about reading and about his own ability to learn. Work is also done on the systematic development of skills in which the child is deficient. The goal of remediation is to enable the individual to function at a level in harmony with his capacity, and to use reading as a tool for further learning and enjoyment.

Diagnostic Study

TONY A. WAS FIRST REFERRED to the Child Guidance Clinic in December, 1965, when he was 7 years old and spending his second year in first grade. At that time he was referred to two departments of the clinic (Social Work and Psychology). A year later he was referred to Reading and Psychiatry. Both referrals were by the school and family doctor.

The Present Problem

Tony was described as an immature and emotionally disturbed boy who daydreamed in school and tired easily. The teacher reported that Tony did not show any interest in learning to read during his first year in school. He had not learned any sight vocabulary and was unable to use any word attack skills to unlock words. He responded rarely to group activities in the classroom. However, at times he did play with classmates in the playground.

Home Situation

Tony, the only child in the family, was adopted at 2 months of age, because of Mr. A.'s strong desire to have a son. Mrs. A. was concerned about the additional responsibilities, bored with the chores of child care, and jealous of the attention her husband gave the baby.

Both parents are working. Mr. A. has experienced a number of unsuccessful business ventures resulting each time in considerable financial losses. For this reason Mrs. A. has worked during most of her married life. Mr. A. is now engaged in a successful and growing business enterprise involving much overtime work. However, his wife anticipates failure and more financial losses with each proposed extension of the business.

Mr. A. came from a home with a domineering, ungiving mother and a passive father. He still resents the bullying and beatings from his elder brother.

Mrs. A. was one of ten children. She was unable to continue her education beyond grade ten because her parents were experiencing financial difficulty in sending two of her brothers through the university. She has worked from an early age, first as a clerk and later as a secretary.

There has been much conflict in the present marriage, with one reported separation. At that time both became involved with older persons.

Developmental History

Tony spent the first two months of his life in the hospital until he was adopted. He was a healthy, active baby. Developmental milestones were normal. There is a history of enuresis, masturbation, and thumb-sucking continuing until age 7. Tony has had the usual childhood diseases and a recurrent congested chest condition. He is physically a small boy for his age. He has always had a poor appetite.

Mother feels that Tony is a sensitive, depressed, unhappy child who finds it difficult to make friends.

He is fond of television and likes to be read to. Father is disappointed in Tony's lack of skill and interest in sports as well as school.

Psychological Findings

8 Jan./65 *Revised Stanford Binet* ('60 L-M) I.Q. 113
Wechsler Intelligence Scale for Children

Performance Scale I.Q.	104
Picture Completion	13
Picture Arrangement	14
Block Design	10
Object Assembly	8
Coding	8

Bender Visual Motor Gestalt Test
House-Tree-Person Test (color)

The psychologist reported that Tony was quiet but cooperative. He attended well and worked fairly consistently throughout the test interview. The quality of response on the vocabulary and other verbal tests was of a high level. There was some suggestion that anxiety could be interfering with functioning. There was some intertest variability in the

WISC Performance Scale, Picture Completion and Picture Arrangement being high and Object Assembly and Coding rather low.

Performance on the *Bender Visual Motor Gestalt Test* was perceptually adequate, but the results suggested poor control and lack of judgment. H.T.P. drawings were immature and suggestive of some perceptual motor problem.

Reading Department Report

Tests Given:

Schonell Graded Reading Vocabulary Test—recognized no words
Dolch Basic Sight Vocabulary—recognized 3 words (a, I, yellow)
Harrison-Stroud Reading Readiness
Illinois Test of Psycholinguistic Ability
Benton Visual Retention Test
Boning Adaptation of the Strang Sentence Completion Test [1]

Screening tests:

Keystone Visual Survey Test—Normal
Spache Binocular Reading Test—Normal
Maico Puretone Audiometer Test—Normal
Speech Evaluation—Normal
Laterality—right-eyed, footed and handed

Tony was seen as an immature, dependent, rather anxious boy whose ability to plan and organize appeared inadequate. He was greatly concerned about "being good" and the consequences of not "being good" in terms of his religious training. His feelings about school were rather ambivalent, and he tended to see himself as unable to cope with the problem of school achievement and with the social pressures in his life.

The tests indicated that Tony had the specific overall skills requisite to begin learning to read. Visual perception was accurate and meaningful. He had some difficulty in recall of visual sequences but responses in this area tended to be inconsistent.

Tests of auditory skills revealed limited power in distinguishing words beginning with the same sound and in the ability to listen to stories and make meaningful associations. In general the auditory area tended to be weak.

[1] See Albert J. Harris, *How to Increase Reading Ability*, 5th Edition (New York: David McKay Co., 1970), p. 465.

Language usage seemed average for his age. Motor development was somewhat immature and motor control tended to fluctuate.

In general, immaturity, dependency, anxiety, poor self-concept, grave concern about his own behavior, and ambivalent feelings about learning, combined with pressures from his home, appeared to be factors inhibiting greater utilization of his potential ability.

Psychiatric Report

Although Tony's problem on referral was inability to read, there was a generalized underachievement in all areas of academic and social functioning. Tony had apparently shown some autistic behavior from an early age. He disliked being handled, spent a lot of time by himself (although he did play with others on occasion), and masturbated openly. He showed as well thumb-sucking for a long time and enuresis.

One wonders how much of the behavior manifested might be considered constitutional and how much might be in response to a cold, mechanical environment.

It is tempting to speculate that the parents, because of their own backgrounds, would be needful themselves to the point of not having much to give affectionally. Father would be very sensitive to domineering women, would have a poor self-image because of his failures sexually and in providing adequately. This would make him very sensitive to the inadequacies of his son through whom he might wish to achieve in compensation.

Mother would tend to be ambivalent in her attitudes towards males, wanting to be looked after by them, but also having a need to see them fail because of unconscious resentment toward her university-trained brothers. It is interesting that father is the one who suggested adoption, specifying that he wanted a son first, while mother, perhaps doubtful regarding her capacities in the mothering role (because of her own needfulness), expressed anxiety over the increased responsibility.

Tony's autistic behavior had continued with evidence that his affectional needs had not been met. He showed some ego-disintegration in the form of some questionable hallucinations. It is probable that Tony has had considerable conflicts over his adoption and possible underlying fears that he might be deserted. There are strong psychotic potentials and he could probably be considered to be borderline psychotic.

Recommendations. As a result of a conference (January, 1967) in which the findings of the various disciplines involved were considered, it was recommended that treatment should include:

1. Remedial reading instruction.
2. Psychotherapy.
3. Encouragement of school participation in involving Tony in supervised group activities and in providing support in Tony's attempts to learn.
4. Supportive case work with the parents in order to develop their awareness of Tony's affectional needs.
5. Futher investigation of personality characteristics by Psychology Department.

Remedial Program

THE REMEDIAL PROGRAM INCLUDED: Play therapy session with the psychiatrist (once every three weeks), and remedial instruction, undertaken from January, 1967, through May, 1968.

1. January, 1967—June, 1967—twice a week, thirty-six individual sessions
2. July 4, 1967—July 28, 1967—daily sessions, group instruction
3. September, 1967—May, 1968—clinic tutoring service

First Year

Tutoring at first focussed on mastery of a basic sight vocabulary, fostering an interest in reading, an involvement in his own learning, and release of tensions around the problem of learning. Materials used consisted of such games as *Grab, Take, Match, Concentration;* free selection from the *Beginning to Read* series and later transfer into the *Copp Clark Developmental Reading Series,* the authorized series being used in the school.

The first words Tony learned were such functional words as the names of the buses and street names he needed to know to make his way independently to the clinic. The clinician noted that in any game played, Tony had to win. He changed rules and cheated if necessary so that he would get all the points. He also read and reread such stories as *Are You My Mother, Put Me in the Zoo, Green Eggs and Ham, Go, Dog, Go.* At first he was very quiet apart from this constant need to set up the situation so that he could win. In this period of tutoring gains were quite limited, but the school reported greater participation in classroom activity and evidence of satisfaction from extra attention.

At first Tony was very secretive about telling the other children anything about his visits to the clinic, saying just that he was attending a "special school." Gradually he began to share his experiences with his classmates, showing them some of his books. By the end of the year Tony delighted in using the opportunity provided by the teacher to tell of his experiences both en route and during his clinic sessions, thereby gaining considerable prestige in the classroom. His teacher and classmates regarded this as the "highlight" of their day.

Meanwhile a change in Tony's behavior while waiting for his appointment with the psychiatrist or reading clinician was noted. At first he tended to sit very quietly, showing no interest or concern with other clients. After several visits he appeared to become aware of a group of 10- to 12-year-old boys scheduled for group therapy sessions. For some time he merely watched their antics. Shortly thereafter he made friends with these boys and joined them in their antics to the point where considerable concern for his safety resulted.

However, during his regular sessions, apart from some increase in excitability, he tended to be quiet and passive.

A reassessment of reading achievement in June, 1967, yielded the following results:

Tests Given	Grade Score
Gray's Oral Reading Paragraphs	1.0
Schonell Graded Word Vocabulary	1.7
Dolch Basic Sight Vocabulary	recognized 73 words
Metropolitan Achievement Tests	
Primary I form B	
Word Knowledge	1.7
Word Discrimination	1.9
Reading	2.0

Tony, at that time, had a working knowledge of preprimer and primer words and was fairly fluent in reading books at this level. He had begun to develop some confidence in applying known initial consonants to new words. He made good use of context and picture clues. His ability to attend to a task for periods of time appeared to be improving. His behavior continued to be immature, hyperactive, and manipulative. While still an anxious boy, he seemed more at ease and to be showing some involvement in independent reading.

The classroom teacher reported that Tony's attitude, behavior, and performance in the classroom had improved markedly. He was more self-confident, taking part in oral discussions, completing assignments, and showing an interest in reading.

Summer. During the summer tutoring program, in which he had to share the attention of the instructor with a number of children, he became quite a behavior problem. There was a decided swing to disinhibited, boisterous hyperactivity. The instructional program included a more formal approach to mastery of phonics skills.

During the summer he was living with his paternal grandparents and reported to be very unhappy about this.

Psychotherapy

During the first year Tony had eleven sessions with the psychiatrist. As Tony was very reluctant to talk about himself, the session took the form of play therapy. Again it was noted that he could not bear to lose any game and had to cheat in order to be sure of winning.

During this period the psychiatrist noted that Tony had constantly been repressed and inhibited, with a lot of repressed aggression coming out in play sessions. His poor self-image was demonstrated by his great need always to win even if he had to cheat to accomplish this. He used the defense mechanisms of denial and compulsive behavior.

The social worker at this stage reported that marital conflicts continued in the home and that parents had little time for Tony, and were indeed unable to give more support to him.

The psychologist had during this period given Tony the following tests:

Rorschach
Thematic Apperception Test
Wechsler Intelligence Scale for Children—Verbal I.Q. 118,
Performance I.Q. 128,
Full Scale I.Q. 125

Subtest Scores:

Information	11	Picture Completion	15
Comprehension	11	Picture Arrangement	13
Arithmetic	14	Block Design	14
Similarities	13	Object Assembly	17
Vocabulary	15	Coding	11

She reported Tony to be basically introversive, using fantasy to obtain satisfaction. Themes centered around hostility and gratification. He seemed to be easily overstimulated by persons and events, reacting in a confused way and showing poorly controlled behavior. Anxiety related to conflict areas (control of aggression, sex conflicts, and Oedipal pre-occupation) stirred him up and made him over-responsive.

Tony showed a strongly defended personality picture, denial and repression being the chief defense mechanisms. Competition with the father for the mother's attention and affection were prevalent themes of the *TAT*. He saw his father as negative and punitive.

Second Year

A second conference, in October, 1967, was held to review progress and to reconsider treatment plans. While gains had been made in terms of Tony's total adjustment, it was felt that until the parents were able to give more support to him, progress would continue to be slow. Therefore it was decided to encourage the parents to seek counseling with regard to their marital problems, which seemed to impede their ability to give Tony the support he needed. Psychotherapy was to be continued. A more intensive program in reading seemed to be indicated. Therefore, Tony was enrolled in the Clinic Tutoring Program. This is a program for disturbed children which involves daily one-hour sessions at the clinic plus half-time attendance in the home school. Tony's program was designed to coordinate as far as possible with the school's program. Word games, the *Dan Frontier* series, *Building Reading Skills,* and the *Diagnostic Reading Workbooks* were used for reading. *Spelling Goals* Book II and *Laidlaw Patterns in Arithmetic* Book III were also used.

Results. The teacher of this program reported in April, 1968, that in seven months Tony's behavior had changed from that of a hyperactive, immature little boy to that of a much more mature, cooperative, personable child who could fit in with his classmates and be assured of some prestige among them.

His work in reading, spelling, and arithmetic had improved. Successful experiences in learning led to a growth in self confidence with resulting strides in learning. He became increasingly independent and involved in his own learning to the extent that he no longer needed to be directed to his next task but would get his materials and begin working on his own.

Reassessment of reading achievement in May, 1968, showed considerable gains.

	Grade Score	Gains
Gray's Oral Reading Paragraphs	2.8	1.8
Schonell Graded Word Vocabulary	3.4	1.7
Dolch Basic Sight Vocabulary	recognized 188/220 words	
Metropolitan Achievement Tests		
Primary II form A		
Word Knowledge	2.9	1.2
Word Discrimination	3.4	1.5
Reading	3.2	1.2

Tony's rate of academic growth showed significant improvement during the 1967–1968 school year. He became more able to settle down to work and to concentrate on the task at hand, even when the group became somewhat disruptive. Traces of dreaminess were noted at times and there was also evidence of more aggressive behavior than formerly. His motor development was still somewhat immature. Visual and auditory discrimination were adequate and sound blending was satisfactory. He had a knowledge of basic phonic elements and general principles of application, but tended to be slow in word analysis. Effort was well sustained in reading for meaning. He still needed considerable support and structure. He was now able to concentrate reasonably well for designated periods of time.

Because of the improvement in Tony's school achievement and his growth in independence and general adjustment to the learning situation, it was decided that he should return to his home school for full-time attendance. Psychotherapy for Tony and case work with the parents was to be continued.

The psychiatrist, who had seen Tony a total of fourteen times during this school year, reported that progress had been slow. Tony has continued to use denial as a defense mechanism. For example, he would deny being upset when the therapist was changed or when he met other patients being seen by the same therapist, when his actions quite openly showed that he was upset. This denial was also shown when his visits to the Clinic Tutoring Program were discontinued. He has been slow to allow the development of close relationships. There has been a decrease in his need to cheat in order to win, some increased attempt to play games in which he obviously wanted the therapist to win, and some aggressive behavior, sometimes directing a ball, for example, so as to "accidentally" hit the therapist. Attempts to engage Tony in discussion of his problems were uniformly unsuccessful.

Follow-Up

DURING THE SCHOOL YEAR 1968–1969, Tony's school placement was in grade three. The reading clinician has kept in contact with the classroom teacher in order to discuss Tony's progress and continuing needs. Unfortunately the teacher taught the entire class as one unit, and therefore was unable to adjust the program to any great extent to Tony's needs. However, his reading and spelling skills had progressed to the stage where he was able to fit into the program with only minimal problems. On the whole his behavior had improved although there were occasional difficulties, for example, throwing snowballs. The school principal felt that generally Tony was a happier child.

At the end of March, 1969, the reading clinician reassessed Tony's achievement in reading. The results show some uneven gains in achievement:

	Grade Score	Gains
Gray Oral Reading Paragraphs	3.9	1.1
Schonell Graded Reading Vocabulary	3.6	.2
Metropolitan Achievement Tests		
Primary II Form C		
Word Knowledge	3.5	.6
Word Discrimination	3.0	—
Reading	4.9	1.5
Spelling	3.6	1.1

The clinician also reported an increased maturity and a marked decrease in the babyish behavior shown formerly. He was able, too, to win or lose the games played with considerable equanimity. Although friendly and polite, he continued to be rather distant, keeping the conversation on an impersonal level.

During the school year the psychiatrist continued to see Tony at three-week intervals. He has reported that Tony has shown considerable overall improvement, particularly in his self-image. However, much remains to be done in exploration of Tony's feelings about his adoption and his fantasies about his real parents. The relationship established at this time is not sufficiently strong to permit Tony to allow his defenses to be penetrated.

Comment

It is obvious that in this case the basic problems which inhibited Tony's school progress and social development have not yet been successfully overcome. This appears to be largely due to the parents' inability to change their relationship with their adopted son, and to Tony's need to maintain the tight defenses he developed to cope with his life situation. Tony, therefore, is not yet functioning in school at a level that might be expected in terms of his superior intelligence. However, the work done with Tony has made it possible for him to cope much more adequately with school learning and to adjust much more comfortably to both the academic and social demands in his present situation.

Editor's Comments

This report of a very bright boy who was practically a non-reader well into his third year in school is illustrative of cases in which there is good evidence of emotional disturbance preceding school entrance, and little or nothing to suggest a neurological difficulty. The psychiatric use of such terms as "autistic," "ego-disintegration," and "borderline psychotic" indicates a quite severe degree of maladjustment of a kind that is often resistant to treatment in the form of psychotherapy, but less severe than that shown by Raphael (Case 6).

Play therapy once every three weeks was probably deliberately chosen, as supportive therapy on a relatively superficial level is often preferred in such cases to deeper and more intensive forms of psychotherapy, which contain the danger of possibly precipitating a psychotic breakdown.

The remedial program was designed to develop interest and to capitalize on Tony's adequate visual skill at first, with a gradual and quite successful introduction of phonics later. The relatively slow progress shown during the first year of remedial help, followed by accelerated gain during the second year, may have been due to the more intensive remedial program during the second year; however, this pattern of a slow start and acceleration is found in many remedial cases when the beginning level is very low.

The smooth coordination of all five departments of the clinic in the diagnosis, and the participation of three departments—social work, psychiatry, and reading—in the treatment, represents a high level of interprofessional cooperation.

8

Fred

BY RALPH C. PRESTON, PH.D., AND
MARGARET F. WILLSON

Setting

The Reading Clinic of the Graduate School of Education, University of Pennsylvania, established in 1937, is a center for the diagnosis and treatment of reading disabilities, for research on reading instruction and reading disabilities, and for training graduate students in the diagnosis and correction of reading disabilities. The Reading Clinic serves a wide range of applicants: elementary-school children, high school students, undergraduate and graduate students at colleges and universities, and adults from various walks of business and professional life.

A diagnostic examination is required by most applicants. It requires three to five separate sessions, which are usually distributed over several weeks. Reading performance is evaluated in relation to a complex of educational, psychological, and physical factors. After each examining session a conference is held with the parents (or the student or adult). In the final sessions, the clinician tries out the indicated teaching procedures and studies the examinee's response to them. Following the final session, a report containing a summary of findings and recommendations is submitted to parent, student, or adult.

The Reading Clinic provides both individual and group instruction. Individual instruction is offered on a limited basis following a diagnostic examination. Group instruction for high school and college students is provided for those whose reading difficulties are moderate. A discussion group for mothers of children with reading difficulties is scheduled periodically to provide opportunity for group counseling and discussion.

Diagnostic Study

FRED D. FIRST CAME TO US as a virtual non-reader when he was 10 years old and in fifth grade. From the start he exhibited the symptoms of dyslexia. His second-grade achievement on the *Gates Primary Reading*

Tests (see Figure 2) proved highly misleading. Although he had been exposed to the customary basal reader instruction for more than four years, we estimated that his sight vocabulary was confined to about twenty words. He tested on an informal reading survey at the primer level. He could not blend known components of a word (such as *in* and *to* to form *into*). He committed reversals of letters and words in both reading and writing. Today, as a 30-year-old art teacher in a high school, he has not yet shaken off all of these problems. There was never any question about his intellectual capacity. When we first saw him, the *Revised Stanford-Binet Scale* yielded an I.Q. of 121, confirmed two years later by *Wechsler-Bellevue* I.Q.'s of 125 (Verbal) and 123 (Performance).

We have been in almost continuous touch with him during most of the intervening twenty years. We have thus been afforded an opportunity seldom available to clinicians to compile longitudinal data covering critical years in the maturing of a remedial subject. We look upon the construction of Fred's history as an important type of research. It supplies longitudinal data, the paucity of which has sharply limited understanding of reading problems. There has been insufficient examination of the independent variables (factors contributing to, or negating, the remedial process) as they relate to the dependent variables (eventual intellectual functioning and occupational adjustment). We have traced possible relationships in retrospect. Aware of the limitations of such *ex post facto* interpretations, we are nevertheless persuaded that retrospection is an essential approach today, in the absence of means for manipulating the complex variables that contribute to remediation.

Early History and Family Relationships

Fred's parents were teen-agers and school dropouts when they were married, and were still under 21 when Fred was born, the first of two children. His mother discontinued breast-feeding when Fred was six weeks old because she was badly upset by two situations. Her husband's business failed during this period, and, causing her apparently equal anxiety, Mrs. D. and her husband battled over the naming of the boy. She was Jewish and had wished him to bear the Jewish name of her father; her husband was of Irish descent and a Catholic.

Fred's physical development, except for an allergy which has always plagued him, was smooth in most respects. The dates of his sitting up, walking, and talking were normal. His intellectual interests started early. At 2 he showed above-average interest in picture books. He kept his parents on their toes with his eager questions and his active exploration of his environment.

Fred's boyhood was spent in a home where bickering was constant. Both his father and his mother threatened, separately, to leave from time to time. Fred told our psychiatric consultant, Dr. Gerald H. J. Pearson, that this never disturbed him, whereas his younger sister was frequently worried by it and would go to Fred in distress. He would tell her that the arguing had been going on throughout her life and would say, "It doesn't mean a thing." Despite the contentious home situation, Fred seemed to have normal relations with his parents and typical attitudes toward them. He was exultant when his father, then a truck driver, won a television set in a contest conducted by the company. He once brought a picture of his father to the clinic to show to his tutor and seemed to be proud of him. Fred was, in turn, highly regarded by his parents. He was their favorite child and was indulged much more than his sister.

Personality Characteristics

Both as a child, and now as an adult, Fred has given the appearance of intensity. He has dark eyes, a black mop of hair, and wears thick horn-rimmed glasses. He is sensitive and moody—one day elated, another day depressed. Several of his former tutors remarked that his reading performance was poor on the latter days. Whatever his mood, however, he could, and still can, be counted upon to be vocally articulate. One tutor, newly assigned to him, devoted the first session to a get-acquainted conference. He dryly concluded his matter-of-fact written report of that session with the comment: "Fred not very anxious to end conference." One might say that his ease in oral expression has been his salvation. He is fluent in verbalizing his most pressing problems.

Fred has always impressed us as likable and serious. He never cared for comic strips, *Mad* magazine, or later, *New Yorker* cartoons. Their wit bored him, he said, so he ignored them. Yet many of the stories he wrote in connection with the tutoring, and conversations he had with us, showed some gayety and imagination.

He is able to plan his life and to work with a good deal of independence, and he displays considerable initiative, as will be illustrated at subsequent points in this report.

Because of his steady diet of failure in school, one might expect to find deep-grained personality or behavior disturbances in Fred, but none appear. Dr. Pearson found no evidence of anxiety during the psychiatric interview. While he detected some repression of feelings, he felt this grew out of the parents' quarrels and his feelings about the quarreling more than the school situation. Of possible significance, he felt, was Fred's apparent repression of unpleasant experiences. Fred accounted for his lack of disturbance over his parent's bickering by the fact that he just does not remember things that are unpleasant. Once his uncle commented that Fred must have been disappointed when his father on one occasion gave him no birthday present. Fred was quite surprised and did not believe it, and to this day he cannot remember whether his father gave him a present or not, and, if he did, what the present was. "Oddly enough," said Fred recently, "I can't remember a single teacher or experience at elementary school."

Interests and Aspirations

Fred's difficulty with reading and his daily frustrations and humiliations during his schooling never seemed to smother his enthusiasm for life or his lively and versatile curiosity. His interests have consistently embraced the mechanical, scientific, artistic, and musical areas. In view of his reading and spelling disability, it is not surprising that he has never shown an interest in literary subjects or in activities involving paper and pencil tasks.

As a child, sheer information had great appeal for him—what Havighurst called the preadolescent's interest in "sidelines, oddities, minor details" and "avidness for detail." He would bring to the clinic information ranging from the location of Einstein's home to the nature of atomic energy, from the number killed in motor accidents over the Fourth of July weekend to his diagram of his family tree (complete from both sets of grandparents and ending with eleven cousins).

Among his interests was curiosity about the reading process and about his own disability. He was first taught by Fernald's VAKT method, and wanted to know what the tracing was supposed to do. One tutor, dissatisfied with his slow progress, decided to revert to Fernald's first stage. "Why do I have to trace?" he asked. "That's Stage One, and I passed that with Miss Bonser." He pressed a neurological consultant into explaining the purpose of the examination. He reported to his tutor: "If they find that a part of my brain is damaged, maybe by an accident, all the lessons in the world couldn't help me, and I'll never be able to read." In his 20s, he continued to want to know "exactly" what caused his reading disability.

Many of Fred's interests have run to popular patterns. He ran through a succession of preoccupations of many children: a pet rabbit, a magician's kit, magnets, stamps, and the like. When he was 11 his interests focussed upon a football outfit and a B-B gun. At 14 he began showing an interest in clothes. He appeared at the clinic one day in the then-popular "zoot suit," startling his tutor so that she jotted down his attire: "Blue-and-white checked shirt, white tie with a blue stripe, blue-gray outsize sport jacket, terra cotta trousers, blue suède loafers, yellow Argyle socks, a fashionable Hollywood haircut, all punctuated with his horn-rimmed glasses." His interest in fashionable appearance has not flagged. Today he sports prominent sideburns, turtleneck shirts, and other up-to-the-minute adornments.

When entering high school his worries were typical of adolescents. He announced one day: "I gotta learn to dance before Friday." He felt that a rash due to allergy spoiled his appearance: "My allergy always makes me look like I have a cold."

In later years an interest in working with his hands developed. He made furniture and sculptured. Today he reads some, but frequently becomes impatient with it and has discovered that he can keep abreast of the world remarkably well by means of television. "McLuhan hit the nail on the head," he exclaimed recently. " 'Forget type! Look at nature! Notice how people behave in life, in the movies, on TV! Listen to people talk!' He's right. You don't have to depend on the paper any more to learn about the weather, or to read a book if you want to know about South Africa. Universities haven't learned yet that the age when reading and learning were one and the same thing is coming to an end." This might be dismissed as rationalization, but the significant fact is that Fred discovered McLuhan, understood his message, and related it to his own appetite for a richer intellectual life.

Fred has always had ambitious vocational aspirations. As a child he talked of becoming a scientist or an engineer—aspirations that would require a college education. "That's why I want to learn to read," he volunteered. During his adolescence architecture attracted him, and so did teaching.

On all sides he was advised to be "realistic" and to reset his sights. An English teacher who worked with him in eleventh grade, sympathetic and understanding, explained to him his limitations and urged him to abandon academic study once he completed high school. Another English teacher remarked: "Fred is a wonderful boy—all wool and a yard wide. Everyone likes him, both his classmates and his teachers. But I cannot see how he can do college work in English." She declined to believe he had above-average intelligence, and recommended that he attend a technical institute and forget college. A professional counselor to whom we referred Fred when he was 18 concluded: "My feeling is very strong that this boy should go into trade training as an apprentice. I would suggest the trade of tool-and-die maker."

School Experiences

Fred moved through the Philadelphia public schools from kindergarten to high school graduation, repeating only the third grade. His movement occurred during a period when "continuous progress" was the standard practice of most school systems of the country, and regular promotion was unrelated to achievement. A quick review of Fred's report cards will make that evident.

No marks or grades were given to pupils in first grade, but Fred's teacher wrote that he was lagging badly in his reading. From grades two through six, thirty reports were issued on which the symbols S (Satisfactory), U (Unsatisfactory), and I (Improvement) were recorded. More than three-fourths of his marks in reading and spelling were U's. In other subjects he received a preponderance of S's.

In junior and senior high school, letter marks were assigned. In the twelve semester reports, his marks in English (which embraced reading and spelling) were four C's, seven D's, and one E. Marks above C were rare on his record in any subject except shop, in which he received A's consistently. Even in art, the subject which was to become his vocation, he had only a C average. During his senior year he achieved a C average and was graduated. He spent an additional year as a postgraduate student in another high school, earning respectable final grades in algebra (86) and biology (82), but failing English (50).

Discouraging to him as his marks were, they were matched in their dampening effect upon his morale by the superficial and often callous reactions of some of his teachers. In their written comments on his report cards they attributed his poor performance to a defect in character in hortatory sentences including:

He needs to work very hard to keep up with his group in reading.
He must wake up and not to be so lazy, or he will fail.
He must learn to concentrate.

His failure in school was not confined to academic performance. For example, at the graduation exercises at the end of sixth grade, each of the fifty-one pupils in the class was given a part in the program. Fred had been given a line to recite, too; but then the teacher withdrew it, and he became the only child in his class without a part in the program. Again, in eighth grade he was elected president of his class. The teacher gave him a sheet of announcements to read at a class meeting. Because of his reading disability Fred had to call upon the vice president to read the sheet, whereupon the entire class, including Fred, had a good laugh. However, the teacher told him following the meeting that he was obviously not qualified to be president, and the honor went to someone else.

Remedial Program

DURING THE FIRST TEN YEARS of Fred's association with the Reading Clinic, he had approximately 300 hours of instruction with seven tutors, three of whom were professionals on the staff of the clinic, the remaining four being graduate students selected for their maturity and their exceptional understanding of the remedial process, remedial techniques, and insight into the human and personal factors involved in teaching. During his 20s, Fred had approximately fifty additional hours. Over the years, he had skilled and resourceful teachers and tutors.

We do not wish to exaggerate the potency of the clinic's role in Fred's development. The 350 hours of clinical instruction must be viewed against the ten thousand and more hours he spent in school and college, not to mention his contacts with psychiatrists, counselors, and other specialized personnel. Nevertheless, we do believe it was crucial and deserves a detailed description.

Initially, Fernald's method for extreme cases [1] was employed with Fred at the Reading Clinic. This continued for two-and-a-half years for periods of one hour, varying between two and three days a week. While he slowly began to learn, there were, as mentioned earlier, discouraging days of regression. After learning to file his words correctly, one day he misfiled several, due to confusion of "S" and "G" on the file tabs. One day he learned five words with apparent thoroughness, only to forget four of them the next day. The method proved only partially successful in assist-

[1] For a more detailed description of the Fernald kinesthetic method, see Cases 1 and 2.

ing Fred to associate the visual images and the sounds and meanings of printed words. Progress was slow and unspectacular. Fred exhibited a high degree of resistance to forming phoneme-grapheme correspondences and to acquiring a sight vocabulary, despite apparently ample motivation and a succession of talented and normally successful tutors. However, progress did take place. The remedial program was gradually broadened, with decreasing need for saying and writing letters and words and with increasing emphasis on decoding (phonics). Subsequently, emphasis was placed upon study skills and composition.

Advancement in terms of test scores is shown in Figure 2. It will be

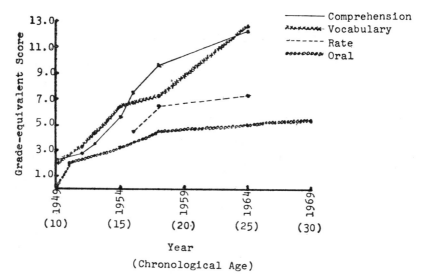

Fig. 2. Fred's achievement in reading, 1949–1969.

noted that the most satisfactory eventual achievement was in vocabulary and comprehension, and that progress in oral reading was relatively slight. To some extent this is due to the limitations of oral reading tests and does not reveal oral reading competence when a reading passage contains relevance and interest. At age 30, we administered the revision of *Gray's Oral Reading Test*. He achieved a fifth-grade score. Yet, at the same sitting, he read orally, without an error, two paragraphs from a newspaper describing the settlement of a sit-in demonstration at a local university, containing such words as *negotiating, advisory,* and *policies* which appear as difficult structurally as those missed in the test; however, these appeared in reporting an up-to-the-minute event in which he had formed an intense personal interest.

A dramatic turning point occurred when he was 15, when he voluntarily returned to the clinic. Like many of our serious reading disability cases, Fred would return for surprise visits at academically stressful periods of his life. School was proving unusually oppressive. He was in the lowest academic group; he was finding his classmates intellectually and socially uncongenial; school discipline was at an all-time low. Frequently, Fred would walk out of a classroom when the class was in session, in despair over the noise and disorder—often with the tacit approval of a sympathetic teacher. Sometimes, on these occasions, he would cut one or two classes and go downtown to a movie. This was far from a satisfying life for Fred. He said he really had to learn to read better. He told of a stack of magazines at home that he wanted badly to be able to read, and of his desire to go to college.

So tutoring resumed. At 16 he became an independent reader, able to achieve considerable satisfaction from the process. In analyzing his record, it is difficult for us to put a finger on the elements that finally yielded success. One certainly was his heightened motivation. A state of "readiness" had emerged, not dissimilar to the "readiness" which one can observe suddenly to occur in a 5- or 6-year-old. Oral reading remained difficult for him. An informal reading survey placed him at the fourth-reader level. A year later, it moved up to the fifth-reader level. But his comprehension scores shot ahead to the junior high school level, and he could read adult books and periodicals with absorption and profit. He began evaluating the content of his reading for the first time. "My, that character is convincing," he once remarked. Another time he commented: "It's good to be smart and to know what a chapter is about by *reading* it!" His work at school picked up. He came in elated one day. He had achieved the highest mark in his class on a grammar test—a C+! "How do you figure out how to pronounce words from the dictionary?" he wanted to know. This initiated a series of lessons for him, in which he engaged wholeheartedly and learned the desired skill quickly.

About this time he became interested in increasing his rate of reading and asked for a chance to practice with a tachistoscope and a reading accelerator. When he found them unhelpful, his tutor taught him the technique of skimming—a process which also proved uncomfortable for him. He has not learned to read rapidly, and is now reconciled to his present rate.

Another aspect of Fred's language disability which has shown little progress is the perceptive process, reflected in its most conspicuous practical form in his spelling. At 10, immediately after studying a word by tracing and saying it, he wrote *nit* for *night, evr* for *ever, lit* for *like,* etc.; at 13, he made such errors as writing *detals* for *details* and *certn* for *certain;* at 16, he wrote *hade* for *had, sead* for *said,* and *tuy* for *tie;* at 18, he wrote *roe hous* for *row house, fater* for *fatter;* at 28, it was *brige* for *bridge, funn* for *fun,* and a continuing flurry of reversals. (Sometimes, he reported, he would catch himself saying *was* for *saw* and *no* for *on* in his speech.) At 30, in drawing a map to direct a clinician, who desired to visit him, to the school in which he worked, he hesitated in writing Allen Road. "Damn!" he exclaimed. "I can never remember whether Allen has one "l" or two." His map showed *Carbondal* (for *Carbondale*) and *Kliff* (for *Cliff*) Street. His insecurity in spelling has resulted in an eagerness to avoid it. "I would rather do anything than write," he once said. "It's the hardest thing in the world."

One of Fred's follow-up visits to the clinic was interesting in view of our recently formulated hypothesis that perceptual cases such as Fred respond best to the Fernald method and that linguistic materials are best with cases in which there is a strong emotional base.[2] Fred was 26 and requested additional instruction in study skills to aid him in two college courses he was then taking. He offered, in exchange, to help the clinic by "teaching." We had just completed a screening of another young adult, who tested at the preprimer level. The evidence indicated that his failure to learn was caused by a serious emotional disorder. Thus, we recommended that a linguistic reader be used. Fred began to work with the case. At the outset, Fred was attracted by the book's neat organization by three-letter words of minimal contrast. He approached us after the first lesson and asked, with a show of anger, "Why didn't you teach *me* by this method?" After only a few lessons, however, Fred rushed into the clinician's office and pleaded: "*Please* find another teacher for this man. I find I can't read one word from another, so I don't know whether he is reading correctly or not." Fred's old perceptual problem continued to haunt him in this area as well as in spelling. This was also seen by Fred's recent responses to the *Bender Visual Motor Gestalt Test*—his drawings suggested that he continued to be anxious over perceptual challenges.

[2]Margaret F. Willson, "Clinical Teaching and Dyslexia," *Reading Teacher,* 21 (May, 1968), 730–733.

Follow-Up

College and Career

After high school, Fred thought of becoming an architect. He realized that, with his poor school record and his reading and writing disability, he would have to plan one step at a time. He applied to an art institute which was an approved four-year college. With a strong letter of support from the Reading Clinic, the admissions officer told Fred he could try out at summer school. He passed the summer courses, and was admitted to the art and crafts program—a non-degree program that did not include academic courses. He worked diligently and graduated on schedule—but without a degree, of course.

During his institute days he had various part-time jobs, one of which, teaching art in an elementary school, led to a determination to become a teacher. But he was told by everyone that without a degree it would be difficult to get a job in a public school. "People were wrong about me so many times that I didn't take this kind of talk seriously," he said. After a year in the army, the superintendent of a small school district, impressed by Fred's personality and art credentials, helped him to secure an emergency teaching certificate and gave him the job of teaching art to the schools of the district. "I didn't use the lesson-plan book, nobody bugged me, and I got along fine," he relates.

He thought he had sufficiently recovered from his academic setbacks to make another try at it. While teaching, he returned to his art school for an evening course in English composition. With permission, he dictated the required compositions to a friend, and passed the course with a C. He also took a course in sociology. He found the subject matter fascinating and claims that to this day he recalls everything that was said in the classroom. But he could not read the textbook rapidly enough to keep abreast of the reading assignments. So he had one of his students stay after school to read the book to him. The examination was multiple-choice —a type with which he had acquired considerable success—and he passed.

About this time he got married to a highly literate young woman, a teacher descended from a long line of renowned and brilliant teachers. "Her family had not known that a chap like me existed!" he chuckled.

His emergency certificate ran out, and he decided to return to the art institute and take the academic courses that would complete requirements for a degree and would lead to a standard teaching certificate.

Again, he found some of the courses entrancing. "I didn't bother with the textbooks," he reported. "I just stayed awake during class." After much agony and struggle, many conferences with his instructors, and flexibility on the part of some instructors in providing Fred with alternative ways of demonstrating his achievement of course objectives, he earned a baccalaureate degree and obtained a regular teaching certificate. Today he is a successful art teacher and, in the opinion of at least one well-known art educator, on the way to becoming a distinguished one.

Fred's Analysis of His Problem

"I know a few fellows with my kind of reading problem," said Fred, "who gave up as kids and quit trying to educate themselves."

He was asked, "Why did you always bounce back after being flattened out by a teacher or a professor or a classmate?"

"I don't know why I was so determined to get educated," he answered. "My mother had a lot to do with it. There were others, too, who supported me when I needed support most. They reminded me that I was important and they treated me with respect. It also helped to be skillful and creative with my hands. That gave me tremendous self-confidence." He continued:

> In a way, I'm an authority on reading problems. No one who doesn't have a reading problem like mine knows the hell you experience every time you are laughed at or scolded or looked down upon. There are compensations, of course. If I had licked the reading problem in first grade, I would have become another well-adjusted bore. I might have become a successful salesman or engineer. It's a frightening thought. I would never have developed what I think—and what others have told me—is my talent. I would not have become an artist and art teacher.
>
> Today, I don't read for fun. I never read fiction or comic strips. I like the *content* of reading, but I really don't enjoy reading itself. Some articles in *National Geographic* and *Harper's* are good and I read them. Others are full of words you never hear spoken and they turn out to be impossible. When I start reading such an article, I drop the magazine in disgust.
>
> As I think about my own experiences, I come to the conclusion that kids who have difficulty in learning to read need experiences in drawing natural objects—trees, fruit, clouds, the human figure—before they begin on letters. So many kids have never *seen* things as they exist in nature. Take color. Many kids have never known or gotten excited by blues or yellows. They've never really looked at them. That drawing test [*Bender Gestalt*] has the kind of activities kids with reading problems should be doing. If they can't recognize squares and circles, if they can't copy them,

how can they ever recognize and copy *a*'s, *b*'s, and *c*'s? The secret of art, and also the secret of reading and writing, is knowing how to look for cues. You look for cues and you stick with those you learn you can depend on.

Discussion

OUR CONCLUSIONS AND INTERPRETATIONS are offered tentatively.

1. In working with bright children who exhibit dyslexic symptoms, there is a temptation to terminate instruction after a year or so, on the assumption that their intelligence will carry them forward once they have received an initial boost. This practice should be reconsidered. Progress is slow, and clinical work should be set up for each individual on a long-term basis. The client should be invited to return for further diagnosis and treatment whenever he feels the need for additional help. A dyslexic is apt to develop his skills over a lifetime, and his progress is apt to be slow.

2. Individual instruction is essential. Wasteful expenditure of time occurs at each change of tutors, so a low tutor turnover is desirable.

3. The Fernald method is an effective approach for the child with severe perceptual difficulties, but it is slow and often proves discouraging to the learner. Perhaps Fred would have progressed more quickly if he had been given training at the outset directly calculated to improve his weak visual memory and weak perception of spatial forms.

4. The child's insecurity and depression caused by the disability calls for much positive encouragement from teachers and tutors. Few dyslexics can be counted upon to have Fred's doggedness and determination. Clinic and school should be in close communication and their respective roles coordinated and mutually respected.

5. Oral reading performance and reader level are inadequate indicators of the bright, older dyslexic's present functional level or of his potential. The underlying perceptual problem may persist into adulthood, yet the individual may learn to cope with his problem even though he may never eliminate it, and he may learn to meet the demands of his chosen career. Teachers and counselors should be cautious in giving advice and should avoid discouraging him from working toward his goals. The dramatic success of the dyslexics reported by Rawson [3] deserves wide study.

[3] Margaret B. Rawson, *Developmental Language Disability: Adult Accomplishments of Dyslexic Boys* (Baltimore: Johns Hopkins Press, 1968).

6. Report cards and grades may be quite damaging to morale and serve dubious ends. Teachers need to be less judgmental than some of them tend to be, and could be helpful by concentrating upon supplying pupils and their parents with constructive information about possible next steps.

Editor's Comments

Relatively few reading clinics have been in operation long enough, have maintained continuing contact with cases through adulthood, and have kept the accumulation of records dating back to first contacts, to make possible the writing of a case report covering twenty years. Thus this case is unique in our collection in the length of contact, and in portraying the career of a man with a very persistent reading disability.

The maintainance of emotional stability and drive despite early and repeated discouraging educational experiences is a most interesting feature of this case. Early psychiatric examination gave no sign of neurotic tendencies. One may guess that the continuing interest and availability of the clinic and gradually improving success in meeting school standards, as well as support and encouragement from his mother, helped Fred to keep on striving.

The choice of art and art teaching as a career is an example of the Adlerian notion that superior achievement is sometimes the result of great effort to overcome a felt weakness. In becoming a teacher, one can make up for many unhappy experiences as a pupil; and the field of art requires less use of reading and writing than any of the usual academic subjects. The relatively specific nature of Fred's visual perception difficulty is shown by his later success in art; other men with similar severe reading problems have become surgeons and sculptors, occupations which also require superior visual perception and visualization. Whether or not direct teaching of visual discrimination skills in early childhood can, as Fred himself suggested, prevent disabilities like his from developing is an important research issue at the present time.

9

Jack

BY SISTER M. JULITTA, O.S.F.

Setting

The Cardinal Stritch College Reading Clinic began in 1943 under Sister Nila's direction in connection with a course in remedial reading taught by Sisters Nila and Chrysostom. In 1944, the work was continued as an extra activity by Sister Julitta with Sister Nila acting as general director. In 1947, to meet the needs of veterans returning to school, at the request of several colleges and universities the clinic work was extended from elementary grade pupils to adult levels. The clinic has always had as its major objectives:

1. Assistance to children and adults in attaining their personal potential in the field of reading.
2. Promoting better reading instruction as a preventive measure through education of teachers in the graduate division, annual conference, and consultant services as well as a materials library for study of materials.
3. Research in the field of reading to find better methods and to interest educators in the values of research findings in improving reading instruction.

The clinic works with all age levels and with various types of problems: corrective and remedial, skills programs, and personal growth courses. The broader scope of cases accepted and the inclusion of developmental skills programs, especially for those of superior ability, is in line with the philosophy held over the years that each individual must be assisted in attaining his personal potential in order to realize real happiness in utilizing God-given talent. Although the original intent was to limit the services to those of average and above average intelligence, those with 80 and above in intelligence are accepted because it seemed the group from 80 to 90 were most lacking in services. It is also our belief that those with lower intelligence require continued daily help not possible in our set-up.

The services are limited to diagnostic testing and corrective work in the area of reading. Referrals are made to various disciplines when need arises, e.g., to the neurologist, the vision specialist, the psychiatrist and psychologist. The child will then work with the specialists and the clinician will follow through on the recommendations. Therefore, our tests are limited to the individual mental tests, educational, general, and diagnostic tests, and informal checks and observations.

The staff includes: nine members who work full-time in the field of reading; three mainly in the college with some work in the clinic; two members mainly in the college with continual contact with the clinic to keep actual contact with children and adults, one of whom has her doctoral degree in the field of reading; five who work in the clinic in diagnosis and teaching, three of whom have their Master's degree in reading and two have a Bachelor plus special courses in the field of reading; graduate students doing their practicum in teaching and testing; and some part-time staff members during the summer and several part-time during the year who have their preparation for teaching and following through on the therapy but do not do the diagnosis work.

Instructional work is eclectic depending on the findings of the tests and possible modes of learning. Various materials and texts are used including basal texts, high interest, low difficulty books, trade books, and skill materials. Tapes, pacing instruments, and tachistoscopic devices are also used as indicated, but emphasis is on teacher-pupil work.

Diagnostic Study

JACK R. WAS REFERRED TO THE CLINIC by his parents because he was experiencing difficulty in school and found the content areas which required reading very difficult. He was 12 years 9 months old and in seventh grade. According to the parents, this reading difficulty, existing since the lower grades, was now posing a rather serious problem as more and more reading was required for progress in the various school subjects.

During the interviews and testing, Jack was slow in responding and his replies were not always clear. He was a rather quiet boy, evidently desirous of completing the tasks. It appeared to the examiner that he would willingly conform to the situation at hand.

Background Information

Developmental. From an interview with the parents and home information questionnaire, it was noted that there were some difficulties at birth due to induced labor. Forceps were used, but evidently there were no serious long-range problems. However, Jack has a slight hip deformity which bothers him if he becomes fatigued from long periods of use in sports. Whether this defect was a result of the circumstances at birth is a question.

The parent report would indicate a pattern of rather early development. Jack began to crawl at 5 to 6 months of age, walk at 10 to 11 months of age; he cut teeth at 4 months. His speech, as the parents remembered it, showed very early development.

Physically, Jack has had generally good health. His only illnesses were measles and chicken pox, with no complications. The hip deformity did cause trouble and it was necessary for Jack to have braces from 2 to 4 years of age. Aside from this, the physical history was limited to a visual defect—strabismus, for which he had surgery. According to the parent this was successful. Glasses were worn temporarily and then the problem was apparently cleared. No visual training followed this surgery.

The mother reported that Jack had been converted to right handedness when he was a baby. It is questionable whether there would have been certainty about the handedness at that early age.

Socially, Jack seemed to have made excellent adjustments. From the parent reports and the comments made by Jack, his friends were approximately his age. He was the first child in the family and had only one sister, three years younger than himself. His play activities were with other boys of the neighborhood and at school. His interests were chiefly outdoor sports, including riding horses and bicycles, engaging in swimming, boating, and ice skating, some chasing games, and football. Soccer also was on his list.

He found enjoyment in parties and talking over the phone, as well as in movies of a mystery and adventure type. This was carried over into interest in reading books involving mysteries, people and heroes, science fiction, and teen-age stories about growing up. The series *Encyclopedia Brown* was his favorite—"the *best* books I ever read." Records, ping-pong, and jazz, in addition to a chemistry set and slot car racing, completed the picture of rather normal and varied boyish interests.

Emotionally, there seem to have been no real problems. There seems to have been a relaxed home environment for the most part. He was immature for his age in responsibility, which may have resulted from some over-protection on account of his earlier problems with vision and the hip deformity.

Educationally, Jack seemed to have gone through the usual school life with its variations in teachers. He had one year of nursery and two years of kindergarten, and began first grade at 6 years. There were no retentions. Aside from his parent's comments that he had a strong dislike for reading, social studies, and industrial arts, and an interest in mathematics and spelling, there was no indication of problems except Jack's remark, which seemed rather mature for him, "I never had a teacher who made reading and learning stimulating." Despite the type of books Jack said he liked, later remarks would seem to indicate he had read very little in the last year or two. According to the parents, Jack never read; yet, some of his remarks would indicate that he did do some reading, but probably had discontinued practically all except required reading at the time of the contact. The parents wished to act on their own and at their request no information was obtained directly from the school.

Factors Influencing Reading Success

Results of the *Revised Stanford-Binet Intelligence Scale,* Form L-M, indicated low average ability (I.Q. 93) with a basal age of 10 years and a ceiling at the Average Adult level. Generally, the performance was rather mediocre except for ability to generalize. His highest success was in directional orientation. Areas of weakness were evident in both verbal and picture absurdities, problem solving, and memory for sentences and digits in reverse. During the tests, Jack was willing to continue and exhibited more than average persistence.

Observations of use of language and vocabulary development indicated average ability, as well as average ability in listening comprehension according to informal test evaluations. A screening test of hearing indicated no deficiencies at any frequency.

In the Keystone Telebinocular screening tests of vision, suppression of vision in the left eye at distance, serious fusional difficulties at near point, and muscular imbalance at near and far point were apparent. The parents were advised to seek professional assistance for functional vision problems. The following report from Marguerite Eberl, O.D., the clinic's vision consultant, gave an understanding of the difficulties Jack encountered in reading because of the vision problem.

> Jack had surgery on his left eye when he was in third grade, because his eye turned in. His eyes are now cosmetically straight, but his coordination is poor, particularly at the reading distance.
>
> On the Keystone Progress of Fusion Unit [testing his ability to use both eyes together], he rates 60% at distance, but only 40% at near.
>
> Under fine fixation tests of prolonged use his vision either doubled or he suppressed the vision of his left eye.
>
> In four tests of hand and eye coordination, each with increasing diffi-

culty, he showed unsteadiness of both eye and hand, with some doubling, and in the last two tests all targets doubled.

His vision without correction was 20/20 in his right eye, both at distance and near, but his left was a blurry 20/40 in both distance and near tests.

All of the above manifestations are, we believe, severe contributing causes to his reading difficulty. They would cause him to lose his place, and would also cause comprehension to be low. This would also be the reason why he could read better with his right eye alone than when both eyes are open.

This would ordinarily be a case for visual training. However, since his vision improved with lenses to 20/20 both far and near, we are giving him lenses to be worn for school (except for sports) and for all close work and study at home.

There is a possibility that his binocular pattern may improve with lenses.

Considering background factors, intellectual ability, language development, and sensory factors, it would seem that Jack should be able to read at approximately average level for his age if attention were given to the vision problem, motivation, compensation for memory deficiencies, and attitudes toward school work and reading in particular. The inadequate eye-hand coordination apparently stemmed from the vision problems.

Reading Evaluation and Diagnosis

The results of several reading tests or sections were as follows:

	Grade Score
California Reading—Junior High School	
Vocabulary	6.9
Reading Comprehension	7.1
Total	7.0
Wide Range Achievement Test	
Reading	5.8
Spelling	6.3
Gray Standardized Oral Reading Paragraphs	4.2
Durrell Analysis of Reading Difficulties	
Word Flash	High 6th
Word Analysis	Med. 6th
Visual Memory for Word Form	Med. 4th
Stanford Achievement Test	
Advanced Study Skills	6.2

A study of the results on the *California* would indicate only minor retardation in reading. Results of the rest of that battery, however, indicated deficiencies in mathematics, science, and general vocabulary, while Jack rated several months above his grade placement in social studies vocabulary. In comprehension, questions involving inference, organization, and knowledge of parts of books caused real difficulty. In both the *California* and *Stanford* Study Skills, Jack was deficient in map reading skills. Rate in both silent reading (measured by informal tests) and in oral reading (measured by the *Gray Oral Reading*) was low: fifth grade and fourth grade, respectively. Jack had no understanding of flexibility of rate. All of his reading was done at a uniform pace, ignoring possibilities of scanning or rapid reading according to special circumstances. This slow rate was a factor in his dislike for any reading, as a book seemed to mean an endless task to Jack.

Much of Jack's difficulty stemmed from word recognition habits and low motivation for reading or finding out. There was a strange discrepancy noted in his oral reading. On some of the low level paragraphs Jack made a large number of errors, while on more difficult paragraphs he read with fewer word errors. Comprehension and word recognition errors showed practically no relationship. At the third-grade level, Jack made eight word recognition errors but scored perfect in comprehension; while at the sixth-grade level, he made six word recognition errors and was unable to answer any of the comprehension questions. At the tenth-grade level, at which Jack was frustrated, he had about two and a half out of four points in comprehension. The highest number of errors was in repetitions, while a close second was gross mispronunciations, with substitutions ranking third. There were very few instances of asking for help, or of such errors as omissions, insertions, and partial mispronunciations.

A study of the errors in the oral reading and word perception tests revealed a pattern of observing only the initial elements of the word and ignoring contextual clues for checking accuracy of his word recognition. There evidently was little interest as he seriously violated meanings through miscalling words, but did not make any corrections. While the errors at the lower level were probably due to lack of interest, the errors at higher levels were due to inability to analyze the unknown words. In both situations meaning suffered without any apparent concern on Jack's part. In addition, one could note certain factors in word recognition: deficiency in noting or recalling configuration patterns; syllable errors by way of omission and change of syllables; and errors in vowel sounds.

An evaluation of Jack's knowledge of phonics revealed ability to distinguish accurately between long and short sounds of vowels, knowledge of phonograms but with a little insecurity, and knowledge of initial sounds, common digraphs, and blends. His knowledge of syllabication principles was spotty. Although he understood the use of the dictionary key, he was unable to apply this to word analysis. Apparently the need was for guidance and practice in application of principles rather than the knowledge of individual elements.

Summarized, Jack's problem seemed to be corrective in nature with functional vision problems, inaccurate perception and memory of form, low motivation for reading, and some immaturity in accepting responsibility as contributing factors. There may have been some inadequacies in his reading instruction in some of his school years. The major stress seemed to have been on general comprehension rather than reading for varied purposes and for definite information.

Remedial Program

AT THE COMPLETION of the diagnostic study a plan for Jack's remedial work was drawn up (in December, 1967) by the clinic director.

Recommendations for Corrective Work

The instructional work should be initiated at the fifth-grade level or transition fifth- to sixth-grade level, with special emphasis on guidance in basic skills in word perception and meaning vocabulary as well as approaches to various comprehension skills, especially organizational skills including main ideas and details.

Word Perception and Meaning. A review of the basic principles of phonetic and structural analysis should be given with special attention to practical application. Due to the erratic and gross errors made in perception, special guidance should be given in studying the whole word from left to right and noting the elements of the words. Although the general sensory approach would be visual-auditory, there is need to utilize a kinesthetic approach by writing the word carefully, and noting the order and sequence of elements. In an effort to improve visual memory for word forms, various techniques should be tried, e.g.: 1) display of word for observation, after which Jack is called on to find the word among a group of similar words, 2) tachistoscopic work through the use of the Flashmeter or any other quick flashing device, followed by reproduction of the word, 3) typing the word for attention to details and sequence of elements.

Another needed aspect for improving word perception which should be utilized is the checking of words with context. Another help would be reading which requires accuracy in words for true meaning, e.g., problems, directions, and science. Excellent material for the word perception work can be found interspersed throughout *Basic Reading Skills for Junior High School* (Scott, Foresman). In addition, there is need for much functional application of contextual, phonetic, and structural analysis as well as dictionary work, within the actual reading situations.

Closely allied to the work in perception will be enrichment of word meanings and concepts. Structural elements as affixes and root words can be of valuable help in improving word collection, either in card file or notebook form. In addition to the word, there would be analysis aids for correct pronunciation and contextual clues for word perception and word meaning. Interesting aspects of the word, as origin or peculiar usage, will add to the fun. This will serve as a means of building interests in words.

Comprehension and Study Skills. Within a developmental sequence of readings it will be possible not only to make word perception and meaning aids functional, but also to improve comprehension. Since much of Jack's problem has its roots in lack of motivation and interest, materials used should meet his special interests. Two possible choices which reach out to his expressed interests are the Classmate Edition of *A Call to Adventure* (Lyons and Carnahan) and *Let's Read*, Book I (Holt, Rinehart and Winston). For effectiveness, it will be necessary to stimulate interest and active thinking through building background and suggesting highly challenging activities or problems before reading. Much of the work will be silent reading with different types of questions for effecting varied approaches to reading. Introduction to varied and flexible rates can be done through utilizing the exercises for different purposes, such as: a general overview, suggesting skimming; a detailed reading of a biography for study of character and building a time line for recall of facts, to set the stage for a slower paced reading; or a rapid reading to note the highlights of a narrative.

Since some selections are suggestive of reading for main points, an opening can be made to practice work on this important skill. To supplement and give additional practice, it is suggested that the *New Practice Readers,* Books E and F (Webster) be used. Preliminary to the use of the materials in print, a more concrete approach could be used by employing pictures with a straightforward message. The theme of the picture or the message is sought; then the details within the picture which support the real message are also found. This can be followed by taking phrases from a selection and have Jack determine the generalization or main point. The article in the practice book is then read so that he sees the points within the total selection. These and similar aids can be carried through to improve the power to select the main ideas and details. Following this, it might be well to carry organization skills to longer passages to be found in the books suggested previously.

It is possible to relate skills of map and chart reading to special selections within the books indicated, especially the selections in *A Call to Adventure.*

Shorter selections found in the McCall, Crabbs *Standard Test Lessons in Reading* (Teachers College Press) or in some of the SRA kits will serve for initiation in speed and comprehension while longer selections in *Let's Read* can be used for timing to give power to speed up reading in various situations.

Developing Reading Habits. Although direct urging is not desirable, it is hoped that if the teacher can reverse Jack's early remark, "I never had a teacher who made reading and learning interesting," he will finally wish to read a book. Another factor in creating an interest in reading is a follow through on correction of his functional vision problem. No one enjoys doing a task which, unconsciously or consciously, is uncomfortable. Prolonged reading in the present situation would be an uninviting task from simply this standpoint, but it also is uninviting when concentration is taken from the reading act to compensate for a vision problem. *Popular Mechanics* or some current magazine or sports articles from the daily paper would probably have special appeal to Jack.

With correction of the vision problem and corrective work in reading, Jack should be able within another year to find greater pleasure in reading and improve his class work.

Remedial Program, Spring, 1968

Conditioned by distance and time availability, Jack attended the clinic one semester for one session a week and guidance for daily work at home between the sessions. Materials and procedures used followed in general the plan outlined above. The materials were at fifth- and transition fifth- to sixth-grade reading difficulty levels.

Selections were taken from the developmental books and emphasis was placed on discussion aimed at stimulating thinking, especially in the areas of weighing facts, making generalizations, and distinguishing between main points and supporting details. In word study, formal work was done along the lines suggested; additional work included selected lessons from *Phonics We Use, E* (Lyons and Carnahan). Some study guides aimed at utilization of word perception skills to words encountered in the reading were also used.

Results. Check tests were administered at the close of the semester consisting of fifteen lessons once weekly, to determine gains as measured by the standardized tests. The results were as follows:

		Gain
California Reading Test—Junior High School		
Meaning Vocabulary	8.0	1.1
Reading Comprehension	8.0	.7
Total	8.1	1.1
Wide Range Achievement Test		
Spelling	7.8	2.0

In studying the test responses, it was noted that Jack had a similar vocabulary profile, with social studies leading, as he had had at the initial diagnosis. In comprehension, Jack improved on responses to inference type questions but was still experiencing some difficulties. He no longer had difficulty related to book orientation and tables of contents. Unfortunately, he did not complete the test in the stipulated time and thus did not complete the responses related to organization of content which came near the end of the test. He had, however, made considerable improvement in following directions.

In evaluating Jack's work lesson to lesson, it was noted that he continued to experience difficulty in syllabication and use of dictionary skills. In organizational skills, he had made progress in getting the gist of what he read and noting the main point, but found real difficulty in recognizing sequential order and in locational skills. Little improvement was made in oral reading fluency and phrasing, partly because of the limited work in this area and because of the serious difficulty he apparently encounters in this phase of reading. Then too, he lacks a real need for oral reading or oral interpretation.

The parents followed through on the visual examination and Jack was fitted with glasses for reading. He continued with periodic checks by Mrs. Eberl who noted that the lenses evidently were quite effective.

During this semester Jack cooperated well with the clinician and followed through fairly well on the home study directed by the clinician. An intensive period of work during the summer session between seventh and eighth grade was recommended.

Follow-Up

DUE TO JACK'S ACCEPTANCE in the reading center at his school during the summer session and the distance from the Reading Clinic, Jack stopped coming to the clinic at the close of the spring session. He attended the school reading center for the summer, and then entered eighth grade but did not have additional reading help. In March, 1969, Jack came to the clinic for a follow-up of his reading. He also checked with Marguerite Eberl, O.D., to determine the progress made in vision; her report follows:

Jack was given lenses last year to coordinate his eyes. His right eye was very slightly hyperopic (far-sighted) but his left eye had a fairly high amount of hyperopic astigmatism. His vision in his left eye was 20/40 both far and near but was brought up to 20/20 with the correcting lens.

He was told that visual training might be necessary if lenses did not bring about the desired results. However this has not been necessary, since improvement in his visual pattern was noted as early as three months after wearing his glasses.

When he came in last year he reported that sometimes he would read with his right eye alone because objects would double when keeping both eyes open. He now uses both eyes equally well with his glasses on.

He does not see double with his lenses off either, and this causes him to tend to forget to put them on. We explained to Jack that his new pattern will hold his eyes together for a time, but that this might in time deteriorate, and he now understands that he should continue to wear them at least for all close work.

Diagnostic Check-Up

Jack came for a re-evaluation of his reading in March, 1969. At this meeting Jack came after school and it was expected that he would find it difficult to respond. However, he was his usual self—cooperative and compliant without special evidence of real enjoyment. He did, however, make some comments about his work and seemed more interested in self-improvement at this visit. He also asked several times how he was doing and how his answers were.

Potential. To re-evaluate his mental ability the *Wechsler Intelligence Scale for Children* was administered. The results were: Performance I.Q., 83; Verbal I.Q., 111; Full Scale I.Q., 95. In studying the results, there was a much greater similarity in results on the verbal subtests than on the performance subtests, which had wide variations. Information was the lowest in the verbal section and the Digit Span test, second lowest. Tests of Comprehension, Artihmetic, Vocabulary and Similarities were about one year above his chronological age level. In the performance tests, Jack seemed to lose on the bonus points for speed. He scored very low on Picture Arrangement while his highest rating in performance area was in Picture Completion. The other tests (Coding, Block Design, and Object Assembly) were one to two years below his chronological age. Jack apparently possessed good ability in gaining practical information, generalizing, and arithmetical reasoning in the verbal scale and in perceptual and conceptual abilities in a visual picture situation. In the ability to react to the whole while relating to the parts, Jack was definitely weak. In fact, he did not seem able to see what was wrong in the Object Assembly. His weakest point, however, was in sizing up the total situation in Picture Arrangement.

Although he found difficulty in Block Design, he showed real persistence, a trait evident in his first visit with us. In fact, he seemed challenged to try the different tasks. The general result of the tests were similar to the results on the *Binet* scale previously administered, but the *WISC* did accentuate the differences between his performance and verbal ability.

Reading Achievement. A brief check was made of his reading achievement and spelling. The results which follow serve as interesting comparison.

Due to the lateness of the hour, the spelling test was omitted at this time. The reading section of the *Wide Range Achievement* had not been given in May, 1968, as the clinician felt she had a good picture of his ability to analyze words and was certain he needed considerably more help. Since *WRAT* does not have additional forms, it seemed unwise to repeat it often.

	Grade Score December, 1967	Grade Score May, 1968	Grade Score March, 1969
California Junior High School Test			
Vocabulary	6.9	8.0	6.9
Reading Comprehension	7.1	8.0	8.5
Total	7.0	8.1	7.7
Wide Range Achievement Test			
Reading	6.3	—	7.1
Spelling	5.8	7.8	—

Considerable change was noted in vocabulary, both in the score change and in the pattern. Previously, Jack had been highest in social studies vocabulary, but, at this time, Jack scored considerably better in science vocabulary and was below level in social studies, general, and literature vocabulary.

Although he had shown considerable interest in the *WISC* test, he showed some reluctance toward taking the reading tests. On the *California,* it was significant that he omitted the section which contained considerable work in inference type of responses, remarking that this was difficult so he would go on to the next part. As he used the entire time allowance for the test, he did not return to the section containing the inferential type of questions; however, the last section was completed and he showed improvement over his initial performances in answering questions on organization.

In word recognition, he had not gained much since his work with us. His errors were of a similar nature but not as erratic. It was evident that he was in need of further help in accurate visual perception of form and quicker perception of words. It is probably this difficulty which makes reading slow and accounts for his statement: "I read what I need to for class but then I do not read other things."

General Evaluation

The interview with Jack at this time gave considerable insight into possibilities of improvement. It was very evident that he had improved considerably in self-concept even though his reading had not shown this much improvement.

He stated that he was now doing better in school and had better grades, and indicated some satisfaction with his work. The relief of the visual problem, as mentioned by Jack, helped him to be more comfortable when he read. This improvement in functional aspects of vision would account for some of his gains in comprehension despite minimal vocabulary gains. Then too, he seemed more mature emotionally.

Jack's reading was now classified as corrective-developmental with specific deficiency in word perception and in the thinking abilities involved in inferential types of responses. Generally, Jack is at transition seventh- to eighth-grade difficulty level, but requires more basic work in word perception.

Shortly before the end of the meeting, Jack suddenly said: "Could I get back in the clinic this summer?" This spontaneous request on Jack's part said in essence: "I am ready for the work now." His mother was informed of this request and she seemed very willing that he attend during the coming summer session despite the distance.

Recommendations

The work during the summer will be at the junior high school level with emphasis on a skills program in comprehension and approaches to study. It seems advisable to have Jack attend in a small group class interested in beginning high school reading skills. In addition, a special time will be given to bring up his word perception power with the idea of improving his comprehension and increasing his speed of reading. Special areas of work will be in:

1. General comprehension compared to specific types of comprehension
2. Methods of assimilating and organizing the ideas from a printed page
3. Developing flexibility through practice in scanning, recalling purpose, and then deciding technique and speed to be used
4. Browsing in books and magazines for informative and stimulating articles and stories with opportunities for discussion
5. Working on speed according to manner selected by him: instrument, timing with stop watch, special speed techniques, or combination. By giving Jack a choice, a better response is expected from him.

It seems that an intensive summer's work would help Jack at this particular time to come closer to his reading potential and make reading a more pleasant occupation rather than the chore it has been. At the time of the writing of this report it is anticipated that Jack will attend the summer session of the Reading Clinic.

Editor's Comments

The case of Jack was selected by the editor from among several submitted by Sister Julitta, in order to have one case representing the group in which previously undiagnosed difficulties in near-point vision and eye coordination seem highly significant. Although Jack's strabismus had been treated by surgery and he wore glasses for a short time after the operation, he was left with impaired vision in the left eye and a tendency to see double. This apparently had not been noted until he was given visual screening tests in the reading clinic, leading to an examination by the clinic's vision consultant and successful treatment of the condition with glasses. If these visual problems had been treated earlier, both Jack's reading and his ability on performance tests might have benefited.

Despite Jack's eye condition, his silent reading test scores at the time of the diagnostic study would not have singled him out in a junior high school as needing attention. Thus his parents' recognition of his study difficulties, and their initiative in seeking help at the reading clinic, explain why he received special help when thousands of children with poorer reading scores do not.

It may be noted that the reading skills taught in the clinic and the materials used did not differ greatly from those commonly employed in junior high school corrective reading classes. However, the personal attention inherent in individual tutoring allowed a closer fit to Jack's needs and tempo of learning than is possible in most corrective reading programs. The quite satisfactory gains after only one semester would seem attributable to relief of his visual problems as well as to the fifteen clinical lessons.

10

Randy

BY DONALD NEVILLE, Ph.D.

Setting

This case is from the files of the Child Study Center at George Peabody College for Teachers in Nashville, Tennessee. The author, who is a past director of the center, wishes to express his gratitude to the current director, Dr. James J. Stack, for permission to use this case material.

The Child Study Center is a non-residential service agency and a practicum facility for graduate students in psychology, education, and special education. Emphasis is placed on interdisciplinary endeavor involving psychology, education, and social work, with consultation in psychiatry, neurology, and pediatrics.

Stimulation of underdeveloped learning capacities at the center may utilize a variety of techniques including remedial education, play therapy, activity therapy, and tutorial therapy, as well as teaching machines and operant conditioning. The concern is with emotional and personality factors as well as with subject matter and skills. Children of all ages and ranges of intelligence may participate. In addition to work with children, several types of programs for parents are in operation. A six-week summer program in reading provides small group instruction one hour a day, five days a week.

Diagnostic Study

Background

Randy, a male Caucasian who was 11 years and 8 months old, was referred to the center because of his inability to learn to read. At the time of the referral, Randy's fifth-grade teacher noted standardized test results which placed his achievement level at grade 1.7. Both teacher and parents indicated that they felt Randy had a "reading block."

The background information which follows was acquired from forms completed by the mother and an interview with the mother. The usual procedure at the center was to conduct an initial interview with both parents. However, in this instance only Mrs. H. appeared for the interview. She stated that Mr. H. had to work and that she felt she could give us all the information that was needed. The interviewer noted that, while Mrs. H. did not appear unduly anxious, the interview was of the question-answer type and most of the information was garnered as a result of direct questioning.

Personal and Family. Randy was brought to the center after much urging by the school personnel. The family included two older brothers whose ages were 19 and 15, and two younger sisters, 9 and 6 years of age. During the initial interview it was learned that both of Randy's older brothers had experienced difficulties in reading which required special tutoring. In both instances the tutoring was performed by primary teachers. Mrs. H. was uncertain as to the effectiveness of the "reading lessons." The girls, it was reported, had no reading problems.

Mr. and Mrs. H., both 40 years of age, had been married for twenty-one years and neither had gone beyond the eighth grade in school. They were born in an adjoining Tennessee county and moved to this city when they were married. Mr. H. owned a small retail business. Because of the necessity for keeping the business open about eighteen hours per day, Mr. H. worked from about 7:00 A.M. until about 4:00 P.M. and Mrs. H. worked from about 4:00 P.M. until 11:00 or 12:00 P.M.

Randy's reading difficulties were noted by his first-grade teacher. He attended first grade at Lee School and repeated it at Johnston School where he completed the elementary grades. During the previous two summers Randy had had special tutoring in reading by a teacher who lived near the family. However, Mrs. H. could see no positive results from this special help. There were no remedial or corrective reading services at Johnston School.

Mrs. H. reported essentially normal birth and development except in the acquisition of language. She stated that Randy began using words at 18 to 24 months but that no attempt to use communicative units containing more than one or at the most two words occurred before his third year.

No behavioral problems were reported. Randy seemed to get along normally with his brothers and sisters. Also, he had several close friends. Activities with this group included football, cowboys and Indians, parties, and movies. Randy was not seen as a discipline problem; but when punishment was deemed necessary, it was administered by the parent at hand. Disciplinary action usually consisted of sending him to his room or an occasional "spanking with a belt" administered by the father.

Mrs. H. stated that Randy was on his own when it came to completing homework assignments. While Mrs. H. was usually at work in the evening, she reported that he was sent to his room to work on his assignments. His father did not assist him and she doubted if the assignments were completed very often. Mrs. H. was not certain whether the assignments were special ones or if they were the usual fifth-grade work. It appeared that the thought that parental assistance might be needed or appropriate had never occurred to either parent. The interviewer had the feeling that school work was something which the parents viewed as either beyond their competencies or none of their business. The net result seemed to be that the goals of the school were viewed as unrelated to the home.

School. From the school report, it was noted that Randy's behavior was generally described as differing from that of the average fifth-grader. It was stated that his interest level was far below average, his leadership ability below average, the amount of assistance required from the teacher above average, and relationships with peers as very limited. In addition, the school reported little or no communicative relationship with parents. While several attempts had been made to set up conferences with the parents, the parents' work schedule had usually prevented these conferences from occurring.

The only standardized test scores reported were on achievement tests. At the end of the fourth grade Randy's average achievement was at 1.7 grade level, upon completing third grade it was also 1.7, and at the end of second grade it was 2.0 level. It was concluded that little or no increment in achievement had occurred after second grade.

The school reported that Randy appeared, for all practical purposes, to be a non-reader. This seemed to mean that he could consistently identify only a very limited number of words. The teacher was particularly concerned about Randy's tendency to reverse words and letters in both reading and writing. In this connection, the teacher noted that Randy was left-handed.

Following standard procedure, the department of pupil personnel of the local school system was contacted in order to ascertain if any further pertinent information was available. It was found that a school psychologist had administered a *Revised Stanford-Binet Intelligence Scale* two months previously. Randy achieved an M.A. of 10–8 and an I.Q. of 94. The school psychologist recommended that Randy be referred to the Child Study Center and noted that he appeared to be able to recognize only two words: Randy and Mother. An additional comment suggested that Randy had exhibited much "fidgety" behavior and had appeared "very anxious" during the testing.

Medical. The report from the physician summarized his findings in the statement that Randy appeared to have "no gross physical defects." Randy's height was 61 inches and his weight 112 pounds. The physician commented that Randy's physical development was occurring within normal limits but that he was slightly ahead of his age group. Randy's medical history included the usual childhood diseases, but no serious or unusual illnesses were reported. Vision and hearing were both reported to be normal. Neurological impairment was noted to be unlikely.[1]

Test Results

The purpose of this section is to present the information regarding Randy's performance on specific tests. The scores and the behavioral data relative to each instrument are presented separately. This section will be concluded with a summary of the diagnostic findings regarded to be important to the treatment plan. The tests administered were: the *Wechsler Intelligence Scale for Children* (*WISC*), the *Keystone Telebinocular*, the *Maico Audiometer*, the *Wepman Test of Auditory Discrimination*, the *Durrell Analysis of Reading Difficulty*, the *Thorndike Handwriting Scale* and the *Bender Visual Motor Gestalt Test*.

Wechsler Intelligence Scale for Children (*WISC*). Table 3 shows Randy's score on each of the *WISC* subtests and the Verbal, Performance, and Full Scale I.Q.'s. From this table it can be seen that Randy's Full Scale I.Q. would be borderline according to Wechsler's classification system. Further, using the test age as an indication of functioning level, it is observed that the mean test age on verbal subtests is 9–0 and on performance subtests 8–0.

In order to examine strengths and weaknesses on the *WISC*, a pattern analysis suggested by Davis[2] was used. Table 4 shows that Randy had a

---

[1] See results of later neurological examination, summarized in footnote 5.

[2] Davis, Frederick B., *Educational Measurements and Their Interpretations* (Belmont, Calif.: Wadsworth Publishing Co., 1961), p. 152.

Table 3. Summary of Randy's *WISC* Scores

	Scaled Score	*Test Age*
Verbal Tests		
1. Information	7	9–2
2. Comprehension	6	8–2
3. Arithmetic	9	10–10
4. Similarities	8	9–10
5. Vocabulary	5	8–2
6. Digit Span	7	7–10
	42 (35)	Average 9–0
Performance Tests		
7. Picture Completion	10	11–2
8. Picture Arrangement	5	7–6
9. Block Design	5	7–2
10. Object Assembly	6	7–6
11. Coding	4	6–10
	30	Average 8–0

Verbal I.Q., 81; Performance I.Q., 72; Full Scale I.Q., 75.

total of thirteen significant (15-percent level) differences among his sub-test scaled scores. On the basis of chance one might expect 8.25 differences. From Table 3 it can be concluded that the nine-point difference favoring the Verbal I.Q. reaches a 15-percent level of significance also.

A further examination of Table 4 indicates that the Arithmetic, Picture Completion, and Similarities subtests were comparatively high and contribute to all of the significant differences. The significantly low scores were not as concentrated and were shared by six subtests: namely, Comprehension, Vocabulary, Picture Arrangement, Block Design, Object Assembly, and Coding. However, two of them, Vocabulary and Coding, account for six of the thirteen significant differences.

The behavioral comments made by the *WISC* examiner were as follows:

1. Was not consistent in use of hands; usually used left but on Block Design and Object Assembly used right hand first and then both.

2. Responses often of poor quality; on Comprehension full credit was given for only two items and on Similarities for only one.

Table 4. *WISC* Pattern Analysis for Randy's Scores

Subtest	Scaled Score	1	2	3	4	Subtest 5	6	7	8	9	10
1	7										
2	6	1									
3	9	−2	−3*								
4	8	−1	−2	1							
5	5	2	1	4*	3*						
6	7	0	−1	2	1	2					
7	10	−3	−4*	−1	−2	−5*	−3				
8	5	2	1	4*	3	0	2	5*			
9	5	2	1	4*	3	0	2	5*	0		
10	6	1	0	3	2	−1	1	4*	−1	−1	
11	4	3	2	5*	4*	1	3	6*	1	1	2

Expected
Differences = 55 × .15 = 8.25

*Actual
Differences = 13 (15-percent level)

3. Difficulty in visual perceptual tasks: on Block Design and Object Assembly work progressed one piece at a time with seemingly little idea of the whole; on Coding a line was skipped and then completed after discovery of error.

Keystone Telebinocular. Randy showed the same restless, talkative behavior on the *Telebinocular* that he tended to exhibit during the other educational tests. The results indicated normal vision with the possible exception of stereopsis (depth perception). However, it was not clear whether Randy ever understood the directions for this subtest. It was further noted that Randy never was able to indicate right or left without confusion. In fact, the examiner finally directed him to point rather than to attempt to indicate direction by saying right or left. Randy seemed relieved and sometimes pointed with his left hand and sometimes with his right.

Maico Audiometer. Randy's performance on the audiometric evaluation was erratic. He seemed unable to sit and concentrate on the task at hand. His responses indicated hearing losses which ranged from 50 decibels at 8000 cycles per second to 10 decibels at 500 and 4000 cycles per second. The pattern of losses in the right ear did not differ from those in the left ear. These results indicated the need for a complete audiometric evaluation and Randy was referred to the Speech and Hearing Center. The results of their evaluation indicated essentially normal hearing but suggested defects in auditory discrimination.

Wepman Test of Auditory Discrimination. In order to reduce the examiner variable, Forms I and II of this test were tape recorded by a graduate student majoring in speech pathology. Examiners at the Child Study Center used these tapes when the *Wepman* was administered. Randy was given Form II with the following results: 1) one Y error (heard the two pronunciations of "wedge" as different) and 2) seven X errors (did not hear a difference). Four of the seven X errors occurred in stimulus words where the differences were in ending sounds and the other three were in words where the vowel sound was the difference. According to the *Wepman* Test Manual, a total of more than six errors suggests inadequate development for five-year-olds. Thus, Randy's performance resulting in eight errors would indicate serious lack of development in this skill.

Durrell Anaylsis of Reading Difficulty. In order to observe his reading behavior, the *Durrell Analysis of Reading Difficulty* was administered. The results were as follows:

Oral Reading—1L (Low first grade)
Silent Reading—0 correct (Below grade 1)
Listening Comprehension—Grade 6
Naming Letters: Capital 14 correct; Small 18 correct
Matching Letters: Capital 4 correct; Small 1 correct
Writing Letters: Capital 13 correct; Small 20 correct
Visual Memory of Words, Primary: 7 correct (Below grade 1)
Hearing Sounds in Words, Primary: 6 correct (Below grade 1)
    Five of the six correct responses were on beginning sounds.
Spelling: none correct (Below grade 1).

Behaviorally, Randy was again restless and talkative. During the administration of this test he found it necessary to get up from his seat and walk around the room on several occasions. It appeared that he was virtually a non-reader and indeed was generally unable to perform those skills that would be considered necessary prerequisites for beginning formal reading instruction. In addition, during this session Randy complained of headaches and stomach pains.

The one area in which Randy performed at a relatively high level was that of listening comprehension. On this subtest, material of sixth-grade reading difficulty was read to Randy and he was able to answer seven of the eight comprehension questions. The selection was on the history of baseball. It is doubtful that it covered factual material which he had learned from another source, since he missed no more than one question on any of the listening comprehension selections below sixth grade.

On the spelling test Randy spelled none of the words correctly. Some of his errors were as follows: *run* was spelled *n, night* was spelled *i, back* was spelled *af, look* was spelled *o*. During this test Randy was encouraged to write any letters he thought might be in the word even if he knew he could not spell the entire word. No letter or word reversals were noted.

Thorndike Handwriting Scale. For this measure Randy was asked to copy the first story from the *Durrell Analysis of Reading Difficulty.* In general, his writing matched sample number five on the scale, which represents the poorest quality of writing for fourth-grade children. The characteristics noted were: a mixture of cursive and manuscript letter forms, generally poorly formed letters, little uniformity in slant or size, and a line slant average of about 14 degrees, and ranging from 10 to 20 degrees. The line slant was in the downward direction three times and upward once. Randy wrote at the rate of 22 letters per minute which is less than the average rate for second graders (35 letters per minute). Again, no reversals were noted. Following the first task Randy was asked to copy the next *Durrell* selection on lined paper. While the formation of letters was not significantly better, he was able to write on the lines and letter size was more consistent.

Harris Tests of Lateral Dominance. According to this instrument Randy would be classified in the crossed dominance category. His knowledge of left and right was confused, a common finding among young children but quite untypical at his age. His hand dominance was rated as moderate left, and his eye and foot dominance as moderate right. According to Harris's data, Randy's performance on the test of lateral dominance, classifying him as left-handed and right-eyed, indicates that he falls in a classification in which it is doubtful if there are significant differences between unclassified and reading disability groups.[3]

[3] Albert J. Harris, *How to Increase Reading Ability*, 5th ed. (New York: David McKay Co., 1970), p. 238. Although crossed dominance is not in itself significantly related to reading disability according to the Harris data, persistence of confusion on left and right to Randy's age is very unusual and strongly suggestive of a neurological immaturity or defect (Editor).

Bender Visual Motor Gestalt Test. This test was administered in the usual way. Randy was asked to copy the designs and no time limit was applied. The examiner made no notation of specific behavior during the administration of this test. The performance was scored by using the scheme devised by Koppitz.[4]

Figure A.	No Score	Score 0
Figure 1.	Distortion of Shape (4)	1
Figure 2.	Rotation (7)	1
Figure 3.	Distortion of Shape (15)	1
Figure 4.	No Score	0
Figure 5.	Distortion of Shape (15)	
	Rotation (16)	2
Figure 6.	No Score	0
Figure 7.	Integration (23)	1
Figure 8.	No Score	0
		Total: 6

In the Koppitz system, a "no score" designation indicates an acceptable reproduction. Thus, the higher the score, the less mature the performance. The numbers in parentheses represent Koppitz's error classification on each figure.

In Randy's case, the total score of six represented most nearly the mean score of children between the ages of 6–6 and 6–11 in the Koppitz norm sample. Utilizing the standard deviation for the appropriate age groups, Randy's performance was between the ages of 5–6 and 8–11 and was below that expected of third graders. It was concluded that in the area of visual motor integration, Randy's performance was several years below that expected for his age group.

Summary

Potential. From the foregoing information it appears that Randy had the necessary general potential to read at a level which was substantially higher than the "non-reader" level at which he was then achieving. This was especially true if one examined those skills or behaviors which might be characterized as verbal.

[4] Elizabeth M. Koppitz, *The Bender Gestalt for Young Children* (New York: Grune & Stratton, Inc., 1964).

If the test ages of the *WISC* Verbal subtests are averaged, the mean test age is 9–0. Roughly, this might be interpreted to indicate that Randy had the verbal skills to achieve at a beginning fourth-grade level in reading. Also, when Randy's performance on the Listening Comprehension Test of the *Durrell Analysis of Reading Difficulty* is examined, it is seen that he understood verbal material estimated to be of sixth-grade reading difficulty. In addition, the results of the basic visual and hearing tests would indicate that Randy had no serious impairments in these areas.

The conclusion that Randy possessed the verbal skills necessary to achieve at a fourth-grade level was also supported by the results of the *Stanford-Binet* administered by the school psychologist. On this instrument he achieved an I.Q. of 94 and an M.A. of 10–8 (CA 11–5). It was our opinion that this score probably overestimated Randy's potential, but the results easily support a reading expectancy of at least fourth grade insofar as verbal ability is concerned.

Basic Perceptual Skills. This area of behavior was measured by the *Wepman Auditory Discrimination Test, Harris Tests of Lateral Dominance, Bender Visual Motor Gestalt Test,* and selected subtests of the *WISC.* In general, Randy exhibited substantial difficulties, primarily in the visual and auditory sensory modes. From the history (playing of sports) and clinical observation of performance on the other tests, motor ability was judged to be less impaired than auditory and visual perception. Also, Randy's ability to write on a line as compared to his slant writing on non-lined paper suggested that the motor skills related to writing were superior to the visual skills.

On all of the above mentioned measures, Randy's performance was far below what would be considered average for his age level and substantially below his estimated verbal abilities. The one exception to this statement was the *Harris,* where Randy's eyedness and handedness were not in a problem category, but his confusion of left and right indicated a degree of immaturity.

Performance on the *WISC* subtests of Block Design and Coding were indicative of visual perceptive impairment, as was that on the *Bender.* The *Wepman* and related measures on the *Durrell* (Hearing Sounds in Words and Spelling) indicated serious difficulties in auditory perceptive skills.

Because of the above results and the overall Performance–Verbal I.Q. differential, the probability of neurological impairment was considered.

It was agreed that a neurological examination would be recommended to the parents.

Reading and Related Skills. Randy's performance on skills directly reflecting reading and related school achievement was at a very low level. On the actual reading tests he was classified as a non-reader. On most of the *Durrell* subtests measuring specific reading-related behaviors (e.g., matching letters, visual memory of words, etc.), he also performed at a level judged to be beginning first grade or below.

The only exceptions to his generally low achievement were Randy's ability to understand sixth-grade material read to him and his perform- ance on the Arithmetic subtest of the *WISC*. On the latter measure, where he achieved his highest verbal subtest score, he had a test age of 10–10 and scaled score of 9.

Attitudes Toward Reading. In this instance, no specific tests of emo- tional adjustment were administered. It did appear clear, however, that negative attitudes toward learning were playing an important role in in- hibiting Randy's learning of reading skills. His behavior in the testing situation indicated that he responded to school learning tasks with a phobic-type reaction. At times Randy physically removed himself from the task, and at other times he complained of stomach pains and related physical discomfort when confronted with reading tasks.

Remedial Program

Overview

From the data gathered during the diagnostic activities, there ap- peared to be four major assumptions on which to base the instructional- treatment program.

1. In terms of general language skills, Randy possessed the potential to achieve reading competency well beyond the level at which he was operating.

2. The basic visual-auditory perceptive behaviors necessary to achieve even beginning decoding skills were beyond Randy's current ability. There was a possibility that motor and/or associational deficits were present and that these deficits were related to neurological impairment.

3. Randy's attitude toward reading and related academic tasks were such that his ability to involve himself actively in the process of learning

was seriously impaired. Thus, the instructional program should be aimed at altering these attitudes as well as providing instruction in areas of skill deficits.

4. The prognosis for any significant involvement of Randy's parents in the treatment program was guarded. However, it was felt that it was important to urge the family to agree to a neurological examination for Randy and to assist them in carrying out any program of medication which might be recommended by the neurologist.[5]

Ideally, the treatment would have included daily tutorial sessions, but because of transportation problems, Randy could only be seen three days a week for about one hour per day.

The instructional program was based on the above assumptions and was planned in three phases. Phase I was basically a desensitization concept. It had two major objectives: to reduce the anxiety-phobic responses to learning situations and to increase skills in the basic auditory-visual perceptive areas.

Phase II was to be an instructional program stressing beginning reading skills in an individual tutorial setting. Initial plans for this phase indicated that the basic approach would be organized in terms of a combination of the Fernald and Gillingham approaches. Language-experience type reading materials would be used and initially whole words would be taught kinesthetically. However, after a basic number of words had been learned (40–50), a phonic instructional program similar to the type described by Gillingham would be introduced. During the remainder of Phase II, instructional techniques similar to those suggested by both Gillingham and Fernald would be used.

Phase III would be characterized by small group instruction and the use of less individually tailored techniques and more commercially prepared, school-type materials. The specific skill instruction would be continued from Phase II.

Phase I

In conceptualizing Phase I as a desensitization process, activities along three continua were planned, namely, visual, auditory, and environmental.

[5] After several recommendations to the parents, Randy was seen by a neurologist who reported that Randy undoubtedly had "diffuse neurological involvement" but that medication was not recommended. No other specific information was obtained from this examination.

In devising activities along these continua, it was planned to avoid any direct confrontation with the printed page. Thus, books and other formal reading materials were not present.

Perhaps it will be best to describe the environmental continuum first, since it represented an organizational notion and therefore influenced the plans for both the visual and auditory activities. It was felt that Randy would learn best and easiest in situations unlike those with which he was confronted at school. It was necessary to alter both the physical environment and the presentation of materials.

In the beginning Randy's sessions were structured to be game-like, and no pencil-paper activities were used. The room in which tutoring occurred was not furnished like the typical school or tutoring room. The tutor and Randy sat on the floor and worked on the floor or on a coffee table. No school-type furniture was present. Since the Child Study Center was located in a converted house, it was fairly easy to provide a non-school environment. The physical environment was slightly altered as Phase I progressed so that by the end of eighteen weeks he and the tutor were working at a table and using a chalk board. However, no books or paper and pencil exercises were used.

The visual continuum began with reading readiness types of visual discrimination. To the extent possible, interactions with the tasks were carried on in an informal way. Randy was never asked to complete a page of work by using a pencil or other marking device. For example, the tutor would often say that she had a game to play which involved finding the thing which was different. Initially, she would begin with actual objects and then move to material from readiness books where the items had been cut out and were presented one at a time. Some Frostig and Continental Press visual training materials were also used. During the final stages of this phase Randy was presented with letter matching tasks. The letters were on 3- by 5-inch cards with the stimulus letter at the top and the response choices along the bottom. In the beginning, only two or three responses which could be easily discriminated were provided. As the program continued the number of response choices and the difficulty level of the discrimination task was increased.

The auditory continuum began with the identification of various sounds which were played on a tape recorder. Randy was then asked to identify loud versus soft sounds and high versus low sounds. Later in the program letter sounds were played, the task being to tell whether the sounds were the same or different. They were not identified as letter sounds and no attempt was made to attach letter names to the sounds. After the letter sounds, words which began and ended with the same sounds were introduced with the task being to identify similarities and differences.

The visual, auditory, and environmental continua progressed concurrently and sequences were arranged in a way that almost guaranteed success. If there was any doubt about the increment between two sequences being too great, it was reduced.

This phase continued for about eighteen weeks. At that point, it was felt that Randy had made extensive progress toward both of the initial objectives. He could now engage in the learning process so that personal involvement was evident, and he had also progressed so that basic visual and auditory perception skills were present. Evaluation at this stage consisted of estimating Randy's ability to match letters and to make auditory discriminations.

It will be remembered that initially Randy was able to match only four upper-case letters and one lower-case letter correctly. The technique used for evaluation was to make four sets of cards, two with upper case and two with lower case letters. One upper case deck was shuffled and then the other was arranged in the same order. The decks were divided into three piles; two piles had nine cards and one eight. Randy was asked to match the cards from the first pile of the lower case deck with the cards from the first pile in the second deck. The procedure was repeated for the remainder of the lower case and for all of the upper case letters. Randy was able to match all of the upper case letters correctly and twenty of the lower case. He missed *m, z, s, q, n,* and *p.* It is suspected that he would have missed *b* and *d* if they had been in the same pile. However, this performance seemed to indicate that there had been substantial progress in visual perceptive skills.

For evaluation of progress in auditory discrimination, Form I of the *Wepman* was administered. The result was four X errors and no Y errors. Randy's errors were all in words where the vowel sound determined the difference. This time he made no errors in ending sounds.

Phase II

This phase was planned so that its primary goals were instructional in nature. While it was still necessary to be certain that success was experienced, it was felt that Randy could cope with a beginning reading program based primarily on instructional goals.

Initially, the Fernald method was used exclusively. Randy selected the words he wanted to learn and they were taught by tracing. Also, a file box of the words he learned was kept so that frequent review was possible. The cards also served the important purpose of providing Randy with constant feedback. He would count the cards almost daily and then verbalize the number of additional words he had learned that day or so far that week.

By using the tape recorder, it was possible gradually to encourage Randy to tell a story or describe something he had seen. The tutor would then type these verbal productions and Randy would choose the words he wanted to learn.

It was early during this phase of treatment that Randy began riding the bus and sessions changed to five days per week. On one particular day he misread a sign and got on the wrong bus. This appeared to be a critical experience. While the tutor was fearful it would discourage Randy, the opposite proved to be true. Rather, it appeared to give him a "real reason" for needing to read, and his motivation improved at an accelerated rate.

After about eight weeks Randy had mastered fifty-nine words. The Gillingham approach of teaching the names and sounds of individual letters was begun while continuing the Fernald approach. The Gillingham approach was altered in sequence so that in the beginning only those letters which represented initial sounds in words Randy had already mastered through the Fernald approach were presented. However, letters were presented in initial and final positions.

After eight additional weeks, it was decided to evaluate Randy's decoding ability informally. To do this a list of words from a first-grade reading skills checklist devised by Walter Barbe [6] was used. Of this list of 175 words, Randy correctly identified 103. The words were typed on 3- by 5-inch index cards, four to a card, and Randy was asked to read them. In addition to the 103, he was able to identify about 72 other words he had learned but which were not on the list.

Behaviorally Randy seemed to have changed also. While he had not yet suggested that conventional books be used, he was bringing in comic

[6] W. B. Barbe, *Educator's Guide to Personalized Reading Instruction* (Englewood Cliffs, N.J.: Prentice-Hall, Inc., 1961), p. 152.

books and the sports page of the local paper as material for tutoring lessons. It also seemed obvious that in informal situations Randy could identify words which he had missed on the evaluative list.

It was decided that Phase II would be continued for about four more weeks. During this time a concerted effort was made to get Randy to interact with formal reading material like newspapers, comic books, and magazines. During the first two weeks of this period, Randy began to voice physical complaints again. This was interpreted to indicate that the interaction with formal reading material was being overly emphasized so attempts were continued but their frequency was reduced.

An additional eight weeks passed before it was felt that Randy should be evaluated for the purpose of moving to Phase III. This time the Word Recognition section of a *Gates Advanced Primary Reading Test* was used. However, to maintain the idea of non-school material, the test was cut up item by item and presented as though it was a daily activity rather than a test. Randy was asked to point to the correct word rather than mark it. Randy made a raw score of 10 with a grade level of 2.5. Only 21 of the 48 items were attempted; the examiner stopped when Randy had missed seven consecutive answers.

From the test results and Randy's behavior, it seemed to be appropriate to move on to Phase III. This was discussed with Randy and he tentatively consented to try working with a group.

Phase II had lasted just over six months. This meant that Randy had been seen for a total of almost eleven consecutive months. During this time he had experienced three different tutors. Two had been graduate students and one a regular staff member. During Phase III, the staff member continued as the tutor. The supervision had been consistent in that the author had served as supervisor throughout.

The school reported significant changes in Randy's behavior. He was participating in class activities although, of course, the skill deficit was still a major inhibiting factor. Randy was now in the first months of sixth grade. He was much impressed with his new teacher, and indeed her influence and understanding attitude was thought to be a major factor in his future progress.

Phase III

This phase began with an instructional group of two fifth-grade and two sixth-grade boys. Later during this phase the group was increased to six by adding two more fifth-grade boys. None of the group attended the same school and they were not acquainted with each other before they entered the tutorial sessions.

The objectives for Randy were: 1) to help him to be able to interact with school-type reading materials, 2) to help him to profit from instruction in a group rather than individually, and 3) to develop skills which would allow him to function nearer to his optimal level.

To accomplish the instructional activities in the group, it was planned to divide the one-hour period into two types of activities. First, a total group lesson lasting twenty to thirty minutes was planned. The specific activities were varied and included such things as: skill instruction, sharing experiences, composing a story, or oral reading. The second activity was to stress independent work, such as practicing a specific skill, or reading from a story or book. It was to include only minimal supervision from the tutor.

In Randy's case the independent activities centered around two types of materials. The specific skill aspect was handled through the Sullivan Remedial Program (*Programmed Reading;* Behavior Research Laboratories) and the reading aspect with easy stories about sports figures. During the initial portion of this phase Randy needed the close attention of the tutor to encourage him to persevere at the designated task but as the phase continued, encouragement was needed less and less frequently.

During Phase III Randy agreed to the tutor's suggestion that he share part of a story with the group by reading several pages to them. He practiced it with the tutor and finally shared it with them. He was amazed when one group member said he thought that was a good story and suggested Randy share it with his class at school. Randy decided he could not read to the "whole class" but, at the tutor's suggestion, thought he might tape record it and play it for the class. When the classroom teacher was consulted, she was very agreeable and went ahead to make specific plans with Randy. The story was recorded at the center. However, when the time arrived, Randy became so anxious that he had to leave the room while it was played. After the story he received much positive reaction from his teacher and fellow students.

He shared stories this way about ten times and finally agreed to read one in person. He was successful, according to the teacher, but the next time he wanted to record the story again. The sharing continued, and sometimes he would read the selection personally and other times record it.

Initially it was planned to evaluate the group by administering formal tests about every three months. However, at the end of the first three months it was felt that they were not ready for this. The group was still very anxious and uneasy about "tests." As a result, it was decided to evaluate Randy by asking him to read orally several pages from the book he was reading.

The tutor selected a portion which Randy had not read and prepared ten comprehension questions. The passage was evaluated by means of a readability formula, and Betts' criteria for instructional and independent reading levels were applied.

The Dale-Chall formula was used and it rated the passage as fourth grade or below in reading difficulty. The Spache formula was then applied and the book was rated as high third grade.

Randy read the passage of 137 words with six errors, not counting repetitions, and he was able to answer eight of the ten comprehension questions. It was thus concluded that Randy's instructional reading level was about high third grade. No attempts were made to estimate his independent or frustration levels.

After three additional months, the group was evaluated with a formal test. The Word Recognition and Paragraph Reading subtests of the *Gates Advanced Primary Reading Test* were given. Randy's performance on this test rated him at 3.7 grade level on Word Recognition and 2.9 grade level on Paragraph Reading. Behaviorally, he was reading high-interest, low-vocabulary books estimated to be at third and fourth grades in reading difficulty.

Phase III continued for another three months with a continuation of the program described before. Again *Gates* tests were administered, but this time the *Basic Reading Test* level was used. Randy's grade scores were: Reading Vocabulary, 4.7, and Level of Comprehension, 4.3.

The formal test results generally agreed with our observations of Randy's level of functioning. Also the teacher reported success with using fourth-grade material in classroom instruction.

It was now June and Randy had been at the center about twenty-one months. After discussing it with Randy and his mother, it was decided to discontinue at the center, at least for the summer. The decision was based on the fact that Randy had made substantial progress in attitude change and achievement and that he was on a baseball team. It was important to him to play on the team and coming to the center would have interfered with this. A tutor who lived near the family was located and the case was discussed with her. She worked with Randy during the summer and reported "slow progress."

Follow-Up

IN EARLY OCTOBER another conference was held with Randy and his mother, and it was decided not to reestablish any special tutoring program. According to the school (junior high), Randy was not doing grade level work; but since they were using homogeneous grouping, he was able to keep up with his group.

The school was contacted about February of that year and the report was substantially the same. The parents or Randy have not been contacted directly since then. However, a recent article in the local paper noted that Randy had been cited as an outstanding sophomore lineman for the football team at his high school.

It was our evaluation that this case represented a moderately successful effort. The goal of assisting Randy to reach a reading level of practical literacy had been achieved. In addition, he was able to function in the school setting at a marginally successful level. It was believed that these achievements represented realistic achievement levels for a boy with Randy's combination of abilities and disabilities.

Editor's Comments

The poor showing that Randy made on the WISC, with a Full Scale I.Q. of 75, would have barred him from some remedial programs that set minimum I.Q.'s, but the gain he made, from non-reader to fourth grade in two years, indicated the correctness of estimating his ability to profit from remedial attention by comparing his potential reading level with his attained reading level.

The three-phase plan for remediation employed with Randy is a good example of considering both long-term and short-term goals from the start, and planning accordingly. The first or readiness phase seems to have been quite successful both in developing positive motivation and in establishing perceptual readiness. The remedial procedures in the second phase combined widely used kinesthetic and phonic procedures. The return of Randy's hypochondriacal complaints when an effort to stress printed material was made a little too early is a fine example of the indirect ways in which pupils tell remedial teachers when something is wrong. In the third phase, the transition to group lessons, formal reading materials, and to reading in his regular classroom was accomplished gradually and successfully. Thus the major objectives were achieved, and one can hope that the program in his slow junior high class encouraged his continuing growth in reading as well as in athletics.

11

Annette

BY HELEN K. SMITH, PH.D.

Setting

The Reading Clinic of the University of Chicago is one of the oldest and best-known in the country. Started by Guy T. Buswell, its directors have included Helen M. Robinson, Josephine Piekarz Ives, and Helen K. Smith. The Reading Clinic is a service agency, a training facility, and a research center. For doctoral candidates in reading, one of the requirements has been spending a year or more as a clinician-teacher in the Reading Clinic.

A diagnostic study usually includes psychological testing, detailed analysis of reading and other skills, screening tests of vision and hearing, and interviews. Many kinds of specialized medical and other examinations are available when needed through cooperative arrangements with other units of the university.

Remedial teaching is usually individual, sometimes in a very small group. The teaching plan is eclectic and, being based on the diagnostic analysis, is somewhat different for each child. It is the policy of the clinic to continue with each child until success in regular school is well established.

Diagnostic Study

Background

Annette was referred to the University of Chicago Reading Clinic by a psychologist who was also a speech and language specialist. He had recently examined her to try to determine the source of her learning problems in school. He urged her parents to make an appointment at the Reading Clinic for a diagnostic reading examination for Annette because he thought her school difficulties stemmed from her poor reading. At the time of the diagnosis Annette was 11 years 3 months old and had just completed the fifth grade in a suburban public school.

Case History

Mr. and Mrs. M. reported that their daughter had experienced no problems of any kind until she was 17 months old. Her birth was normal in every respect, and she had been a healthy, happy baby. She began walking at 14 months and talking in words of three or more words when she was approximately 19 months old.

Annette fell from her baby carriage onto the cement sidewalk and incurred a skull fracture, a lineal fracture of the left temporal bone, when she was 17 months old. She was unconscious for approximately two hours. She was examined by both her pediatrician and a neurosurgeon immediately after the accident occurred. Her parents noticed that Annette became irritable, impatient, and "sensitive in the head area" after her accident.

Annette had not had any serious illnesses. She had a mild case of measles when she was 7 and mild cases of mumps and chicken pox when she was 8, with no unusual reactions to any of these illnesses. Her parents reported that there had been no history of speech, visual, or auditory difficulties, or any physical disability.

The first in a family of three children, Annette has two brothers. At the time of the diagnosis, one was an A student in the third grade and the other was a first grader who scored high on all tests administered to him. The third grader was a "bookworm" who "read on a high-school level." Sometimes Annette is jealous of her brothers and wonders why they can do their school work faster and more easily than she can.

Mr. M. is president of a retail business, and Mrs. M. helps him on a part-time basis as bookkeeper, saleslady, and buyer. She has never worked on a full-time basis and has been able to give much time to her children. The only other person who lives in the household is a full-time housekeeper whose relationship with the family has been quite good. Mrs. M. attended a state university one year; Mr. M. attended a local college for two years. Neither parent had experienced any learning difficulties at any time in their education. Mrs. M. is an avid reader, but Mr. M. does not read very much because of a severe visual problem. Both are in good health.

It was evident that both parents wanted only the best for their children. They were willing to do anything to facilitate their children's education and were able financially to seek the services that were needed.

Because of her sincere interest in her children, Mrs. M. appeared to place pressures upon her children but was not aware that she did. She stated that she had a difficult time accepting the fact that her daughter had a learning problem. When she was told that Annette's problem was not her fault, she relaxed and became more accepting of the situation.

Annette attended a nursery school for one-and-a-half years, from age 3½ to 5 years; this experience was followed by one year in kindergarten. She attended the public schools in Chicago until she was in the fourth grade. Because the parents felt that the classes of forty-five pupils in Chicago were too large, they moved to one of the suburbs. Annette's school problems dated from the first grade when she had a "terrible time in reading, spelling, and arithmetic." When Annette was in kindergarten, Mrs. M. noted that she had poor eye-hand coordination. She further stated that the other children in the family had the same kind of problem, but it had not interfered with their learning at later times. Annette repeated the first semester of the second grade because of problems in reading, arithmetic, and spelling. Since that time, she has had many difficulties in school but has not repeated any other grade.

Mrs. M. thought that Annette was taught to read by the sight method with no attention being given to phonics during the first grade. She read and spelled backwards, both words and lines of print, but she had overcome that problem by the time of the diagnosis. She still has trouble with easy words, such as *there;* she continues to confuse the order of letters when she is spelling, and she still has difficulty "hearing phonics." The parents had sought different kinds of help for Annette. When she was in the third grade, an aunt, who was an accredited third-grade teacher, taught her phonics once or twice each week. She attended a summer-school session the year before she came to the Reading Clinic, but the extra work did not seem to help Annette. In addition, Mrs. M. attempted to tutor Annette throughout her entire school career.

Annette becomes angry and frustrated in school when she cannot answer questions, according to the parents. She has attempted to escape into an "I can't" atmosphere quite frequently and has lost confidence in herself. Annette realizes that she has ability but that "she has something in her head that means she will learn differently from other children."

She likes to read interesting books, such as fairy tales and stories about the Pilgrims, but she dislikes reading science books. She is interested in sports and does well in them, especially baseball and kickball. During the last year or two, she has enjoyed playing with younger children, probably because it is difficult for her to compete with children her age.

Report from Referring Agency

Prior to the reading diagnostic examination, Annette had been examined by a number of specialists: psychologists, neurologists, and refractionists. It was the strong belief of both the neurologist and the referring psychologist that the accident Annette experienced when she was a baby was the source of her learning problems.

The report from the psychologist who referred Annette to the Reading Clinic revealed that she was a very bright girl. On the *Wechsler Intelligence Scale for Children*, administered to Annette when she was 10 years 10 months old, Annette earned a Full Scale I.Q. of 125. Her Verbal Scale I.Q. was 130 while her Performance Scale I.Q. was 113. Her lowest scaled scores were in Coding, Object Assembly, and Block Design. The discrepancy of seventeen points between the Verbal and the Performance I.Q.'s was greater than that found in most children and was one indication to the psychologist of the possibility of some brain impairment.

To verify or to negate the foregoing impression, different standardized individual tests were administered, especially those that included visual-performance tasks. Very definite indications of brain impairment were found on these tests. On the *Raven Progressive Matrices* test she scored at only the fifth percentile for all children her age; on this test she showed a marked lack of ability to utilize visual forms in an organized or controlled manner. On the *Graham-Kendall Memory for Designs,* a test of visual form memory, her abilities were at the borderline brain-impaired level. The results of the Articulation Test indicated moderate impairment. She had difficulty with the final *l* and *r* sounds and showed a mild dysarthria due to poor tongue movement.

The psychologist, who was also a speech therapist, summarized his findings as follows: "There is no question of her intelligence (capacity) or her cooperativeness, and on test or observation, of her stability. But she needs some reassurance and specificity for an attack on learning to read, to do arithmetic, to spell, etc. Since her auditory verbal learning is potentially so good, it appears that phonics might be the proper approach.

"There is also no question in my mind of brain injury. She is a girl capable of learning, but because of the brain injury, she is unable to apply herself without very individualized instruction.

"I think she would be a good risk for a specialized program."

Prior to her evaluation by the referring psychologist, Annette had been examined by a neurologist. His brief report indicated that no major disturbances were noted. Some involvement of the left side of the brain was reported, but it was not "brain damage like that found in cerebral palsy." On the EEG some abnormal rhythms were found.

Capacity to Read

Since it is the policy of the Reading Clinic not to repeat tests if they had been given within a year of the time of the reading examination by an authorized examiner, the *Wechsler Intelligence Test for Children,* usually given in the Reading Clinic, was not repeated. The results of this test, administered by the referring psychologist, were used to provide an estimate of the level at which Annette could be expected to read if all other factors for learning were present. Depending upon which I.Q. score was used, it was estimated that Annette should be able to read at the seventh- or eighth-grade levels.

She was also given the *Sequential Tests of Educational Progress,* Listening Test, Form 4A, to estimate her ability to understand material that was read to her. When compared on this test with beginning sixth graders, Annette's rank was slightly below average; she ranked within the percentile band of 23–40. The results tended to be in harmony with the observations made by the referring psychologist that she had "difficulty holding things in mind . . . loses track." The examiner tentatively considered the results to indicate that such problems as lack of careful listening and ability to retain might be among the factors preventing Annette from utilizing her above-average capacities.

Reading Achievement

Annette was given the *Development Reading Tests* for the Intermediate Grades, Form IR-A, to evaluate her general achievement in silent reading. Her scores were as follows:

Area	Grade Equivalent
Basic Vocabulary	4.5
Reading to Retain Information	2.5
Reading to Organize	4.1
Reading to Evaluate—Interpret	3.2
Reading to Appreciate	4.4
Average Comprehension	3.6

As can be noted, Annette's general achievement in vocabulary was equivalent to that of an average student in the middle of fourth grade, and her comprehension was similar to that of the typical student in the middle of the third grade. Because Annette was unable to complete some of the subtests within the time limit, she was permitted to continue each subtest without time limits. Although Annette was able to answer a number of additional questions correctly, she made great and laborious effort to do so. As she neared the end of the test, Annette remarked, "It's getting harder to remember the story," another indication of her problems in retention. At this point, the examiner hypothesized that the difference in her performance on the timed and untimed sections of the test might be due to many factors, one of which might be insufficient word recognition skills.

The *Gray Oral Reading Test*, Form A, was used to appraise Annette's oral reading ability. Her score on this test was at grade level 1.5. Her errors on this test were primarily repetitions of words and phrases and substitutions of one word for another, as *distance* for *dense, earlier* for *eager, preserved* for *previously*, and *opinions* for *opponents*. Annette attempted to work out some unknown words, but her efforts were very ineffective. She commented that she tried to correct herself as soon as she could; these efforts accounted, in large part, for her many repetitions. She was able to recognize quite readily many of the basic sight words, but she was unable to unlock successfully words that she did not recognize. When she substituted one word for another, she said a word that began with the same sound and that was approximately the same length as the printed word. She was aware of her problems and made a conscious effort to improve her reading accuracy as she proceeded with her reading. When asked questions on the passages she had read, she was able to recall some of the significant details, especially on the selections in which word recognition was not a problem.

Since Annette's reading potential was estimated to be at seventh- to eighth-grade level and her reading test scores ranged from first- to fourth-grade levels, Annette was seriously disabled in reading.

Analysis of Reading Difficulties

Since it was determined that Annette was not reading as well as could be expected, she was given several additional tests to pinpoint specific strengths and weaknesses in her reading.

The *Word Discrimination Test,* Form A, by Huelsman [1] was administered to determine how well Annette was able to use such visual characteristics of words as length, internal details, and general shape to discriminate among them. Of the 96 items on the test she had 69 correct, which was equivalent to a 4.2 grade level. She appeared to have difficulty discriminating between the letters *m, n,* and *r.* When the items became difficult for her, she lost her confidence and quit.

In the conference with the parent, Mrs. M. stated that Annette had trouble with little words. Although the evidence gained by the diagnostician from the other tests pointed to the fact that Annette seemed to have a substantial sight vocabulary, she was shown the Dolch 220 *Basic Sight Vocabulary Words* to determine if there were any of these words that troubled her. She had little trouble with these words as she recognized instantly 212 of them. She miscalled five others, which she later corrected.

Parts of the *Boyd Test of Phonic Skills,*[2] a test designed and used in the University of Chicago Reading Clinic, were administered to explore Annette's application of phonic and structural analysis skills to nonsense words. Annette was quite successful in her use of single consonants, consonant blends, and consonant digraphs, except for *th.* She had some difficulty with the vowels controlled by *r* and *l* and with dipthongs. She did not know when to use the short or the long vowel sounds, and she was confused about the *c* and *g* sounds. She was quite inconsistent in her pronunciation of multisyllablic words. The results of this test showed that she had learned the sounds for most letters, and was able to use some of them at times in the identification of words. She also showed some evidence of being able to use syllabication in unlocking multisyllabic words. However, it was evident that Annette needed both instruction and a review of the specific skills in which she was weak, and much practice in applying these skills to new words in a meaningful context.

Because success in phonic skills is dependent upon the ability to discriminate between sounds, and because the *Boyd Test of Phonic Skills* revealed that Annette had some difficulty with phonics, the *Wepman Auditory Discrimination Test,* Form II, in which words with similar sounds have been paired, was administered. Although Annette was quite restless and flighty at the time of this test, she performed quite satis-

[1] Charles B. Huelsman, *Word Discrimination Test* (Oxford, Ohio: Miami University Alumni Association).

[2] Helen M. Robinson and Helen K. Smith, *Clinical Studies in Reading,* III (Chicago: University of Chicago Press, 1968).

factorily. The results confirmed the referring psychologist's view that Annette's potential auditory verbal learning was quite good.

When the results of the foregoing tests were considered together, it was determined that Annette needed instruction in word recognition skills, including the noting of important visual details; instruction in and a review of syllabication; and the application of these skills to new words. In addition, the tests revealed that Annette needed help in comprehension, so that she might progress in her understanding and enjoyment of the materials she reads as she gains skill in learning to unlock words. The diagnostician believed that Annette had reached the stage in reading development in which her basic skills should be further developed and consolidated so that reading could be more functional and more enjoyable than it was at the time of the diagnosis.

Inhibiting Factors

At this stage in the diagnosis the examiner attempted to determine what factors might be present which could inhibit progress in reading. Annette passed the hearing screening test on the *Maico Audiometer* at all frequencies. All visual tests on the Bausch and Lomb *Ortho-Rater* were passed except for far acuity. Since Annette's vision had been checked regularly, it was suggested to the parents that it would be wise for Annette's refractionist to continue his observation of her visual development so that any needs could be met as they arose.

The several specialists who had examined Annette, including the referring psychologist, strongly believed that neurological problems resulting from the early accident interfered with her academic progress. Her performance on visual performance tests, her behavioral characteristics, and the results of professional examinations gave considerable evidence of brain impairment as an interfering factor. However, Annette's reading levels were more advanced than those of other pupils in the clinic who had been diagnosed by specialists as brain-impaired. Though not a disturbed child, it was apparent that she felt pressures and that she had little confidence in her own abilities. Mrs. M. was at times so tense herself about Annette's reading problem that she attempted to tutor Annette even though she was untrained in the teaching of reading. This anxiety might be reflected in Annette's reading disability.

During the reading diagnosis, Annette was very cooperative. She grew more restless as the testing continued and became somewhat noisy, quite distractable, and flighty. She was aware of her flightiness and said, "I don't know why I am so silly today." At times she made irrelevant statements as "I hate big kids" and "I love to read—not books."

The diagnostician tentatively concluded that a number of factors might be inhibiting Annette's progress in reading. However, she was quick to point out that in spite of these interfering factors and her slow rate in learning to read, she had come a long way and should be praised for the gains she had made. Because Annette had made progress in reading, because she could attend to tasks when she was being tested, and because she cooperated with the examiner very well, it appeared that Annette could profit from remedial instruction in reading from someone trained in remedial techniques.

It was recommended that Annette's reading instruction should begin with instruction and review in word attack, especially in the skills in which gaps were found, and in comprehension of both oral and silent reading; in the application of reading skills to meaningful context; and in reading for enjoyment. For the latter, it was suggested that books with a vocabulary load on the second- or low third-grade level with a higher interest level would be appropriate for Annette.

Evaluation of Annette's reading progress should be made periodically, and changes in the emphasis in instruction should be in harmony with her needs.

Remedial Program

ANNETTE BEGAN REMEDIAL READING INSTRUCTION in the Reading Clinic immediately after the diagnostic reading examination. She came to the clinic for four years with the exception of two summer sessions. During the school year she came to the Reading Clinic three times a week for fifty-minute periods; in the summer she reported for instruction five days a week for instructional periods of the same length. With the exception of two summer sessions, Annette was taught by the same clinician, Mrs. Lowe, who is the person principally responsible for Annette's later progress in reading and for much of her development as a person.

The First Year

Areas of Remediation. Initially, instruction was based upon the findings of the reading diagnostic examination. However, diagnosis was a continuous process, and as Mrs. Lowe worked with Annette, changes were made in instruction to meet her changing needs. At first, gaps in her word recognition skills were recognized and provided for; ample review of other word recognition skills was included throughout the first year of instruction and as needed at later times.

Annette required many ways to study word recognition principles before she was secure in the application of them. For example, she was confused about the generalizations for the sounds of *c* and *g* and their application. When Mrs. Lowe wrote on the board words including the sounds being taught, Annette had little trouble forming the generalizations but needed many opportunities to apply the generalization in meaningful situations. Pictures illustrating the *c* and *g* sounds were used to reinforce the principles Annette was learning. Care was taken that the pictures were not confusing for her because of too many things to see and to do at once. The generalization was typed and kept before her if she needed to refer to it.

Working with her, Mrs. Lowe learned that she was much more facile in hearing sounds at the beginning of words than at the ends of words, had much difficulty in taking a sound out of a word, and needed much practice in applying the generalizations to unknown words. Mrs. Lowe prepared special paragraphs in which she incorporated examples of the generalizations being studied. It was explained to Annette that constant review and application would help her retain what she learned. Each rule or generalization was also typed on a sheet of paper so that she could refer to it in school. As she made progress in word recognition, she evaluated her own performance by saying, "I'm getting better at this all the time."

At the same time that Annette was studying word recognition skills, she was working for fluency in her oral reading. Since she had difficulty hearing the endings of words, she dropped the last parts of some words as she read; she skipped lines until she was given a marker to use; she read slowly but attempted to be expressive. Except when the clinician wished to evaluate her oral reading, Annette was given the opportunity to read silently before she read orally. All stimuli except the sentence Annette was reading were covered by a file card; with this plan she found it easier to follow the print. Much of her oral reading was done with plays. Like the real actresses she knew about, she practiced her oral reading. When it was sufficiently good, she and Mrs. Lowe prepared tape recordings with sound effects, which were later played at her home or school.

When Annette told Mrs. Lowe she could not find one of her spelling words in the dictionary, she was given immediate help in using the dictionary. She insisted that she did not like the dictionary because it made her "dizzy to go back and forth in it."

Many ways were provided so that Annette could apply skills she was learning. Her comprehension in silent reading was checked. She learned how to distinguish important details from irrelevant ones, how to determine the central thought, and how to follow a sequence of events. Although she sometimes read materials and answered questions from published materials, she often told the clinician she much preferred the "home-made" exercises prepared by Mrs. Lowe.

Since one of the goals of remedial reading instruction is to help the student become an independent reader, efforts were made early in the instructional period to help Annette develop independence. Mrs. Lowe was careful at all times to let her know the purpose of each part of the lesson and the structure of each clinic session. When she began new tasks, Mrs. Lowe helped her with several examples before she was permitted to work on her own. Structure was an absolute necessity for Annette; yet, probably because she was bright, she became bored with the same structures if used more than once or twice. A schedule of the activities to be accomplished during the period helped to keep Annette's attention on the work at hand.

Behavioral Traits. Throughout the year Mrs. Lowe found that Annette's behavior was quite erratic. At times she went straight to work when she came to the clinic. At other times she was highly distractable—every sound would set her on new tangents. She was noisy at times, but she was not an uncontrollable child. She wished to cooperate and to learn; at the same time, she had little ability to remember things from one day to the next. Before she began a task at hand, she was certain in her own mind that she could not accomplish it. She was usually so friendly and chatty that it was difficult to stop her from visiting. As might be expected, her attention span fluctuated. On some days it was so short that learning was minimal; on other days she was able to attend to and complete tasks within the tutoring period. From the first, she realized some of her problems and might say at the end of instruction, "I don't know why I acted the way I did today."

Evaluation. Evaluation of Annette's status in reading was made each time she came to the clinic. In addition, at several times throughout the year both formal and informal methods were used to assess Annette's progress and to determine changes in her reading needs.

For example, at the end of her first summer session in the clinic both the *Gray Oral Reading Test,* Form D, and the *Developmental Reading Tests,* Form IR-B, were administered. On the oral test she showed a gain of one year, with accompanying improvement in comprehension. Comprehension gains were significant on the silent reading test, but there were no measurable gains in vocabulary. However, the clinician observed that Annette had shown improvement in her regular day-to-day performance in attacking new words, recognizing old ones, and comprehending materials she read. Her silent reading showed slight improvement also when the Form IR-B, of the *Developmental Reading Tests* was administered.

At the end of the first year Annette took the *Diagnostic Reading Test,* Pupil Progress Series, Elementary Form A,[3] to gain another estimate of her reading. The results were as follows:

Area of Reading	*Grade Equivalent*
Rate of Reading for Meaning	3.2
Reading Comprehension	4.9

An examination of the subtest scores revealed that Annette was able to recall information, could locate information well but slowly, and could read for descriptions. She continued to have difficulty determining the main ideas and following directions. She was able to follow simple direction with a limited number of tasks but became confused as the directions became more complicated. She appeared to be relaxed during the test except for the section on following directions, which disturbed her greatly.

Although Annette had made progress, continued work in the Reading Clinic was recommended because of the many deficiences in reading that still remained. She was about to enter the seventh grade.

The Second Year

Areas of Instruction. During the second year that Annette attended the

---

[3] Oliver F. Anderbalter, R. Stephen Gawkoski, and Ruth Colestock, *Diagnostic Reading,* Pupil Progress Series (Chicago: Scholastic Testing Services, Inc.).

clinic, emphasis was placed upon the development of comprehension abilities. She worked upon sentence comprehension, particularly key words, descriptive words, and connecting words which, when understood, increase the understanding of sentences. She learned to use her understanding of key words in sentences to compose phrases for outlines. She learned to place the main ideas and details of a selection into an outline and to identify paragraphs with implied main ideas and to write such main ideas in her own words.

Instruction also included the application of the word attack skills which Annette had learned or reviewed. The visual details of the beginning and ends of words were stressed; roots and affixes were noted. Annette was generally more confident about word attack skills than she had been formerly.

As Mrs. Lowe worked with Annette, she realized that her vocabulary was quite limited. She already knew that words had many different meanings and that words are often quite specific and should be used properly. She had looked up the meaning of words in the dictionary and had seen how analyzing words into parts had improved her word attack skills. She also knew how analyzing sentences into parts had increased her comprehension. At this time she needed to learn how understanding parts of words could help in the understanding of the entire word and how the meanings of idioms and figurative language must be understood to comprehend the materials to the fullest extent.

Using her experiences at camp from the previous summer, Annette wrote a play about her first day there. She and Mrs. Lowe discussed the ways to make her play "hang together," such as a character's anticipating what would come next or a narrator's stating what would be the next event. After she finished her play, each day she selected three words for which to find substitutes. At this time the thesaurus was introduced. She spent several days rewriting the play and selecting more appropriate words for the ones she had originally used. After she had rehearsed her play, she and her teacher recorded it. The recording, like earlier ones, was played for her parents and for her gym teacher whom she liked very much.

Annette prepared a list of words for social studies on file cards. She worked on the parts of words and attempted to detect base words. She practiced reducing answers to essential words and phrases, wrote stories in which she used sensory words and learned when they were appropriately used, and wrote a brief description of the weather for three out of four days in which she used as many sensory words as possible. She learned how descriptions could be dull and boring without sensory words.

At this time in the instructional program the basic reading skills being learned in the Reading Clinic were related to Annette's work in school. For example, sentence structure in reading was related to sentence structure in grammar and writing. She had experiences with map reading and the vocabulary of maps. Annette learned how to read mathematics problems (both words and symbols), how to understand graphic examples, and how to read for the basic main ideas and details in mathematics. She also learned to use the devices of the author to facilitate understanding, such as headings, review pages, dark print.

Behavioral Traits. Annette's use of what she had learned was at times frustrated by the overwhelming amount of materials presented in her school classes, or the varied ability of teachers to differentiate instruction for her. In some classes too much had been expected and in others, too little. For example, in English Annette was capable of much better writing than that which had sometimes been accepted. When asked why she did not write as well as she could, she stated that she was not required to check her compositions. Being an intelligent child, Annette knew when she was not sufficiently challenged. Sometimes confusion for Annette resulted and was reflected in her instructional periods in the clinic.

She had improved in her ability to make herself clear when she asked questions of Mrs. Lowe. When the clinician introduced new ideas, she did not lose confidence and panic as quickly as she had in the past. Early in her instruction she became quite upset if Mrs. Lowe was uncertain about anything, for she expected her to know everything. During her second year in the clinic, Annette gradually was able to accept that Mrs. Lowe did not know all of the answers and that they could seek the answers together. She slowly learned that uncertainties did not have to mean utter chaos.

Annette still needed encouragement to control her feelings of doubt or meaninglessness when solving problems or answering questions. She continued a tendency to cling to a way of doing things that was inappropriate to the matter at hand, or to choose a mechanical solution because it was more easily understood. She often missed the significant as opposed to the unimportant details.

Mrs. Lowe gradually added new stimuli to the teaching situation, such as more colorful clothes, more materials, a ticking timer, which Annette usually could ignore. She had bad days at times, when every visual and auditory stimulus, including her own thoughts, intruded. Medication was begun this year and after its start, Annette became noticeably calmer and more controlled. This year she was less rigid and negative and would do things she was not wildly excited about if she understood their purpose.

Evaluation. On the Advanced Form A of the *Diagnostic Reading Test,* Pupil Progress Series, given in May, Annette attained a grade level score of 5.7 in Rate of Reading for Meaning and 7.1 in Reading Comprehension. At this time she was able to complete three of the six sections of the test within the time limits. When she was allowed to complete the other three sections, her accuracy was unusually high. Her gains on the subtest of Reading for Directions, the section which a year ago disturbed Annette so much, were particularly significant. From both observation and test results Annette's progress in reading was evident.

Annette was not ready to be dismissed from the clinic because her reading skills were not adequate for the demands of her seventh-grade school work. She wished to continue, and her parents were eager for her to continue in her instruction. Though progress at times seemed very slow, Mr. and Mrs. M. had been prepared for this fact. They saw changes in Annette and appreciated the support Mrs. Lowe had given Annette.

The Third Year

Areas of Instruction. At the beginning of the third year in the Reading Clinic, Annette was in eighth grade. She and Mrs. Lowe discussed the areas of reading and decided work in all four areas was still needed: word recognition, vocabulary, comprehension, and rate. Annette worked to consolidate these skills and to apply them to school assignments. She read easy materials to develop fluency and learn to skim. She was given instruction in skimming lists and tables, skimming for a single word in a sentence, skimming for several words in a sentence, identifying the key words in a question for which to skim in an accompanying story, skimming for words with similar meanings to those in a question, skimming to locate information, and skimming to get the general idea. All materials used for skimming were well within her word recognition and word meaning abilities.

One of the state requirements for students in the upper grades in Illinois is the passing of tests on the state and national constitutions. Because Annette was fearful of the foregoing task, Mrs. Lowe incorporated work on both constitutions in the reading instructional periods. Annette learned to outline the materials she read, answered study questions given to her by her classroom teacher, and set purposes for reading. A structured plan was given to Annette for her study work: she listed the big points (categorizing) and then arranged the small details under each large idea. Because she continued to have difficulty in reading the materials about the constitutions assigned to the class, her classroom teacher lent her a book that contained a simplified description of the writing of the Constitution and of the principal ideas of the Constitution itself. For the reading in this book she selected important ideas, formulated her own questions on the content, outlined ideas, selected key words, and took tests on the constitutions devised by Mrs. Lowe. She was successful when she took the test but realized that she could not have passed the test if Mrs. Lowe had not given her instruction on reading the materials. The foregoing is an example of one of the many meaningful ways in which Annette was able to apply the reading skills she had learned.

Behavioral Traits. Annette's attitude towards reading and her work habits improved considerably this year. She was quite comfortable with Mrs. Lowe and talked freely and confidentially to her. One time she said, "We haven't gotten mad at each other once during these three years."

Though she was still distractable at times, she was showing signs of maturing. For example, she made a schedule on her own for the homework she needed to do one night. This led to other kinds of schedules which she prepared and followed. She also prepared tests for herself on material she was reading for her classwork. She recognized that she was able to skim while others in her class could not, and she was proud of her achievement.

Evaluation. At the end of the year Annette was given Advanced Form B of the *Diagnostic Reading Test*, Pupil Progress Series. Her grade equivalent score for rate of reading was 7.2 as compared with 5.7 on Form A administered a year before. Her comprehension score was higher, too, with an 8.4 as compared with 7.1. One of the subtests was devoted to vocabulary; here again Annette showed considerable improvement. It appeared that the area of Annette's greatest growth, aside from rate, was in vocabulary. Annette's rate, vocabulary, and comprehension scores were more equalized than they had been before.

Annette would enter high school (ninth grade) in the fall. There were still recognizable gaps in her reading development, ones which were not assessed on standardized tests. She needed help especially in inferential reading. She needed to understand idioms, figurative language, and specialized vocabularies better than she did. In addition, some attention should be given to the development of flexibility of rate and specific study skills.

The Fourth Year

Areas of Remedial Instruction. The emphasis in instruction during Annette's final year in the Reading Clinic was placed upon the application of reading skills to her school work, this work including summarizing, note taking, outlining, science reading, history reading, and inferential reading. She was encouraged to use the SQ3R method of studying,[4] library facilities, and materials. Introductory work in rate of reading was begun to help Annette become conscious of developing flexibility in rate according to the purpose for reading and the difficulty of the material.

She found research techniques to be extremely difficult. As in the past, she worked better within a structured plan. This time the structure was more complicated than ones used previously. The following sequential steps were used for the reading for the research report: to understand the question asked, to recall what she knew about the subject already, to find out what resources were available on the topics, to locate and evaluate these resources, to read, and to take notes. She later organized her notes laboriously, and finally prepared her report.

Annette read longer selections than she had previously and worked for deeper meanings. Some of the ideas in the selections had many ramifications, some too obscure for Annette at this time. Work was continued on relationships, organization, writing as well as reading, and incidental spelling. Spelling had been troublesome to Annette from the beginning. She was early taught to proofread especially because of her reading problem, because of the irregularities of the English language, and because of her carelessness. This Annette had not liked and often forgot to do. By this time in her development she had become a little more independent in correcting her own spelling than she was previously.

Behavioral Traits. Annette matured a great deal this year. She was developing sensitivity about herself and others and was taking more and more responsibility for herself. She was an active girl, enthusiastic about sports in which she excelled. It was believed that if she could be as active

---

[4] Francis P. Robinson, *Effective Reading* (New York: Harper and Row, 1962).

in her pursuit of learning in school as she is otherwise, she would make gains academically as well as socially. It was evident that she accomplished more when she was challenged than when she was allowed to coast along or given tasks that were too repetitious or easy. Some of her learning problems were still present, but Annette wished people to expect more of her than they did. Mrs. Lowe felt that, in this respect, all should accede to her wishes.

Evaluation. Standardized tests were administered to Annette to obtain an objective evaluation of her reading. She was given the *California Reading Test,* Junior High Level, Form W, Reading Comprehension section only, because it included skills that were similar to those which had been taught. Her grade score on this section was 8.4. Her subtest scores varied greatly; her excellent performance in following directions and reference skills tended to offset the difficulties she had with interpretive reading.

She was also given Form 2A of the *Cooperative Reading Comprehension* test. The percentile band ranks for Annette were as follows: Vocabulary, 28–9; Level of Comprehension, 6–29; and Speed of Comprehension, 1–15. The results of the tests seemed to indicate some gains, but again continuing needs in reading. She had made good progress in study skills as well as in vocabulary; she gained somewhat in rate, but her progress was uneven. Her awareness of a variety of rates was much greater, however. Both Annette and her teacher agreed that she probably should have been pushed harder on interpretive reading skills. However, a conscious choice was made to relate her reading lessons as closely as possible to her school assignments, most of which did not require interpretive or critical reading abilities.

At this time (end of ninth grade) Annette wished to be on her own, and all concerned agreed that she should be able to pursue this independence. She was permitted to drop her special reading tutoring with the understanding that Mrs. Lowe would be available for help if it seemed advisable. The following recommendations were made:

1. Annette should be responsible for her own school assignments without home pressures or assistance unless she requested it. Annette wanted to see what she could do by herself. From her discussions with Mrs. Lowe it was felt that she would try to be honest with herself if she were in trouble.

2. Mrs. Lowe would consult her teachers in the fall to discuss what

Annette's teachers might do to give her the help she needed in school. It was thought that her English teacher might be able to provide lessons in the kinds of comprehension she needed.

Leisure Reading

One of the goals of remedial instruction in reading is to gain enjoyment from reading. Annette understandably at first did not really enjoy reading. After her reading skills became better developed, she would read easy books if she understood the purpose of such reading. Riddles and puns were used at first, but Annette felt that the latter were not funny at all; she called them "sick humor." For awhile, she enjoyed the books of Louisa May Alcott and other similar ones.

Later Mrs. Lowe made a special effort to provide beautiful books for Annette's pleasure reading—those with especially fine literary value and artistic qualities. The time toward the end of the instructional period was set aside for special things, like these lovely books or poems or activities which Annette liked best to do. She responded very well to these experiences which, it was hoped, would increase her interest in reading. The looking at and reading from these particular books relieved Annette from the pressures she sometimes felt from the study-type reading during the instructional period.

Although Annette found more enjoyment in reading at the end of the instruction than she did at the beginning, Mrs. Lowe was not certain that she really sought reading for her own enjoyment. She simply liked to do other things better. She still did not do enough reading and therefore did not get enough practice in reading easy materials. Since she tended to resist reading even more when everyone wanted her to read for enjoyment, it was decided not to press her in these matters. Rather, it was more fruitful if interesting books were suggested to her. Though her skills had improved a great deal, true enjoyment of reading was lacking.

Communication between Clinician and Classroom Teachers

From the first, it was often necessary for Mrs. Lowe to meet with Annette's classroom teachers. Some did not understand her problem or what the clinic was attempting to do, Mrs. Lowe was consulted by the school in regard to placement in classes within the school and selection of subjects when Annette entered high school. One of the difficulties Annette experienced in school was the pressure of trying to compete with others when the schools she attended ranked above the national norms. Through the combined judgments of teachers, clinician, parents, and Annette schedules were made and revised.

Mrs. Lowe helped Annette's classroom teachers by listing the special kinds of difficulties Annette had exhibited in the clinic. The following were among the problems listed:

1. Some difficulty in the handling of visual materials. This problem seems to be reflected in her reading and spelling.

2. A slight speech problem, which had disappeared as she matured. While the articulation problems were resolved for the most part, Annette still has some difficulty expressing herself orally in a specific and organized way. This situation may reflect her lack of confidence, rather than a speech problem.

3. Some trouble in sequencing and organization and a tendency to focus on parts rather than the whole. The foregoing seemed to influence her ability to organize her work for recall and select important from unimportant details. She needs to understand and be reminded of the relationships in everything she does.

4. A tendency to be distracted by various stimuli around her. This has improved with maturity, but she may have days when she is unable to focus attention as she should.

5. Uncertainties about her abilities to control her environment. In the early days Annette was upset by changes in routine or by new ideas and developments. At the same time, she was easily bored by dull repetition and welcomed the chance to learn the same material with a different approach. The foregoing reflected Annette's intelligence and imagination as well as her need for security.

6. Annette sometimes forgets what she hears as well as what she reads. She needs to feel that she can ask questions to clarify an assignment or an idea. She needs to have the purpose for what she does clearly in mind.

Through her work with Annette, Mrs. Lowe was able to determine procedures which were useful in Annette's instruction. These were shared with Annette's teachers from time to time:

1. When Annette was particularly talkative, it helped to give her an assignment; make clear the limitations of time, space, and task; and leave the room. This removed the clinician as a source of stimulation.

2. Preparing Annette beforehand for a task at school or in the clinic

was a great help. Keeping a schedule on the board was also helpful to her.

3. Annette was encouraged to jot down an unrelated thought or question rather than interrupting the lesson for it. This practice exercised some control over the consequences of her distractability.

4. When Annette did not understand a direction or an explanation, she rewrote it. This increased her understanding and provided a way to give her greater confidence in her ability to control her environment. This procedure was another way of helping her to learn how to solve her problems rather than giving up in despair.

5. It is important to expect enough from Annette, but it is equally important to recognize that she may have problems doing the work expected. She realizes when a teacher makes things too easy for her and when a teacher is not really interested. She knows quite a bit about her situation and the reasons for it. She will cooperate with her teachers, but she may need some help to prevent her learning problems from becoming a crutch.

6. Annette should be encouraged to be independent, but her errors should be discussed with her and corrected so that she will not continue to repeat them.

7. Because she has read slowly, Annette does not readily pick up a book to read, even an easy one. She needs encouragement to do so. She is reading more fluently now and cannot improve her reading without reading. All should help her, but not force her, to gain interest in reading.

8. It is important for all teachers, including those in the Reading Clinic, to work together so that Annette will have a systematic and consistent approach to the work, and the efforts of her teachers will reinforce each other.

Evaluation by Specialists in Other Disciplines

From time to time, contacts were made with other specialists who worked with Annette. Though she continued to show some signs of impairment, all specialists felt that she should continue to be in a regular classroom and be treated as a normal child who had special problems. As Annette matured, her problems decreased; in addition, she developed better control over them. The referring psychologist wrote in his report of his re-evaluation of Annette: "I think that the last four years have been good ones for her intellectually, and she should be treated as a relatively normal child with a need for special instruction."

Follow-Up

ANNETTE HAS COMPLETED her sophomore year in high school. She apparently has enjoyed being on her own. She contacted Mrs. Lowe several times mostly to chat. In the early part of the year she had difficulty interpreting poetry and asked Mrs. Lowe to help her. Two lessons were sufficient to clarify the assignments. Both her maturity and her understanding of herself appeared to increase. Her final grades were still not in harmony with her ability, but they were satisfactory. She continued to need to know the purpose of her reading and to have structure within which to work. In the areas that interested her the most, she continued to be willing to go beyond the surface. At this time she has tentatively decided to be a physical education teacher. Since she has skills in this area, she would probably do well if her academic status continues to improve.

To Mrs. Lowe and others in the Reading Clinic, Annette was both a joy and a challenge. Her progress will continue to be observed, largely because of the sincere interest all in the clinic had in Annette.

Editor's Comments

For each poor reader who, like Annette, incurs some brain injury from a fall, there are many whose parents feel guilty because they think their child suffered permanent neurological damage due to their negligence, despite medical assurance that there is no evidence of such damage. In spite of her neurological problem, Annette had a reading disability much less severe than most of the children described in this book.

Annette also demonstrates that developmental changes take place in a reading disability as a child grows older. The tendency to read and spell backwards, which the mother described as very marked in the first grade, had cleared up by the time of the diagnostic study at age 11.

Although Annette's word recognition difficulties had been mainly overcome in the first year of remedial work, it took three more years before her comprehension skills, her self-confidence, and her emotional stability had developed to the point where she felt that she could keep going in a suburban secondary school on her own. The description of the upper-level reading skills stressed in the second, third, and fourth years is well worth careful reading.

Remedial teachers are sometimes not too successful in establishing helpful relationships with a child's teachers in school. Mrs. Lowe's approach to this problem had three main elements: 1) she described Annette's special difficulties, as they were apparent in the clinic; 2) she described some of the procedures she had found to be useful in her work with Annette; and 3) she did not try to tell the teacher how to handle Annette in the classroom. Such an approach is much less likely to arouse antagonism and resistance than a more authoritative type of presentation.

12

Mary Lynn

By DOROTHY KENDALL BRACKEN AND
JIMMYE DOBBS HAYS

Setting

The Reading Clinic at Southern Methodist University in Dallas, Texas, provides diagnostic and remedial services, reading improvement programs for normal or mildly retarded readers at elementary, secondary, college, and adult levels, and teacher training services.

An individual diagnosis includes testing of reading capacity, vision, and directional attack (using an eye-movement camera), as well as detailed diagnostic testing of specific reading skills and interview and case-history data. The remedial service provides individualized instruction based on the diagnostic findings. During the spring and fall semesters the tutoring schedule is three fifty-minute sessions, or two eighty-minute sessions, per week. In the summer term students attend two hours a day, five days a week, for five weeks.

Diagnostic Study

MARY LYNN WAS BROUGHT to the Reading Clinic for diagnosis in February, 1967, when she was 8.9 years old and in third grade. The parents made the initial contact because they were concerned about her progress in school. At the close of the school year she was retained in third grade. She had one month of remedial instruction in the summer of 1967, attended for two semesters in 1967–1968, and terminated at the end of May, 1968.

Physical Information

Mary Lynn was a tall, thin girl. She had short, straight, brown hair and wore glasses. She was subject to colds and attacks of asthmatic bronchitis. Her difficult breathing, running nose, and watering eyes were a hindrance in her work at school and in the clinic. This was called to the attention of the parents by the clinician in early February, 1968. As a result, her pediatrician referred her to an allergist and her health and work improved.

Emotional Characteristics

Mary Lynn came to the Reading Clinic with a fearful attitude toward reading and school work in general. The demands placed upon her in her third-grade classroom had been too great, and she had experienced daily failure in academic activities. Her anxiety was demonstrated in many ways. She hid her school work from her parents and was embarrassed by her grades; she was unable to concentrate on her work to the extent that, when she entered the clinic, it was all that she could do to listen to a simple story, such as *Go Dog Go* (Beginner Books). When working with the clinician, she frequently attempted to direct the conversation away from reading-related activities.

Mary Lynn was a sensitive and affectionate child. She related well to adults and sought adult approval and attention. She had difficulty in relating to children. Other children often teased and bullied her, and when this happened she withdrew or sought adult protection.

Family Background

Mary Lynn's parents were high school graduates who did not attend college. Both of her parents were concerned about her poor progress in school and were probably responsible, in part, for some of the anxiety that Mary Lynn felt in school and in reading situations. This was evidenced by the importance they had placed upon grades and by their statement that Mary Lynn's room was filled with books, none of which she could read. Her father was a sales representative for a manufacturing company; her mother was a housewife. She was an only child.

Interests

Much of Mary Lynn's conversation was about animals and she usually chose books about animals. The family had a dog and she was responsible for feeding him.

After school and on weekends Mary Lynn played with her friends, with her toys, or watched television. She seemed to enjoy being outdoors. Her favorite toys were her Barbie Dolls.

Vision, Hearing, and Speech

Mary Lynn spoke with clear diction and had a good speaking vocabulary. She conversed well on many topics and enjoyed conversing with persons of all ages.

Her glasses were fitted just before the diagnosis in February, 1967, at which time the *Keystone Visual Survey Test* was administered on the telebinocular. Her glasses were made with a correction for astigmatism. With glasses she scored 5 percent usable vision for her left eye at near point on the *Keystone Visual Survey Test*. Her reading clinician recommended that Mary Lynn's vision be re-examined. As a result, her glasses were corrected.

The *Wepman Auditory Discrimination Test* was given to Mary Lynn. Since only two items were missed, one of likenesses and one of differences, there seemed little question of her ability in auditory discrimination. Also, Mary Lynn made a perfect score on the Auditory Blending section of the *Gates-McKillop Reading Diagnostic Tests* and did well on the listening potential test of the *Spache Diagnostic Reading Scales*. Her auditory discrimination abilities were satisfactory.

Eye-Movement Photograph

An eye-movement photograph was made February 6, 1967, using the *Reading Eye*.[1] According to the eye-movement evaluation, she scored below grade 1 on all of the reading performance profile ratings. Her directional attack was poor, showing 34 percent regressions. Her average span of recognition was .37 words and her average duration of fixation was .39 seconds. She had unusually prolonged durations. The photograph revealed tremors, slight head movement, and some vocalization. Her comprehension on a first grade card was 90 percent.

Leavell Hand-Eye Coordinator Tests [2]

The score on this test was borderline. The subject was in a hyperactive state when the test was administered and the clinician concluded, after informal observation, that no problem was indicated in this area, es-

---

[1] *The Reading Eye,* Educational Developmental Laboratories (New York: Huntington).

[2] Ullin W. Leavell, *Hand-Eye Coordinator Tests* (Meadville, Pennsylvania: Keystone View Co., 1961).

pecially since the significance of preference and dominance, its measurement, and its relation to the reading act is questionable.

Leavell Hand-Eye Coordinator Tests

Hand-Foot Preference (5)	R 4
Eye-Ear Preference (5)	R 3
Hand Dexterity Performance (5)	R 5
Pointed Objects (10)	L-R 6
Incomplete Objects (5)	L-R 3
Moving Objects (10)	L-R 9
Total	32

Intelligence

The *Wechsler Intelligence Scale for Children* was administered to Mary Lynn when her chronological age was 8.9. She scored a Verbal I.Q. of 108, a Performance I.Q. of 99, and a Full Scale I.Q. of 104. An analysis of her subtest scores follows:

Good g meas.		*Poor g meas.*		*Verbal Comprehension*	
Vocab.	12	Dig. Span	9	Vocab.	12
Infor.	15	Coding	13	Infor.	15
Arith.	8	Ob. Assembly	8	Comp.	11
Comp.	11	Mazes	—	Simil.	13
Simil.	13	Pic. Comp.	10		
Pic. Arr.	9				
Bl. Des.	10				
Total	78/7	Total	40/4	Total	51/4
	11		10		13

Perceptual Organization		*Freedom from Distractability*	
Bl. Design	10	Digit Span	9
Obj. Assmb.	8	Arithmetic	8
Total	18/2	Total	17/2
	9		9

Mary Lynn seemed to be strong in areas that showed perceptiveness to her environment, common sense, good memory function, and abstract thinking. She was weak in attention span, power of concentration, quantitative abilities, and persistence at a task. Since her global scores were fairly close together, probably there was no psychologically significant emotional problem; however, there was evidence of anxiety.

Reading Tests

Mary Lynn was administered the *Gates Advanced Primary Reading Tests* (Form 1) on February 7, 1967. In December, 1967, she was given Form 2 of the same test. By this time she had been retained in the third grade. The results are compared as follows:

Gates Advanced Primary

Form 1		Form 2	
(Date of original diagnosis: 2/7/67)		(Date of re-testing after 5 mos. remedial help: 12/8/67)	
C. A. = 8.9, Grade 3		C. A. = 9.6, Grade 3 (repeating)	
Word Recognition		*Word Recognition*	
Reading Grade	2.86	Reading Grade	4.2
Reading Age	8.1	Reading Age	9.4
Paragraph Reading		*Paragraph Reading*	
Reading Grade	3.1	Reading Grade	4.1
Reading Age	8.3	Reading Age	9.3

Mary Lynn was enrolled in the Reading Clinic program for ten months. Since she was retained in third grade, her reading ability, after ten months of instruction in the Reading Clinic, was probably equal to that of most other pupils in her grade.

At the time of the original diagnosis Mary Lynn was also given Form 1 of the *Gates-McKillop Reading Diagnostic Test*. Mary Lynn's frustration level of oral reading was shown to be at the third grade, third month. Although she was below grade level on flash word presentation, she appeared above grade level on flash phrase presentation. Her knowledge of letter and vowel sounds and her auditory discrimination revealed normal progress.

Gates-McKillop Reading Diagnostic Test

Form 1	
(Date of testing 2/7/67) C. A. = 8.9, Grade	3.5
Oral Reading	3.3
Words: Flash Presentation	3.4
Phrases: Flash Presentation	4.2
Letter sounds	22/26 NP
Vowels	8/10 NP
Auditory blending	15/15 NP

Mary Lynn was given the *Spache Diagnostic Reading Scales*. Her instructional reading level, as measured by her oral reading, was shown to be third-grade level. Her independent reading level, as measured by Spache's test, measured fourth-grade. However, Spache determines this level differently than many other reading specialists. Most authorities would say that Mary Lynn's independent reading level was at second grade. Mary Lynn's potential reading level, as measured by her listening comprehension, showed that she should have been able to read at a sixth-grade reading comprehension level, if her reading skills were as advanced as were her listening comprehension skills.

Although Mary Lynn read laboriously and hesitatingly, her comprehension was excellent. From her responses to the *Spache* test, it was noted that she relied on context and configuration as clues for decoding. While it was evident that she read faster while reading silently, head and lip movements were very apparent. Additional observations were: Mary Lynn always left the book flat on the desk where it was placed, never moving it or holding it; she often read the difficult words correctly, but missed words of four letters or less; and she lost her place several times while reading orally, at times skipping entire lines of print.

Spache Diagnostic Reading Scales
(Date of Testing 3/7/68) C. A. = 9.6

Instructional Level	—3rd
Independent Level	—4th
Potential Level	—6th

Additional Information as Secured by an Analysis of Student's Responses on Reading Tests:

Gates-McKillop Reading Diagnostic Test—Form I

I. *Oral Reading*

Omissions	3	Wrong order	0
Additions	1	Wrong beginnings	1
Repetitions	4	Wrong middles	2
Mispronunciations	3	Wrong endings	1
Full reversals	0	Wrong several parts	0
Reversal of parts	0		

Errors Made on Oral Reading:
to added (So he ran *to* the rat into his hole)
pick for *peek*

Errors Made on Oral Reading:

    small for *smile*

    The for *He*

    And for *Then*

    a for *the*

    the for *this*

    Talk, stuck, and *dull* were not attempted

It appears that Mary Lynn added *to* in the above mentioned sentence because she was reading partly contextually and was thinking faster than she was reading. Her errors of saying *pick* for *peek* and *small* for *smile* show that she was using the initial consonants and initial consonant blends and then guessing the rest of the word from contextual or configuration clues. She did not apply the double *e* sound in *peek* or the final silent *e* rule in *smile*. Calling *the* for *he, and* for *then, a* for *the,* and *the* for *this* might mean that she did not read carefully enough, or that perhaps she was concentrating so hard on the more difficult words that she gave little thought to the easier words. However, she could have been depending upon configuration to a great extent and, since these words look so similar, was unable to detect the differences between these words in print.

    IV. *Phrases: Flash Presentation*

Errors Made:

    slide for *sled*

    read first for *ride fast*

    step for *ship*

    bright for *bring*

As in her oral reading, Mary Lynn correctly pronounced the initial consonant or the initial consonant blend but seemed to depend chiefly on configuration clues for the rest of the word. Again, she did not apply the final silent *e* rule. Nor did she correctly pronounce the short sounds of the vowels *i* and *e*.

    V. *Knowledge of Word Parts: Word Attack*

    V-1. *Recognizing and Blending Common Word Parts.*

This test shows that Mary Lynn knew all of the initial consonant blends tested and usually correctly pronounced the final consonant sound or blend. Her knowledge of short vowel sounds appeared to be very weak. Again, she did not apply the vowel-consonant-final *e* rule. Half of the time when asked, Mary Lynn correctly identified the word after it had been broken into pronounceable patterns for her.

V-2. *Giving Letter Sounds:*
Errors:

uh for *o*   *uh* for *a*
didn't know *x*   short *i* for *e*

Mary Lynn did not know the sounds of the vowels *a*, *o*, and *e*. Also, she did not know the sound of *x*.

VI. *Recognizing the Visual Forms of Sounds:*
VI-4. *Vowels:*

said *a* for short *e*
said *e* for short *i*

As indicated on all of the preceding subtests of the *Gates-McKillop*, Mary Lynn did not know the short vowel sounds of *e* and *i*.

VII. *Auditory Blending:*

Since Mary Lynn made a perfect score on this subtest and an almost perfect score on the *Wepman Auditory Discrimination Test*, it appears that she had good auditory discrimination abilities.

Spache Diagnostic Reading Scales:
Oral Reading:

Omissions	13	Wrong Order	1
Additions	4	Wrong Beginnings	17
Repetitions	1	Wrong Middles	5
Mispronunciations	15	Wrong Endings	7
Full Reversals	0	Wrong Several Parts	10
Reversal of Parts	1		

Errors Made in Oral Reading:

When for *The*   *they* for *them*
the hill for *again*   *and* for *or*
he for *they*   *campaign* for *company*
doesn't for *does not*   *a* for *was*
the for *he has*   *thruggling* for *thrilling*
in for *to*   *and around* for *one ring* (in "A big
from for *off* (later corrected)   clown rode around one ring.")
cat for *kitten* (later corrected)   *cried* for *carried*
and for *with*   *whip* for *for whip*
on for *in*   *his head hat* for *one hand and*
clang for *clad*   *clicking* for *cracking*
the for *in*   *another* for *other*
and for *with*   **have been** for *must be*

An analysis of Mary Lynn's errors seems to indicate that she depended greatly on context, often substituting words that gave the story meaning. An example of this was when she read, "When he rides it quickly down *the hill*," instead of *down again*.

The types of errors Mary Lynn made on the *Gates Advanced Primary Test* (Form 1) followed a fairly consistent pattern. On the word recognition section, Mary Lynn always called the initial consonant sound correctly and often the initial consonant blend. However, from there to the end of the word she seemed to attack the word by means of configuration or guessing. It is possible that she may not have had some of these words which were tested in her speaking and listening vocabulary, or she may not have been able to call to mind the word for which the picture stood, and since her sight vocabulary was so weak, she was not able to associate the correct word with the picture. It appears that Mary Lynn may not have been looking "all the way through the word." Her performance on this test showed a weakness in analyzing the medial and final parts of words. Her comprehension scores on the Advanced Paragraph Reading section showed she was almost on grade level both times she took the test. Since her sight vocabulary was weak at the time of the administration of Form 1, it is likely that, to a large degree, she was depending on contextual clues to meaning. As was pointed out earlier, her sight vocabulary appeared greatly improved on Form 2.

Summary of Diagnosis as Derived from Errors on Reading Tests

Mary Lynn appeared to be quite strong in using initial consonants, initial consonant blends, context, and configuration as clues to word analysis. However, she tended to depend too much on context and configuration clues to make up for other reading deficiencies. Her knowledge of short vowel sounds and of the general rules that determine the sound of a vowel was quite poor. She did not apply the vowel-consonant-final *e* rule. Often she guessed at a word after identifying the initial sounds rather than looking "all the way through the word." She did not seem to know how to break a word down into pronounceable patterns. Furthermore, her sight vocabulary was deficient.

Remedial Program

THE PROGRAM AS OUTLINED in this report covered a period of one month in summer, and two semesters, beginning in June, 1967, and ending in

May, 1968. Each semester consisted of fifty hours of instruction. The original program was planned on the basis of the results of diagnostic testing. Information obtained through diagnostic teaching and observation altered the form of the program during administration. The pupil's program consisted of the following materials and activities:

Controlled Reader.[3] At the beginning of her first term in the Reading Clinic in June, 1967, Mary Lynn used the EDL *Controlled Reader* materials at Book 1 level. She was placed in Book 2 in October, 1967. The clinician prescribed the controlled reader for two reasons: first, because the diagnostic tests indicated poor directional attack, and second, because Mary Lynn enjoyed working with machines and so was able to maintain attention for longer periods of time.

Flash-X.[4] The EDL *Flash-X* was used to aid in the development of Mary Lynn's sight vocabulary and for improvement of visual memory. Since she displayed very poor sight recognition of words of similar configuration in oral reading and on the *Gates-McKillop Reading Diagnostic Tests*, basic sight vocabulary wheels were used and individual word wheels were created for her by the clinician, using words with which she had difficulty in oral reading.

Working with Sounds, Level A. Since Mary Lynn displayed a poor knowledge of vowel sounds on the diagnostic tests, *Working with Sounds*, Level A (Barnell Loft), was used to help her learn the sounds of letters. She worked well in this workbook and showed progress in phonic analysis skills.

Eye and Ear Fun, Books 2 and 3. After Mary Lynn completed *Working with Sounds* she began the *Eye and Ear Fun* Workbooks (Webster). These workbooks provide short drills in working with blends, vowel and consonant combinations, and syllabication. The clinician assigned selected pages from these books to meet the pupil's particular needs, rather than having the pupil work through the entire workbook. Mary Lynn had difficulty in following the directions given for the exercises and could not use this material independently.

The Magic World of Dr. Spello. Selected pages from *The Magic World of Dr. Spello* (Webster) were used. In addition, the clinician tape-recorded instruction to accompany several pages of practice exercises designed for teaching the sounds of letters and syllabication. Mary Lynn

[3] *Controlled Reader,* Educational Developmental Laboratories (New York: Huntington).
[4] *Flash-X,* Educational Developmental Laboratories (New York: Huntington).

could function independently in this activity. She was able to operate the tape recorder herself, and her control over the recorder seemed to give her a feeling of confidence.

Reading Stories from Books. Stories from the *Dolch Basic Vocabulary Books* (Garrard) and from the *Beginner Books* (Random House) were read orally to Mary Lynn. She followed the words in the books, and after hearing a story in this way, she discussed the story with the clinician, often reading selected passages aloud. This activity seemed to help Mary Lynn improve in rhythm and intonation, and contributed to the development of her sight vocabulary. She thoroughly enjoyed this, and it helped her to realize that reading can be fun. After she had heard a number of stories, her program was somewhat altered and she selected books at her instructional level to read without always having the assistance of the clinician; however, occasionally the clinician would revert to the original procedure.

Oral and Silent Reading. Mary Lynn read *Dog Stories* and *Horse Stories* from the Dolch Basic Vocabulary Books Series and became so interested in her reading that she brought books from home to read in the clinic.

Both oral and silent reading were taught diagnostically. Mary Lynn read parts of the stories orally and the clinician kept a record of her errors to use as a guide in planning additional instruction.

Her difficulties in silent reading and in reading comprehension were noted for the same purpose. Immediate instruction was sometimes given when difficulties were noted; however, the clinician was careful to avoid frequent interruptions and unnecessary corrections that would diminish the pleasure of reading the story.

Mary Lynn kept a list of the books that she had read in the Reading Clinic and often displayed it with pride.

Language Master. Words and phrases with which Mary Lynn had difficulty were placed on Language Master cards (Bell and Howell). Mary Lynn worked with five or six cards for usually no more than five minutes at any one time. When she could recognize the words or phrases at sight, new words were put on cards.

S.R.A. Listening Skill Builders, C. Mary Lynn enjoyed using the tape recorder so much that the clinician had her start working with the *S.R.A. Listening Skill Builders* (Science Research Associates). Mary Lynn listened to the tape-recorded story and then answered comprehension questions. Previous to working with this material she had often missed questions involving inference, and this activity helped her in learning to comprehend inferred meaning.

S.R.A. Reading Laboratory, Elementary. In January, 1968, Mary Lynn began working independently with the *S.R.A. Reading Power Builders.* The clinician felt that she needed to become more independent in her learning and the *Reading Skill Builders* provided many needed reading skills activities as well as an opportunity for Mary Lynn to practice independent and, to a limited degree, self-directed learning.

Final Testing

Eye-Movement Photograph Record. A final eye-movement photograph was made on March 27, 1968. Mary Lynn's relative efficiency has improved from a grade equivalent of 1.0 to 4.5. However, her directional attack is still poor. Her component grade ratings on the reading performance profile have improved greatly in all areas except in number of regressions. Her grade ratings were all below first grade on the initial test. The final test shows her above grade level in all areas except regressions. It appears that she has difficulty focusing quickly each time she returns her eyes to the beginning of a line of print.

The Gates-McKillop Reading Diagnostic Test (Form II) was given on May 1, 1968. Although Mary Lynn's oral reading score has improved only slightly, her ability to break words into syllables and pronounce them has improved greatly. Also, her basic sight vocabulary has increased. Mary Lynn's knowledge of letters and letter sounds appears to be normal. She is above her present grade level in oral vocabulary, ability to attack unknown words, ability to recognize and blend common word parts, ability to recognize the visual form of the sounds of nonsense words, and in her knowledge of vowel sounds.

Gates-McKillop Reading Diagnostic Test, Form II

Oral reading grade	3.5 L-M
Words: Flash	3.9 M
Words: Untimed	4.5 H
Phrases: Flash	3.9 M
Recognizing & Blending Common Word Parts	5.0 H
Giving Letter Sounds	21/26 M
Naming Capital Letters	PS NP
Naming Lower-Case Letters	PS NP
Nonsense Words	4.8 H

Gates-McKillop Reading Diagnostic Test, Form II

Initial Letters	PS	NP
Final Letters	13/14	NP
Vowels	5.0	H
Auditory Blending	14½/15	L-M
Spelling	3.5	L
Oral Vocabulary	5.8	H
Syllabication	4.1	M
Auditory Discrimination	13/14	NP

Errors Made:

I. *Oral Reading:*

Omissions	1	Wrong Order	0
Additions	2	Wrong Beginnings	4
Repetitions	4	Wrong Middles	8
Mispronunciations	14	Wrong Endings	7
Full Reversals	0	Wrong Several Parts	4
Reversal of Parts	0		

Types of Errors:

was for *were*	*dismand* for *dismay*
a for *the*	*the hall* for *a hole*
How for *Now*	*I'm* for *I am*
pall for *pal*	*an* for *the*
cat for *cats*	*idot* for *idiot*
he for *she*	*embras* for *embarrass*
big for *bad*	*proof* for *profound*
squaled for *squealed*	

II. *Words: Flash Presentation*

adventure for *avenue*	*convince* for *conversation*
jewel for *jealous*	*absent* for *acquaintance*
victory for *victorious*	*musical* for *musician*
refuse for *reference*	

Words Mary Lynn said she did not know were these:

landscape	*difficulty*
courage	*comprehend*
candidate	*performance*
discontent	*certificate*
celebration	*organization*

III. *Words: Untimed Presentation*

I'll for *ill*	*copperhead* for *comprehend*
for tune for *fortune*	*tributry* for *tributary*
crill for *cruel*	*difnife* for *dignify*
muscle for *muzzle*	*her itence* for *inheritance*
adventure for *avenue*	*re fer ence* for *reference*
spirit for *sprit*	*suspication* for *suspicion*
conrage for *courage*	*mountains* for *mountainous*
freighter for *feature*	*musical* for *musician*
revault for *revolt*	*diskiplin* for *discipline*
persecut for *persecute*	*perpesual* for *perpetual*

Often on her second response for a word Mary Lynn would guess. She made many errors on the middle part of a word and some on the ending of a word.

Often she missed the vowel-consonant-final *e* rule.

IV. *Phrases: Flash Presentation*
ran fast for *run fast*
under a table for *under the table*
this is new for *that is new*
then it blew for *then it blows*
wear your hat for *ear a new hat*
see my new dress for *see my best dress*

V–1. *Recognizing and Blending Common Word Parts*

-id for *-ed*	*-ill* for *-ell*
wish for *wh*	*tw* for *st*
-um for *-ome*	*tw* for *sw*
-asph for *-asp*	*-it* for *ite*

V–2. *Giving Letter Sounds*

Ya for *u*	*e* for *i*
wa for *y*	*K* for *g*
ik for *x*	

VI–3. *Final Letters*
z for *j*

VI–4. *Vowels*
o for *u*

VIII–3. *Syllabication*

orli for *olri*   *irlat* for *irliate*
etof for *etfo*   *ingrin* for *igarind*
igeest for *igast*   *willclow* for *wacolow*
lighter for *lither*   *rolafo* for *roleafo*
placorn for *placorow*   *antray* for *ayterha*
indrall for *indarill*   *arknid* for *arknide*

Types of errors on syllabication:

Identifying the VCCV pattern in the middle and on the end of words.

Identifying the VCV pattern in the middle of words.

Pronounces a three-syllable word as two.

Doesn't use the position of the vowel as a clue to pronunciation.

Doesn't know the sound of *th*.

Gates Advanced Primary (Form 3)

Mary Lynn's score on the *Gates Advanced Primary Tests* (Form 3), Paragraph Reading, has improved from a reading grade score of 3.1 when she entered the clinic to 5.2. Her score on Word Recognition has improved from a reading grade of 2.86 when she entered the clinic to 3.8.

Advanced Word Recognition
(given 4/25/68) C.A. = 9.10
Reading grade   3.8
Reading Age   9.0
Errors:

kitten for *kitchen*   *triumph* for *trumpeter*
meant for *meat*   *tremble* for *trench*
magnify for *magnet*   *pulse* for *pulpit*
spake for *spank*   *velocity* for *velociped*
courtship for *courthouse*   *propsect* for *prospector*
thirty for *thirsty*   *emperor* for *embark*

Paragraph Reading
(given 4/4/68) C.A. = 9.10
Reading grade   5.2
Reading age   10.4
Errors:

Didn't read carefully enough to detect answer.

Didn't read all of paragraph. Only followed half of the directions given in two paragraphs.

Discussion

AT THE END of the remedial instruction period in May, 1968, Mary Lynn was working up to grade level (high third) in her word analysis abilities; however, she was repeating third grade and was reading below the expected ability level indicated by her chronological and mental ages.

In light of her reading performance at the time she entered the Reading Clinic, she made notable progress both in her reading abilities and in her attitude toward reading. Many of her anxiety symptoms disappeared and her parents reported that, although she was repeating third grade, she was much happier and was performing better in school.

Before coming to the Reading Clinic, learning to read seemed an overwhelming and mysterious process to Mary Lynn, but during her instruction in the clinic she was made aware of the purpose of each learning task that was assigned and was able to recognize and evaluate her own progress. By using a diagnostic approach in teaching, the clinician was able to present needed skills to Mary Lynn in small, manageable parts, and Mary Lynn was aware of the skill that was being developed.

For many pupils, anxiety may be used effectively as a motivating device, and many work well under the pressure of competition. Mary Lynn did not respond to pressure, neither did she work well in group situations. In her regular school situations the anxiety produced by normal competition and by common motivating devices such as grades or gold stars often made learning impossible for her.

The progress in reading that Mary Lynn made was in part due to the support the clinician gave her, by accepting her and her performance without criticism, by planning learning tasks to assure success, and by using teaching approaches that were unlike those with which she had experienced previous failure.

It was recommended that Mary Lynn continue to receive instruction in the Reading Clinic in September, 1968, because she was still not working up to the level of her potential ability and because she did not learn well in group situations. However, there has been no further contact with Mary Lynn or her parents.

Editor's Comments

Some children, like Mary Lynn, do failing work in school despite achievement test scores that are not far below average. Her need for help was emphasized by the school's decision to have her repeat the third grade.

Two physical conditions, a visual defect and allergic bronchitis, may have been significant causes of Mary Lynn's school problems. The visual problem was not discovered and glasses prescribed until just before the diagnostic examination in February. Since an error in the glasses was discovered and corrected almost immediately, and little progress was shown during the spring term, it is evident that correction of vision was not sufficient in itself to produce a significant improvement in school work. The correction of her allergic bronchitis came when her remedial instruction was more than half over, and while it is said to have improved her work as well as her health, substantial progress had already been made in the remedial program. There was no evidence to suggest a neurological difficulty. If Mary Lynn had been a bright child, she might have become a successful reader despite these health problems.

This case report is the only one in the collection in which eye-movement photography was used in diagnosis, and is also helpful in giving the specific errors on reading tests on which diagnostic conclusions and remedial planning were based, allowing the reader to make an independent analysis of the errors.

The remedial program was an eclectic one, involving sight vocabulary, phonics, and oral and silent reading, and it emphasized motivation as well as skills. The clinic's desire to continue until a close approximation to potential would be obtained, and the parents' breaking contact when grade level in reading had been reached, illustrates a divergence in viewpoint that is quite common in clinical practice.

13

David

BY LAWRENCE GOLD, Ph.D.*

Setting

The Learning Center, located in Binghampton, New York, was a regional supplementary services project sponsored by nineteen school districts on the southern border of New York State. The program was funded by the U.S. Office of Education under provisions of Title III of the Elementary and Secondary Education Act of 1965. The principal objective was to provide clinical services to pupils with severe disability in reading and related skills. Criteria for enrollment included underachievement of at least two years below grade level in grades three through six, and one year below in grades one and two. Pupils had to be of normal intelligence or above and not eligible for placement in special classes for the emotionally disturbed or perceptually handicapped. Terms such as "developmental dyslexia" and "specific language disability" have been used to describe the target population of the program.

The Learning Center was staffed by a director, a school psychologist, a social worker, and ten teachers. Medical specialists from the disciplines of psychiatry, neurology, and ophthalmology were available for diagnosis and staff consultation. Additional medical services were processed through the family or the school district.

The combined pupil population of the school districts affiliated with the program was in excess of 65,000. Some four hundred pupils were seen for intensive diagnosis and treatment during the three-year period the program was in operation. Pupils received individual or small group instruction in hourly sessions held twice weekly on alternate days. They were bused in from distances of as much as twenty miles, since in most

* Many individuals contributed to the development of this study. Specific acknowledgement is made of the assistance of Dr. David M. Bloom (neurologist), Dr. Ivan Fras (psychiatrist), and Dr. Francis J. Gilroy (opthalmologist), and staff members Miss Anne M. Lynch and Mr. Frank Beylo. Other individuals must remain anonymous to protect the identity of the client. Full responsibility for errors of interpretation and omission is assumed by the author.

instances comparable facilities and services were not available in the school districts.

Diagnostic Study

DAVID HAD BEEN ATTENDING the learning center for a little more than fourteen months when this report was written. He was fairly representative of the pupils enrolled, mostly boys, in age, severity of learning disability, and school history. He was untypical in the limited academic progress he had made in the remedial program.

General Impression

David was a handsome, well-developed boy 9 years 10 months old at the time of initial contact. There was some indication of hyperactivity, but he was able to sustain attention for reasonable periods of time. He enjoyed talking about his experiences, particularly those associated with a horse he rode after school and on weekends. In discussion about his schoolwork he clearly indicated that he was unhappy because it was difficult. Attendance at the Learning Center was both an opportunity to avoid frustration in school and a means to communicate with a sympathetic adult.

School History

David entered kindergarten at age 5 years 6 months. He was considered a healthy child before and during the school years, and had no known health problem during the period of tutorial instruction.

Although he received passing marks in most subjects throughout the grades, these were given out of concern for his emotional reaction rather than for achievement. This report was started while he was in the middle of fourth grade and his teacher indicated that she was unable to grade him on interim reports because of his very low achievement.

David received speech therapy in kindergarten. A report in March of that year indicated that he continued to have difficulty with the *s* and *sh* sounds. Progress was observed, however, in his pronunciation of *l*, *ch*, and *th*. His tendency to use "baby talk" on occasion was first observed in kindergarten and was to continue in later grades. During a parent conference held in February, the kindergarten teacher noted that he had a good oral vocabulary. His number concepts were poor, his art work was immature, and he could not carry a tune. Throughout kindergarten he displayed symptoms of latent hostility and aggression, such as hitting other children or deliberately knocking down their building blocks. He cried a great deal at the beginning of the year, particularly on Monday mornings.

In a summary report at the end of kindergarten the teacher noted that his speech articulation was poor and that he continued to have difficulty with number identification, although he could count objects up to 12. He could not recognize his name in print by the end of the year. On the *Metropolitan Readiness Tests* (1964 edition) he had the most difficulty with the subtests of Matching (a test of visual perception), Numbers, and Copying (a test of visual perception and motor control). His receptive verbal skills were average. The predicted readiness score was classified as "D" which indicated a need for individualized help in the first grade.

The first-grade teacher observed that David was having difficulty recognizing the letters of the alphabet. She wrote in February, 1965, that his oral language ability was quite well developed. "His experiences seem so grown up that it is a little difficult to understand his lack of academic ability." In arithmetic he was unable to identify the numerals 6, 8, and 9, and his numerical concepts continued to be poor.

In June, 1965, the teacher had observed little improvement in basic academic skills. His crying on Monday mornings and his constant teasing of other pupils indicated emotional problems. She felt that "some of the trouble would disappear if he would concentrate on his own work and not be concerned with what other children were doing." She recommended that he repeat the first grade.

His repetition of the first grade appears to have produced little change in achievement. The February, 1966, report noted that he was having difficulty with common words like *mother* and *father*. He did not know the sounds of some letters. In addition, he had difficulty staying at an assignment for any length of time. "He likes to talk all the time. He needs to listen more."

In grade two there was further indication of poor adjustment to the school setting. The same pattern of behavior as in the previous grades was apparent. He frequently cried, particularly on Monday mornings. He interrupted the class periodically, asking irrelevant questions. Except for his ability to express himself well orally, he was seriously below the class in all aspects of achievement.

The first achievement test on record was administered in November,

1967, in the third grade. His scores on the *New York State Reading Test* and *Arithmetic Test* were both at the tenth percentile.

The referral application for enrollment in the program of the Learning Center was completed by the third-grade teacher in October, 1967. The application provided a rating scale in which five areas were rated from 1 (below average) to 5 (above average) in comparison to the class as a whole. David received a rating of 1 in General Reading Level, Reading in Subject Areas, and Ability in Arithmetic. His Personal and Social Adjustment was rated 3 (average) and his General Attitude Toward School was rated 2.

His fourth-grade teacher was visited in January, 1969, in connection with the development of this report. It was a new school which had opened the previous September and even more than the old one, tended to enroll pupils from families of middle to upper-middle socioeconomic level. The pupils were grouped heterogeneously and the general achievement level of David's class was well above the national norm. His academic difficulties became more apparent in this new setting.

His fourth-grade teacher noted that he was unable to participate in most of the class activities. He could not read the assigned text and his arithmetic skills were limited to addition. He continued to use his fingers for simple addition, and subtraction work was begun without success. He could copy from the board, but he could not read what he copied nor could he write from oral dictation. His written communication and spelling were equally poor.

Nevertheless, his teacher noted his eagerness to participate in classroom activities. He demonstrated considerable sophistication in his ability to relate his weekend experiences to the class. He also demonstrated fairly good mechanical ability and was the official "fixer" in the class. Instruction in physical education, art, and music was offered by special teachers. He performed well in these areas and he was particularly successful in the physical education class.

His demeanor in the classroom continued to be a problem. He sought ways to disturb the class routine or direct attention to himself. The teacher was quite sympathetic to the academic frustration which he faced. Every effort was made to provide independent seat work and individualized instruction in the basic skills. He clearly was the poorest achiever in the class and did not fit into even the lowest of the instructional groups. When report cards were issued in January he received none since the teacher felt unable to grade him. One positive note was that his crying on Monday mornings was no longer observed. Indeed, he seemed to enjoy this period, for it was partly used to share weekend experiences with the class.

Parent Interviews

Staff social worker and both parents.   Jan., '68
Staff social worker and mother.   Apr., '68
Psychiatric consultant and paternal grandmother.   May, '68
Staff social worker and mother.   Dec., '68
Director of Learning Center and both parents.   Feb., '69

The information in this section is a composite of details and impressions acquired during the parent interviews. All conferences were held at the Learning Center and usually in the evening, as both parents held full-time jobs. Despite the distance from their home to the center and the inconvenience of the hour, the parents were eager to meet with staff members to share information.

David was an only child and the parents did not wish additional children. They were in their late twenties when he was born. The paternal grandparents lived in close proximity on land shared by both families. Both parents had worked in responsible positions since their marriage, except for the period of the mother's pregnancy. The paternal grandmother was largely responsible for the daytime supervision of David from the time he was 4 months old.

The mother required hospitalization on several occasions during the pregnancy, which was complicated by high blood pressure and retention of fluids (the staff neurologist thought she had the condition known as preeclampsia). She considered herself a nervous person and had received medication at the time of pregnancy and on several occasions since then.

David was a full-term baby and delivery was without complications. He weighed 8 pounds, 8 ounces, at birth and developmental history was normal, except that he began to talk late (at 14 months) and distinct speech patterns did not evolve until 18 months. Toilet control and walking both occurred prior to 12 months of age.

He had the usual childhood illnesses, including measles (age 3), chicken pox (age 5), whooping cough (age 6), and mumps (age 7). High fever was noted only at the time he had measles. Periodic medical evaluations were provided by the family physician and David was reported to be in excellent general health.

For the most part the parents did not consider David difficult to raise, although they thought he was a nervous child. On occasions he displayed marked irritability and even temper tantrums. At age 2 he was hospitalized for a broken leg and his behavior required one parent to stay with him at all times. He would not permit the hospital staff to provide the usual medications unless a parent was present.

Both parents provided discipline when necesssary, although that meted out by the father was far more severe and even erratic. Common reasons for punishment included failure notices sent home by the school and neglect of assigned chores, such as cleaning his room. The punishment usually consisted of restricting David to the house and grounds for several weeks and denial of use of television. David complained bitterly about these restrictions to his teachers at the center.

The father was clearly the dominant individual in the family, and did most of the talking during the interviews attended by both parents. He was proud of the material possessions he had acquired, which included a motor boat, tractor, and elaborate camping and hunting equipment. David was permitted to drive the boat and tractor with minimum supervision. The family enjoyed many recreational activities as a unit and throughout the year they went hunting, fishing, or camping on the weekends. The father was not concerned that David did not have any close friends and insisted only that David fight to win if he should come into conflict with his peers.

The parents were concerned about David's failing in school. In the early part of the third grade, prior to David's enrollment in the center, they tried home tutoring upon the recommendation of the classroom teacher. The father forced David to read and spend more time with homework. David soon displayed symptoms of a "nervous breakdown" and the family physician advised the discontinuation of further home instruction.

Neither parent had completed high school because of dislike for school (father) and financial reasons (mother). The paternal grandfather could barely read, and several of David's maternal relatives had experienced considerable difficulty in school, including one referred to the center for reading disability.

Every effort was made to provide David with material possessions, including toys, sporting equipment, musical instruments, and his own color television. The parents were proud of David's mechanical ability and the responsibility he had shown in caring for a neighbor's horses after school. He was very fond of horses and the family had owned one for several years. While his parents were eager for him to do well in school, they felt that he could be happy, as they were, by developing marketable skills and indulging in recreational activities.

Psychological Tests

Given on September, 1967, C.A. 9–7.
Wechsler Intelligence Scale for Children
Bender Visual Motor Gestalt Test
Ellis Visual Designs Test
Wide Range Achievement Test
Tests of Learning Rate
Given on April, 1968, C.A. 10–1.
Rorschach Test

The school district psychologist provided the initial battery of tests when David entered the third grade. The results were used to support the referral application for enrollment in the Learning Center. The center psychologist provided an additional evaluation later in the school year in response to a request by the center teacher.

The initial battery of tests was administered over a period of several days. On the whole David was pleasant and cooperative, although he was sensitive to routine noises which occurred outside the testing room and manifested other signs of distractibility.

The results of the *WISC* test were as follows:

I.Q. Rating
Verbal Scale	89
Performance Scale	92
Full Scale	89

Scaled Subtest Scores

Verbal		Nonverbal	
Information	9	Picture Completion	11
Comprehension	12	Picture Arrangement	8
Arithmetic	6	Block Design	10
Similarities	–	Object Assembly	9
Vocabulary	8	Coding	5
Digit Span	6		

The Verbal and Full Scale I.Q.'s placed him at the upper limit of the Dull Normal range, and the Performance I.Q. was near the lower limit of the Average range. Analyses of the subtest scores confirmed his difficulty with numerical concepts and indicated a considerable degree of anxiety and distractibility (Arithmetic and Digit Span). Inability to sustain attention and poor perceptual-motor integration were also noted (Coding). His ability to verbalize well and his wide range of experiences may have contributed to the relatively high Comprehension score.

The figures on the *Bender Visual Motor Gestalt Test* were reproduced on paper with little regard for order, and designs 7 and 8 were slightly distorted. On the *Ellis Visual Designs Test* few of the ten designs were reproduced correctly, and his total score was in the lowest quartile of the normative population. The results of these tests suggested impairment in perceptual-motor and perceptual-memory processes.

On the *Wide Range Achievement Test* he scored 1.8 in Reading; 2.3 in Spelling; and 2.6 in Arithmetic. In reading words he responded only to initial consonant clues and guessed at the remainder, usually incorrectly.

Two learning rate tests were applied.[1]

The first required responses to visual cues (pictures of common objects) and the second to auditory cues (common words presented orally). David demonstrated no notable difference in learning rate using these differentiated modalities and he reached an early plateau on both tests.

The staff psychologist administered the *Rorschach* in April, 1968, after David had been in the tutorial program four months. The *Rorschach* interpretation suggested that David had angry and destructive impulses. There were indications of deep resentment and hostility, apparently as a result of continued academic and interpersonal frustrations. These reactions were considered appropriate under the circumstances and were not viewed as essential pathological.

Medical Reports

Psychiatric Evaluation	May, 1968
Electroencephalogram Study	November, 1968
Neurological Evaluation	January, 1969
Ophthalmological Evaluation	February, 1969

The Learning Center made arrangements to provide selected medical evaluations for pupils enrolled in the program. The information presented

[1] Edith Meyer Tayler, *Psychological Appraisal of Children With Cerebral Defects* (Cambridge: Harvard University Press, 1959), pp. 423–429.

below is based on reports received by the center and on follow-up discussion with each of the consultants.

The psychiatric report noted that David had very few friends. He described his horse and dog as his brother and sister and denied that he
wanted siblings. He used mechanisms of isolation to deal with his feelings, especially those of aggression. An interview with the paternal grandmother suggested that David had a history of hyperactivity, distractibility,
and low tolerance for frustration. He also employed some counterphobic
defenses and obsessive-compulsive reactions. The diagnosis was made of
developmental dyslexia complicated by symptoms associated with psycho-
neurosis. Continued enrollment in the program of the Learning Center
was recommended.

The neurological evaluation indicated that nerves, reflexes, sensation,
gait and stance, and sensory apparatus were intact and functioning within
normal range. There were, however, atypical mirror movements of the
fingers. When David touched each of the fingers in one hand with the
thumb, mirror movements also occurred in the other hand.

The electroencephalogram was considered somewhat abnormal, for it
revealed intermittent slow waves over the cerebral hemispheres and the
central regions. The diagnosis of minimal brain injury was made by the
neurologist as a result of the "soft signs" revealed by these evaluations.
It was his opinion that this diagnosis was consistent with David's educational history and the available psychological data.

The ophthalmological report indicated that external examination of the
eyes was normal. Distant vision without correction was 20/20 in each
eye. Muscle balance was well within normal limits, although David
showed mild esophoria (eyes tend to turn in) at distance and near vision.
On the *Worth 4-Dot Test* fusion for near and distant vision was normal.
Stereopsis (depth perception) was found normal on the *Wirt* test. A
mild condition of hyperopic astigmatism (farsightedness) was observed,
but a corrective prescription was not deemed necessary. The ophthalmological report concluded that David's visual performance was within normal limits and did not require further attention.

On informal tests of space and body orientation the results were poor.
He tended to confuse his right and left hand when asked to perform
movements, and he reversed directions when told to draw an arrow pointing to the right and left. The ophthalmologist noted that David had been
ambidextrous as a younger child, according to information provided by

his mother. On examination, however, he appeared right-handed, right-eyed, and right-footed.

Visual and Auditory Screening

The *School Vision Tester* (Bausch & Lomb) was used to screen referrals for more intensive evaluations of visual performance. The instrument provides tests for distance acuity, near-point vision (farsightedness), and muscle balance (phoria). The *Tritone Audiometer* (Eckstein Bros.) can test hearing response at three decibel levels (25, 40, and 60) for each of three frequencies (500, 2000, 4000), and was used for screening gross hearing loss.

David passed all tests on both instruments. He was referred for additional ophthalmological evaluation (as noted above) to confirm the findings of screening instrument and to explore the possibility of eye pathology.

Reading and Related Skills

December, 1968   Grade 3

Sample Graded Word Lists
Word Analysis Record
Informal Reading Inventory
Informal Spelling Inventory
Writing Sample

The diagnosis of reading and related skills was performed by the center teacher under the supervision of the director. The pupil was first seen for a preliminary screening to determine whether the minimum criteria for enrollment were met. After enrollment in the program others tests were administered.

The level of basal reader sight vocabulary was evaluated by *Sample Graded Word Lists*.[2] Each list contains ten words common to basal readers at reading levels from preprimer through grade five. Difficulty with more than two or three words in any list suggests that the pupil will find typical books of a similar grade level too difficult for instructional purposes. David was able to read at sight all the words on the preprimer list without any errors. At the primer level he read nine of the ten words correctly

[2] Albert J. Harris, *How to Increase Reading Ability*, 5th ed. (New York: David McKay Co., 1970), p. 178.

(he said *store* for *story*). On the first reader level he was able to identify seven words (he could not read *cry, gate,* and *well*) and only three words (*music, often,* and *cannot*) at the grade-two level. He was not able to identify any of the words on the remaining lists.

His ability to utilize phonics for the analysis of words was evaluated by means of a locally produced test. David experienced considerable difficulty with most of the phonic elements. He was able to respond to initial consonants (except *m*) and vowels, and some of the compound words. He clearly was deficient in his knowledge of consonant blends and digraphs, short and long vowels, and vowels controlled by *r, l,* and *w*. The results confirmed the impression that David responded primarily to the initial letter of a word and guessed the remainder according to general configuration or context.

A basal series was used to administer an informal reading inventory. Criteria used at the center required the pupil to read without error a minimum of 95 percent of the words in a basal reader with good comprehension. David's instructional level tested at beginning primer. His reading in higher level basal material was characterized by gross omissions, reversals (*saw* for *was*), and many mispronunciations.

Informal evaluations of spelling and writing indicated severe underachievement in these areas as well. He was able to spell correctly some common words at the first-grade level. Beyond that he experienced considerable difficulty. Typical errors included *ent* for *eat, tar* for *took, jut* for *just,* and *coal* for *cold*. In each instance he was able to record the correct initial consonant, but could not follow through on the remainder of the word. The writing sample he produced was confined to simple phrases of three or four words, each which he was able to spell.

The informal evaluations indicated that comprehension was not a major factor in David's reading disability. He was able to provide the meaning of words, sentences, and passages, when he was able to recognize the words. He was able to identify most of the letters in the alphabet and some of the words introduced at the first-grade level. He was deemed to be reading at a level at least two years below his actual grade placement in school, and three years below that of typical pupils his age (he had repeated grade one).

Diagnostic Summary

The most obvious feature of David's academic history was the extreme underachievement in basic subjects. In verbal (except oral communication) and numerical areas he was achieving at a level no higher than first grade, although he had attended kindergarten, repeated first grade, and had relatively good attendance throughout more than four years of school.

The following factors were identified as having contributed to the learning disability: 1) emotional immaturity stemming from an authoritarian father and the absence of the mother during the daytime after a minimum period of postnatal care; 2) an intellectual level in the lower end of the normal range, although the subtest scatter suggested a somewhat higher potential; 3) an inadequate level of readiness in perceptual ability and numerical concepts at the time formal schoolwork was introduced; 4) the probability of minimal impairment of the central nervous system; and 5) the lack of provision for systematic individualized instruction, particularly in the primary grades. A number of these factors may have interacted during the school years to reinforce the learning disability.

The term developmental dyslexia has been applied to pupils, mostly boys, of average ability or above who experience unusual difficulty in acquiring the basic skills in reading and related areas. These pupils do not manifest frank brain damage, nor is the learning disability primarily due to emotional factors. Immature developmental patterns of speech and handedness have been observed in this group, as well as indications of educational disability in members of the immediate or distant family. Since the condition is related to impairment in the central nervous system, the prognosis for complete recovery as a result of tutorial instruction is usually guarded.

David's learning disability was deemed to be primarily associated with developmental dyslexia, complicated by emotional problems. The recommendation was made for enrollment in the program of the Learning Center, and he had attended a total of eighty hourly sessions at the time this report was written.

Remedial Program

First Semester: December, 1967, to June, 1968

David entered the tutorial program in the middle of the school year. It was not possible to provide him with individual instruction at that time, and he was placed in a group with another boy who was somewhat younger although reading at about the same instructional level.

The teacher was serving an internship at the Learning Center and had previously taught five years in the primary grades. She held a master's degree in elementary education and had taken several courses in remedial reading. She was an unusually sensitive person who was able to generate a friendly and supportive milieu.

Instruction was offered twice a week. Each session consisted of fifty minutes of tutoring followed by ten minutes of creative crafts or quiet games in the activity room. David attended forty sessions between December, 1967, and June, 1968.

David's classroom teacher was kept informed about the tutorial program by means of 1) visits by the center teacher, 2) periodic progress reports which indicated the instructional level in reading and the skills most in need of attention, and 3) the occasional sharing of instructional material for review purposes.

Materials

The following instructional materials were used during the semester:

Books	Level	Company
Pony Rider	P_p	Benefic Press
Cattle Drive	P	Benefic Press
Pony Ring	P	Benefic Press
Dan Frontier and the Big Cat	P	Benefic Press
Dan Frontier with the Indians	1^2	Benefic Press
Jim Forest and the Trapper	1^2	Harr Wagner
Lands of Pleasure	1^2	Macmillan

Workbooks		
Phonics We Use (Books B and C)	1, 2	Lyons & Carnahan
Building Reading Skills (Streamliner)	2	McCormick-Mathers

Supplementary Material		
Linguistic Block Series		Scott, Foresman
The First Rolling Reader		Scott, Foresman
The Second Rolling Reader		Scott, Foresman
Phonetic Quizmo		Milton Bradley
Group Word Teaching Game		Garrard
Picture-Word Cards		Garrard
Basic Sight Vocabulary Cards		Garrard
Phonics We Use-Learning Games Kit		Lyons & Carnahan

Supplementary Material

| Consonant Pictures for Peg Board | Ideal |
| Blends and Digraphs Pictures for Peg Board | Ideal |

Equipment

| Language Master | Bell & Howell |

Overhead projector
Tape Recorder
Primary typewriter

Procedures

Objectives. The remedial program was designed primarily to develop word identification skills, including those of word analysis (phonics and structural analysis) and word recognition (sight vocabulary). Emphasis on comprehension as an instructional objective was avoided. The related skills of spelling and writing also received some attention. Every effort was made to offer instruction in a supportive manner, since his past failures in learning to read had generated a strong dislike for formal instruction.

Selection of Books. David was usually given a choice of three or four books from which he selected one for reading instruction. The first book he read was *Dan Frontier and the Big Cat,* and this was followed by *Pony Ring, Pony Rider,* and *Cattle Drive.* These books satisfied his great interest in horses and provided a convenient source of motivation for reading.

He preferred reading from supplementary readers since they contained story selections that were relatively short. He read each book in its entirety before going on to the next, and he had such a good feeling about completing a book that on several occasions he preferred to reread one before selecting a new title. He enjoyed the farm stories in *Lands of Pleasure,* and this was the only basal reader he used during the semester.

Word Identification Skills. Although phonic and kinesthetic techniques were employed to some extent, David appeared to learn word identification skills most efficiently through a visual approach. The *Dolch Picture-Word Cards* and *Basic Vocabulary Cards* were introduced and reviewed periodically until he was able to read most of the common nouns and about half of the basic sight words. Words from the supplementary readers were placed on index cards and their special features were noted and the words later reviewed. *The Language Master* provided a means for reinforcement of word recognition skills during independent seatwork. Last, the games (*Linguistic Block Series* and *Group Word Teaching Game*) provided an interesting form of review for words learned through the visual method.

David knew most of the initial consonants but he experienced occasional difficulty with *f, m, q, v,* and *w.* These and other phonetic elements, particularly consonant blends and vowel digraphs, were taught by the *Consonant Pictures* and *Blends and Digraphs Pictures* placed on peg board. Kinesthetic reinforcement was provided by means of the overhead projector. David traced the phonic element (presented either in isolation or in the context of a word) on the chalkboard after the teacher wrote the original on a transparency and projected it. The typewriter was introduced to focus attention on the specific letters and letter combinations of words. *Phonetic Quizmo* and selected games from *Phonics We Use— Learning Games Kit* enhanced motivation for reviewing phonics when he played with the other boy in the group.

The linguistic or phonogram approach was used with success. He was able to learn some basic word patterns (such as *band, hand, sand*) as well as the sounds of individual letters (*b, h,* and *s*). During oral reading a word he did not recognize was isolated for review by this procedure if it contained a significant phonogram.

Language Development. David enjoyed talking about his experiences, which included many trips and recreational activities with his family on the weekends. The teacher recorded some of these presentations in the form of experience stories for later silent reading. David occasionally drew pictures to accompany the stories and he took pride in his ability to read material he had presented orally. Spelling, writing, and typing were developed from these experience stories.

Oral Reading. During the early sessions almost all reading was oral. His typical attitude was that he could not read by himself. He required assurance from the tutor during oral reading, that he was reading correctly. Gradually, some silent reading was done in connection with the experience stories and supplementary readers.

Behavioral Pattern. David could not work effectively on independent seatwork. He became restless and distractible. When the tutor was working with the other boy, David deliberately made noises or dropped his book or pencil to attract attention. For the most part each boy worked independently and the tutor shared the time between them. On appropriate occasions, such as during the use of instructional games, they worked together. David used these occasions to make critical statements directed at the other boy. He was particularly abusive if he happened to lose a game. In June the teacher made the recommendation that David should be provided with individual instruction after the summer recess.

Motivation. Motivation for learning to read was maintained by 1) the utilization of books that contained themes relating to horses and farms, 2) the use of games and manipulative equipment, 3) the application of individualized instruction in a supportive setting, 4) the use of experience stories, and 5) the involvement of David in the selection of appropriate activities.

David enjoyed coming to the Learning Center. In May, 1968, a *Pupil Attitude Inventory* was administered to him orally. He answered each question with a response that indicated that his attitude toward the center was very positive. His reply to the question "What do you like most about coming here?" was "The game room," and to the question "What do you like least about coming here?" "Nothing."

Results

Several tests and informal reading inventories were administered to assess the effectiveness of the tutorial program. The results are given in Table 5.

Table 5. David's Results on Achievement Tests

	First Semester		Second Semester		
	12/67	6/68	9/68	1/69	3/69
Grade Placement:	3.4	3.9	4.1	4.5	4.7
Metropolitan Primary II					
Word Knowledge		1.8	1.9	2.2	
Reading		2.0	1.8	2.2	
Stanford Primary II					
Arithmetic Computation			1.9	1.7	
Basal Reader Instructional					
Level	Primer	1^2	Primer	1^2	2^1
Sample Graded Word List					
Number Correct			13	24	27
Wide Range Achievement					
Reading			1.8		2.5
Spelling			2.3		2.5
Arithmetic			2.6		3.0

During the semester David had made slow but discernible progress. He had learned the sounds of the letters of the alphabet that he did not know and some of the consonant blends. He was able to identify at sight most of the common nouns and many sight words normally introduced at the first-grade level. His instructional level in reading had progressed from primer to first reader (1²) level. His spelling and writing skills had made little improvement, possibly because insufficient time was spent on these areas.

His self-concept appeared to have improved somewhat, and perhaps for the first time since he began school he did not complain about having to learn. He was proud that he had completed so many books, and on occasion he took them home to read to his grandmother.

The center teacher recommended continuation in the program on an individual basis, with a male teacher if possible.

Second Semester: September, 1968, to March, 1969

David received individual instruction from a male teacher during the second semester. The teacher was serving an internship at the Learning Center and had previously taught ten years at the junior high school level. He held a master's degree in English education and was accustomed to teaching adolescent underachievers. The tutor was receptive to David's need to express his feelings about his experiences at home and in school. Part of each session was devoted to some discussion of David's difficulty with schoolwork or resentment at having to do a family chore. David was encouraged to assist in the selection of instructional materials and a general tone of permissiveness pervaded the instructional program.

During the second semester the same frequency of contact was maintained as before (two alternate days of the week), and David continued to utilize the activity room for approximately ten minutes of each instructional hour. Communication between the center teacher and the classroom teacher was maintained by visits, progress reports, and the sharing of instructional material.

David was in the fourth grade when the second semester began and his age was 10 years 7 months. He attended forty sessions from September, 1968, to March, 1969 (the terminal date of this report) when his chronological age was 11 years 1 month. He was to continue in the program of the Learning Center through June, 1969, and plans were made to provide him with further remedial instruction in the regular school the following year.

Supplementary Diagnostic Study. Given September, 1968, Grade 4.
Metropolitan Achievement Tests (Primary II)
Stanford Achievement Test (Primary II)
Sample Graded Word List
Word Analysis Record
Informal Reading Inventory
Informal Spelling Inventory
Picture Story Language Test (writing sample)
Interest Inventory

A supplementary diagnostic study, mainly of educational achievement,
was provided when David returned from the summer vacation. On the
Metropolitan Achievement Tests he scored 1.9 in Word Knowledge and
1.8 in Reading (see Table 5). These scores were similar to those recorded in June, 1968, (1.8 and 2.0, respectively).

In Arithmetic Computation his grade equivalent was 1.9. His compu-
tational ability was restricted to simple addition and subtraction. He
experienced particular difficulty with horizontal addition, although he
could do similar examples when placed in vertical form.

On a locally constructed set of graded word lists David was able to
identify at sight a total of thirteen first-grade words; nine preprimer and
four primer and 1². The errors he made included *you* (he said *why*),
please (*plant*), *friend* (*find*), *sleep* (*sheep*), and *would* (*cold*).

The informal phonics test indicated that he had maintained improvement in the identification of the basic phonic elements, as noted in June,
1968. He responded correctly to all initial consonants, single vowels, and
most of the consonant blends (the exception was *sm*). He identified three
of the compound words (he said *showday* for *showdown,* and *sunship* for
sunshine), and missed only one (t-ap) of the word synthesis tasks. In
the other categories of the record (short and long vowels, digraphs, and
vowels controlled by *r, l,* and *w*), he continued to do poorly.

The informal reading inventory indicated that his instructional level in
basal reader material had regressed over the vacation period from 1² to
primer (1¹). His spelling showed no improvement since the initial diagnosis in December, 1967.

A sample of his writing in September, 1968, is shown in Fig. 3.

An inquiry into his interests indicated that David's primary interest
centered around horses. His favorite hobby was horseback riding, and most
of his free time was spent in pursuit of this hobby. He liked to read books

about horses, although the subject he liked least in school was reading. He wanted to have a ranch when he was an adult and to learn to read so that he could know more about horses and ranches. The three wishes he made were: 1) to get race horses, stallions, and jumping horses, 2) to be free to go anywhere without asking permission, and 3) to have a .22 caliber rifle.

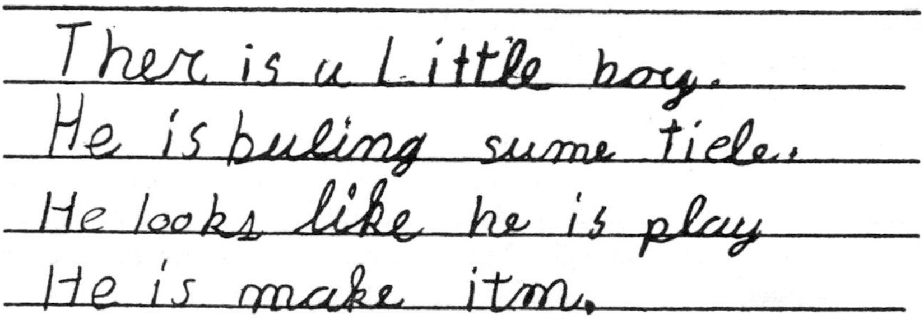

```
There is a little boy.
He is building something.
He looks like he is play
He is make things.
```

Fig. 3. David's writing.

Materials. The following instructional materials were used during the second semester.

Books	Level	Company
Around the City	P	Macmillan
Real and Make-Believe	1²	Harper & Row
Let's Take a Trip	1²	Chandler
Down City Streets	2¹	Follet

Workbook		
Phonics We Use (Book B)	1	Lyons & Carnahan

Supplementary Material

Basic Sight Vocabulary Cards	Garrard
Popper Words (Set I & II)	Garrard
Phonetic Word Cards	Educators Publishing Service
Phonics Drill Cards	Educators Publishing Service

Supplementary Material

| Durrell-Murphy Phonics Practice Program | Harcourt, Brace & World |
| Phonics We Use-Learning Games Kit | Lyons & Carnahan |

Filmstrips

The Rabbit Who Wanted Red Wings	Curriculum Materials Corp.
Mike Fink	Museum Extension Service
Davy Crockett	Museum Extension Service
Paul Bunyan	Museum Extension Service
Daniel Boone, Frontiersman	Film Strip-of-the Month Clubs

Equipment

| "T" Control Portable Cassette Recorder | Craig |
| Primary Typewriter | |

Objectives. During the second semester the instructional objectives were similar to those set for the preceding period. Emphasis was placed on the development of basic word identification skills. More attention was paid to spelling and writing, partly as a reinforcement for word identification, and partly as a result of the expanded use of experience stories as a source of reading material. A supportive milieu was maintained and a counseling-type tutorial program was developed to improve David's attitude about himself and school.

Reading Material. He read about the experiences of children in the city (*Around the City*) and in different settings (*Let's Take a Trip* and *Real and Make-Believe*). He also enjoyed reading about animals (*Down City Streets*). Each book contained some pictures of Negro children, unlike those he selected for reading during the first semester.

Much use was made of experience stories. Those dictated during the preceding session were reviewed and words that caused difficulty were isolated for further practice. The themes of these stories dealt with his recreational activities and reflected some of his social and academic problems. Frequently the experience stories were given to the classroom teacher for use as reading material during independent seatwork activity.

David enjoyed using the filmstrips, most of which portrayed the legendary figures of the frontier period. The filmstrips contained captions that provided an opportunity to review and extend word identification skills.

Word Identification Skills. The visual method (using the *Dolch Popper Words* and *Basic Sight Vocabulary Cards,* as well as basal readers and experience stories) was supplemented by several systematic phonics programs. *The Phonics Drill Cards* consisted of cards with specific elements in isolation. David was taught to associate each element with a sound or word. The *Phonetic Word Cards* and the Durrell-Murphy *Phonics Practice Program* were used to introduce and review the basic phonograms or word patterns. Part of each session was used for specific word identification skills.

Language Development. The introduction of the portable cassette recorder during the second semester tended to promote oral communication. The recorder was very simple to use and David liked reading stories for later playback. Almost all of his reading continued to be oral, and the use of the recorder enabled him to become more aware of his reading errors. Various discussions which David had with the teacher were placed on cassettes for later evaluation by the staff psychologist and the consulting psychiatrist.

Behavioral Pattern. Since instruction was offered individually during the second semester, some of the behavioral problems previously noted did not develop. The tutor was able to establish a fair degree of empathy with David. However, certain unusual patterns began to develop early in the semester. These included a tendency for David to use "baby talk" and make unusual sounds (resembling those of different animals) on various occasions. His ability to sustain attention was very limited on certain days. His actions and comments were erratic at times, while at other times he was able to participate with full effort and attention. The decision to assign him to a male teacher for individual instruction was deemed to be responsible for his improved reaction to the program.

Motivation. Motivation was sustained by 1) the provision for individual instruction, 2) the use of appropriate instructional material (including books, filmstrips, and games), 3) the development of experience stories for periodic review, and 4) the counseling-type tutorial program that permitted David an opportunity to talk about his problems.

Results

In January and March, 1969, selected evaluations were made and the results, together with those from previous evaluations, are indicated in Table 5.

Discernible improvement (although not statistically significant) was noted in the scores of the Word Knowledge and Reading subtests over the period from June, 1968, to January, 1969. No improvement was noted in Arithmetic Computation.

The basal reader instructional level had advanced from primer in December, 1967, when instruction began, to 2 [1] at the time of the last evaluation, in March, 1969. Corresponding to this improvement was the increased number of correct responses on the graded word list. Spelling did not improve during the period of tutorial instruction.

After more than fourteen months of participation in the tutorial program, which included forty sessions each of small group and individual instruction, David had progressed slightly less than one year in functional reading ability. The related communication skills of spelling and writing showed no comparable gains.

Follow-Up Psychological Tests

March, 1969, C. A. 11–1.
Wechsler Intelligence Scale for Children
Bender Visual Motor Gestalt Test
Wide Range Achievement Test

The center psychologist administered selected follow-up tests. The results of both *WISC* administrations appear below:

I. Q. Rating	9/67	3/69
Verbal Scale	89	80
Performance Scale	92	94
Full Scale	89	85
Scaled Subtest Scores		
Information	9	7
Comprehension	12	6
Arithmetic	6	5
Similarities	–	9
Vocabulary	8	8
Digit Span	6	6
Picture Completion	11	10
Picture Arrangement	8	8

Block Design	10	10
Object Assembly	9	10
Coding	5	8

Significant deterioration was observed in the verbal I.Q. rating. This was mainly due to a drop in the Comprehension subtest score, which suggested that David was experiencing increased difficulty in coping with the home and school environment.[3] There was some indication of improvement in attention span and perceptual-motor integration (Coding).

The follow-up administration of the *Bender Visual Motor Gestalt Test* resulted in improved reproduction of figures 7 and 8. Also, the figures were placed in orderly arrangement across the paper, in contrast to the disarray noted at the time of the first evaluation. These changes, together with the increased score on the Coding subtest, suggested a general improvement in David's perceptual-motor and perceptual-memory process.

In the eighteen-month interval between the initial and follow-up evaluations, David's verbal I.Q. rating dropped while tests involving word identification and perceptual-motor skills manifested improvement.

Supplementary Diagnostic Tests

January to March, 1969.
Peabody Picture Vocabulary Test (PPVT)
Developmental Test of Visual Perception (Frostig)
Auditory Discrimination Test (Wepman)
Evaluation of Lateral Preference (LP)
Human Figure Drawing (HFD)

A variety of supplementary diagnostic tests was applied during the latter part of the second semester. Four of these tests had normative data (*PPVT, Frostig, Wepman, HFD*), and one was a research instrument (*LP*) developed at the Learning Center. The results of the tests will be described under the categories of intelligence, maturation, and emotional status.

Intelligence. The *PPVT* was designed to provide an estimate of verbal Intelligence as measured through listening vocabulary. David achieved

---

[3] Alan J. Glaser and Irla Lee Zimmerman, *Clinical Interpretation of the Wechsler Intelligence Scale for Children (WISC)* (New York: Grune & Stratton, 1967), p. 54.

an I.Q. rating of 103 on the *PPVT*, a score that was above those he received on any of the *WISC* scales.

Maturation. The *Frostig* test was developed to evaluate five perceptual skill areas. David manifested distinct weakness in only one of these areas, Test II, Figure-Ground Discrimination. His perceptual age equivalent in this area was only 5 years 6 months.

The *Wepman* test was designed to identify problems in auditory discrimination. Pairs of words are presented orally to the subject, who is required to indicate whether they have a similar or different sound. David made four incorrect responses, three of which involved words with the *th* sound (vow-thou, clothe-clove, fie-thigh). The fourth error involved *sh* (shoal-shawl). These were among the sounds that the speech therapist indicated she had taught when David was in kindergarten.

A lateral preference test was developed at the Learning Center to identify the condition of mixed dominance. The test consisted of a series of tasks using common objects which involved movement of the hand, eye, or foot. David manifested right eye and foot dominance, but incomplete hand dominance. He used his right hand to write his name and completed three of the remaining eight hand preference tasks with the same hand. The left hand was used for the other four tasks. Five supplementary questions on this test required David to identify his right hand, left foot, and in similar fashion other parts of his body. He responded correctly to all questions.

Emotional Status. The human figure drawing was scored according to criteria established by Koppitz.[4] The absence of the neck, hands, and feet, the shading around the face, and the large size of the figure suggested that David continued to have notable emotional difficulty.

Summary

AT THE TIME OF FIRST CONTACT at the Learning Center, David was 9 years 10 months of age and in the middle of the third grade. He had attended kindergarten and repeated grade one. Throughout the school years his teachers had expressed concern about his inability to acquire the basic academic skills. In addition, he manifested behavioral characteristics that were symptomatic of emotional disturbance.

[4] Elizabeth M. Koppitz, *Psychological Evaluation of Children's Human Figure Drawings* (New York: Grune & Stratton, 1968), pp. 331–333.

On the initial intellectual appraisal he received an I.Q. rating of 89 on the *WISC*, which placed him at the upper limit of the Dull Normal range. Subtest scores suggested that he had notable difficulty with numerical concepts and perceptual-motor integration. Anxiety, distractibility, and limited attention span were also manifested. Significant positive factors appeared to be his wide range of experience and his ability to express himself orally.

Diagnostic tests of visual-motor development, learning rate, and academic achievement indicated performances which were poor for his age and grade level. Informal evaluations of reading, spelling, and writing placed his level of achievement in these areas at the middle of grade one. His knowledge of phonic elements was very poor, and his spelling and writing samples demonstrated gross inaccuracies with words of more than three letters.

Neurological evaluation indicated the possibility of minimal brain injury. Visual and auditory processes were deemed to be normal, and his general state of health appeared to be excellent. His mode of environmental adaptation seemed to contain psychoneurotic elements, including counterphobic defenses and obsessive-compulsive reactions.

Both parents expressed concern about David's academic disabilities, and cooperated fully with personnel at the school district and the Learning Center. Parental interviews suggested normal developmental history, except for late talking. He continued to have some speech difficulty during kindergarten, as well as problems with the auditory discrimination of selected speech sounds. Maternal deprivation may have resulted when his mother returned to work after he had attained the age of 4 months. The father appeared to assert an authoritarian role in the family, and tended to encourage David to assume an aggressive demeanor with his peers. Although David had an ample number of toys and access to all kinds of recreational equipment, he very rarely enjoyed them in the company of other children.

The tutorial program was first applied in a group with one other boy, then individually. Instruction was given twice weekly on alternate days, and each session consisted of fifty minutes of basic skills development followed by ten minutes of creative crafts or games in the activity room. David participated in eighty sessions during a fourteen-month period.

The instructional program emphasized the acquisition of word identification skills. Various approaches were utilized, although the visual method appeared to be the most successful. Considerable use was made of phonograms, while phonic and kinesthetic techniques were employed for reinforcement. Experience charts, supplementary and basal readers, games, and audio-visual equipment were used with varying degrees of emphasis throughout the program. A therapeutic environment was generated, particularly during the second semester when individual instruction was provided.

Follow-up evaluations indicated that David's instructional level in basal reader material had progressed from primer to the first half of the second grade. Improvement was recorded in his knowledge of phonics and sight vocabulary, although spelling and writing samples manifested little change. Subtest scores on the second administration of the *WISC* indicated some deterioration in his ability to cope with the home and school environment, and improvement in attention span and perceptual-motor integration.

During the fourteen-month interval of tutorial instruction, David's grade placement in school had extended from the middle of grade three to the latter part of grade four, at which time he was 11 years 1 month old. His general level of reading ability had improved approximately one year (from primer to 2^1), while the related skills of spelling and writing remained almost as deficient as at the onset of tutorial instruction. He continued to manifest symptoms of emotional disturbance, although improvement was noted in his ability to participate in learning activities with sustained effort.

David was considered to be an example of a pupil whose learning disability was related primarily to developmental dyslexia, complicated by emotional factors. Some of his deviant behavior was attributed directly to the learning disability itself, since he faced constant ego deflation throughout the school years. Additional maladaptive patterns appeared to have their source in the home environment.

The progress he made in reading and related skills during the period of enrollment was somewhat below that of the other pupils of similar characteristics. The staff of the center felt that more progress might have been made if his parents were involved in a counseling program. Unfortunately, this service was not available on a systematic basis to the families of pupils in attendance.

Another matter worthy of conjecture is the advisability of a special class for pupils similar to David. Such a class would follow the example of those established for the mentally, physically, and emotionally handicapped. Pupils would meet daily in classes of restricted size with a teacher who had special training. The Learning Center did not utilize this approach since it would have severely limited the number of pupils enrolled in the program. Comparative research is necessary to determine the efficacy of the special class model for pupils with developmental dyslexia.

Editor's Comments

The center at which David was diagnosed and treated was able to make effective use of medical consultants in diagnosis, but was not equipped to provide counseling or psychotherapy, and it was located in an area where facilities for such treatment were very sparse. That a need for modifying parental attitudes was felt by the center staff is evident in the author's concluding comments.

The author has also speculated whether David might have done better in a full-time remedial class, roughly comparable to the settings in Cases 1–4. It should be noted that those cases required three or more years of remedial help before they were ready to return to public school on even a part-time basis, whereas the report on David ends only fifteen months after his remedial program began. David was to receive three more months of help at the center and further remedial teaching in school the following year, so there is time and opportunity for considerable further growth in his reading.

Schools often advise parents to tutor a child at home when he is failing in school. Some parents are able to do this satisfactorily. Many parents, unfortunately, lack the patience and understanding to do this successfully. Not all children respond to parental tutoring by developing symptoms of a "nervous breakdown" as David did, but teachers should realize that if they cannot help a particular child to learn, an untrained and emotionally involved parent may only aggravate the problem by efforts at home tutoring.

The medical and psychological evidence pointing to a neurological basis for David's learning problem is quite strong, and includes the persistence of mixed handedness and figure-ground perception difficulties (*Frostig*) to the age of 10. There does not seem to be, however, a clear basis for differentiating between minimal brain damage and delayed maturation in this case.

14

Jimmy

BY LEON J. WHITSELL, M.D., WILMA BUCKMAN, AND
ALICE J. WHITSELL

Setting

At the University of California School of Medicine in San Francisco, one of the functions of the Child Study Unit and the Pediatric Reading and Language Development Clinic is the training of fourth-year medical students, pediatricians, and other professional personnel in the diagnosis and treatment of children with learning disorders. Eligibility for enrollment in the Reading and Language Development Clinic depends upon the findings of a four-day multidisciplinary study by the Child Study Unit and the Reading and Language Development Clinic staffs. In preparation for this study, the child's physician is required to complete a mimeographed form regarding the child's medical history and development. Another form is sent to the school requesting their observations of the child in areas of academic performance, behavior, and standardized test results.

In this clinic, such a multidisciplinary study of a child with a learning disorder starts with a physical examination by a senior medical student or a pediatrician in training, under the supervision of a senior pediatric consultant. Following this initial examination, the child and his parents have a conjoint diagnostic interview with a senior pediatrician, a psychiatrist, or a psychiatric social worker. Additional evaluations, also attended by the medical student, are done by a neurologist, a psychologist, an educational consultant, and an audiologist-speech pathologist. An electroencephalogram is usually done, and a special ophthalmological examination is scheduled whenever indicated.

On the fourth day, at a staff conference, the team members discuss and integrate their findings into a diagnostic formulation and multiphasic treatment plan. Following this staff conference, the medical student and his consultant meet with the parents and child in a "Summary and Planning Conference" to discuss these findings and recommendations. They help the family understand the many and interrelated facets of the problem, the need and the resources for treatment.

This program, in addition to its direct services to children and parents, was developed as a model for teaching multidisciplinary team participation, and serves as part of an introduction to community medicine for the instruction of medical students and physicians.

Diagnostic Study

Introduction

Jimmy W. was first brought to the Pediatric Reading and Language Development Clinic when he was 8 years 3 months old. He was just then about to repeat the second grade. During the previous year, on the recommendation of his school, he had already attended a private remedial reading clinic near his home for several weeks without any apparent benefit.

Jimmy was referred to our clinic by a neurologist because of a severe reading disability which he had diagnosed as due to "brain damage," after an extensive study which was done in a hospital. This study had included numerous blood tests, two electroencephalograms, an air encephalogram, and cerebrospinal fluid examination.

Both electroencephalograms were reported to show a mild generalized dysrhythmia with possible focal abnormalities in the temporoparietal (side and upper rear parts of the cerebral cortex) regions on both sides. Jimmy's air encephalogram was interpreted as probably normal, although the temporal horn of the left lateral ventricle (a ventricle is a hollow space within the brain, filled with fluid) was very slightly broader and more blunted at the tip than the right temporal horn.

His parents reacted to the diagnosis of "brain damage" at first with disbelief, then catastrophically. Some of the parents' anxiety about Jimmy was reflected by their letter to the clinic asking for appointments: "We are interested in the earliest possible placement of our son in the reading program. We are willing to move to San Francisco in order to make his attendance there possible. . . ."

Medical History

Pregnancy. Jimmy's mother was under medical supervision throughout this pregnancy, which was her third. This pregnancy occurred when her second baby girl was only 9 months old. Both parents felt that this pregnancy had occurred too soon after the second baby. Mrs. W. was quite healthy throughout this third pregnancy, except for a flu-like illness in the fourth month with respiratory symptoms and a high fever for several days, during which she received codeine and other medications.

Birth. Labor was induced at nine months by rupture of the membranes and by the use of pituitary extract. Delivery occurred somewhat precipitously about one hour after induction. Mrs. W. received nitrous oxide anesthesia during the birth, which occurred without any other complications.

Infancy. At birth Jimmy weighed eight pounds and six ounces. He appeared healthy, alert, and responsive. He had a vigorous cry and presented no problems in feeding or sleeping. Throughout infancy he was healthy except for an acute ear infection and an episode of diarrhea for a week. Both of these illnesses occurred when he was between 2 and 3 years old and cleared up without complications. He occasionally banged his head rhythmically during his first 2 or 3 years, especially when tired or upset, but this was never a severe problem.

Development. His early motor development was excellent. Jimmy walked very well with a good sense of balance at 1 year. However, his mother said, "He was a handful." He was always very active, curious, and explored everything.

In language development Jimmy was slower than either of his sisters, but he started to say words at about one year. He was also slower in developing bladder and bowel control. Bed wetting occasionally occurred until he was past 7 years old.

Health. His general health has always been excellent. Jimmy has had very few colds. A second ear infection occurred when he was 7. His tonsils and adenoids were removed after that illness.

Physical Examination

The general physical examination was entirely within normal limits. Jimmy's general physical health and development seemed good. Jimmy gave an immediate, vivid impression of being a well developed young acrobat. A special eye examination disclosed no abnormalities. His hearing was intact.

Neurological Examination

In the neurological examination, he performed well in walking, hopping, and skipping. Jimmy also did unusually well in tests for balance except for slight difficulty in standing on his left foot alone. He was very hyperactive and distractible throughout the examination. In walking toe-to-heel on a line, his associated arm movements were asymmetrical, in that his right hand assumed a rather stiff, dystonic (strained) posture with the palm turned back and outward. This was considered to be an indication of mild occult (hidden, not obvious) cerebral dysfunction, probably involving the basal ganglia (brain centers below the cerebral cortex) or their connecting tracts.

Other subtle indications of abnormalities or immaturities in neurological development were present in several of the tests of higher motor and sensory integrative functions. In the arm extension test and the head rotation test of Hoff and Schilder deficiencies in static postural control were noted. Jimmy's extended arms failed to show any deviation from the target point within twenty seconds in the standard palms-down position (eyes closed). The expected mature response in this test after the age of seven years would be slight upward deviation of the hand used for writing. Carried out again in the palms-up position, this test again showed no vertical deviation of either hand but there was slight lateral deviation of the right hand (8 cm in 20 seconds), which was also considered abnormal for his right handedness.

Passive rotation of Jimmy's head, either to the right or left, while standing with his eyes closed and arms extended, produced paradoxical lateral (sideways) deviation of the occipital arm (the arm nearer the back of the head). Normally, in this test, after the age of 7 or 8 years, the arms remain extended forward in parallel except for slight upward deviation of the chin arm (the one nearer to the face).

The findings in the arm extension and head rotation tests were interpreted as indicating probable immaturity in Jimmy's establishment of sensory-motor integrative processes relating to posture.

Jimmy performed well in all of the ordinary tests for motor coordination, such as the finger-to-nose and heel-to-knee tests. His deep (tendon) reflexes were all somewhat hypoactive; this is a frequent indication of tension in children. There were no pathological toe or finger reflexes except for the isolated finding of a palmomental sign, grade III (contraction of muscles in the chin upon stimulation of the palm of the hand) on the right. This palmomental sign was interpreted as indicating slight dysfunction of his left cerebral hemisphere affecting the cortical sensimotor areas for his right hand and face, or their subcortical connecting pathways. It was felt to be possibly correlated with the dystonic posture of his right hand previously observed in toe-to-heel walking.

Tests of the cranial nerves and of the usual gross modalities of somatic sensation (touch, pain, temperature, vibration, and position senses) were within normal limits.

Dual simultaneous tactile (touch) testing showed rostral (head end) dominance, grade II: on the simultaneous touching of Jimmy's hand and face with his eyes closed, in either a homolateral (same side) or a heterolateral (opposite sides) pattern, there was consistent inattention to (or "extinction" of) the hand stimulus. This persistence of an infantile rostral dominance pattern was considered to be a clear indication of a lack of integration of higher parietal sensory functions, which should probably have become more mature between the ages of 5 to 7 years.

Jimmy's finger localization ability, as tested with double tactile stimuli, was faulty. He gave responses which were correct in only six out of ten trials on the right and in three out of ten trials on the left. This impairment of finger localization (often called "finger agnosia") was felt to reflect a lack of a mature refinement of his body image. Both this finding and the rostral dominance suggested that Jimmy probably had a subtle but important difficulty in using tactile-kinesthetic clues in learning.

Another highly important finding, immediately relevant to Jimmy's reading problems, was that his right-left orientation was insecure, even for parts of his own body, and grossly defective for another person. Right-left orientation generally should be more firmly established than Jimmy's before the age of 7 years for self and before the age of 8 years for another person, particularly in a child of higher general intelligence.

There were several indications that Jimmy probably had mixed or confused cerebral dominance. His occipital hair whorl was noted to be clockwise on the right side. This position of the hair whorl is somewhat correlated with left handedness.

On folding his hands his left thumb was placed on top of his right; on folding his arms, he held his left forearm over his right. He used his left hand for combing his hair. He kicked with his left foot. However, Jimmy used his right hand for eating, writing, batting, and clapping. His right eye was used for sighting through a pinhole and a telescope.

Diagnostic Family Interview

Although both parents were asked to participate in the diagnostic family interview, it was Mrs. W. who brought Jimmy for the study. Mr. W. was out of town on business. In this two-hour interview, the psychiatric social worker and the medical student met with Jimmy and his mother.

With the social worker's help, Mrs. W. expressed her concern and her desire for this evaluation in a straight-forward manner to Jimmy. Jimmy was given support and encouragement to tell his ideas, observation, and concern about his problems at home and at school and his feelings about his parents and school's reactions to him. Both Jimmy and his mother had the opportunity to realize that their concerns and feelings were important and worthy of consideration. The social worker's approach emphasized that there was no need for blame, shame, fear, or secrecy and that open, honest interaction was necessary.

As Jimmy walked into the interview, he appeared as a pallid, well-groomed, conforming 8-year-old boy who behaved in a rather apprehensive, tense, and solemn manner. He responded evasively to most questions with a resentful, whiny "I don't know," accompanied by a light shrug of his shoulders. He glanced furtively at his mother or looked down as she complained and accused him of the innumerable ways he was causing trouble at school and at home.

She focused particularly on her son's failure to assume responsibility for any work and his failure to behave in an acceptable manner. Everything his mother said about him was negative. Mrs. W. did not mention any strengths, attitudes, or other characteristics that would give Jimmy any hope or self-esteem.

Mrs. W. was a stylishly attractive 36-year-old woman, from an upper middle-class family, who appeared intelligent and very conscientious. In a hurt, unsure, disappointed, and often desperate voice and manner, she complained of feeling frustrated ever since Jimmy started to walk and of becoming increasingly desperate over handling him. It infuriated her that Jimmy would not listen, would not remember and follow directions. She felt compelled to repeat everything and to prod him to get him to do anything.

Jimmy's problems also caused a lot of friction and disagreement between his parents. According to Mrs. W., her husband was inclined to be impatient and harsh with Jimmy. Mrs. W. would then usually become annoyed at her husband, but would tend to do the same thing. Jimmy was constantly on the go and getting into things, never knowing why he did this, never completing his tasks, losing his sweaters, and telling innumerable lies.

Family History. Jimmy was the youngest of three children, the only boy with two older sisters, age 9 and 11. Although his sisters were doing well academically, Mrs. W. expressed dissatisfaction with their lack of cooperation in completing tasks and their discontent with life at home. Interchanges between Jimmy and his sisters consisted chiefly of derogatory remarks regarding his poor school performance.

Both parents had attended college but neither graduated. Jimmy's father only completed one year of college. Although he had become a fast reader, he always had trouble with spelling, and his writing was so illegible that he had to use a typewriter. Mrs. W. had completed two years of college. She was good in mathematics but, like her husband, had problems with written work.

Both parents had come from stable homes of an upper socioeconomic level. The fathers of both of Jimmy's parents were very successful career men who provided good physical and economic environments but were absent from their homes on business much of the time. In both families, the mothers were left in charge of the rearing of children and accepted this as their way of life. This pattern was being repeated in Jimmy's home.

Jimmy's parents focused their major attention and greatest concerns on their children's academic and social achievement. Apparently, neither Mr. nor Mrs. W. had much awareness and understanding of their children's feelings or needs for affection, approval, and support.

School History

In kindergarten Jimmy had considerable difficulty in separating from his mother and in joining the other children in group activities. He enjoyed modeling clay and using the carpentry tools, but avoided using crayons, pencils, paints, and scissors if possible.

On the *Metropolitan Readiness Test* at the end of kindergarten, he was classified as a "poor risk."

Jimmy did not do well in anything in the first grade and was constantly a distracting influence on the rest of the class. The only thing he did enjoy was "story time." His first-grade teacher's complaints included: "Lack of initiative, no response to motivation, daydreams continually."

When he first came to the Reading Clinic, Jimmy was repeating the second grade and was at the bottom of the class. His parents believed that Jimmy was not paying attention or applying himself. They were extremely impatient with him.

The report from the school at the time of referral consisted of two pages of complaints. It mentioned only three strengths or positive attributes—his good vocabulary, creative ideas, and his willingness to help in the classroom—but enumerated twelve "does nots." "Jimmy does not listen . . . does not follow directions . . . does not assume responsibility . . . does not work independently . . . does not produce any work . . . does not have desire to learn . . . does not take initiative . . . does not participate in group discussions or oral language activities . . . does not form his letters . . . does not write neatly and legibly . . . does not have satisfactory conduct . . . seems to be in another world most of the time."

His teacher concluded, "Unless Jimmy begins to develop the desire to learn, I feel he will continue to waste his years in school."

Psychological Evaluation

Since the *Wechsler Intelligence Scale for Children* (*WISC*) had already been administered by a well-qualified psychologist only seven months previously, our psychologist, Mrs. Donya Harvin, felt that it was not necessary to repeat this. The scores which were reported when Jimmy was 7 years 7 months old are listed in Table 6.

Table 6. Jimmy's Scores on the *Wechsler Intelligence Scale for Children*

	Age at Time of Testing		
	7–7	9–9	12–10
Verbal Tests*			
Information	16	10	14
Comprehension	15	9	14
Arithmetic	11	8	15
Similarities	8	12	13
Vocabulary	16	13	13
Digit Span	8	6	7
Performance Tests *			
Picture Completion	17	12	12
Picture Arrangement	18	9	12
Block Design	14	14	14
Object Assembly	11	11	12
Coding	4	8	8
Verbal IQ	115	97	116
Performance IQ	120	106	111
Full Scale IQ	119	101	115

*Scaled Scores.

Jimmy's very low Coding score and the relatively low Object Assembly score were considered indications of specific difficulties in figure-ground discrimination and visual-motor coordination functions. The low Object Assembly score suggested a relative immaturity of higher Gestalt function. The very low Coding score reflected difficulty in retaining small units of information and in maintaining spatial interrelationships while transporting visual symbols.

In his very low Digit Span and relatively low Arithmetic subtest scores, Jimmy's difficulties in concentration and in maintaining continuous attention were probably important factors. These same behavioral difficulties probably also had a considerable influence on his poor Coding performance.

On the other hand, the configuration of high Information, Comprehension, and Vocabulary scores reflected his high verbal abilities.

Jimmy's rather low Similarities subtest score indicated a contrasting immaturity or deficit in verbal concept formation and abstract reasoning. His inability to reason abstractly was accompanied by very literal and concrete thinking characteristic of a younger age.

When these findings were considered together, the extreme degree of scatter and the pattern of the scatter in Jimmy's *WISC* subtest scores were felt to be practically diagnostic of a specific learning disability associated with a neurodevelopmental disorder.

On the *Bender Visual Motor Gestalt Test,* done when he was 8 years 3 months old, Jimmy showed deficiencies in visual-motor processes. His copied reproductions of the visually presented figures were made with great effort. There were frequent erasures and inaccuracies in the details of his drawings, although there were no gross distortions of spatial relationships. He was able to reproduce only one figure from memory, and this was rotated.

Jimmy had obvious difficulty in controlling some of the finer hand and finger movements in these tasks. As a result, his laboriously drawn figures were far larger than the original ones. One rotation was observed. Despite these difficulties, his mental age equivalent in the Koppitz quantitative scoring was roughly 8 years.

When he was asked to draw designs from memory on the *Benton Visual Retention Test,* Jimmy also had some mechanical difficulties. He made many erasures and crudely over-drawn lines. Nevertheless, his quantitative rating by the accuracy of visual retention was within the low average to average range.

Jimmy's performance on the Graham and Kendall *Memory-for-Design*

Test showed comparable difficulties and distortions. These findings were felt to corroborate the reliability of his very low Coding score in the *WISC*.

Jimmy's scores in the *Frostig Developmental Test of Visual Perception* are shown in Table 7. His low score in the Form Constancy subtest was thought to indicate an inability to conceptualize and categorize forms on an abstract level. His low score in the Position in Space subtest was correlated with his left-right disorientation and also suggested more general difficulty in grasping the concepts of serial order and sequence.

Table 7. Jimmy's Scores on the *Frostig Developmental Test of Visual Perception*

	Age When Tested	
	8–3	9–9
Eye-Motor Coordination	9–6	10+
Figure Ground	10+	7–0
Form Constancy	7–9	9–0
Position in Space	7–9	7–0
Spacial Relations	9–6	8–3

On the *Goodenough Draw-A-Man Test* Jimmy drew his man slowly and carefully. He thought of many details. Although the drawing was primitive in structure, the concept was clear, and the features were symmetrical. There was a big smile on the man's face. Jimmy's I.Q. equivalent in this test was 114.

A further indication of Jimmy's intelligence was found in the mental age estimate of 8 years 11 months in the *Peabody Picture Vocabulary Test*, obtained when he was 8 years 3 months.

Jimmy obtained a high score of 94 on the *Lincoln-Oseretsky Motor Development Scale,* corresponding to the 95th percentile for his chronological age. This high score gave quantitative confirmation to his generally excellent motor skills observed in the neurological examination. Jimmy's weakest points for his age in this scale were his inability to maintain rhythm in tapping alternate sides with his feet and fingers (subtest item 6), his slowness in winding thread on a spool (item 14), and other tests for accuracy and speed of fine finger and hand movements (items 17 and 18).

Educational Evaluation

In the educational consultant's evaluation, Jimmy appeared to have some compensatory strengths in auditory channels. For example, on the Auditory Word Discrimination section of the *Monroe Reading Aptitude Tests* he made a perfect score. Also, he made no errors on *Wepman Test of Auditory Discrimination.*

However, in the Visual Memory section of the *Monroe* tests, Jimmy made a very low score because of several reversals, in keeping with his poor left-right orientation.

In the *Durrell Analysis of Reading Difficulties,* he failed in oral reading at the first grade level. Jimmy could not recognize *drinks, does, get,* or *wet;* he misread *go* for *like.* He was unable to read silently, but achieved a perfect score in listening comprehension at the third-grade level.

Table 8. Jimmy's Scores on the *Durrell Analysis of Reading Difficulty*

		Age When Tested	
	8–3	*9–9*	*11–6*
Oral Reading	Failed 1st grade	Middle 3rd grade	Low 6th grade
Silent	Unable to read silently	Middle 3rd grade	Low 6th grade
Listening Comprehension	3rd grade	5th grade	Above 6th grade
Word Recognition	Low 1st grade	Low 4th grade	Middle 6th grade
Visual Memory	1.5	3.0	4.0
Auditory Discrimination	Failed	3.5	Not tested
Phonic Spelling	Not tested	Not tested	4th grade
Spelling	1 word	2nd grade	3rd grade

Jimmy showed poor skills in word recognition and analysis. He only recognized correctly seven out of twenty words at the first-grade level. Among his errors he read *make* for *little, my* for *me,* and *car* for *run.* Jimmy was able to identify all of the letters, only confusing *b* and *d,* but could not repeat or write the alphabet in sequence.

His visual memory in the *Durrell Analysis* was poor, scoring at 1.5 grade level. He was unable to attach the correct sound to any consonant or vowel letter; his phonic skills were nil.

Jimmy held the pencil awkwardly; he had trouble in staying on a line and forming letters. *Run* and *look* were the only words he could print correctly on the *Durrell* spelling test. He attempted to spell *go*, printing first *e* and then mirrored *g*. He also printed *see* correctly. (See Fig. 4.)

His oral language was excellent on the whole. However, Jimmy's pronunciation of "birfday" indicated some residual immaturity of his speech.

The educational consultant's summary and impression stated: "This boy is having severe difficulties learning to read. He is confused about

Fig. 4. Jimmy's spelling on the first administration of the *Durrell Spelling Test*.

direction of letters and is not noting visual details. He has no skills in the use of phonics and almost no sight vocabulary. He can listen well and comprehends, if you can hold his attention. He seems able to hear differences in sounds but does not attach letters to sounds at all. In spite of a fair score in visual memory, he is not making use of this in spelling. He is confused over direction, espcially in writing. He needs extra help as soon as possible. The program should be planned to use his skills and correct his confusions."

Formulation and Treatment Plan

We felt that there were clear indications from these evaluations that both Jimmy and his parents had serious emotional problems that were contributing significantly to Jimmy's learning difficulties. However, it was our conclusion that the psychological test results and the findings of the educational consultant probably reflected a constitutionally determined cerebral dysfunction affecting the development of certain specific higher cognitive intellectual skills.

Therefore, our initial plan for treatment involved the simultaneous use of remedial educational help and psychotherapeutic counseling of his parents. Within a few weeks after starting the remedial reading program, however, it became clear that Jimmy should also have a trial of medication directed at control of his hyperactivity and difficulty in concentration.

Remedial Program

Initial Counseling and Medical Treatment

In several counseling sessions with Mrs. W., the neurologist stressed a hopeful prognosis. He tried to make it clear that the term "brain damage" was inappropriate for this case, since Jimmy's degree of dysfunction could have developed without a frank lesion or anomaly of the brain. Since Mrs. Walcott had considerable difficulty in accepting this formulation, several counseling sessions were necessary for a better understanding.

Several weeks after Jimmy had been in our remedial reading program, it was apparent that his general hyperactivity, impulsiveness, restlessness, distractibility, and short attention span were greatly interfering with his work. We regarded these symptoms as manifestations of an impulse control deficit—a hyperkinetic behavior syndrome—presumably associated with imbalances in the relationships of the reticular activating system in the brain stem (lower brain centers) with the limbic system and neocortex (higher brain centers).

When we realized that even the highly structured, carefully planned individual tutoring remedial sessions were inadequate for the control of Jimmy's hyperactivity, we decided that he should have a trial of medication. Our first choice was dextro-amphetamine sulphate, because of the long history of its effective use for the treatment of hyperkinetic children and its extremely low incidence of long-term side effects.[1]

Jimmy started receiving this drug in very small doses, 2.5 mg. three times

---

[1]This paradoxical calming effect of amphetamines and related stimulant drugs in hyperkinetic children is thought to result from their action in stimulating the reticular activating system and possibly inhibiting the limbic system, permitting more optimal balance between these structures and the neocortex. Because of their different sites of action on the brain, the barbiturates and minor tranquilizers, such as meprobamate (Miltown®, Equanil®), often aggravate hyperkinetic behavior disorders.

daily before 4 P.M. Gradually, over a period of a few weeks, the dose was increased to 5 mg. three times daily.

When this dosage level was reached, Jimmy seemed slightly less hyperactive in the clinic and at school but he complained a great deal of stomachache, and his appetite was poor. Because of the persistence of these complaints, which we regarded as side effects, dextro-amphetamine was stopped after several months.

Jimmy was then given methylphenidate acetate (Ritalin®), a newer non-amphetamine compound, which has actions and uses similar to the amphetamines, but with less frequent gastrointestinal side effects. Starting with a dose of 5 mg. three times daily before 4 P.M., there were periodic changes during the next several weeks until he reached a dose of 20 mg. three times a day. Within a few days after reaching this dose, both his remedial teacher and classroom teacher reported a dramatic improvement in his behavior, which they both characterized as "almost unbelievable."

At the time of his latest re-evaluation at the clinic, when Jimmy was 12 years, 10 months old, he was still receiving methylphenidate, 20 mg. twice daily on school days. For the previous six months he had seemed to be more mature and better able to pay attention and concentrate at school, even with one less dose daily.

Throughout the approximately four-year period that Jimmy took this drug, there have been no disturbing side effects. Jimmy has always been able to stop it on school holidays, weekends, and vacation periods without any withdrawal symptoms, such as increased irritability. He has shown no tendency to either habituation or to a drug dependence. The dose has never had to be increased from its initially optimal level. It is our prediction that as Jimmy's brain becomes more completely mature during adolescence, he may no longer require this type of medication.

Educational Treatment

Our long-range educational plan for this boy was initially aimed at: 1) building up solid skills in the relationships between sounds (his strength) and written symbols (his weakness), 2) improving his hand-eye coordination, and 3) integrating visual, auditory, and tactile-kinesthetic modalities for his use in reading, spelling, and wrting.

It was clear that, before these aspects of training could be undertaken, some changes in his attitude and behavior had to be effected. Also, it was essential that his confusion with left and right be straightened out before work on letter recognition could begin.

In the first lessons his remedial teacher attempted to establish rapport and to provide a highly structured learning situation. There were four children in his class. All were 8 years old and had reading problems. They were scheduled for a one-hour lesson twice a week.

Upon entering the classroom for the first lesson, Jimmy dived under the table and began drawing a swastika on the floor with chalk. Its meaning was clearer than a "four-letter word" which Jimmy probably could not have spelled. His resentment and hostility were at once apparent. However, the incorrect arms on his design gave the teacher an opening wedge, and she was able to show him the correct way to draw the symbol at the board. This led into a discussion of left and right and the offer of other materials for drawing, such as felt pens, crayons, paint, etc., at the table.

It was evident then that Jimmy was impossible to manage in a group, as he demanded constant attention and was a distracting influence to the others. In fact, his own distractability was so extreme and his attention span so short that it seemed impossible that even individual tutoring could be carried out effectively for more than a few minutes without very careful planning. He was dismissed after twenty minutes.

At his second visit to the clinic Jimmy had an individual lesson, which was broken into four segments of approximately fifteen minutes each with a change of pace. It was soon discovered that even this was too long to expect him to pay attention. His remedial teacher then settled on units of ten minutes with a "Behavior Chart" to be marked as each task was completed. He marked his own chart with the teacher at the end of each lesson. After eight individual lessons, he was allowed to join the group, still marking his chart.

During the next several months, parts of each lesson involved the use of exercises to develop better control of his pencil and establish left-to-right orientation and sequencing. Also included in each lesson were exercises in listening, tracing, copying, and a game.

One sample lesson looked like this:

1:00–1:10   Copy a peg board design
1:10–1:20   Trace name on plastic overlay
1:20–1:30   Sort cards (matching initial consonants—using a *Language Master*)
1:30–1:40   Use Link Letters to spell "at" words (for encouraging left to right progression)

1:40–2:00   Play a game—choice of Blockhead, Pick Up Sticks, High Up
(for finger control)

This is a sample of one day's "Behavior Chart":

Job	Not Completed	Completed	Good	Fair	Poor
Peg Board		X	X		
Name-tracing		X	X		
Sorting sound cards					
with Language Master		X		X	
Link Letters ("at" words)		X			X
A Game		X	X		

Tactile-kinesthetic techniques did not prove particularly useful for Jimmy, as predicted from certain of his neurological signs (rostral dominance and poor finger localization ability). We also decided not to include any formal motor training except for exercises to improve his handwriting and visual-motor coordination. Although Jimmy had shown minor abnormalities in some of his motor functions, we felt that any treatment techniques directed primarily at his gross motility pattern were contraindicated. He already had achieved generally superior gross motor skills, which possibly represented the strongest aspect of his ego development.

We felt that any special emphasis on motor training would be inappropriate, wasteful, and probably harmful by complicating Jimmy's and his family's understanding of his problem and by taking away time for help in improving his academic skills. Being forced to undergo a complicated ritual of regressive patterned exercises would, we felt, have been confusing and highly humiliating to this sensitive, already disturbed boy. For similar reasons, no special attempt was made to influence the establishment of Jimmy's cerebral dominance.

Jimmy's first clinic teacher thought that Jimmy had most difficulty performing tasks requiring sustained attention, fine motor control of his pencil, visual memory, and left-right orientation. She also noted that he tended to react intensely in an initially negative manner to any oral instruction. He appeared to have enormous bottled-up violence. Whenever he had a spare moment for drawing he made pictures of explosions, bombs dropping, or army tanks with guns blazing.

Jimmy was extremely alert to noises outside the classroom or building and would go to the door or window to investigate at the slightest opportunity. He could not tolerate failure or criticism. He refused to consider any material that looked "babyish" to him; he completely rejected primers or primary workbooks even though these were at his appropriate reading level.

The one consistent way to get Jimmy's attention was by providing a structured program that required little in the way of verbal instructions from the teacher. A seatwork paper, peg board design, tracing materials, or the Pythagoras Puzzle, with materials already laid out, began the lesson without comments by the teacher. Some of the *Frostig* work sheets on Form Constancy and Position in Space were used because of his difficulty with figures.

Jimmy also enjoyed using clay, templets of different shapes, puzzles, and a labyrinth game. Timed activities appealed to his highly competitive spirit, but these were only useful when he did them alone, competing against his own time. In group games he always had to be the winner.

Jimmy greatly enjoyed using the *Language Master* for practice in sound discrimination, sound-letter association activities, and sound blending words. It provided a depersonalized form of teaching, and the additional use of earphones gave him the opportunity to work alone and without auditory distraction for a full ten minutes. Since Jimmy's auditory distractibility seemed to be even a greater problem than his visual attention difficulties, we felt that the use of earphones at a desk was far more effective for him than having to work in a cubicle.

Several months after starting at the clinic, his remedial teacher invited Jimmy to a party at her home with her own children and other guests. This was done in the hope of improving their relationship, since he still regarded all authority figures as "poison."

Jimmy obviously enjoyed the party but it was hard on his teacher, as well as on the other guests. He was into everything, insisted on being first for all games, pouted if he lost, and was generally too noisy and boisterous. However, although his clinic teacher was uncertain about having improved their relationship, she felt she learned a lot more about him from the experience.

Jimmy's oral language expression was excellent—far above average—but it was difficult for his clinic teacher to get spontaneous oral expression from him, either alone or in the group. His favorite responses to questions were, "No," or "I don't know." Therefore, another objective during the first year was to encourage spontaneous verbal expression in complete sentences. Short experience stories and class discussions of current news became a part of each lesson. His clinic teacher would not answer any of his questions or requests unless he used full sentences.

Throughout the whole first year, the average length of time for any effective work period was ten minutes. Before Jimmy left each session, he and his teacher would mark his chart and plan for the following lesson. In spite of all this, his gains were very small.

Second Year

The turning point was very dramatic. It happened immediately after his medication was changed to a more effective dose. This was not until early in the second year of the program. His clinic teacher suddenly reported noticing a striking change.

It now became possible to stretch his work periods to fifteen and then twenty minutes. He accepted criticism and suggestions from classmates. He also accepted the authority of the teacher and was able to wait for his turn and for his rewards. He began to insist on completing one job before starting another. When Jimmy finished his first paper of any length (twenty words) without error and presented it to his mother at the end of a lesson, she promptly burst into tears.

Jimmy had all along been building up very solid concepts of sound-letter associations and had developed skill in sound-blending. The order of presentation and progression of Jimmy's instruction in phonics followed the plan outlined in Gillingham's *Remedial Training for Children with Specific Disability in Reading, Spelling, and Penmanship*, sixth edition. (Educators Publishing Service).

These skills suddenly became useful to him in reading and spelling. He was willing to try to express himself in writing, as long as the teacher accepted his errors in spelling without too much criticism.

Jimmy particularly enjoyed using the bulletin-type typewriter because of the large print. Printed materials that were now effectively used with him included: the Lippincott Primer and its accompanying workbook and, especially, the *New Practice Readers*, Book A (Webster), since the level of interest was very important to him.

When his spelling errors began to concern him, his clinic teacher started a card file box for Jimmy's use only. Here, the words were selected from his reading lesson or written work. They were chiefly the non-phonetic words. He was encouraged to draw a stimulus picture in the upper right-hand corner to encourage rapid word recognition. These cards were filed alphabetically. The picture was covered or erased when it was no longer needed.

Games that proved effective during the second year were: *Grab, Phonic Rummy, Consonant Lotto, Vowel Lotto,* and Whitman's *Sentence Fun.* Jimmy also enjoyed playing Concentration, using home-made sets of cards, first with pairs of matching pictures and then with printed word pairs.

During the second year at the clinic, when Jimmy was 9 years 9 months old, he was re-evaluated by psychological and achievement tests. (See Tables 6 and 7). Also the *Durrell Analysis of Reading Difficulty* was repeated. (See Table 8.) Jimmy had improved considerably in word recognition, had mastered the sound-letter associations of consonants, consonant blends, and most short vowels, and could now use his auditory skills to blend sounds into words, both as a means of attacking new words and for spelling. Our educational consultant advised that he continue in the remedial program.

At the time of these tests Jimmy's achievement scores showed satisfactory improvement over those obtained previously, although it was obvious that he still needed more remedial help.

Somewhat enigmatically, his scores on the *Wechsler Intelligence Scale for Children* were lower than those obtained at the age of 7 years 7 months (see Table 6). We interpreted these findings as reflecting either a considerable degree of residual emotional disturbance, or quite possibly a stage of temporary apathy and lessened motivation, such as is frequently encountered in children during a mid-phase of the remedial work. A few months later, when his mother asked for additional psychiatric help, we were more completely able to understand these contradictory test results.

Third Year

In the third year in the remedial program, Jimmy was assigned to another clinic teacher. He was then in the fourth grade in public school. His clinic teachers were pleased with his progress but he was still at the bottom of his school class in achievement. This difference in opinion was hard for him to reconcile.

His clinic teacher found that he needed constant encouragement, and that any criticism had to be quietly or privately given to be effective. In the remedial group he was much better able to follow oral instructions and stay with a task until it was completed. Now that his visual confusions were largely overcome, he progressed rapidly in learning to connect sounds with letters.

Jimmy had excellent auditory skills and learned to blend sounds into words without any difficulty. He had some difficulty learning to count the syllables in a word from just hearing it. His teacher had him "pace off" the words, taking a step for each new syllable. We found that he learned each principle of phonics better if he drew the conclusion and formulated the rule himself, as in developing the rule for silent "e" endings. His clinic teacher noted, "Once he gets an idea, it is a solid concept. He enjoys being analytical."

Early in Jimmy's third year in the clinic, his parents received another call from his school, reporting on how poorly he was doing. Mrs. W. felt she could not relay this message to Jimmy and asked for advice about a change of schools. Before giving advice on this point, Jimmy's school principal and teacher were invited to a conference with our clinic personnel.

His school was located in a well-to-do neighborhood attended largely by children from upper middle-class homes. It had a reputation for high achievement on standard group tests, and the average I.Q. of its students was reported to be 115. The principal was obviously unhappy over Jimmy's underachievement, particularly because of his high recorded intelligence.

Both Mrs. W. and Jimmy often worked on his school assignments two or three hours a night. These nightly sessions were stormy, and the results were still not acceptable to the principal. She continually berated both Jimmy and his mother for his lack of effort. Before school each day, she called him into her office, scolded him for his "sloppy papers," and then phoned his mother urging her to give him more help with his homework.

From a constructive standpoint this conference was unsuccessful, inasmuch as Jimmy's teacher and principal were unable to accept the neurological and psychological findings as relevant, and so did not change their position even slightly. They considered our remedial educational program merely another way to "protect" Jimmy. Their standards were firm and they indicated that Jimmy must either measure up or face the consequences. His principal predicted, "He will never make it to junior high at this rate."

It was hard for our staff to believe the principal's accounts of tearing up his homework papers because they were unreadable, since the staff knew he had often spent as long as two hours on them. Jimmy's teacher seemed to be confused about the problem. The principal's comments and manner appeared to reflect a highly rigid attitude that could not be expected to change.

In contrast to our more common experience with other cases, this particular conference had an adverse effect, as those involved at the school seemed determined to see their worst predictions come true. After continuing their attempts for a few months longer to get the school to cooperate, the parents were able to arrange for Jimmy's transfer to another school.

Later in the third year of the remedial program, Jimmy began to use the *Gates-Peardon* exercises on grasping the general significance of a story and predicting the outcome, third-grade level. He could hold his own in group discussions that followed reading any type of material and could refer back to the text to prove his point. He was admired by the other members of his group for this ability.

He had much drill in the application of his phonic rules to spelling, using games and the *Language Master* machine. Some of the more advanced games used at this time included the *Dolch Syllable Game* and Sally Child's *Magic Squares*. Kottmeyer's *Conquests in Reading* (Webster) was used as a workbook.

At the end of Jimmy's third year in the remedial reading program, we felt he had acquired good work attack skills and good work habits. He was reading easily at his appropriate grade level. He was also reading for pleasure. Jimmy was then considered graduated from the clinic with an option to return if necessary.

At that time the *Durrell Analysis of Reading Difficulty* showed that he was reading at grade level with very little difficulty (see Table 8). Spelling and handwriting were still below his grade placement. His drawing of a map of North America from memory showed that he was still having difficulty with visual memory. However, his oral explanation of his Social Studies program showed a fine grasp of the subject matter. On the *Gates Reading Survey*, Form I, Jimmy's grade scores were: Vocabulary 6.8, Comprehension 7.9.

Conjoint Family Therapy

Ironically, shortly after Jimmy had begun the third year of remedial work and had shown great improvement in his ability to read and spell, Mrs. W. telephoned the psychiatric social worker to request additional help. She complained Jimmy was stealing and "always" had since he was very young, age 3 or 4.

The social worker met with Mr. and Mrs. W. and Jimmy to evaluate the problem further. Mrs. W. brought out, and Jimmy reluctantly confirmed, that he had been stealing money repeatedly at home and most recently had taken various objects from the school and from the home of relatives. Also, in spite of Jimmy's improvement in reading and spelling skills, he was again failing in school.

Here the therapist pointed out that stealing might possibly be considered a symptom of some other difficulty relating to Jimmy's development. In this case, conjoint family therapy was recommended. Initially, Mrs. W. questioned whether "we" (the parents and the social worker) "could do this with Jimmy there." The parents subsequently accepted the idea that therapy might appropriately involve the whole family, and that all would benefit from learning how to cope with their mutual problems in open, honest, forthright interactions with each other.

This conjoint psychotherapy extended over a six-month period with one and one-half hour sessions at weekly interviews. It was Mrs. W. who took the initiative and maintained the family in therapy.

Jimmy's stealing turned out to be the overt expression of a more pervasive problem affecting each member of the family. An extreme poverty of interaction and communication prevailed between the children and parents, whether by words, touch, or body or eye contact. When an interaction between parent and child did occur, it was a critical, disparaging, blaming verbal attack.

The parents neither blamed nor supported each other; they focused criticism on one of the children, usually Jimmy. They were critical of his lack of responsibility in assuming or completing a school or home task. As if preprogrammed, each child defended himself with a similar stereotyped pattern of blame and attack on his parents or siblings. When this was not going on there was dead silence.

Initially, when Mr. and Mrs. W. complained about Jimmy's persistent stealing and lying, they expressed themselves in a paradoxically hurt, but smiling and indecisive manner. During these discussions Jimmy often broke into poorly suppressed laughter which his parents ignored. Significantly, Jimmy's parents had made no effort to help Jimmy return the stolen goods.

On being encouraged to express their feelings more openly, they told Jimmy they were embarrassed, disappointed, and angry. Mr. and Mrs. W. said they wanted to trust Jimmy, but had not given him an allowance or the opportunity to earn money, fearing he would use the money foolishly. After realizing that they might be depriving Jimmy of learning about the responsible use of money, they were able to negotiate openly with Jimmy for an allowance of sixty cents a week.

It was significant that Jimmy frequently had almost no contact with his father during the week. Mr. W. usually came home after 8 P.M. when Jimmy and his sisters had already had their dinner, completed their homework, and been sent to bed. Mr. W. explained that for years, Jimmy's "I don't know" answers had so infuriated him he would spank the boy and send him to his room.

In describing his day, from awakening in the morning to falling asleep at night, Jimmy expressed feelings of loneliness and of being told constantly what to do, like a robot. His flat tone of voice and slumped posture reflected these feelings. Mrs. W. expressed amazement and chagrin when she heard Jimmy describe these feelings.

Gradually Mr. W. became able to allow Jimmy to express more of his feelings and thoughts, but was only able to give Jimmy terse, begrudging approval. Upon watching this change, Mrs. W. observed, "I see we have only communicated what we did not like, our disapproval of Jimmy . . . we have not let him know when we were pleased with him."

Jimmy's stealing had gradually ceased, and he had begun to assume responsibility for his daily chores without having to be angrily reminded. With a rare smile, Jimmy acknowledged this improvement and explained, "My father spends more time with me and my father and mother praise me now."

However, Mr. and Mrs. W. still complained of Jimmy's poor cooperation and inattentiveness. Slowly, Mrs. W. became more aware of how she was still taking over the responsibility for completing Jimmy's homework to protect him from school failure, and from his father's anger at being asked to help with the homework. Somewhat diffidently, Mr. W. defended and resisted any change of this family pattern of two generations, in which wives took over the raising of the children. Gradually, they were able to develop more mutually acceptable ways of helping Jimmy to handle the initiative and responsibility for completing his tasks.

Therapy continued, working on open, honest communication of feelings, expectations and validations of good efforts and achievements. Frequently, the parents resorted to their old patterns of defensive intellectualizations and logic, instead of responding to and acknowledging the children's feelings and ideas as a way of helping them to grow toward self-esteem, autonomy, and independence. Rather hesitantly, Jimmy expressed his feelings that his parents often "wanted him out of the way," by asking him "to go elsewhere, to his room, or outside to play." He read the message, "We don't want you." Mr. and Mrs. W. expressed dismay and insisted they did not intend to give Jimmy such a message.

In later sessions, Jimmy was more openly able to express his need for more autonomy in regard to his own homework. "Mom forces herself on me . . . You stay on top of me . . . You watch all my movements." Both parents expressed a pessimistic attitude about Jimmy's ability to be responsible. Mr. W. was reluctant to spend more time with his son, but later when Jimmy suggested that after completing his homework he would like to play a game of Monopoly with his father, Mr. W. agreed, "I will try."

Jimmy continued to improve in taking responsibility for his work and behavior. In school his grades improved and he earned good report cards. The threat of being expelled from school was gone.

Toward the completion of these therapeutic sessions, Mr. W. had actively taken over some of the tutoring. Jimmy was asserting himself openly and courageously in his growth toward autonomy. He was able to let his parents know how he felt about his problems. Mr. and Mrs. W. became more aware of how their ambitions for their son had been hollow and meaningless to him.

Jimmy's recurrent school failure following the initially successful remediation of his specific learning disability appeared to result from a pattern of passive-aggressive resistance and sabotage, associated with parental anxieties and pressure. In our view, the intensive, specific remedial educational help which this boy received would have been largely wasted if the medical and psychotherapeutic aspects of treatment had not been simultaneously available and appropriately utilized.

Follow-Up

JIMMY'S LAST EVALUATION at the clinic was done when he was 12 years 10 months old, nearly two years after his leaving the remedial reading program, and in sixth grade. We found him still improving and reading above his actual grade placement. A follow-up family interview showed indications of continuing improvement both at home and at school.

His psychological test results at this follow-up study are shown in Tables 6 and 7.

In the *WISC* at 12 years 10 months, Jimmy's I.Q. scores were within a

Table 9. Jimmy's Grade Scores on the *Wide Range Achievement Test*

	School Placement		
	2.0	3.6	6.8
Reading	1.7	3.6	8.4
Spelling	1.8	2.8	5.0
Arithmetic	1.8	3.6	5.9

few points of those obtained at age 7 years 7 months. These results tended to verify our impression that the generally lower scores obtained at age 9 years 10 months reflected the influence of his severe inner emotional turmoil related to his family's problems.

The scores on Jimmy's last *WISC*, at age 12 years 10 months, showed substantial improvement in the Similarities subtest, probably reflecting his improved abilities in abstract reasoning. His improved score in the Arithmetic subtest indicated improved ability to concentrate and maintain continuous attention.

On the other hand, his low scores in Digit Span and Coding reflected some residual limitation of his ability to retain and mentally transport the interrelationships of symbols from either an auditory or a visual input source.

During the following summer, his first clinic teacher had another party. She invited Jimmy and couldn't believe her eyes when she saw him. He was calm and poised. He insisted on helping to serve the refreshments and waited patiently for his turn at games. On leaving, he expressed his thanks and reminded her sheepishly of the other party. He said he enjoyed this party much more than the previous one.

Conclusion

In this case, the child's specific reading disability appeared to be the manifestation of a neurodevelopmental disorder with multiple indications of a constitutionally determined cerebral dysfunction. His learning problems were complicated by a severe hyperkinetic behavior disorder and a seriously disturbed family situation.

This case history illustrates the value of a multidisciplinary approach to the diagnosis and treatment of a specific reading disability that fails to respond readily to standard remedial techniques. By a careful integration of the diagnostic findings of each member of a multidisciplinary team, a comprehensive individualized therapeutic program can be developed and carried out.

Through the continuing participation of the multidisciplinary team, the proper utilization of multisensory remedial educational methods, simultaneously with any relevant medical or psychiatric modes of therapy, can lead to a successful result which may not be otherwise attainable.

Editor's Comments

Because Dr. Whitsell was known to have a special interest in the use of drugs for treatment of behavioral disorders, he was asked to select a case in which medication played a significant role. As it happened, both medication and psychotherapy proved to be important in this case. The detailed presentation of neurological and psychological findings may have presented vocabulary problems to the reader, despite editorial efforts to provide parenthetical explanations, but it was felt desirable to retain this rich material.

There are many points that could be discussed at length concerning this fascinating case—the value of trying more than one drug, and more than one dosage; the diagnostic significance of a drop in I.Q. while a child is learning to read; the reasons for preferring a structured phonic approach in this case; what can be done about an unsatisfactory school situation; etc. To the editor, however, the most interesting part of the section on remediation is the reluctance of the parents to admit their concern over Jimmy's stealing (not mentioned till late in the second year), and the graphic, if brief, description of the conjoint family therapy that followed. This form of group therapy would seem to be very well suited to families in which parents and children are locked in a repeating cycle of mutual misunderstanding and retaliation. Without resolution of the parent-child difficulties, it seems probable that Jimmy would have remained an academic failure, despite the quite adequate level of reading proficiency that he had reached.

15

Nannette

BY ARCHIE A. SILVER, M.D., AND ROSA A. HAGIN, Ph.D.

Setting

Dr. Silver has supplied the following description of the setting:

The material presented in our report comes from our own private practice. The methods and techniques used are those which we have developed
through the years at the New York University Medical Center. Our initial
work was done in the early 1950's when we attempted to devise methods
of identifying the subtle defects hidden in the child with a reading disability and in one with minimal structural brain damage. By the early
1960's we attempted to devise and systematically evaluate methods for
training based upon the specific defects uncovered in each child.

Our experience during these years has ranged through every problem
encountered in a practice of psychiatry and psychology and in a child
psychiatry clinic of a busy general hospital serving a population largely
from the lower east side of New York. Dr. Hagin's psychological and educational contributions, added to Dr. Silver's medical, neurological, and
psychiatric ones, contributed to a more complete understanding of the
patient. In addition, the facilities of a large medical center and the challenging questions from medical students and residents are continually
available.

Diagnostic Study

THIS REPORT WILL FOCUS on the diagnosis, management, and outcome
of the language problems in a bright girl who has evidence of a structural
defect of the central nervous system. It will touch briefly on the reading
problems of her two siblings and will outline the familial background to
these problems.

This report is a segment in the history of a family, the interrelationships
of emotional and biological factors in their successes and their failures,
and the methods used to help them. The segment we will observe extends

in time from December, 1958, to April, 1969; the people we will observe include three children, their parents and grandparents, their aunts and uncles, and a number of their cousins. The scene is New York City and its environs.

Nan's First Examination, Age 2

Our observation of this family begins in December, 1958, when Nannette, the middle child, was 2 years 3 months of age. Mary, the older daughter, was then 4½, and William was a boy of 12 months. The initial problem was not, of course, reading. It was that Nan would cry most of the night, an intense, persistent wail continuing for several hours, exhausting her parents. This had been going on since Nan was about 10 months of age, sometimes improving with Butisol and Compazine given by her pediatrician, but sometimes, as in the months preceding her referral, unremitting in spite of medication. By day, however, as in her first appearance at our office, Nan was an alert, appealing, slight, dark-haired little girl with deep brown, trusting eyes, who, without anxiety, left her mother in the waiting room and, holding on to the examiner's hand, walked into the playroom.

It was noted that part of these few yards were done on tiptoe and that if the examiner withdrew his hand Nan stumbled. In the playroom she accepted dolls, playing with them as though this was what she had done every day. She was hypokinetic (underactive). Her speech consisted of pertinent sentences at at least a three-year level; her comprehension of verbal material and her vocabulary were both excellent. On the motor side, however, her enunciation was not clear; her hand grasp when manipulating crayons or when making a tower of four blocks was awkward and still palmar; and the equilibrium problem and predominance of extensor tone in the lower extremities was again noted—with that, there was marked anxiety on antigravity play. Her muscle tone was increased throughout, there was a facial asymmetry with the left side smaller than the right, the pupils were eccentric (not in the center of the iris) and there was sustained nystagmoid movement (jerky eye movements) on left lateral gaze. The deep reflexes were increased throughout.

Search for the origin of these neurological signs revealed that despite weekly hormone injections, there was persistent staining throughout the first six months of pregnancy with Nan. The labor itself was induced, prolonged (twenty-two hours), and difficult because of slow dilatation. Birth weight was six pounds, twelve ounces. The neonatal period and well into the sixth month was characterized by "continual crying," with night time screaming, irritability and startle to sudden loud noises, and irregular bowel function. She was a tumultuous bed rocker, bouncing her crib off the wall.

Her father was a grim-jawed individual, controlling his feelings with a deliberate rigidity, but in fact extremely insecure as to his ability, driving himself to compulsive and demanding work patterns. Although his intelligence is superior and although he did manage to graduate from a small college, his academic record was a poor one and on questioning he admitted that he reads very slowly and always "had trouble" reading. On examination, although he was right-handed, it was his left hand which was elevated on the extension test. His father, Nan's grandfather, was left-handed, had no formal education, and could read only with difficulty.

Nan's mother, although physically a large, soft, pink woman struggling with overweight, was emotionally very hard, demanding, and immoveable. Her speech was rapid and incisive, and, not surprisingly, she grimly said, "A few beltings will help Nan." She was an avid, rapid reader who had found reading an escape from her own parents' arguments as a child. Her father was also left-handed. He was always dependent on his wife's income (from a circulating book library). He was not examined by us but is described by his daughter as never interested in reading, his handwriting illegible and childish, and his spelling impossible.

We were faced then with a complex of problems: a child with evidence suggestive of a structural defect of the central nervous system, in a grim and demanding household, with a family pattern of reading problems observed in the father and in both grandfathers.

While our immediate therapeutic efforts were directed at relieving the presenting problem of a non-sleeping, night-wailing child, our long-range view for this family included not only psychotherapeutic help for the parents but also an alertness to the possible development of language problems in Nan and in her siblings.

Relief of the immediate problem was not difficult. It was more difficult to impress the need for psychotherapy on the parents and to insure the children's return for our evaluation as they grew older.

Nan at Four Years

It was not until two years later, when Nan was 4 years and 4 months of age, that she was brought to us again. This time, however, it was not Nan who precipitated the visit but her mother's fractured toe. This injury occurred when the mother, exploding in anger at her older daughter Mary's difficulty with second-grade arithmetic, kicked out and missed the child but hit a kitchen cabinet with her toe. The father, at least, agreed to the family's need for psychotherapeutic help and, equally important, we were able to evaluate Nan once again and to examine her older sibling, Mary.

Nan at age 4½ was the same bright, appealing child we had seen some two years before, with the same need for physical support and reluctance to climb. Muscle tone was still increased, more so on the left where cogwheeling (a form of rotary motion) was noted on extension of the left arm at the elbow. She still had not clearly established a preferred hand, but seemed equally facile with both. Visual-motor functioning was not yet at a five-year level and visual discrimination of wedges in various spatial orientations was not correct. Her comprehension of verbal material was excellent and her enunciation had improved.

Our concern here, in addition to the continuing abnormality in muscle tone and synergy and in equilibrium, was twofold: 1) that visual perception seemed poor for this bright child; and 2) emotional problems characterized by depression and withdrawal were evident. In retrospect, training to improve her spatial discrimination and orientation and to enhance a dominant cerebral hemisphere should have been started then.

Mary. The older daughter, however, presented an immediate problem. In the second grade of a demanding and exacting school, she was having a difficult time, in spite of reading tutoring at school and continued help with homework at home. In contrast to Nan's alertness, Mary was a sad, dull-eyed child, physically large for her age, who looked at the world with fear and with anticipation of rejection. She complained that she is "not good" at school, has to work very hard to understand arithmetic, and needs constant support and encouragement.

On neurological examination Mary's muscle tone and synergy were normal, cranial nerves intact, reflexes within normal limits. There was, however, abnormality in: on extension of the arms, although she is right-handed, it was the left arm that was elevated; the extended arms tended to converge. There were marked errors on testing for right-left discrimination in herself, in her mirrored image, and in drawings of the body; finger gnosis [1] was impaired with respect to her age and intelligence. There was difficulty with praxis (action, movement) and her grasp of the

---

[1] Ability to identify, without looking, which finger has been touched.

pencil was still immature. Perceptually there were defects in visual discrimination, in visual figure-background perception, and in visual-motor functioning, in all of which there was extreme difficulty with diagonals. On the *Bender Gestalt*, for example, a stellate (star-shaped) diamond was produced in A and on 7, and diagonal groupings were flattened to the horizontal or to the vertical. Auditory perception revealed no difficulty in discrimination, but errors in auditory sequencing and in intermodal auditory-visual association. On the *Wechsler Intelligence Scale for Children* she functioned in the high average range (Full Scale I.Q. 107, Verbal I.Q. 103, Performance I.Q. 110).

Mary was then a child with better than average intelligence who, despite continued support at school, was beginning to falter. She represents a child with the syndrome of specific or developmental language disability, with her major problems in right-left orientation, visual-motor functioning, auditory sequencing, and auditory-visual associations.

Remedial work was then begun with Mary and, at the same time, her father entered what was to prove some two years of successful psychotherapy. With this background and with our alerting her school to Nan's problems in equilibrium, praxis, and perception, it was hoped that remedial work might not be necessary for Nan.

Nan at Age Seven

Kindergarten and first grade were completed by Nan with no turmoil, but as she became 7 years old and entered second grade and into the lowest reading group, a reluctant and abashed child began conveying home notes from school. These notes, telling her parents that "Nan does not write well, her handwriting is getting bad, and she is erasing on her page" stirred up her mother's flushed anger again and caused Nan to retreat into her own pleasureable fantasy.

Examination at that time revealed a mildly hypokinetic and dejected child. Her gait was slightly broadbased and flatfooted, she could not balance on one foot, nor could she perform heel to toe walking. In the upper extremities her gross motor coordination was more adequate, but a distinct difference in muscle tone was apparent, with the left greater than the right and with cog-wheeling on the left. Synkinesis (involuntary, useless movement that accompanies a voluntary movement) was marked on both sides. The cranial nerves revealed again the pull of the right corner of the mouth and the pupils were mildly eccentric (off center). There was no nystagmus, and caloric testing revealed a sensitive vestibular apparatus. The deep reflexes in the lower extremities were brisk but equal; in the upper extremities slightly increased on the left.

In spite of excellent fine motor coordination as seen in the finger to finger testing, praxis was impaired with marked difficulty in her ability to imitate the position of the examiner's hands and of drawings of hands. Her pencil grasp, too, was immature and awkward and her handwriting labored and immature, with many reversals noted. On extension of the arms, although she was right-handed, it was the left hand which was elevated, and the outstretched arms tended to converge. There were errors in right-left orientation, particularly in her mirrored image. Her speech in content revealed excellent comprehension and excellent vocabulary (see psychological test data below), but there was a slight articulation defect. She could not, however, correctly write the words she was able to say. The electroencephalogram at that time was diffusely abnormal with high-voltage slow waves throughout, consistent with cerebral dysfunction.

Neurological study, then, continued to reveal problems in equilibrium, in praxis, in muscle tone and synergy, in tests of clear cut cerebral dominance, in right-left orientation, and in the ability to translate the spoken word into writing.

Psychiatric examination revealed a depressed child, beginning to be overweight, occasionally scratching the mild neurodermatitis (skin rash of neurological origin) on her arms and on the back of her neck. Her ambivalence to her mother was characterized by a dream, "My mother was hit by a car and had to go to the hospital. I brought her flowers." Concerning her sister Mary she reported a dream, "We were at the beach, Mary went too far out in the water and was drowned. I was afraid to tell my mother." This mixture of resentment and displaced resentment alternated with her fear and guilt. She was bewildered by her school problems, began to feel thoroughly stupid and unloved. Her reaction was a passive resistance to her mother and to the world, and a surreptitious eating and hoarding of candy and cookies, the wrappers of which she carefully arranged for her mother to find.

During psychological study Nan related easily. She was spontaneous, cooperative, playful, and at times a little giggly. However, she worked hard and accomplished the following battery in a little over two hours:

Wechsler Intelligence Scale for Children (Verbal I.Q. 123, Performance I.Q. 115, Full Scale I.Q. 121)

Wide Range Oral Reading Test, Grade 3.3
Wide Range Spelling Test, Grade 2.8
Metropolitan Reading Test (Word Knowledge 2.9; Word Discrimination
2.9; Comprehension 3.3)
Rorschach
Goodenough, Bender Drawings
Perceptual Battery

Her Full Scale I.Q. of 121 on the *WISC* (92nd percentile) put her within the superior intellectual group. Distribution of subtest scores was:

Verbal Scale		*Performance Scale*	
Information	17	Picture Completion	13
Comprehension	11	Picture Arrangement	14
Arithmetic	15	Block Design	10
Similarities	9	Object Assembly	11
Vocabulary	18	Coding	13
Digit Span	12		

She did best with those tests tapping verbal facility. She was alert to the world around her and showed good understanding of relevant social behavior. She showed that she was able to improvise with number relationships on the Arithmetic Reasoning test. Her response to some of the Comprehension items, however, was surprisingly immature. She tended in these responses not to take the initiative herself but either to depend upon an adult or to accept the consequences of the happening described. She also had a low scaled score (9) on the test of conceptual thinking (Similarities), in which her responses described concrete or functional relationships rather than abstract qualities. She also had difficulty with Object Assembly, with her lowest scores on the two items which tapped body image. Her approach to the Block Design test was that of segmenting and then trying to assemble the parts into a Gestalt. Even so, she made errors in figure-background and reversals of the orientation of split sides.

In view of an approximate mental age of 9 years, Nan might be expected to achieve educational test scores at the fourth-grade level at that time. Achievement test scores were above grade placement although not appropriate to expectancy. Oral reading was carefully and slowly done. Her writing was also slow and careful, probably because much emphasis was placed upon "good" writing at school. Nan's reading comprehension was also lower than expectancy, as seen by the scores of high second to low third grade on the *Metropolitan Achievement Test*.

Perceptually she worked very slowly, and on the drawings placed heavy pressure on the pencil. There was much evidence on the *Bender* of constriction in her reproduction of the designs. There was also evidence of difficulty with diagonals and with mild angulation problems. She had more difficulty with the *Marble Board* test. However, this, too, she managed with great effort and trial and error. The final results were fairly good, particularly the later designs, because she seemed to learn as she went along. However, early in the test there were signs of an erratic approach and omissions and displacements. Here, as on the *Bender*, she managed to get some diagonals correct eventually.

No errors in auditory discrimination were elicited on the *Wepman* test. Marked difficulty with auditory sequencing was apparent. No errors were seen on the finger schema but right-left discrimination was sometimes incorrect. Her figure drawings had large heads, displaced arms, and slanted to the left. Upon questioning about preferred writing hand, Nan says she sometimes gets tired writing with her right hand and then uses her left. She says that this writing is not very good.

Nan's first figure drawing was described by her as a "good little girl." The second drawing, described as a "good little boy" was less well differentiated than the first. Her associations emphasize the fact that they were playing together well and had been rewarded with ice cream cones.

Nan's response to the *Rorschach* was appropriate to the superior intelligence demonstrated on the cognitive measures. Her playful manner on cognitive measures contrasted with the fears the *Rorschach* revealed. While Nan was only reasonably productive, responses were rich and well elaborated. She felt insignificant and vulnerable both to threats from the environment and to inner anxieties. She was all too aware of these anxieties and demonstrated marked sensitivity to her feelings. For example, the response to Card VII was "the jittery nerves of a ballerina like I sometimes are." On the inquiry, she said "she's shaking because she's scared, she never performed before." While this sensitivity gave evidence of the emotional resources this child has, it also suggested her greater vulnerability to stress. Depression, unusual for a child of this age, underlined the record. While in day-to-day behavior Nan had learned to use constriction, this defense was not seen in the *Rorschach* protocol. Indeed, the characteristic reaction here seemed to be either to ignore attempts at adult control or to act out explosively.

Table 10. Neurological and Perceptual Findings in Three Siblings at about Age 7 Years

	Mary at 7 yrs., 11 mos.	Nan at 7 yrs., 6 mos.	William at 7 yrs.
WISC	FS 107 V 103 P 110	FS 121 V 123 P 115	FS 121 V 123 P 110
I. NEUROLOGICAL			
Kinetic pattern	N	hypokinetic	N
Muscle tone	N	increased, cog-wheel left	N
Gross coordination and equilibrium	N	poor; marked defect	N
Fine coordination	N	N	N
Synkinesis	+	+++	+++
Deep reflexes	N	left > right	N
Cranial nerves	N	mouth pulled to right	lag in blink of right eye
Extension test	left elevated	left elevated	no clearcut pattern
Praxis	poor	poor	poor
Right-left discrim-ination	errors	errors	errors
II. PERCEPTION			
Visual			
Discrimination	+	+	++
Figure-background	+++	++	+++
Visual-motor	+++	++	+++
Auditory			
Discrimination	++	N	+
Sequencing	++	++	++
Body-Image			
Finger gnosis	N	N	+
Drawing	+++	++	+++
Time concept	++	++	++
III. INTERMODAL	+++	+++	+++

Note: Plus signs indicate the presence of abnormal responses; the number used indicates the severity of the symptom, with three the most severe. N means normal.

Diagnostic Summary. Our evaluation of Nan led to a number of conclusions. This was a child with a family history of specific language disability who, in addition, had evidence on neurological examination of a central nervous system defect. Despite superior cognitive resources, she was managing a marginal level of achievement at school. She was, moreover, living in an emotionally constricting atmosphere. The exchange of complaints between her mother and her school further endangered the self-concept of this confused, frightened, and discouraged little girl. It was felt that at this point her mother had to be involved in her own psychotherapy, and that Nan urgently needed remedial teaching directed at her language disability and supportive psychotherapeutic help as indicated.

Remedial Program

INTERVENTION FOR NAN WAS FOCUSED upon her language disability, which we regarded as severe because of the discrepancy between her *potential* and her *actual* school achievement and the emotional havoc this was creating. Although she was able to earn scores on educational tests close to her current grade placement, the level of intellectual functioning demonstrated on individual intelligence examination suggested that her expectancy was at least two years above grade placement. The purposes of educational intervention were not only to offer help with her problems in perception and language, but also give her concrete evidence that she could achieve. This would help her realize her intellectual promise and learn more effective ways of dealing with frustration than withdrawing into fantasy or striking out like a bull in a china shop.

Tutoring was started in November, 1964, during the fall of her third grade, with a one-hour session per week, and continued until June, 1966. More frequent sessions would have been preferred, but were not possible. The idea of tutoring appealed to Nan and she readily accepted the goals which were set with her: 1) to learn to organize what she saw and heard, 2) to learn to put ideas down on paper, 3) to improve her understanding of what she read. These sessions would not be used to do her school assignments, but we could always take time for any specific work which she found hard.

The School Situation

Nan's school offered a highly structured curriculum in a highly pressured atmosphere. Reading was done from a basal reading series with the class divided into three reading groups. Nan was painfully aware that she was in the lowest group. Additional work in phonics was given by an itinerant teacher who drilled all classes in phonics generalizations, often inappropriate for Nan's reading level. She was able to make the rote responses required in these lessons, but could not apply these generalizations to unlock new words when she was reading. Spelling lessons at school consisted of words selected from an official list. These, too, were learned by rote with no contextual application provided. Furthermore, in Nan's class it was required that words be written without erasures in order to be considered correct on the final test given on Friday of each week.

The principal of Nan's school had great personal investment in the achievement levels of the pupils. She saw any modification to meet the needs of individuals as a compromise of her standards. The classroom teacher, none too warm to begin with, was intimidated by the atmosphere of the "tight ship" that prevailed in the school. She regarded Nan as a somewhat limited youngster intellectually and a decided handicap in her own daily struggle to meet the school's inflexible standards.

It has been our practice to encourage cooperation and exchange of information with the schools, and particularly with the classroom teachers, of the children we work with. Efforts to open channels of communication with Nan's school only confirmed the family's description of it. We were faced with an immovable force which would consider no modification of the existing program. Since no other school arrangements were available, it seemed advisable to maintain open lines of communication with school. Telephone conversations with her principal were arranged to give her some information concerning the high points in Nan's functioning. Attempts were also made to describe the nature of specific language disability, but our feeling is that this administrator considered it delusional thinking to imply that a child might have above-average intelligence and yet fail to learn to read well in her school. Our work with the family required discussion and interpretation of report cards and other written communications from the school with both Nan and her parents. This was particularly important when Nan began to gain in her reading skills, but found that these gains were not reflected in her school marks or report cards. We could only be grateful that she was able to "keep up" if not distinguish herself in the pressured (though well-intentioned) atmosphere of the school.

The Remedial Plan

Four kinds of activities comprised the content taught during the sixty-six tutoring sessions: 1) perceptual stimulation, 2) experience stories, 3) practice with word attack skills, 4) reading comprehension. Initially,

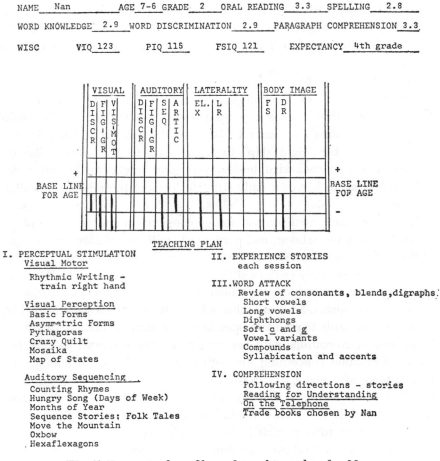

NAME ___Nan_____ AGE _7-6_ GRADE __2___ ORAL READING __3.3___ SPELLING ___2.8___

WORD KNOWLEDGE _2.9_ WORD DISCRIMINATION _2.9__ PARAGRAPH COMPREHENSION _3.3_

WISC   VIQ _123_   PIQ _115_   FSIQ _121_   EXPECTANCY _4th grade_

Fig. 5. Perceptual profile and teaching plan for Nan.

emphasis was placed upon the development of accuracy of perception; as these skills were acquired, there was a shift of emphasis to their application in language arts activities. Perceptual training was directed toward areas of deficit as outlined in the perceptual profile which was based upon the results of our initial evaluation. Figure 5 presents the data together with the teaching plan that was utilized. Teaching techniques are drawn from the pool of such techniques developed in the course of a study funded by the Carnegie Corporation of New York.[1]

Writing. Because of the praxic problems that Nan demonstrated, the Rhythmic Writing technique was valuable in her retraining program. This technique was adapted from the work of Roach and Kephart [2] but is used by us, not so much as a test of perceptual-motor functioning, but as an approach for teaching left to right progression, awareness of directionality, and accuracy in the reproduction of increasingly complex motor patterns. The only materials required are a chalkboard large enough to extend beyond the child's outstretched arms, eraser, and white chalk. The child stands at the center point of the board and, using the preferred hand, traces or reproduces, on his own, motifs presented by the teacher. These motifs are repeated rhythmically by the child.

At first, it may be necessary for the teacher to write an entire line and ask the child to trace over it. As the child gains skill, there is gradual reduction in cues, so that he may trace only the beginning of the motif and continue on his own, and then he may follow trails she makes with the eraser tip on the chalky surface of the board, and finally he may write the entire motif on his own.

The motifs are simple at first, but may become more complex as the child's skills permit. They contain elements that can be combined to teach the motor patterns required in cursive writing. The variations are endless; frequently the children themselves originate new motifs, and enjoy naming them. It is important to restrict the writing to the preferred hand. Many children with reading problems, like Nan, tend to use the left hand on the left side of the board, switching to the right hand as they reach the mid-line.

Nan began this practice with the simple horizontal and vertical lines of Wayne's Fences:

[1] A. A. Silver, R. A. Hagin, and M. F. Hersh, Reading Disability: Teaching Through Stimulation of Deficit Perceptual Areas," *American Journal of Orthopsychiatry*, XXXVII (1967), 744–752. A. A. Silver and R. A. Hagin, "Specific Reading Disability: Teaching by Stimulation of Deficit Perceptual Areas," Final report in preparation.

[2] E. Roach and N. C. Kephart, *The Purdue Perceptual-Motor Survey* (Columbus, Ohio: Charles E. Merrill Books, Inc., 1966), pp. 53–58.

and Bruce's Bridges:

These led to more complex motifs such as Caterpillars:

and Craig's Snowmen:

and Greg's Double Diamonds:

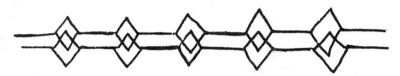

As these and other motifs were mastered at the chalkboard, a transition was made to paper and pencil. Correct grip on the pencil, slant of the notebook parallel to the writing arm, and comfortable writing position to permit ease of movement across the page were taught at this time. It was especially important that Nan work on these skills, for cursive writing was being introduced during that year at school. Her approach to the formation of the letters had been to try to segment them, drawing the shapes in inconsistent fashion. By June of the first year of tutoring she was able to make all of the lower case letters correctly. Some of the capitals were difficult for her and practice with them continued during the second year of tutoring.

Form Perception. Nan also worked to improve perception of form. We usually teach these skills through three stages: 1) matching, 2) copying, and 3) recall. Nan had little difficulty with the first stage, having by now mastered problems in discrimination. Copying was difficult for her because of her praxic difficulties; recall brought out errors in orientation of asymmetric figures.

Form perception was taught through the use of both basic and asymmetric forms which have been described elsewhere. Puzzle-toys such as *Pythagoras, Crazy Quilt, Mosaika,* and a jigsaw puzzle map of the states were also used. The three stages of matching, copying, and recall were also used with these puzzles because it was felt that a trial-and-error approach did not effect improvement in form perception.

Two sheets of paper were provided for each design to be built; one contained the outline of the figure and the other the elements of the design. At first Nan was encouraged to superimpose each piece of the puzzle upon the correct place of the sheet on which the design elements were drawn. When these discriminations were made easily, she was asked to place the pieces on the outline sheet with the elements sheet available to copy. Finally, when the design could be copied easily, the elements sheet was removed from sight and she was asked to recall the solutions of the puzzles.

Sequence. As Nan gained skills in the organization of figures in space, she was also helped to sequence sounds in time. This work began with patterns of sounds tapped on the table top, simple counting tasks, rote repetition of the days of the week, and the months. Meaningful sequences of directions were also used. Such puzzles and pocket games as *Move the Mountain* and *Oxbow* were useful because they involved the repetition of a series of moves utilizing left-right and up-down directions.

Once Nan had learned them herself, she was encouraged to teach the solutions to her parents and her brother and sister. This teaching not only added to her self-confidence, but gave her further practice in sensing correct orientation in space and in verbalizing the direction correctly.

To give Nan practice with the sequencing of ideas, a number of folk tales were used. She particularly enjoyed retelling *The Old Woman and the Pig* and *The Tawny, Scrawny Lion* [3] to parents, siblings, and anyone else who would listen. The sequencing of the ideas of stories led naturally to the sequencing of content. The principle of sequencing was used at the close of every lesson, at which time Nan was asked to review what she had done. At first she would recall activities only tangentially and in incorrect temporal order. Gradually, she was able to recall the correct sequence of the work we had done, referring to each task by its correct name. These summaries were jotted down by the teacher and Nan soon began to regard them as a record of what she had accomplished. The principle of sequencing was generalized to brief stories (*How to Make Applesauce, How Pearls Are Formed, How to Fold a Hexaflexagon, Differences in the Customs of Americans and Japanese*) and to Nan's plans of stories she was to

[3] Custaf Tenggren, *The Tawny, Scrawny Lion* (New York: Simon and Schuster, 1951).

write. The sequences became forerunners of simple outlines that Nan learned to use to make simple "speeches" or to organize longer written compositions.

The writing of experience stories was utilized from the earliest tutoring sessions. Because Nan had little opportunity for the spontaneous expression of ideas both at home and at school, she enjoyed this activity. She was encouraged to put words down whether or not they were spelled correctly. It was important to accept all she had to say at first, suggesting corrections only with those aspects of her work that clarified the meaning of what she was trying to communicate. Gradually, some work with style was done so that she could, for example, learn to use connectives to express relationships of ideas. Misspelled words were rewritten for her on a separate sheet of paper; phonic principles she knew, word structure, or mnemonic devices were provided where they were appropriate to the learning of a word. Nan then was encouraged to "be the teacher" and make these corrections in her original copy. The changes in her organization and style are illustrated in the following stories she wrote:

Dolly [written during second month of tutoring]
    I know a horse named Dolly. She is a very good horse. I ride bareback now. I like her and she likes me.

The Planetarium [written during seventh month of tutoring]
    Last week I went to the Planetarium. First there was a lecture about the planets. Then there was a movie called *Watchers of the Sky*. After that we went over to some scales that said how much you would weigh on the Sun, Moon, Venus, and Jupiter.

My Trip [written during fifteenth month of tutoring]
    On December 27 we were on our way to Virginia. At Williamsburg we went to many shops. My family saw the Wig Maker's where the saying, 'You flipped your wig!' came from. We went into the Raleigh Tavern, the Silversmith's, and Printshop and the Governor's Palace. I liked the Blacksmith's Shop where I got a horseshoe. All in all I had a great time.

That these stories also served in the expression of feelings generated in the combustible atmosphere at home was also apparent in the choice of subjects. Nan came to one session tearful because her older sister had broken a small purse that she had cherished. The time set aside for story-writing was consumed in angry recriminations on the theme of the uselessness of sisters. The very next week, however, Nan chose to compose a birthday card, which while not distinguished by the clarity of its rhymes, does make a point:

> For Dear Mary
> Happy Birthday, Mary
> Your are the best sister on this hemisphere-y
> When you were eleven
> You acted like you came from heaven
> Now that you're twelve
> Just be yourself
> Soon you'll be thirteen
> And that will be keen!

Word Attack. As auditory and visual perception improved with training, it was possible to work with word attack skills. The approach to this area of reading at school had been by mechanical rules which Nan learned by rote. There was little opportunity for assimilation or application in the reading process because they were presented in isolation. For example, all the short vowels were taught at the same time, and her class was told to "know them by next week." At that point, she was unable to discriminate among the short vowel sounds, much less associate sound and symbol, or select appropriate words in reading context.

After five months of tutoring, Nan was able to demonstrate mastery of consonants, consonant blends, and digraphs. Work continued with specific phonic principles for short vowels, long vowels, vowel variants, diphthongs, "soft sounds," compounds, and syllabication. Words illustrating the specific phonic principles were used both for dictation and oral reading so that the sound-symbol relationships were practiced both in encoding and decoding processes.

Review games were used to permit overlearning of skills so that they would become automatic. Most effective were those with the simplest structure and equipment: Steal the Old Man's Pack played with the Go Fish cards, Vowel Dominoes, Word Jumbles utilizing the tiles of a Scrabble set, and Hangman. The last two games are valuable in drawing attention to such characteristics of word structure as the probable combinations among letters, the number of vowels in syllables, the relationships between consonants and vowels. These games were an integral part of the work of the session and were understood by Nan as an opportunity for rapid practice with new skills rather than as a reward or recreation. Because all sessions were structured with the question "How does this help me with reading, spelling, or writing?" digressions were never a problem with Nan. She was well aware of her goals and settled down to reaching them in a businesslike fashion. She needed no extrinsic rewards; a sense of accomplishment was all the motivation she needed.

Comprehension. As soon as word attack skills permitted, work with the comprehension of contextual material was introduced. Although she had much work with factual comprehension at school, Nan needed practice with comprehension tasks that required her to organize details in order to follow directions, to draw inferences from material she had read, or to select the specific word meanings. The *Reading for Understanding* kit (Science Research Associates) was useful in alerting her to contextual cues. Much work with following written directions was done, because Nan, like many children with reading disabilities, worked so hard at decoding the words that the message often became fragmented or lost in the process. Reading simple contextual material that required the application of the ideas (e.g., to play a game from the rules she had just read, to draw a plan of a swing to be built) was more appropriate and challenging than selecting a multiple-choice answer or responding to written questions. Nan also enjoyed dramatizing plays, stories, and poems. Because of the "here and now" quality of the conversations, the *On the Telephone* books [4] were particular favorites.

Eventually Nan began to read on her own. *Suzy the Ballet Horse* was the first of a number of books she brought to her session to share "the best part" with her teacher. She was encouraged to read books well below her instructional level in her free reading. It was most important that she have the opportunity to consolidate reading skills with easy material, rather than to struggle along (or worse yet, skip over) more difficult words in books judged appropriate for her age level.

Results

The improvement seen as tutoring sessions progressed was confirmed in objective evaluation. Gains in ability to organize visual stimuli and to reproduce them were demonstrated in the successive administrations of the *Bender Gestalt Test.* Auditory discrimination, never a serious problem, continued to be accurate. Auditory sequencing tasks, initially difficult for Nan, were done easily on retest. Figure drawings were better organized. Response to the finger schema test was now correct, as was right-left

---

[4] R. H. Turner, *When People Talk . . . On the Telephone,* Books A and B (New York: Teachers College Press, Columbia University, 1965).

discrimination on herself. There were, however, some evidences of confusion in pointing out right and left on others. The extension test, initially ambilateral, was now strongly right-hand elevated. Achievement test scores (Table 11) show that these gains in perception were also accom-

Table 11. Nannette's Educational Test Scores

		Tutoring Period			
School Grade	Mar., 1964 2	Nov., 1964 3	Jan., 1966 4	June, 1966 4	Jan., 1968 6
Wide Range Oral Reading	3.3	3.5	5.7	7.6	7.9
Wide Range Spelling	2.8	3.1	3.7	4.2	5.6
Metropolitan Reading					
Word Knowl- ledge	2.9 (Pri. II)		5.7 (Elem.)	6.2 (Int.)	
Paragraph Reading	3.3		7.2 (Elem.)	6.3 (Int.)	10.0+ (Adv.)

panied by improved achievement in oral reading, spelling, and reading comprehension.

Follow-Up

REEXAMINATION IN APRIL, 1969, when Nan was 12 years, 7 months old and in the seventh grade of a suburban junior high school, indicated continued improvement not only in academic skills but also in her emotional development. She is now a tall child, physically well into adolescence. She enjoys reading and reads omnivorously, but she complains of difficulty in spelling and does "not like to do lab reports."

Her approach to tasks is still slow and deliberate, with a self-critical undercurrent. Her depression, however, has lifted. She appears interested and assured, aware of her good intelligence and ability to reason as well as of her problems. She is sensitive to and enjoys the physical world of nature. She relates well to her classmates and does not feel unloved when her mother insists that she pick her clothes off the floor.

Neurologically, her old problems of equilibrium, her abnormality in muscle tone and synergy, can still be found. Cerebral dominance, however, as measured by the extension test, appears clearly established.

Summary and Discussion

IN SUMMARY, WE HAVE ATTEMPTED to review our findings and our management of a child now almost 13 years old whom we have known for over ten years. Our diagnosis revealed the presence of a non-specific structural defect of the central nervous system in a child of potentially superior intellectual ability, whose two siblings were suffering from a developmental (specific) language disability and whose parents created a grim atmosphere of tension and rejection. Our study further revealed the presence of a reading disability in the father and suggested a reading disability in both grandfathers; a maternal cousin (a child of the maternal grandfather's sister) was also examined and found to have a specific reading disability.

In management we elected to treat the parents psychotherapeutically, and the children with remedial education directed at their specific perceptual and cognitive defects which our diagnosis revealed. The course of Nan's sixty-six remedial sessions has been given in detail, recounting the methods used in correcting her praxic errors, her struggles with visual figure-ground perception and visual-motor functions, her confusion in auditory sequencing, and her inadequately established cerebral dominance. With the hypothesized neurological basis for reading thus attained, it was possible to sequence more complex cognitive material.

In retrospect, our efforts at perceptual training might have started when Nan was 4½ years old, and her mother's psychotherapy might have started even sooner. We recognize also that other workers may have chosen therapeutic procedures and techniques different from those we elected. We chose to present this case to illustrate the complex combination of biological and psychological factors that must be unraveled in the understanding and treatment of a child with learning problems and to illustrate the use of perceptual training in building the neurological basis for learning.

Editor's Comments

It is most unusual to find a reading disability case in which diagnostic examinations began at the age of two, long before reading instruction started. It is also quite unusual for diagnostic evidence to indicate the presence of both a familial basis for reading disability, and in addition the presence of a non-specific structural defect of the central nervous system in one of the children. Third, when both a familial trend and some brain damage are indicated, it is surprising to find the child's reading before remedial help to be up to grade level, although well below the potential indicated by superior general intelligence.

In recent years Drs. Silver and Hagin have become advocates of planning remedial activities directly to correct diagnosed weakness in specific physical and psychological abilities. The description of the procedures followed with Nannette for training specific motor, perceptual, and cognitive functions is the first such description they have given in a specific case report; further details on their methods will unquestionably be eagerly awaited. In this case a handwriting difficulty seems to have needed and received more attention than the relatively milder reading problem, at least in the early stages. In evaluating the total results, the emphasis the authors place on the parental improvement from psychotherapy should not be overlooked.

16

Mark

BY EDWIN M. COLE, M.D.

Setting

The material reported here is derived from casework in the Language Clinic of the Massachusetts General Hospital. Methods of evaluation and recording that are described are in current use in the clinic. For the most part they are adaptations of methods used in this author's private practice.

The Language Clinic is one of the "specialty" clinics within the neurological department of the Massachusetts General Hospital because its orientation is neurological. This writer established it in 1934 for the study and treatment of language problems, and it has continued with this primary purpose ever since. Language is communication, and language problems include both speech and reading. The clinic is, therefore, staffed with therapists from both orientations.

The work of the reading clinic is based upon the original work of Dr. Samuel T. Orton, with remedial techniques devised by Anna Gillingham and Bessie Stillman in consultation with Dr. Orton. It is natural that through the years we have altered techniques somewhat, using material and methods derived from our own experience. Nevertheless, we find our original base to be valid, and essentially we adhere to it at the present time.

Our reading clinic receives patients referred by other clinics in the hospital such as pediatric, neurological, psychiatric, or eye. In addition children are referred by schools, by individual teachers and pediatricians, and by various community agencies.

To facilitate evaluation of patient material, in addition to using other clinics within the hospital, such as the Eye Clinic for vision checks and the Ear Clinic for checks on hearing, we have established the Cortical Function Laboratory as our own psychological testing laboratory where experienced clinical psychologists administer psychological and academic achievement tests. In our experience, evaluation of children with specific reading disability (developmental dyslexia) requires specialized skills, the result of both psychological training and the actual experience of working with patients who suffer from this particular disability.

Therefore, we have found it necessary to establish our own training course, within our clinic, for teachers or tutors who wish to acquire sufficient knowledge and experience for the treatment of dyslexic children. In fact, we have found it quite impossible to count on teachers who have not been so trained.

These teacher trainees do most of the teaching in the Language Clinic. Their course is a practicum in which each trainee spends three hundred hours at the clinic. After a short period of orientation and initial instruction in techniques, each trainee tutors three pupils individually. The pupils come to the clinic three times a week for a lesson of one hour. It takes approximately one academic year to complete the training course which, in addition to the closely supervised teaching, includes weekly seminars and conferences.

Diagnostic Study

In March, 1967, a 12-year-old, left-handed boy, Mark M., was brought in by his mother because of his persisting difficulty in learning to read and spell. He was a student in the sixth grade of a local parochial school. He had visited various clinics in an attempt to overcome his difficulty, as well as an optometrist who advised eye exercises which he had followed for a brief time. A report from an oculist who gave Mark a visual examination in 1967 indicated normal vision.

Case History

The history obtained from Mrs. M. is as follows: Mark was the product of a second pregnancy, a full-term delivery, and at birth he seemed to be healthy in every way. As a matter of fact, physical health has been one of his strong points. He has never lost time from school on account of illness. Developmental milestones seemed normal. He walked at 18 months and he talked at about the same time, without any marked cluttering in his speech. He has never stuttered or stammered. So far as self-care training is concerned, he has always seemed to resist suggestions. He seems to prefer to do things "in his own sweet time," but there has been no outstandingly poor performance in development of skill in self-feeding, dressing, or toilet training.

Mark appears physically well-coordinated. A thorough physical examination in 1964 had revealed nothing relevant to his learning difficulty. He is an excellent skater and has been successful on the drums in a bugle corps. But baseball gives him problems. He can't decide whether to bat, catch, and throw with his left hand or his right. Mark is the oldest child; none of his sublings has apparently had scholastic difficulties.

Schooling. At 4½ Mark entered kindergarten in the Boston public school system. After one year there, he enrolled in the local Catholic parish school. He did very poorly and was asked to repeat the first grade, which he did. Mrs. M. recalls that Mark had to repeat the grade because he seemed to be able to do absolutely nothing. She also recalls the teacher telling her early in his schooling that "the boy is a walking encyclopedia and can answer anything as long as he doesn't have to write it down." The mother also recalls that in the first grade he had severe letter confusions. *B's* and *d's* were continually confused, and there were other examples of the same thing. There were also reversals of letter order in words. One that Mrs. M. recalls is Mark's tendency to write his first name as "Karm."

When Mark was in the second grade Mrs. M. began to seek help. She took him to a private high school where they were supposed to understand reading problems, but she felt that nothing was accomplished there. He was given some tutoring, but the school continued to claim that there was no such thing as a reading disability. She then learned of a center doing specialized testing and individual tutoring, and Mark went there for one school year, and intensively during the summer, when he was scheduled for lessons five times a week over a six-week period. In reporting Mark's work to us, the teacher at the center said that although Mark had just completed the fifth grade, when he started there his reading tested at first-grade level. His potential in reading was definitely several grades higher than his actual reading level. He found even the first-grade book used in the course very difficult, as also the elementary phonics workbook. He never showed ill-will, but he carried on in a very lazy sort of way at the reading center. He found it very difficult to pay attention to the task at hand. His mother admitted that he was quite lazy. During the twenty summer lessons (some were missed because of absence) there was little progress. In October, 1967, Mark once again began going to the center, but only once a week. Even this attendance was irregular, because of his mother's sickness and other matters. In March, 1967, the family decided to terminate Mark's lessons at the center.

During the history taking, Mrs. M. made the following statement: "All the articles I've read about dyslexia I could have written myself, based on my own experience and that of my son." Mark is now in the eighth grade of the same parochial school in which he started.

Examination

With this history and clinical evaluation at hand, it seemed advisable for Mark to go through our usual test procedures for evaluation of reading disabilities, although, at that time, from the evidence we felt reasonably sure of the diagnosis: specific reading disability.

When seen in the Cortical Function Laboratory, the results of the psychological testing administered in the reading center in December, 1966, were made available. The *Wechsler Intelligence Scale for Children* had been administered with the following results:

Verbal Tests	Scaled Score	Performance Tests	Scaled Score
Information	8	Picture completion	8
Comprehension	13	Picture arrangement	7
Arithmetic	6	Block design	10
Similarities	12	Object assembly	(spoiled)
Vocabulary	15	Coding B	7

Verbal Scale—total scaled score 54, I.Q. 105
Performance Scale--(pro-rated) 40, I.Q. 86
Full Scale—94, I.Q. 96

Since this test data was only three months old, it was not thought necessary to repeat the *WISC*.

The examiner at the laboratory found Mark to be a pleasant and apparently well-motivated boy, although he appeared to daydream frequently while working on the achievement tests.

Results of tests given on June 2, 1967, were as follows:

Gray Oral Reading Paragraphs	Grade 2.3
Stanford Achievement Elem., Form L	
Word Meaning	Grade 2.7 (94% acc.)
Paragraph Meaning	Grade 2.0 (55% acc.)
Spelling (dictated)	Grade 3.3

Although oral reading was still slow, especially for the more difficult material, there was less tendency to substitute words of similar visual configuration than the year before. His lips moved during the silent reading. The accuracy of his reading comprehension had improved considerably, for the relatively easy level on which he was tested. Spelling, though scoring lower than a year ago, was of better overall quality; he showed he could carry sounds better. His tendency to work quickly without taking time to think affected his spelling adversely.

On the basis of data derived from the clinical evaluation, as well as the detailed testing, it seemed clear that Mark's educational problem was the result of a severe specific reading disability (developmental dyslexia). At his mother's request we enrolled him for therapy, starting in October, 1967.

Remedial Program

First Year

When Mark enrolled, his school was most cooperative about excusing him, and he came to the clinic for lessons three times a week. These lessons consisted of individual tutoring with a trainee who was enrolled in the training course. The tutor-trainee was a mature woman who had started her training course the previous summer, so that when she started work with Mark she had already had about one hundred hours of supervised teaching experience at the Language Clinic.

Mark's attitude from the very beginning has been good. It has never been necessary to use games or special motivating devices to hold his interest. From the first lesson he has been able to see his own progress and the usefulness of the tools he was given to improve his reading and spelling.

Mark is left-handed, and he wrote with his left hand in an awkwardly hooked position, the hand above the line. According to the history he formerly was ambidextrous. He was able to shift into the straight, correct left-handed position, with the paper slanted correctly for left-handed writing. His writing is slow in the correct position, but nevertheless he is able to produce quite legible writing.

Since the tests he had been given prior to his first lesson indicated that word recognition was weak and phonic skills almost nonexistent, his teacher began with the letters of the alphabet, teaching the consonant sounds (except for soft c and g and the voiced sound of s) and the short sounds of the vowels. Mark knew most of the consonant sounds but was not sure of the short vowel sounds. In order to build this knowledge we provided drill with nonsense syllables using short vowels with consonant blends in the consonant-vowel-consonant pattern. This was done with syllables to read, followed by similar syllables to write so that he would develop the ability to make the association between letters and their sounds.

At the same time, Mark was presented with the rule for adding a suffix to a one-syllable word ending with a consonant. Because this rule is largely concerned with words with short vowels, it fitted appropriately and made it possible to keep the material with a consistent sound-to-symbol relationship. In response to Mark's enthusiasm and interest he was given some homework for additional practice in adding suffixes to one-syllable words. For the oral reading part of each lesson, *Royal Road, Book* 2,[1] proved to be appropriate. In general, the Gillingham sequence was followed with procedures for reinforcement as outlined in the Gillingham manual, and in succeeding lessons additional phonograms were presented, reviewed, and written.[2]

By November, 1967, Mark had been taught basic principles of syllable division so that he could read phonetic polysyllables. He had learned the vowel-consonant *e* concept, the effect of *r* on preceding vowels, and he began to learn some of the vowel digraphs such as *ea, ai, oa,* etc. Because he now had tools for reading, he began to read aloud in one of the Discovery books, *George Washington Carver.* His reading was slow; some words had to be supplied for him, but, on the whole, he was able to handle the material, and he enjoyed the book.

Spelling continued with additional rules and generalizations. He still had some trouble with short vowel discrimination and practice in auditory discrimination was required. It has been a constant challenge to help lengthen his limited auditory span. A part of each lesson was dictation of words and sentences to develop this retention.

Mark had a quick understanding of material presented. This was true of principles of word attack as well as spelling rules and generalizations. From the very beginning of his lessons here, he has used with care and attentiveness the techniques he has been taught for reading. In spelling he can apply the rules in a list of words of one type. When sentences are dictated, however, he continues to omit endings, to spell phonetically with no thought of word structure (*hopt* for *hopped*), and gives evidence of auditory discrimination difficulties (*lift* for *left*).

---

[1] *Royal Road Readers.* American distributors: Educator's Publishing Service, Cambridge, Mass.

[2] Anna Gillingham and Bessie W. Stillman. *Remedial Training for Children with Special Disability in Reading, Spelling, and Penmanship,* 7th ed. (Cambridge, Mass.: Educators Publishing Service, 1966).

Early in December, 1967, after two months' lessons, Mark took the *Morrison-McCall Spelling Scale* on which he scored at grade 3.1. This test quite clearly showed Mark's auditory difficulties with discrimination and sequence, and his weak visual memory. This appeared in efforts to spell by memory (*whis* for *with*) as well as in attempts to spell non-phonetic words by sound (*dun* for *done* and *eneyway* for *anyway*). Sound confusions and limited sequencing appeared in such words as *miruly* for *nearly* and *thayfod* for *therefore*.

Mark's attendance was regular and his attitude continued to be most cooperative. His lessons continued until the end of May, 1968. He completed *George Washington Carver* and read a simplified version of *Treasure Island*.

Daily work in spelling and dictation was showing results as long as the words were phonetic or words that he could reason out. It was still necessary to provide plenty of time, with admonitions about thinking before writing. *Morrison-McCall* tests given later in the spring showed slight improvement, but lack of visual memory together with auditory weakness produced such attempts as *atimted* for *attempt, compleat* for *complete*, and *repher* for *refer*.

Achievement tests were readministered in May, 1968, with the following results:

Gray Oral Reading Paragraphs	Grade 4.2
Stanford Achievement Prim. II, Form W	
Word Meaning	Grade 3.8:(100% acc.)
Paragraph Meaning	Grade 4.4 (81% acc.)
Spelling (dictated)	Grade 3.1

Second Year

Mark discontinued lessons for the summer because he was going to camp. Actually, although he had gone to a camp for several previous summers, he stayed at home in 1968 and worked with his father. In September, 1968, he returned to the Language Clinic, again coming in the morning. Mark had retained most of what he had learned about letter sounds, syllable division, and basic word-attack skills. He began reading a book of Robin Hood stories at an easy fourth-grade level. This he is able to handle well but still slowly. Sight vocabulary is still limited and he has to work out many of the words slowly and thoughtfully. An attempt to increase the speed of his reading results in guessing, substitutions, and regressions. His comprehension is excellent, not only for strictly factual material but also for inference and implication.

Spelling still lags behind. He remembers the rules and generalizations he had learned last year, but he has had too little practice for any writing to be automatic. When reminded, he can apply what he has been taught, but unless his thinking is specifically directed to these rules, he tends to spell by sound only, with complete disregard for word structure. When this difficulty is compounded—as it is—with auditory perception problems not yet overcome, the resulting spelling leaves much to be desired.

When Mrs. M. was interviewed again in December, 1968, she said that she realizes Mark has never done any pleasure reading, but that he is determined to stick by the training course he is having at the hospital. Coming to the hospital has meant missing a couple of classes each morning, and he is marked down in school because of this. When Mrs. M. suggested to her son that perhaps he could go on his own and drop the work in the clinic, he demurred and insisted that he was going to continue coming in here because this, in our clinic, is where he was learning to read. Mrs. M. notes that the teachers in his school who, at first, hadn't ever heard of reading disability and felt there was no such condition, now seem to understand the problems better and are more accepting of Mark and his difficulty. The result is that he seems more content. This year Mrs. M. notes that he is buckling down and working, and applying himself much better to all his schoolwork. The mother certainly feels encouraged. Mrs. M. states that next year, when Mark is to enter the ninth grade, she hopes to have him go to a trade vocational school where he will have excellent training of that sort, because she feels an ordinary academically oriented high school program would not be the right place for Mark.

When asked about Mark's attitude about his own handicap, Mrs. M. said he doesn't say much about it or display any strong feeling, except one of determination to overcome it. Mrs. M. has been rather protective of Mark, has tried to explain matters to him, has tried to give him a good understanding of his problem, and in this connection has read articles on dyslexia and has certainly become very understanding herself. This degree of understanding has been difficult for the father to achieve, and he has seemed to feel very threatened by having a son who does not make progress and learn as he should. At times he becomes quite harsh with his son, still using corporal punishment when he feels it necessary.

Cortical Function Laboratory Test Report

In January, 1969, the *WISC* was repeated in our own laboratory since the previous testing of December, 1966, had been reported from another laboratory. Our psychologist reports as follows:

Mark, who is now 13 years and 10 months old, is a left-handed boy, who was tested here originally only on achievement tests, as he had the *WISC* elsewhere a very short time before his first evaluation here. At this time he was referred specifically for retesting on the *WISC*. He is currently in the eighth grade in a parochial school and is considering the possibility of going to a technical high school, where he would like to study mechanical engineering.

Mark is a big boy, who seemed socially mature in the sense of assuming responsibility about money (he worked last summer and saved the money he earned for skis), but it was my impression that he was rather naive and somewhat dependent about relating to people. In the test situation he often waited for extra directions or help, displaying a certain passivity rather than taking initiative. He showed strong enthusiasm, however, about his outside interests, which include skiing and performing in the drum and bugle corps. In the latter he has taken part in many competitions and is proud of what they have been able to achieve with hard work.

At this time the obtained scores on the *Wechsler Intelligence Scale for Children* were as follows: Full Scale I.Q. 95, Verbal I.Q. 97, Performance I.Q. 93.

The Full Scale I.Q. is almost identical to that reported in the spring of 1967, but the present Verbal score is somewhat lower and the Performance somewhat higher than the respective scores reported then. At the present time, stronger verbal potential was suggested by his readily stating a good proportion of similarities in abstract terms and also by his relatively extensive knowledge of vocabulary. His verbalization in general was not very articulate, but some of his own word usage was good, and he brought into his definitions some special information. However, on a specific test of information there were quite a few scattered errors, with spotty successes over quite a range. Mental arithmetic reasoning was poor for his age and level. Auditory span for digits (four forward, four backward) was limited for his age and level. On the Performance Scale, there was less variability among the subtest scores, but qualitatively several things were noted. His awkward hooked left-handed position slowed his work on Coding. He worked quickly on the Picture Arrangement items but made sequence errors on the more complex items. He assembled puzzle pieces accurately, but on the Block Designs he had marked difficulty with spatial orientation, making multiple errors on one design and finally accepting a solution that involved reversals.

Consistent with his limited auditory memory span, he also did poorly for his age at a tapping test for reproducing sequential patterns observed visually.

Impression from psychological testing. This is a left-handed boy whose present mental ability measures as average but whose present performance suggests stronger verbal potential. He seems handicapped by limited span for sequences in both auditory and visual material and by considerable difficulty with spatial orientation. His awkward left-handed position penalizes him in rate of using the pencil. He feels that because of his lessons here he misses out in the continuity of schoolwork, and his low scores on the WISC Arithmetic and Information subtests would tend to support the impression that there are some gaps in what he has acquired at school.

Further Remedial Work

As this report was completed (in March, 1969), Mark was still attending the clinic and planned to do so until school ended in June. Progress is continuing at an unspectacular rate and is more satisfactory in reading than in spelling. By June, 1969, his reading comprehension should be at a fifth-grade level.

Mark will graduate from elementary school (eighth grade) in June and plans to enter the vocational program mentioned above in September. The school he will attend has a corrective reading program, in which he can receive some further help, and it is not expected that he will return to the clinic.

Discussion

Quite clearly, this is a boy severely handicapped in his schoolwork by a specific reading disability (developmental dyslexia). He has had years of discouragement, and although he has average ability, his achievement is generally depressed in all subjects. The family and clinical evaluations demonstrate many of the typical findings associated with this condition. We feel all these background and performance data are of diagnostic significance.

We have indicated the direction of therapy, and tests show that progress is very slow. This, unfortunately, tends to be the rule in cases of average endowment, a severe visual-spatial confusion of the specific reading disability type, and many years of discouragement that result from the inevitable school failure which is in itself consequent to the student's inability to read and spell in a useful way.

Editor's Comments

Mark had the misfortune to enter first grade at the very young age of 5½, and with low average intelligence, some immaturity in reading readiness would normally be expected. In Mark's case this was complicated by delayed establishment of hand dominance and a marked directional confusion, with many letter and word reversals. These problems might be expected to be accentuated if the class is quite large and the instruction in reading is not adapted to individual rates and styles of learning. Thus even when there is a predisposition toward developing a reading disability, environmental factors may have an important bearing on the severity of the problem. Since Mark's mother is the only other member of the family noted as having had difficulty with reading, the familial basis is quite different from that in the more typical family containing several male members with language disabilities.

Mark had had tutoring elsewhere for more than a year and a half, and had progressed from first-grade to second-grade level before coming to Dr. Cole's attention, so that this report is mainly concerned with his later progress in remedial teaching. He obviously was ready for and profited from intensive phonics instruction, and came to rely on it so much that he made excessive use of phonics in his spelling. Mark's rate of progress in remediation, described as "unspectacular," is fairly typical of children with a combination of a severe disability and average or below average intelligence.

Appendix A

AN ALPHABETICAL LIST OF TESTS

Pertinent information is given in the list below concerning the tests that have been mentioned earlier in this book. In addition, a few recent tests of interest to reading specialists have been included, although not mentioned earlier. All tests, regardless of type, have been arranged in a single alphabetical order for easy reference. When forms are not mentioned the test has only one form. Information is based on the publishers' catalogs available when this list was compiled. Since revisions, new forms, new manuals, etc., are issued from time to time, before ordering any test it is desirable to write to the publisher for the current catalog.

Before deciding which test to use, it is advisable to make a tentative selection of a few tests that might be suitable and to order a specimen set of each for careful study. For large-scale testing programs, it is also desirable to consider the practicality and cost of hand-scoring, use of special answer sheets, or use of the various test-scoring services that are now available.

The names of publishers are abbreviated to save space. Full names and addresses of the publishers are given in Appendix B.

The listings below are very brief and are not evaluative. For detailed descriptions and critical evaluations of reading tests the most useful source is *Reading Tests and Reviews,* edited by O. K. Buros, Gryphon Press, 1968. This volume includes all of the reviews of reading tests that had appeared in the six *Mental Measurements Yearbooks.* Detailed descriptions and evaluations of psychological tests may be found in those yearbooks, also published by Gryphon Press.

Academic Promise Tests. A scholastic aptitude battery for grades six through nine, with separate tests of verbal, numerical, abstract reasoning, and language usage abilities; gives verbal, non-verbal, and total scores. PSYCHOLOGICAL.

American School Achievement Tests
Primary I Battery, grade 1, word recognition, word meaning, numbers.
Primary II Reading, grades 2–3, sentence, word, and paragraph meaning.
Intermediate Reading, grades 4–6, vocabulary and paragraph meaning.
Advanced Reading, grades 7–9, vocabulary and paragraph meaning. BOBBS

American School Reading Readiness Tests, Revised Edition, Form X. Kindergarten—beginning grade 1. Group administration. Separate norms for those who have and have not attended kindergarten. BOBBS

Ammons Full-Range Picture Vocabulary Test. Preschool to adult. An individually administered test of verbal intelligence in which answer is given by pointing to one of four pictures. Forms A, B. PSYCHOLOGICAL TEST

A O School Vision Screening Test. A revised, portable version of the *Massachusetts Vision Test.* Designed for quick screening to find pupils who need more complete visual examination. AMERICAN OPTICAL

Arthur Point Scale of Performance Tests. Age 4 to adult. An individually administered scale of non-language tests to be used only by trained psychologists. Form I, revised form II. STOELTING

Berry-Buktenica Geometric Form Reproduction Test. Ages 5–10. A visual-motor test involving copying, matching, and tracing designs. AUTHOR: San Francisco Medical Center

Bender Visual Motor Gestalt Test. A clinical test of ability to copy visual designs. PSYCHOLOGICAL

Benton Visual Retention Test, Revised. An individual test of ability to draw designs from memory. PSYCHOLOGICAL

Botel Reading Inventory. Grades 1–12. A group of tests for determining reading instructional levels. Includes tests of phonics, word recognition, word opposites reading, and word opposites listening; mainly group-administered. FOLLETT

Brown-Carlsen Listening Comprehension Test. Grades 9–13. A group test of ability to comprehend spoken English language. HARCOURT

California Phonics Survey. Grades 7–college. A group test with eight subtests of aspects of phonic knowledge. CALIFORNIA

California Reading Tests, WXYZ Series, 1963 Norms. *Lower primary,* grades 1, 2; *Primary,* grades 3, lower 4; *Elementary,* grades 4–6; *Junior High,* grades 7–9; *Advanced,* grades 9–college. Each test has two main parts, vocabulary and comprehension, with several subtests in each part. Two to four forms at each level. Also included in the *California Achievement Test* batteries. CALIFORNIA

California Short-Form Test of Mental Maturity, 1963 Revision. Eight levels, kindergarten–college. A group test of intelligence providing separate language M.A.'s and I.Q.'s as well as total. CALIFORNIA

California Tests of Mental Maturity (Long Form), 1963 Revision. *Level 0,* kindergarten–grade 1; *Level 1,* grades 1–3; *Level 2,* grades 4–8; *Level 3,* grades 7–9; *Level 4,* grades 9–12; *Level 5,* grade 12–college. An analytical group intelligence test. Reading and non-reading items are used for testing memory, attention, spatial relationships, reasoning, and vocabulary. Provides separate M.A.'s and I.Q.'s for language (reading), non-language (no reading), and total scores. CALIFORNIA

California Test of Personality. *Primary,* kindergarten–grade 3; *Elementary,* grades 4–8; *Intermediate,* grades 7–10; *Secondary,* grade 9–college. An analytical group personality questionnaire providing scores on self-adjustment and social adjustment. CALIFORNIA

Chicago Non-Verbal Examination. Age 7–adult. A non-verbal group intelligence test requiring no reading; can be given in pantomime to the deaf and non-English speaking. PSYCHOLOGICAL

Children's Apperception Test. Ages 4–10. An individually administered projective test of personality, to be used only by trained psychologists. PSYCHOLOGICAL

Comprehensive Tests of Basic Skills. A series of achievement test batteries: *Level 1*, grades 2.5–4; *Level 2*, grades 4–6; *Level 3*, grades 6–8; *Level 4*, grades 8–12. Reading vocabulary and comprehension included at each level. CALIFORNIA

Cooperative English Tests: Reading Comprehension. Forms 1A, B, C for grades 12–14; Forms 2A, B, C for grades 9–12. Provides scores for level of comprehension, rate of comprehension, and vocabulary. ETS

Cooperative Primary Tests. Achievement test batteries for grades 1–2 and 2–3; forms A, B at each level. Include a pilot test to give practice in test-taking; and tests of listening, word analysis, mathematics, reading, and writing skills. ETS

Cornell-Coxe Performance Ability Scale. Ages 6–15. An individual non-language performance scale for measuring intelligence, for use by trained psychologists. STOELTING

Culture Fair Intelligence Tests. Ages 4–adult. Group tests of general intelligence not requiring any reading and relatively free from educational and cultural influences. *Scale 1*, ages 4–8, one form; *Scale 2*, ages 8–13 and average adults, Forms A, B; Scale 3, ages 14–college and superior adult, Forms A, B. IPAT

D.A.T. Verbal Reasoning, Numerical Ability, and Abstract Reasoning Tests. Grades 8–12. These three elements of the Differential Aptitude Tests provide the equivalent of an intelligence or scholastic aptitude measure; only the verbal reasoning test requires any reading. PSYCHOLOGICAL

Davis Reading Test. *Series 2*, grades 8–11; *Series 1*, grades 11–13; Forms A, B, C, D each series. Provides two scores, level of comprehension and rate of comprehension. PSYCHOLOGICAL

Detroit Alpha Intelligence Test. Grades 4–8. A group intelligence test with eight subtests, giving separate verbal (reading) and non-verbal scores. BOBBS

Detroit Beginning First-Grade Intelligence Test, Revised. Beginning grade 1. A group intelligence test with ten short subtests, requiring no reading. HARCOURT

Detroit Tests of Learning Aptitude. Ages 4–adult. An individual intelligence test battery containing nineteen subtests, each with separate mental age norms, allowing a flexible choice of tests for diagnostic purposes. BOBBS

Developmental Reading Tests
Readiness Test, beginning first grade.
Lower Primary, grades 1.5–2.9. Basic vocabulary test, comprehension test. Forms A, B, C

Upper Primary, grades 2.5–3.9. Basic vocabulary, comprehension. Forms A, B, C

New Intermediate, grades 4–6. Vocabulary, reading for information, reading for relationships, literal comprehension, reading for interpretation, reading for appreciation. Forms A, B. LYONS

Diagnostic Reading Tests. A series of survey and diagnostic tests from grade 1–college.

Kindergarten–grade 4. Reading readiness; Survey section, Booklet 1, grade 1; Booklet II, grade 2; Booklet III, grades 3, 4; Section IV, Word Attack, Part 1, Oral.

Lower Level, grades 4–6. Booklet I, comprehension and word attack; Booklet II, vocabulary and rate; Section IV, word attack, oral, for individual administration. Forms A, B, each booklet.

Higher Level, grades 7–college. Includes a Survey Test of vocabulary, comprehension, and rate, with seven forms, A to H; and a Diagnostic Battery with eight separate booklets: vocabulary, silent comprehension, auditory comprehension, general rate, rate in social studies, rate in science, oral word attack (individual), and silent word attack; forms A, B, each part. COMMITTEE

Dolch Basic Sight Word Test. The 220 words of the *Dolch Basic Sight Words List* arranged on one sheet of paper for testing. GARRARD

Doren Diagnostic Reading Test. Grades 2–8. A group test for detailed testing of word attack skills. Beginning sounds, sight words, rhyming, whole word recognition, words within words, speech consonants, bleeding, vowels, ending sounds, discriminate guessing, letter recognition. AMERICAN GUIDANCE

Durkin-Meshover Phonics Knowledge Survey. Any grade. Individually administered test of knowledge of phonics, with subtests. TEACHERS

Durrell Analysis of Reading Difficulty: New Edition. A battery of diagnostic tests for intensive analysis of reading difficulties. Includes a set of reading paragraphs, a cardboard tachistoscope, word lists, and a record blank. Provides tests of oral and silent reading, listening comprehension, word analysis, phonics, faulty pronunciation, writing, and spelling. HARCOURT

Durrell Listening-Reading Series. *Primary,* grades 1–3.5; *Intermediate,* grades 3.5–6; *Advanced,* grades 7–9. Group tests of listening (vocabulary and sentences) and reading (vocabulary and sentences) standardized on the same population. Forms DE, EF. HARCOURT

EDL Reading Eye. A portable eye-movement camera. Accessories include sixty-four reading test selections, grade 1–adult. EDL

EDL Reading Versatility Tests. *Basic,* grades 5–8; *Intermediate,* grades 8–12; *Advanced,* college. Covers reading of fiction, non-fiction, skimming, and scanning. Three equated forms at each level. EDL

First Grade Screening Test. A group test for detecting potential learning difficulties. Includes items on social and emotional adjustment as well as intellectual and perceptual abilities. AMERICAN GUIDANCE

Marianne Frostig Developmental Test of Visual Perception. Ages 4–8. A group test with five subtests: eye-motor coordination, figure-ground, constancy of shape, position in space, spatial relationships. FOLLETT

Gates-MacGinitie Readiness Skills Test. Beginning first grade. Listening comprehension, auditory discrimination, visual discrimination, following directions, letter recognition, visual-motor coordination, auditory blending. A word recognition test is also included to detect early readers. TEACHERS

Gates-MacGinitie Reading Tests. *Primary A*, grade 1; *Primary B*, grade 2; *Primary C*, grade 3; each contains two parts, vocabulary and comprehension; Forms 1, 2, each level. Primary CS, speed and accuracy for grades 2, 3; Forms 1, 2, 3. *Survey D*, grades 4–6; speed and accuracy, vocabulary, and comprehension. Forms 1, 2, 3. *Survey E*, grades 7–9; speed and accuracy, vocabulary, comprehension. Forms 1, 2, 3. TEACHERS

Gates-McKillop Reading Diagnostic Tests. Battery of tests for individual diagnosis of retarded readers from non-reader up. Paragraphs for oral reading; word perception, flashed and untimed; phrase perception; syllabication, letter names and sounds, visual and auditory blending, spelling. Forms 1, 2. TEACHERS

Gillingham-Childs Phonics Proficiency Scales. Individual tests of letter-sound correspondences, reading and spelling of real and nonsense words, consonant clusters, vowels, syllable division, etc. EDUCATORS

Gilmore Oral Reading Test, New Edition. Grades 1–8. An individual test of oral reading. Ten reading paragraphs of increasing difficulty, separate record booklet; scored for accuracy, comprehension, and rate. Forms C, D. Older forms A, B, also available. HARCOURT

Goodenough-Harris Drawing Test. Ages 3–12. Provides an objective method for scoring children's drawings of the human figure as a measure of nonverbal intelligence. HARCOURT

Gray Oral Reading Tests. Grades 1–10. An individually administered oral reading test with thirteen graded reading passages in each form, separate record booklets; accuracy and rate combined in a composite score. Separate norms for boys and girls. Forms A, B, C, D. BOBBS

Gray Standardized Oral Reading Check Tests. Grades 1–8. A series of very brief oral reading tests. *Set I*, grades 1,2; *Set II*, grades 2–4; *Set III*, grades 4–6; *Set IV*, grades 6–8. Five forms in each set. BOBBS

Gray Standardized Oral Reading Paragraphs. Grades 1–8. An oral reading test containing twelve graded paragraphs; accuracy and rate combined in one score. BOBBS

Harris Tests of Lateral Dominance, Third Edition. Ages 6–adult. A set of brief tests of hand, eye, and foot dominance. PSYCHOLOGICAL

Harrison-Stroud Reading Readiness Profiles. A readiness test with five subtests: using symbols, visual discrimination, using context, auditory discrimination, using context and auditory clues; also letter names. HOUGHTON

Henmon-Nelson Tests of Mental Ability, Revised. Levels for grades 3–6, 6–9, 9–12. A self-marking group intelligence test that requires reading. HOUGHTON

Illinois Tests of Psycholinguistic Abilities, Revised. Ages 4–9. Eleven individually administered subtests measuring abilities basic in communcation. ILLINOIS

Iowa Every-Pupil Tests of Basic Skills. *Elementary*, grades 3–5; *Advanced*, grades 5–9. Test A, Silent Reading Comprehension, includes paragraph comprehension and vocabulary. Test B, Work-Study Skills, including map reading, use of references, reading of graphs, charts, tables. Series also includes language and arithmetic. Form O. HOUGHTON

Iowa Silent Reading Tests: New Edition. *Elementary*, grades 4–8; *Advanced*, high school and college. Analytical silent reading tests including rate, comprehension, vocabulary, sentence and paragraph meaning, locating information. Forms Am, Bm, Cm, Dm, each level. HARCOURT

Iowa Tests of Basic Skills. Grades 3–8. Tests for all grades in one reusable booklet. Test V, vocabulary; Test R, reading comprehension; Test W, work-study skills. Forms 1, 2, 3, 4. HOUGHTON

Iowa Tests of Educational Development. Grades 9–12. Contains nine tests in four major curriculum areas: English, mathematics, natural sciences, and social studies. Reading score based on separate reading tests for social studies, science, and literary materials. SRA

Kelley-Greene Reading Comprehension Test. Grades 9–13. A survey silent reading test involving paragraph comprehension, finding answers to questions, retention of information read, estimate of rate. HARCOURT

Keystone Tests of Binocular Skill. An adaptation of the *Gray Standardized Oral Reading Check Tests* for use with the *Keystone Telebinocular*. Equivalent oral reading selections are read with each eye separately and with binocular vision. KEYSTONE

Keystone Visual-Survey Service for Schools. Grade 1 and up. Includes a *Telebinocular* (stereoscopic instrument) and twelve stereographs providing measures of near and far acuity, muscle balance, depth perception, and fusion; also color vision. KEYSTONE

Keystone Visual-Survey Short Tests. Grade 1 and up. Three stereographs provide a brief screening test of several visual functions. KEYSTONE

Kindergarten Evaluation of Learning Potential: KELP. A teaching program mainly for disadvantaged children, including provisions for evaluation of readiness by the teacher. CALIFORNIA

Kuhlmann-Anderson Measure of Academic Potential, 6th and 7th editions. Nine levels, one for each grade, kindergarten-grade 6, one for 7–8, one for grades 9–12. A group test of general intelligence with ten subtests per level. Content below fifth grade is largely non-reading. PSYCHOLOGICAL

Kuhlmann-Finch Intelligence Tests. Tests I–IV for grades 1–6, junior high school test, senior high school test. Group intelligence tests, completely nonverbal in lowest two levels, and largely nonverbal in upper levels. AMERICAN GUIDANCE

Leavell Language-Development Service. No age limits. The Hand-Eye Coordinator consists of a slanted surface on which are mounted stereoscopic lenses and clips for holding stereoscopic materials which are traced or copied. KEYSTONE

Lee-Clark Reading Readiness Test, 1962 Revision. Kindergarten-beginning grade 1. Contains four tests of visual discrimination of letter symbols and word shapes. CALIFORNIA

Let's Look at Children. Materials designed for use both in teaching and in assessing the readiness of first-grade children, particularly the disadvantaged. ETS

Lincoln Diagnostic Spelling Tests. *Intermediate,* Grades 5–8; *Advanced,* grades 8–12. Designed to disclose causes or areas of difficulty; pronunciation, enunciation, and use of rules. BOBBS

Lorge-Thorndike Intelligence Tests, Multi-Level Edition. Grades 3–13. Materials for all grades in a single reusable booklet which contains eight levels of difficulty. Provides verbal, nonverbal, and total scores. A separate level edition is also available. HOUGHTON

Macmillan Reader Placement Test. Grades 1–3. Individual test containing graded book samples and word lists. MACMILLAN

Macmillan Reading Readiness Test. End of kindergarten, beginning grade 1. Subtests include a quantified rating scale, visual perception, auditory perception, vocabulary, and concepts. Separate norms provided for disadvantaged children. MACMILLAN

Massachusetts Vision Tests. See *A O School Vision Screening Test*

McCullough Word Analysis Tests. Grades 4–8. Group tests of seven word attack skills: initial consonant clusters, comparing vowel sounds, matching symbols with vowel sounds, identifying phonetic respellings, using a pronunciation key, dividing between syllables, finding a root word. GINN

Metropolitan Achievement Tests, Revised (1958–62).
   Primary I Battery, end of grade 1. Word knowledge, word discrimination, reading, arithmetic. Forms A, B.
   Primary II Battery, grade 2.0–3.5. Word knowledge, word discrimination, reading, spelling, arithmetic. Forms A, B.
   Elementary Reading, grades 3, 4. Paragraph comprehension, vocabulary. Forms A, B.
   Intermediate Reading, grades 5, 6; *Advanced Reading,* grades 7, 8. Paragraph comprehension, vocabulary. Forms A, B. HARCOURT

Metropolitan Readiness Tests, 1965 Revision. Beginning grade 1. Word meaning, listening, matching, alphabet, numbers, and copying. Forms A, B. HARCOURT

Minnesota Percepto-Diagnostic Test. Children and adults. A clinical test intended to assist in the diagnosis of neurological dysfunction. Three designs to be copied in different settings. CLINICAL

Monroe Diagnostic Reading Examination. Poor readers, any age. Individually administered battery of tests include oral reading, word recognition and discrimination, mirror reading, other supplementary tests. STOELTING

Monroe Reading Aptitude Tests. Beginning grade 1 and non-readers to age 9, for measuring readiness for reading instruction. Includes visual, auditory, perception, and memory; motor control; speed and articulation in speech; language development. Mainly group administration, some subtests to be given individually. HOUGHTON

Monroe Standardized Silent Reading Tests. Test I, grades 3–5; Test II, grades 6–8; Test III, high school. Very brief tests of rate of comprehension. Forms 1, 2, 3. BOBBS

Monroe-Sherman Group Diagnostic Reading Aptitude and Achievement Tests. Grade 3 and up. Achievement tests include paragraph meaning, rate, and word discrimination; arithmetic and spelling tests also included. Aptitude tests include visual memory, auditory memory and discrimination, motor speed, oral vocabulary. NEVINS

Murphy-Durrell Reading Readiness Analysis. Beginning first grade. Includes subtests on visual discrimination, auditory discrimination (phonemes), letter names, and learning rate. HARCOURT

Nelson-Denny Reading Test, Revised. High school and college. Vocabulary and paragraph comprehension. Forms A, B. HOUGHTON

Nelson Silent Reading Test, Revised. Grades 3–9. Vocabulary and paragraph comprehension. Forms A, B. HOUGHTON

Ortho-Rater. Master model for rapid testing of large numbers of adults or adolescents; modified model for school use with children. Available with two sets of slides; a short set for very rapid screening, and a set of twelve tests for more comprehensive visual screening. BAUSCH & LOMB

Oseretsky Motor Proficiency Tests. Ages 4–16. An age scale of tests of motor proficiency. AMERICAN GUIDANCE

Otis Quick-Scoring Mental Ability Tests. *Alpha Short Form,* grades 1–4. A group intelligence test requiring no reading. Same booklet is used for a verbal directions test and a nonverbal test. *Beta Test,* grades 4–9; *Gamma Test,* high school and college; group tests of the omnibus type requiring reading. Forms Em, Fm each level. HARCOURT

Otis-Lennon Mental Ability Tests. Revisions of the Otis series of verbal intelligence tests. *Primary I,* kindergarten; *Primary II,* first half of grade 1; *Elementary,* I, grades 1.5–3.9; *Elementary II,* grades 4–6; *Intermediate,* grades 7–9; *Advanced,* grades 10–12. Forms J, K, each level. HARCOURT

Peabody Library Information Tests. Grades 4–13. A group test of skill and information in the use of the library. AMERICAN GUIDANCE

Peabody Picture Vocabulary Test. Ages 2–18. A vocabulary test requiring only the choice of one out of four pictures. Forms A, B. AMERICAN GUIDANCE

Pintner General Ability Tests: Verbal Series, Revised 1965.
> *Pintner-Cunningham Primary Test,* Revised 1965. Kindergarten–grade 2. A group intelligence test requiring no reading. Forms A, B.
> *Pintner-Durost Elementary Test,* grades 2–4. Scale 1, picture content, and Scale 2, reading content.
> *Pintner Intermediate Test,* grades 4–9, a group test requiring reading. HARCOURT

Primary Reading Profiles, 1967 Edition. *Level 1,* grade 1.5 to 2.5; *Level 2,* 2.5 to 3.5. Each has five subtests: aptitude for reading, auditory association, word recognition, word attack, reading comprehension. HOUGHTON

Psychoeducational Profile of Basic Learning Abilities. Ages 2–14. A booklet for use by psychologists in summarizing data from various sources concerning motor integration, perception, language, social-personal adaptivity, and intellectual functioning. CONSULTING

Purdue Perceptual-Motor Survey. Ages 4–10. A series of tests for motor control and flexibility, visual-motor coordination, laterality, and directionality. MERRILL

Raven Progressive Matrices. A nonverbal group test of general intelligence. Form 1938, ages 8–adult; Form 1947, ages 5–11. English norms. PSYCHOLOGICAL

Reading Tests for New York State Elementary Schools. *Beginning grade 3.* Word recognition, paragraph comprehension. Forms A, B. *Beginning grade 6.* Word recognition, paragraph comprehension, rate. Forms A, B. Distributed by the New York State Education Department free to schools within the state.

Revised Stanford-Binet Intelligence Scale, Third Edition (1960). Ages 2 to adult. Individual test of general intelligence, for use by trained psychologists. Form L–M. HOUGHTON

Rorschach Technique. Preschool to adult. A projective test of a personality using inkblots, for trained psychologists. PSYCHOLOGICAL

Roswell-Chall Blending Test. A brief test of ability to hear the sounds of a word pronounced separately and recognize and say the word. ESSAY

Roswell-Chall Diagnostic Reading Test. A short series of tests for analyzing phonic knowledge and skills. ESSAY

School and College Ability Tests—SCAT Series II. Group test of scholastic aptitude. Levels 1–5 cover grades 4–14. Three forms of Level 1 (college); two forms for each other level. Provides verbal, quantitative, and total scores. ETS

Schrammel-Gray High School and College Reading Test. Grades 7–12 and college. Rate, comprehension, and comprehension-efficiency. BOBBS

Screening Tests for Identifying Children with Specific Language Disability (Slingerland). Levels for grades 1–2, 2–3, and 3–4. Intended for use in locating children who have or are likely to develop disabilities in reading, spelling, and handwriting. Visual copying, memory, and discrimination; three auditory group tests; one individual auditory test. EDUCATORS

Sequental Tests of Educational Progress—STEP. *Level 4,* grades 4–6; *Level 3,* grades 7–9; *Level 2,* grades 10–12; *Level 1,* college. A battery of achievement tests including tests of reading comprehension and listening comprehension. Forms A, B, each test and level. ETS

Silent Reading Diagnostic Tests. Grade 3 and up. Group test providing a detailed analysis of many word recognition and phonic skills, with eleven subtests. LYONS

Southern California Test Battery for Assessment of Dysfunction. Includes four clinical assessments: kinesthesia and tactile perception tests; figure-ground visual perception tests; motor accuracy test; and Ayers space test. WESTERN

Spache Binocular Reading Test. Grade 1 and up. Individual test to measure the relative participation of each eye in reading. Uses stereoscopic slides with different words omitted on each side. Three levels of difficulty. For use in a *Telebinocular* or stereoscope. KEYSTONE

Spache Diagnostic Reading Scales. Grade 1 and up. An individually administered battery of tests including three word lists, twenty-two graded reading passages, and six supplementary phonics tests. CALIFORNIA

SRA Achievement Series: Reading. *Grades 1, 2.* Verbal-pictorial association, language perception, comprehension, vocabulary. *Grades 2–4, Grades 4–6, Grades 6–9,* comprehension and vocabulary. Forms A, B. *Grades 4–6,* Word-study skills, Forms A, B. SRA

SRA Reading Record. Grades 8–13, adult. Ten subtests with short time limits: rate, comprehension, paragraph meaning, directory, map-table-graph, advertisement, index, technical vocabulary, sentence meaning, general vocabulary. SRA

Standard Reading Inventory. Grade 1 and up. Individual tests including recognition vocabulary, oral reading errors, oral and silent comprehension, oral and silent speed. PIONEER

Stanford-Binet. *See* **Revised Stanford-Binet Intelligence Scale.**

Stanford Diagnostic Reading Test. *Level I,* grades 2.5–4.5; *Level II,* grades 4.5–8.5. Group tests with separate measures of comprehension, vocabulary, syllabication, auditory skills, phonic analysis, and rate. HARCOURT

Stanford Reading Tests, 1964 Revision. *Primary I,* grades 1.5–2.4. Word reading, paragraph meaning, oral vocabulary, word study skills. *Primary II,* grades 2.5–3.9. Word meaning, paragraph meaning, word study skills. *Intermediate I,* grades 4.0–5.4; *Intermediate II,* grades 5.5–6.9; *Advanced,* grades 7–9.9. Word meaning, paragraph meaning. Forms W, X, Y, each level. HARCOURT

STAR: Screening Test of Academic Readiness. Kindergarten. A group intelligence test. PRIORITY

START: Screening Test for the Assignment of Remedial Treatments. Ages 4–6. Group tests of visual memory, auditory memory, visual copying, visual discrimination. PRIORITY

Thematic Apperception Test. Ages 6 to adult. A projective test of personality for use only by trained psychologists. PSYCHOLOGICAL

Traxler High School Reading Test, Revised 1967. Grades 10–12. Rate of reading and comprehension of easy material; finding main ideas in factual paragraphs. Forms A, B. BOBBS

Traxler Silent Reading Test. Grades 7–10. Rate, comprehension, word meaning, paragraph meaning. Forms 1, 2, 3, 4. BOBBS

Tyler-Kimber Study Skills Inventory. Grade 9–college. Use of reference books, card catalog, index, interpreting maps and graphs, etc. CONSULTING

Valett Developmental Survey of Basic Learning Abilities. Ages 2–7. A compendium of 233 tasks in seven areas: motor integration, tactile discrimination, auditory discrimination, visual motor coordination, visual discrimination, language development, conceptual development. CONSULTING

Van Alstyne Picture Vocabulary Test. Mental ages 2–7. A vocabulary test of sixty items, each requiring only a choice of one out of four pictures. HARCOURT

Wechsler Adult Intelligence Scale. Age 16–adult. An individual intelligence scale for use only by trained psychologists. Provides Verbal, Performance, and Full Scale I.Q.'s. PSYCHOLOGICAL

Wechsler Intelligence Scale for Children (*WISC*). Ages 5–15. An individual intelligence scale for use only by trained psychologists. Gives Verbal, Performance, and Full Scale I.Q.'s. PSYCHOLOGICAL

Wechsler Preschool and Primary Scale of Intelligence. Ages 4–6.5. An individual intelligence scale similar to the *WISC*. Provides Verbal, Performance, and Full Scale I.Q.'s. PSYCHOLOGICAL

Wepman Auditory Discrimination Test. Ages 5–9. Tests ability to distinguish whether two spoken words are the same or slightly different. LANGUAGE

Wide Range Achievement Test, Revised Edition (1965). Age 5–adult. An individual test of word recognition, spelling, and arithmetic computation. PSYCHOLOGICAL

Williams Reading Tests, Revised. *Test I*, grade 1, *Test II*, grades 2–3, word recognition and comprehension. *Tests for grades 4–9*, vocabulary in paragraph context. Forms A, B. BOBBS

Appendix B

A LIST OF PUBLISHERS AND THEIR ADDRESSES

The following list contains, in alphabetical order, the names and addresses of the publishers of the books and tests mentioned elsewhere in this book. It also contains some entries of producers and distributors of audio-visual materials, materials for special education, etc., although their products may not have been mentioned. Only one office is listed for each publisher. The abbreviated name of the publisher is listed in italics, followed by full name and address.

Abelard. Abelard-Schuman, Ltd., 6 W. 57 St., New York, N.Y. 10019

Abingdon. Abingdon Press, 201 Eighth Ave. S., Nashville, Tenn. 37203

Aladdin. Aladdin Books, see American Book Co.

Allyn. Allyn & Bacon, Inc., Rockleigh, N.J. 07647

Americana, Mundelein, Ill. 60060

American Book. American Book-Van Nostrand Co., 55 Fifth Ave., New York, N.Y. 10003

American Ed. American Education Publishers, Inc. 55 High St., Middletown, Conn. 06457

American Guidance. American Guidance Service, Inc., Circle Pines, Minn. 55014

American Library. American Library Association, 50 E. Huron St., Chicago, Ill. 60611

American Opt. American Optical Co., Southbridge, Mass.

Appleton. Appleton-Century-Crofts, see Meredith Corp.

Audio-Visual. Audio-Visual Research, 1505 Eighth St. S.E., Waseca, Minn. 56093

AVID Division, P.M. & E. Electronics, Inc., 10 Tripps Lane, E. Providence, R.I. 02914

Baldridge. Baldridge Reading Instruction Materials, Inc., 14 Griggs St., Greenwich, Conn. 06830

Barnell Loft, Ltd., 111 South Centre Ave., Rockville Centre, N.Y. 11570

Basic Books, Inc., Publishers, 404 Park Ave. South, New York, N.Y. 10016

Bausch. Bausch & Lomb Optical Co., Rochester, N.Y. 14602

Beckley-Cardy Co., 1900 N. Narragansett Ave., Chicago, Ill. 60639

Beginner. Beginner Books, see Random House

Behavioral. Behavioral Research Laboratories, P.O. Box 577, Palo Alto, Calif. 94302

Bell. Bell & Howell Co., Audio Visual Products Division, 7100 McCormack Road, Chicago, Ill. 60645

Benefic. Benefic Press, 10300 W. Roosevelt Road, Westchester, Ill. 60153, see Beckley-Cardy.

Bobbs. Bobbs-Merrill Co., 4300 W. 62 St., Indianapolis, Ind. 46268

Book Lab Inc., 1449 Thirty-seventh St., Brooklyn, N.Y. 11218

Stanley Bowmar Co., Inc., 4 Broadway, Valhalla, N.Y. 10595

Milton Bradley Co., Springfield, Mass. 01101

Burgess Publishing Co., 428 South 6 St., Minneapolis, Minn. 55415

Cadmus. Cadmus Books, see E. M. Hale

Califone, 5922 Bancroft St., Los Angeles, Calif. 90016

California. California Test Bureau, a Division of McGraw-Hill Book Co., Del Monte Research Park, Monterey, Calif. 93940

Cenco Educational Aids, 2600 S. Kostner Ave., Chicago, Ill. 60623

Childcraft Equipment Co., Inc., 155 E. 23 St., New York, N.Y. 10010

Children's Book Centre, 140 Kensington Church St., London W 8, England

Childrens. Childrens Press, Inc., 1224 W. Van Buren St., Chicago, Ill. 60607

Clinical. Clinical Psychology Publishing Co., Brandon, Vt. 05733

College Skills Center, 101 W. 31 St., New York, N.Y. 10001

Combined Book Exhibit, Inc., Scarborough Park, Albany Post Road, Briarcliffe Manor, N.Y. 10510

Committeee on Diagnostic Reading Tests, Mountain Home, N.C. 28745

Conrad Publishing Co., Box 90, Bismark, N.D. 58501

Consulting. Consulting Psychologists Press, 577 College Ave., Palo Alto, Calif. 94306

Continental Press, Inc., Elizabethtown, Pa., 17022

Coronet Films, Inc., 65 E. South Water St., Chicago, Ill. 60601

Council for Exceptional Children, 1201 Sixteenth St., N.W., Washington, D.C. 20036

Coward. Coward-McCann Inc., 200 Madison Ave., New York, N.Y. 10016

Craig Corporation, 3410 S. La Cienega Boulevard, Los Angeles, Calif. 90016

Creative Playthings, Inc., Edinburg Rd., Cranbury, N.J. 08540

Creative Visuals, Box 310, Big Springs, Tex. 97920

Crowell. Crowell, Collier, & Macmillan, Inc., 866 Third Ave., New York, N.Y. 10022

Curtis Audio Visual Materials, Curtis Publishing Co., Independence Square, Philadelphia, Pa. 19105

Davis A. V. Service, 713 S.W. 12th St., Portland 5, Ore.

Day. John Day Co., 62 W. 45 St., New York, N.Y. 10036

Delacorte Press, see Dial Press

Dell. Dell Publishing Co., 750 Third Ave., New York, N.Y. 10017

Developmental Learning Materials, 3505 N. Ashland St., Chicago, Ill. 60657

Dexter & Westbrook, Ltd., 111 South Centre Ave., Rockville Centre, N.Y. 11571

Dial. The Dial Press, 750 Third Ave., New York, N.Y. 10017

Dick Blick Co., Box 1267, Galesburg, Ill. 61405.

Dodd. Dodd, Mead & Co., Inc., 79 Madison Ave., New York, N.Y. 10016

Doubleday. Doubleday & Co., Inc., 277 Park Ave., New York, N.Y. 10017

Dutton. E. P. Dutton & Co., 201 Park Ave., New York, N.Y. 10003

EB Auditory Products, 4807 W. 118 Place, Hawthorne, Calif. 90250

The Economy Co., Oklahoma City, Okla. 73125

Educational Activities, Inc., Box 392, Freeport, N.Y. 11520

EDL. Educational Developmental Laboratories, Inc., a Division of McGraw-Hill Book Co., Huntington, N.Y. 11743

Educational. Educational and Industrial Testing Service, San Diego, Calif., 92107

Educational Projections Corp., 119 S. Roach St., Jackson, Miss., 39205

ETS. Educational Testing Service, Princeton, N.J. 08540

Educators. Educators Publishing Service, 75 Moulten St., Cambridge, Mass. 02138

Edukaid of Ridgewood, 1250 E. Ridgewood Ave., Ridgewood, N.J. 07450

Electronic Futures, Inc., 57 Dodge Ave., North Haven, Conn. 06473

Embossograf Corp. of America, 38 W. 21 St., New York, N.Y. 10010

Encyclopedia Britannica Educational Corp., 425 N. Michigan Ave., Chicago, Ill. 60611

Essay. Essay Press, Box 5, Planetarium Station, New York, N.Y. 10024

ETA Division, A. Daigger & Co., 159 W. Kinzie St., Chicago, Ill. 60610

Eye Gate House, Inc., 146-01 Archer Ave., Jamaica, N.Y. 11435

Fearon Publishers, 2165 Park St., Palo Alto, Calif. 94306

Field. Field Educational Publications, Inc., 609 Mission St., San Francisco, Calif. 94105

Field Enterprises Educational Corp., Merchandise Mart Plaza, Chicago, Ill. 60654

Follett. Follett Publishing Co., 1010 W. Washington Blvd., Chicago, Ill. 60607

Funk & Wagnalls, a Division of Readers Digest Books, Inc., 380 Madison Ave., New York, N.Y. 10017

Garrard. Garrard Publishing Co., Champaign, Ill. 61820

Ginn. Ginn & Co., Waltham, Mass. 02154

Globe Book Co., 175 Fifth Ave., New York, N.Y. 10010

Golden Gate Junior Books, Box 398, San Carlos, Calif. 94071

Golden. Golden Press, Publishers, 850 Third Ave., New York, N.Y. 10022

Grolier. Grolier Educational Corp., 845 Third Ave., New York, N.Y. 10022

Grossett. Grossett & Dunlap, 51 Madison Ave., New York, N.Y. 10010

Grune & Stratton, Inc., 381 Park Ave. S., New York, N.Y. 10016

The Gryphon Press, Highland Park, N.J. 08904

Hale. E. M. Hale & Co., Eau Claire, Wis. 54701.

C. S. Hammond & Co., 515 Valley St., Maplewood, N.J. 07040

Harcourt. Harcourt, Brace & World, Inc., 757 Third Avenue, New York, N.Y. 10017

Harper. Harper & Row, Publishers, Inc., 49 E. 33 St., New York, N.Y. 10016

Harvey. Harvey House, Inc., Irvington-on-Hudson, N.Y. 10533

Hastings. Hastings House, Publishers, Inc., 151 E. 50 St., New York, N.Y. 10022

D. C. Heath and Co., 285 Columbus Ave., Boston, Mass. 02116

The Highsmith Co., Inc., Fort Atkinson, Wis. 53538

Holiday. Holiday House, Inc., 18 E. 56 St., New York, N.Y. 10022

Holt. Holt, Rinehart & Winston, Inc., 383 Madison Ave. New York, N.Y. 10017

The Horn Book, Inc., 585 Boylston St., Boston, Mass. 02116

Houghton. Houghton Mifflin Co., 2 Park St., Boston, Mass. 02107

Illinois. See University of Illinois Press

Initial Teaching Alphabet Publications, Inc., 20 E. 46 St., New York, N.Y. 10017

IPAT. Institute for Personality and Aptitude Testing, 1602–04 Coronado Drive, Champaign, Ill. 61820

The Instructo Corp., Paoli, Pa. 19301

The Judy Co., 310 N. 2 St., Minneapolis, Minn. 55401

Kenworthy Educational Service, Inc., P.O. Box 3031, 138 Allen St., Buffalo, N.Y. 14205

Keystone. Keystone View Co., Meadville, Pa. 16335

Laidlaw Bros., a Division of Doubleday & Co., 36 Chatham Rd., Summit, N.J. 07901

Language. Language Research Associates, 950 E. 59 St., Chicago, Ill.

Lippincott. J. B. Lippincott Co., E. Washington Square, Philadelphia, Pa. 19105

Little. Little, Brown & Co., 34 Beacon St., Boston, Mass. 02106

International Reading Association, 6 Tyre Ave., Newark, Del. 19711

Lothrop. Lothrop, Lee & Shepard Co., Inc., 419 Park Ave., New York, N.Y. 10016

Lyons. Lyons & Carnahan, Inc., 307 E. 25 St., Chicago, Ill. 60616

Macmillan. The Macmillan Co., 866 Third Ave., New York, N.Y. 10022

Macrae. Macrae Smith Co., 225 S. 15 St., Philadelphia, Pa. 19102

McCormick. McCormick-Mathers Publishing Co., Inc., P.O. Box 2212, Wichita, Kans. 67201

David McKay Co., Inc., 750 Third Ave., New York, N.Y. 10017

Maico Hearing Instrument, Inc., 8 S. Michigan Ave., Chicago, Ill.

Meredith Corp., 440 Park Ave. S., New York, N.Y. 10016

Meredith Press, 250 Park Ave., New York, N.Y. 10017

Merrill. Charles E. Merrill Books, Inc., 1300 Alum Creek Drive, Columbus, Ohio 43216

Messner. Julian Messner, Inc., 1 W 39 St., New York, N.Y. 10036

Morrow. William Morrow & Co., Inc., 425 Park Ave. S., New York, N.Y. 10016

National Council of Teachers of English, 508 S. 6th St., Champaign, Ill. 61820

Nelson. Thomas Nelson & Sons, 1626 Copewood St., Camden, N.J. 08103

Nevins. C. H. Nevins Printing Co., Pittsburgh, Pa.

New Century, see Meredith Corp.

New York Times Teaching Resources, 100 Boylston St., Boston, Mass. 02116

Noble. Noble & Noble, Publishers, Inc., 750 Third Ave., New York, N.Y. 10017

F.A. Owen Publishing Co., 7 Bank St., Dansville, N.Y. 14437

Perceptual Development Laboratories, 6767 Southwest Ave., St. Louis, Mo. 63143

Phonovisual Products, Inc., P.O. Box 5625, Washington, D.C. 20016

Pioneer. Pioneer Printing Co., Bellingham, Wash. 98225

Plays, Inc., Publishers, 8 Arlington St., Boston, Mass. 02116

Portal Press, Inc., a Division of John Wiley & Sons, Inc., 605 Third Ave., New York, N.Y. 10016

Prentice. Prentice-Hall, Inc., Englewood Cliffs, N.J. 07632

Priority. Priority Innovations, Inc., P.O. Box 792, Skokie, Ill. 60076

Psychological. The Psychological Corp., 304 E. 45 St., New York, N.Y. 10017

Psychotechnics, Inc., 7433 N. Harlem Ave., Chicago, Ill. 60648

Rand. Rand-McNally & Co., P.O. Box 7600, Chicago, Ill. 60680

Random. Random House, 457 Madison Ave., New York, N.Y. 10022

Reader's Digest Services, Inc., Educational Division, Pleasantville, N.Y. 10570

The Reading Institute of Boston, 116 Newbury St., Boston, Mass. 02116

The Reading Laboratory, Inc. 55 Day St., Norwalk, Conn. 06854

Remedial Education Press, Kingsbury Center, 2138 Bancroft Place, N.W., Washington, D.C. 20008

Rheem Califone, 5922 Bancroft St., Los Angeles, Calif. 90016

Frank E. Richards, Publisher, 215 Church St., Phoenix, N.Y. 13135

RIME Associates, P.O. Box 252, Paramus, N.J. 07652

Ronald. The Ronald Press Co., 79 Madison Ave., New York, N.Y. 10016

Scholastic Magazines and Book Services, 50 W. 44th St., New York, N.Y. 10036

Schoolhouse Industries, Inc., 170 Central Ave., Farmingdale, N.Y. 11735

Science for Visual Education, Inc., 1345 Diversey Parkway, Chicago, Ill. 60614

SRA. Science Research Associates, Inc., 259 E. Erie St., Chicago, Ill. 60611

Scott. William R. Scott, 333 Sixth Ave., New York, N.Y. 10014

Scott F. Scott, Foresman & Co., Glenview, Ill. 60025

Seabury. The Seabury Press, 815 Second Ave., New York, N.Y. 10017

Silver, Burdett & Co., a Division of General Learning Corp., Box 2000, Morristown, N.J. 07960

Simon & Schuster, Inc., 1 W. 39 St., New York, N.Y. 10018

Singer. L. W. Singer, Inc., a Division of Random House, 501 Madison Ave., New York, N.Y. 10022

Special Child Publications, 4635 Union Bay Place N.E., Seattle, Wash. 98105

Special Education Materials Development Center, 2020 R St., Washington, D.C. 20009

Speech & Language Materials, Inc., P.O. Box 721, Tulsa, Okla. 74101

Spoken Arts, Inc., 59 Locust Ave., New Rochelle, N.Y. 10801

Steck. Steck-Vaughn Co., P.O. Box 2028, Austin, Tex. 78767

Study-Scope Co., P.O. Box 689, Tyler, Tex. 75701

Systems for Education, Inc., 612 N. Michigan Ave., Chicago, Ill. 60611

Teachers. Teachers College Press, Columbia University, 525 W. 120 St., New York, N.Y. 10027

Teaching Resources, Inc., 100 Boylston St., Boston, Mass. 02116

Teaching Technology Corp., 5520 Cleon Ave., N. Hollywood, Calif. 91601

Technifax Corp., 195 Appleton St., Holyoke, Mass. 01040

Tempo Books, see Grosset & Dunlap

3 M Visual Products, 2501 Hudson Rd., St. Paul, Minn. 55119

Tweedy Transparencies, 207 Hollywood Ave., E. Orange, N.J. 07018

University of Chicago Press, 5750 Ellis Ave., Chicago, Ill. 60637

University of Illinois Press, Urbana, Ill. 61801

Vanguard. The Vanguard Press, Inc., 424 Madison Ave., New York, N.Y. 10017

Viking. The Viking Press, Inc., 625 Madison Ave., New York, N.Y. 10022

Wagner. Harr Wagner, see Field Educational Publications

Walck. Henry Z. Walck, Inc., Publishers, 19 Union Square, New York, N.Y. 10003

Warne. Frederick Warne & Co., 101 Fifth Ave., New York, N.Y. 10003

Washington Square Press, Inc., a Division of Simon & Schuster, 630 Fifth Ave., New York, N.Y. 10020

Watts. Frederick Watts, Inc., 575 Lexington Ave., New York, N.Y. 10022

Webster. Webster Division of McGraw-Hill Book Co., Manchester Rd., Manchester, Mo. 63011

Wenkart. Wenkart Phonic Readers, 4 Shady Hill Square, Cambridge, Mass. 02138

Western Publishing Co., School and Library Department, 1220 Mound Ave., Racine, Wis. 53404

Western. Western Psychological Services, 12035 Wilshire Boulevard, Los Angeles, Calif. 90025

Westminster. The Westminster Press, Witherspoon Building, Philadelphia 7, Pa.

Whitman. Albert Whitman & Co., 560 W. Lake St., Chicago, Ill. 60606

Winston. See Holt, Rinehart & Winston

Winter Haven Lions Research Foundation, Inc., Box 112, Winter Haven, Fla. 33880

Word Making Productions, P.O. Box 305, Salt Lake City, Utah 84110

Xerox Corp., Curriculum Programs, 600 Madison Ave., New York, N.Y. 10022

INDEX

Index